SOC

CAPITALISM,

CRITIQUE

SOCIOLOGY, CAPITALISM, CRITIQUE

KLAUS DÖRRE,
STEPHAN LESSENICH,
HARTMUT ROSA

TRANSLATED BY
JAN-PETER HERRMANN
AND LOREN BALHORN

VERSO
London • New York

First published in the English language by Verso 2015
Translation © Jan-Peter Herrmann and Loren Balhorn
First published as *Soziologie – Kapitalismus – Kritik: Eine Debatte*
© Suhrkamp 2009

1 3 5 7 9 10 8 6 4 2

Verso
UK: 6 Meard Street, London W1F 0EG
US: 20 Jay Street, Suite 1010, Brooklyn, NY 11201
www.versobooks.com

Verso is the imprint of New Left Books

ISBN-13: 978-1-78168-932-5 (PB)
ISBN-13: 978-1-78168-931-8 (HC)
eISBN-13: 978-1-78168-933-2 (US)
eISBN-13: 978-1-78168-934-9 (UK)

British Library Cataloguing in Publication Data
A catalogue record for this book is available from the British Library

Library of Congress Cataloging-in-Publication Data

Dörre, Klaus.
[Soziologie – Kapitalismus – Kritik. English]
Sociology – capitalism – critique / Klaus Dörre,
Stephan Lessenich, Hartmut Rosa ; translated by
Jan-Peter Herrmann and Loren Balhorn.
pages cm
"First published as Soziologie - Kapitalismus - Kritik:
Eine Debatte [by] Suhrkamp, 2015."
Includes bibliographical references and index.
ISBN 978-1-78168-932-5 (pbk. : alk. paper) – ISBN
978-1-78168-931-8 (hardcover : alk. paper) – ISBN
978-1-78168-933-2 (ebook : alk. paper) – ISBN 978-
1-78168-934-9 (ebook : alk. paper)
1. Capitalism–Social aspects. 2. Sociology. I.
Lessenich, Stephan. II. Rosa, Hartmut, 1965– III. Title.
HB501.D662713 2015
306.3–dc23
2015005785

Typeset in Minion Pro by MJ & N Gavan, Truro, Cornwall
Printed in the US by Maple Press

Contents

Foreword to the English Edition

As Klaus Schwab, founder of the World Economic Forum in Davos, claimed in 2012, 'Capitalism in its current form does not fit our world.'[1] Pope Francis put it more radically, stating that 'this economic model kills.'[2] More generally, it seems that a certain uneasiness regarding capitalism as such has even reached the social elites. This appears to pose a fitting occasion for a critical sociology. Yet when this book was published in its original German edition in 2009, causing great debate among German sociologists, a sound, scholarly critique of capitalism was in fact lacking. Indeed, sociology was ill prepared for the financial and economic crisis of 2008–2009. Analysis and critique of capitalism had remained confined to the shadows, at least in the German-speaking world. If capitalism was mentioned at all, it was spelled out in the plural while its divergent institutional varieties were dissected. The systemic 'commons' of this social formation was largely ignored analytically.

Our book aims to re-ignite the debate. Yet it is also directed at non-sociologists interested in the anatomy of capitalist societies, their crises and the chances of a post-capitalist transformation. The authors proceed from one common point of departure: modern capitalisms constitute dynamic growth societies. Their relative stability throughout numerous crisis periods rested on economic-technological efficiency and growing material prosperity. A break in this continuity, however, is now occurring in the guise of an economic-ecological double crisis. There is a growing discrepancy between economic growth and general levels of prosperity. Economic growth itself has become a driving force of crisis. For sociology, this raises a question about the mutual interrelations between dynamic self-stabilisation and the principles of legitimation of modern capitalist societies. Our hypothesis reads that the logic of increase and escalation, consisting of an endless chain of *Landnahmen*, accelerations, and activations, may have in fact passed a critical threshold at which capitalist modernity's dynamisation imperatives

---

1 Klaus Schwab on 24 January 2012, as reported by German news channel n-tv.
2 'Franziskus und die Globalisierung, Was der Papst verschweigt', in *Frankfurter Allgemeine Zeitung*, 29 November 2013.

themselves are being questioned. This fundamental assumption represents the common theme of the following sociological debate. The book starts off with three introductory chapters presenting the key concepts in our respective analyses of capitalist dynamics: *Landnahme*, acceleration, and activation. These are followed by criticisms and ripostes by each of the three authors, respectively.

Five years after the first publication of the German edition of this book, European capitalisms have not left the socio-economic crisis behind, not even remotely. Due to unemployment and economic stagnation, ecological threats such as climate change are either being ignored or fatalistically accepted. Moreover, the crisis in Ukraine has re-ignited the cold war between East and West, while the Arab Spring has not only deposed despots, but also created a power vacuum that is being filled, at least partially, by Islamic fundamentalists. However, despite all the crises and convulsions, the capitalist elites seem to be running a tight ship, at least in the historical centres. The year of 2011 saw social movements emerging in opposition to market fundamentalism. Yet with the exception of those Latin American countries with centre-left governments, democratic anti-capitalist political forces are weaker than ever. In fact, currently, it seems more likely that far-right and right-wing populist formations could be successful in instrumentalising widespread dissatisfaction to pave the way towards a new authoritarianism.

While the world stumbles from one crisis to the next, the social sciences largely confine themselves to business as usual. Once again, economists have outpaced sociologists. While Thomas Piketty's hypothesis of permanently growing wealth inequality due to capitalism is being debated all over the world, the German *Wirtschaftsweise* (economic wise men) remain convinced that the heterodox economist has 'shot himself in the foot'.[3] This clinging to old dogmas, immune to new insights or developments, shows that our debate about contemporary capitalism is as relevant as ever. Today, whoever seeks to analyse and criticise capitalism as a social formation still faces – in economics as well as in sociology – a significant challenge. This book is our contribution to this effort. In order to address more recent developments, we have complemented the English edition with three additional chapters at the end of the book. The analytical approaches here take their empirical reference points mainly from European capitalism.

---

3 'Verschärft der Kapitalismus die Ungleichheit oder nicht?', in *ZEIT-online*, 5 June 2014, http://blog.zeit.de/herdentrieb/2014/06/05/verschaerft-der-kapitalismus-die-ungleichheit-oder-nicht. Accessed: 01 December 2014. This statement comes from the neo-Keynesian Bofinger, of all people.

Given that we are particularly interested in the global commonalities of capitalist socialisation (*Vergesellschaftung*), however, we hope that our discussion proves stimulating for readers from the Anglo-Saxon world and beyond, too.

Klaus Dörre, Stephan Lessenich, Hartmut Rosa,
December 2014

Introduction:
Sociology – Capitalism – Critique:
Towards the Revitalisation of an
Elective Affinity

We Are All Socialists Now.
–*Newsweek*, 16 February 2009

Wherever you look these days, the critique of capitalism has all of a sudden become quite fashionable. You could get the impression that critiques of the 'system', which for a long time had been confined to marginal or fringe groups (among for instance social milieus such as students, unionists, and veteran libertarians), and lately seemed to have found their (anti-)institutional home within the alt-globalisation movement, have now made their way into the social mainstream. Whether in the review section of major newspapers or in the catalogues of prestigious publishing houses, from Heiner Geißler's invectives against globalisation to Josef Ackermann's self-incriminating public statements, in this country, anyone keen to go with the times is distancing themselves from capitalism. Even if this condemnation is moralistic, everyone feels obligated to disassociate themselves from the dysfunction and crises of capitalism's latest neo-liberal phase of development. The reader of this book may rightly ask herself at the beginning of this intellectual endeavour: why another tirade against capitalism? Why another book on what is by now a very obvious crisis? Do we really, now that everyone is having a go at the toppled giant, also want to join the fray?

When the three of us came together in the summer of 2007 to develop a scientific-political position on capitalism, still undoubtedly the 'most fateful force in our modern life',[1] we could hardly foresee that it was about to make such an impactful return to the centre of public controversy. Indeed, at that time, the approaching crisis of the financial market-dominated regime of

---

1 M. Weber, *The Protestant Ethic and the Spirit of Capitalism*, 23rd print, London 2001, p. xxxi.

accumulation so prominent over the last decades was beginning to materialise. But the initiative for publishing this book had other, more profound reasons – reasons that have by no means been made redundant by the precipitous increase in public critique of capitalism. For, in our opinion, sociology, which has prematurely been deemed by some observers to be the lucky 'profiteer of the crisis',[2] has to this day failed as an academic discipline equipped to treat the recent, clearly crisis-prone transformations of capitalist society in a manner that meets the standard of a critical-progressive self-understanding.

This is due primarily to the fact that such a self-understanding of the discipline – this is true at least for Germany and the German-speaking world – has been utterly marginal in the recent past. Lately, only a small minority of sociologists has held to the view that sociology, as a science of society, must always contain a critical analysis of the social relations of its time, and that the capitalist structure of its own society is to be placed centre stage, as the analytical point of departure. The post-communist triumph of market liberalism that dominated the last two decades was also, especially in the academic social sciences, accompanied by a sustained 'exhaustion of utopian energies',[3] an essential disavowal of thinking about (or in terms of) societal alternatives to capitalism. In this context, mainstream sociology morphed into a (sometimes more, but usually less critical) scientific accessory to an era in which flagrantly displayed subjection to the market became hegemonic in just about every sphere of life. A political agenda of enabling, or rather educating people with regard to Marktlichkeit[4] had increasingly become an unquestioned and convincing sign of 'modernity'.

To speak of 'capitalism', a term that was publicly proscribed in post-war West Germany, did in fact become analytically acceptable in the local social sciences again after it emerged victorious in the 'systems rivalry' between the West and the East – that is, as long as it was used to differentiate between various institutional regimes of (market-)economic relations in late industrial societies. But even these debates (in this country) on contemporary

---

2 Cf. R. Hoppe, 'Die Kriegsgewinnler', in Der Spiegel 42, Hamburg 2008, p. 75

3 Cf. J. Habermas, 'The New Obscurity: The Crisis of the Welfare State and the Exhaustion of Utopian Energies' (trans. P. Jacobs), Philosophy and Social Criticism 11(2), 1986, pp. 1–18 [orig.'Die Krise des Wohlfahrtstaats und die Erschöpfung utopischer Energien', in J. Habermas, Die neue Unübersichtlichkeit, Frankfurt 1985, pp. 141–63.

4 Cf. F. Nullmeier, 'Vermarktlichung des Sozialstaats', in WSI-Mitteilungen 57 (9) 2004, pp. 495–500. [Trans. Note] Marktlichkeit is a broader term encompassing behaviour and attitudes in line with market requirements for which there is no adequate counterpart in English.

'varieties of capitalism'[5] were generally marked by a tendency to praise the socially-coordinated Rhenish rather than the liberal-competitive American variant. And as soon as German-speaking social science attained a modicum of public recognition, it launched decisively into praise of the 'social market economy', which supposedly – if properly understood – is not even an actual form of capitalism anyway. It thereby acquiesced to a specific discursive formation[6] pervaded by the bodies of knowledge and interpretations of academic economics, in the framework of which professional economists have gained intellectual prerogative in the interpretation of social reality. Even in the face of the looming crisis of the financial markets in June 2008, the economic and social order often referred to as the 'social market economy' managed, in its sixtieth year, to sell itself as the definitive success story of social organisation. In what came to be known as the Jena Manifesto,[7] propagandists of neo-liberal regulatory policy from politics, business, and academia celebrated the social market economy as the only viable guarantor of a prosperous and free life, without alternative. They lamented the ongoing threat presented by a hypertrophic interventionist state that patronised its citizens, crippled their economic initiative and strangled their aspirations for freedom, and which needed to be reigned in by an equally interminable social 'renewal'.

The fact that capitalism, as unregulated as possible (though supposedly moderated by Christian ethics) was being celebrated on our doorstep with such pomp and circumstance (a massive investment of public resources, a downright disarming conceitedness, and a counterfactual energy bordering on the denial of reality) as the exclusive bearer of all that is eternally true, good and beautiful, may have provided the final motivation for our initiative. However, our shared aspiration to articulate such a public position had begun to develop earlier. The institutional framework had already been established in the winter of 2004 as a result of the historically contingent reconstitution of sociology in Jena as a place of critical analysis of contemporary society.

So what is the common point of departure for our reflections, the shared core of our endeavours? We all share the conviction that a great act of 'renewal' is indeed on the horizon, a collective scientific effort to which we seek to contribute with this book: the return of critique to sociology. We

---

5   Cf. P. A. Hall, D. Soskice (ed.), *Varieties of Capitalism*, Oxford 2001.

6   Cf. M. Nonhoff, *Politischer Diskurs und Hegemonie*, Bielefeld 2006; L. Gertenbach, *Die Kultivierung des Marktes*. Berlin, 2007.

7   Cf. 'The Jena Manifesto for the Renewal of the Social Market Economy', at http://www.jenaerallianz.de/fileadmin/marktwirtschaft/downloads/Jena_Manifesto __ket_Economy.pdf.

locate our goal of reviving a critical impulse in academic sociology in the tradition of *critical theory* – a tradition that itself draws much of its inspiration from Marxist theory, which sees critique as one of the primary tasks of sociology, and which holds the emancipation from unjustified domination, or rather from socially created yet socially uncontrollable systemic constraints, as the yardstick for this critique. Our critical impulse rests upon the insight that in 'modern' society – including in its present, 'late modern' formation – sociological diagnostics of society and social critique must first and foremost target capitalism as a form of private profit accumulation, and the social conditions and consequences that it engenders. This relates closely to our shared conviction that a critical theory of (capitalist) society must be systematically tied to an empirically grounded sociological diagnosis of the times. Moreover, we agree that what is needed for a successful revitalisation of sociology as a space of social critique is a conflation of various lines of tradition and development of critical theory – such as (neo-)materialist *and* post-structuralist approaches – in a way that recognises difference but is at the same time oriented towards reconciliation and synthesis. Using this approach, questions of economic exploitation and social inequality feature just as prominently as modes of subjectification and practices of culture formation.

It is in *this* sense of a critical sociology of contemporary capitalism that our three introductory contributions to the present volume should be understood. In them, we diagnose a threefold dynamic of historical-cultural transformation of the capitalist social formation, which we seek to conceptualise utilising the process categories of *Landnahme*,[8] acceleration (*Beschleunigung*), and activation (*Aktivierung*). The foundation of this book is based, firstly, upon the supposition that none of the three approaches hiding behind these labels – as valid as they may be in and of themselves – are capable of encompassing and capturing the objectionable reality of contemporary capitalism in its entire complexity.

Furthermore, we want to show that the reciprocal criticism and recapitulation of our theses and theorems undertaken in this volume represent a way of not only demonstrating their individual strengths and weaknesses,

---

8 [Trans. Note] Literally translated, *Landnahme* means land grabbing, land appropriation, or territorial gain. It refers to internal as well as external capitalist expansion. The concept of *Landnahme* argues that in the long run capitalist societies cannot reproduce themselves on their own foundations. In order to reproduce themselves, they continuously have to occupy and commodify a non-capitalist 'other' (i.e., regions, milieus, groups, activities) in, so to speak, ceaseless repetition of the act of primitive accumulation. Owing to the difficulty of finding a conclusive exact translation, the term *Landnahme* will be used throughout the text.

but also – in the sense of the discursive principle of the dialogical development of knowledge[9] – their productive complementarity with regard to the sociological analysis and critique of the capitalist mode of socialisation[10] of our time. This is not to suggest, of course, that the merging of the three approaches developed here can alone provide a global analysis of the social formation of the present: for nothing could be more presumptuous and further from our thoughts. However, we do hold the conviction that the possibility for the renewal of sociology in a spirit of social critique lies exclusively in scientific-collegial complementation and cooperation. On the path to this book we learned the important lesson that the mutual respect for each other's perspectives significantly heightened our sensitivity to those aspects that each of us had previously dismissed.

What unites the processes of *Landnahme*, acceleration and activation is their reflection of the intrinsic crisis-proneness of capitalist socialisation. In its crises – including the current, financial market-driven crisis, which may turn out to be the most severe since the Great Depression – capitalism reveals its otherwise systematically suppressed or socially marginalised potential for social destruction again and again. Even the supposed – that is, if you believe the apologists – unparalleled *economic* efficiency of late-modern, affluent, 'throwaway' capitalism may be rightfully doubted. But what cannot be ignored are the *social* inefficiencies of that social formation we wish to depict in its current phase of development. The social injuries, dislocations, and depredations this formation constantly produces can only be ignored if one renounces the very ethical standards that 'bourgeois society' set itself in its political revolutions. In the sense of the normative standards of critique of the Enlightenment – freedom, equality, and fraternity – our analyses here may be best understood as a critique of the self-debasement, self-disempowerment and self-destruction wrought upon society under capitalism. At the same time, another aim is to sharpen the understanding of the historical situation and context of these standards of measure, of their ideational and material entrenchment in a social formation. The overcoming of these standards, this entrenchment, is and must always be at the heart of any serious critique of capitalism.

In light of the current renaissance of critique of capitalism – that (for good or ill) old 'system question' – this is the very point at which the ways of critics begin to part. We have placed the necessity of overcoming the

---

9 Cf. P. Zima, *Ideologie und Theorie*, Tübingen 1989; U. Kalbitzer, *Wissenschaftliche Politikberatung als wirtschaftspolitischer Diskurs*, Marburg 2006.

10 [Trans. Note] The term 'socialisation' (*Vergesellschaftung*) is to be understood in a Weberian sense; that is, as the process of integration of individuals into society as a whole and of transforming individual activities into social relations.

capitalist system as the point of departure for our critique, even though we may not agree on how this goal can be reached, or what a path towards this goal would look like. This is not to say that we, as *social scientists*, have assigned ourselves the task of propagating concrete utopian alternatives to the dominant social formation. However, together we seek to develop, through mutual critical engagement with our respective approaches, analytical and diagnostically reliable (and thereby potentially politically viable) standards of measurement for the critique of capitalism. From our position in favour of a critical sociology we thus go beyond a 'sociology of critique'[11] that simply reflects upon the act of critique. In particular, we aim to distance ourselves from those trite varieties of critique of capitalism and their representatives, who exhaust themselves in polemics against single actors within the system (lately these tend to be the 'managers'); or who consider a diluted critical attitude to be a temporary concession to the *zeitgeist* necessary to enhance their own careers. Neither of these variants faces a rosy future (nor should they), for both would go down without a whimper if faced with a revitalisation of the neo-liberal paradigm – a prospect that cannot be ruled out, in spite of the current manifestations of crisis. Only briefly did it seem as if the market propagandists of the past two decades had suffered a serious blow and were in fact retreating – just as it was only briefly that one could fall for the illusion that neo-liberalism had abdicated, that, indeed, the primacy of the economy had been thrown into the dustbin of history. Meanwhile, the soldiers of the free market have begun to gather and regroup: whether in conventions of speech – that neo-liberalism, in its good old German *ordo-liberalist* guise, has always demanded a strong regulatory state (according to the then-current German president: 'Germans can make a contribution to dealing with the crisis'[12]) – or in the discursive attempt to portray the latest crisis as simply yet another chapter in the history of the failure of the state.

How, then, must a sociological critique of capitalism be constituted if it is to represent a radical aspiration that lasts beyond the current moment? In our view it must contain the following three features: it must be *clear*, *complex*, and *collective*. What do we mean by that? Recent political sociology has depicted capitalism as a system with the seemingly inexhaustible power to absorb the energies of social alternatives;[13] the only way this system

---

11   Cf. L. Boltanski Thévenot, 'On Justification: Economies of Worth'. *Princeton Studies in Cultural Sociology*, Princeton University Press, 2006.

12   This is what Horst Köhler said in his 'crisis speech' on 24 March 2009: H. Köhler, 'The credibility of freedom', 2009, at http://www.bundespraesident.de/ SharedDocs/Reden/EN/HorstKoehler/Reden/2009/03/20090324_Rede.html.

13   Cf. T. Künkler, 'Produktivkraft Kritik: Die Subsumtion der Subversion

is incomparably efficient (in this regard) is that it does not allow any real or ideal alternatives to the system to coexist in the long term. Nor can we ourselves, as politically minded scientists within the academic space of actually existing capitalism, simply evade and elude the systemic dynamics of incorporation, and the institutional practices of co-optation in our times. It follows that, in order to not go unheard and fizzle out, the sociological critique of capitalism of the future (that is to say, a sociological critique of capitalism *with a future*) must operate using terms clear in both analytical substance and critical content. These terms must allow for the grasping of the world of capitalist socialisation in all its complexity, and they must be published and popularised in a collective scientific-political effort. Ideally, such terms are then available – beyond the field of science – to social practices of politicisation, which in turn aim at a widening of the horizon of potential social configurations – and thereby point the way toward an alternative practice of socialisation.

For a science of society, however mediated and on whatever kind of winding path, to set itself in relation to such social practices and dynamics, the 'critical' part of its aspiration cannot be just a label. A critical sociology also has intellectual and material, individual and institutional limitations. The critique we present is the critique of the incorporated: a critique of capitalism by three *landgenomme, beschleunigte* and *aktivierte* professors. There is a danger that such a critique may reflect only the personal; that is, it may cultivate a purely personal gesture of consternation. This danger cannot be addressed simply through individual self-reflection; it must be countered by collegial criticism and professional supervision; first, in the smaller circle of the native academic institution, and second, within the wider circle of the scientific community. Jena sociology – keeping in mind today's parameters of critical science – provides the best possible institutional and personal, intellectual and social conditions for the attempt to, firstly, (re-)position our own discipline at home as producers of social critique and secondly, to use this dynamic to seek out links to corresponding activities in other spaces of academic life. From that point on, a renewed critical sociology will be and will have to be about seeking the light of the world outside academia: that of the media and of everyday life. For here, and only here, will the final determination be made whether sociology and the critique of capitalism will find common ground once more – and whether society will notice it.

*   *   *

im neuen Kapitalismus', in R. Eickelpasch, C. Rademacher, P. R. Lobato (ed.), *Metamorphosen des Kapitalismus – und seiner Kritik*, Wiesbaden 2008, pp. 29–47; S. van Dyk, 'Abweichung als Norm – Widerstand als Ressource?', Jena 2009 (ms.).

The work on this book was a truly collective, cooperative, collegial undertaking. Correspondingly, we owe multiple thanks that we would like to express at this point (though we will restrict ourselves for the sake of brevity). We would like to thank, first and foremost, our respective co-authors, who managed against all odds to complete this scientific-social experiment with (preliminary) success. We would, then, like to thank Thomas Barth, who has accompanied and facilitated the evolution of the volume with exceptional intellectual and organisational resourcefulness. We collected many important ideas for our study during two faculty retreats in Tuscany in March of 2008 and of 2009, without which this volume most probably would have never seen the light of day. Accordingly, we would like to extend a big thank you to the team of the Villa Palagione and to all participants of both trips: Thomas Barth, Karina Becker, Michael Behr, Michael Beetz, Peter Bescherer, Tanja Bogusz, Melanie Booth, Uli Brinkmann, Michael Corsten, Susanne Draheim, Silke van Dyk, Margrit Elsner, Dennis Eversberg, Jan Freitag, Lars Gertenbach, Stefanie Graefe, Jannett Grosser, Jens Hälterlein, Tine Haubner, Hajo Holst, Ute Kalbitzer, Christoph Köhler, Cornelia Koppetsch, Martin Langbein, Henning Laux, Diana Lehmann, Oliver Nachtwey, Matthias Neis, Jörg Oberthür, Tilman Reitz, Alexandra Schauer, Karen Schierhorn, Steffen Schmidt, Olaf Struck, Vera Trappmann, Alexandra Wagner, Angela Wenning-Dörre, Torsten Winkler and Franziska Wolf. In addition, we would especially like to thank our faculty colleagues Christoph Köhler, who actively provided help and advice, as well as Heinrich Best and Bruno Hildenbrand, who both kept an eye on our activities with great forbearance, generosity and collegial solidarity. We are delighted to be working with you at the Institute – and, after all is said and done, to share a rock stage with you! The authors would like to give their special thanks to Hans Jürgen Bieling, Frank Deppe, Werner Fricke, Janett Grosser, Oliver Nachtwey, Hans Jürgen Urban, Klaus Peter Wittemann and Volker Wittke (Klaus Dörre); to Thomas Barth, Evi Bunke, Silke van Dyk, Stefanie Graefe and Ute Kalbitzer (Stephan Lessenich); and to Stefan Amann, Ulf Bohmann, Sigrid Engelhardt, Andreas Klinger and David Strecker (Hartmut Rosa). Finally, we would like to thank our publisher Suhrkamp, in particular Mrs Gilmer, Mrs Göhring, and Mr Gelhard, for their faith in our work, and Daniela Neumann for the last corrections to the manuscript. And, of course, Jena and the *genius loci*.

Klaus Dörre, Stephan Lessenich and Hartmut Rosa
Jena, April 2009

Section I

POSITIONS

CHAPTER 1

The New *Landnahme*: Dynamics and Limits of Financial Market Capitalism[1]

KLAUS DÖRRE

I work as a temporary worker in a large company, meaning I am not part of the core workforce. There is no new hiring anyway ... just temping, everywhere. Unfortunately, this kind of capitalism has now been given free rein. Ever since temporary labour laws were loosened up by the government in 2004, the company only hires people on fixed-term contracts. From secretaries to administrators, that's all that's booming. The hiring is done on the basis of the so-called 'BZA collective labour agreements',[2] in which wages are much lower than those of a regular employee. Through these contracts, the employer's obligation to pay an equal wage to temps is circumvented. Compared to my colleagues I only earn two-thirds of their wage, I have five fewer vacation days, no bonuses, only half of the overtime pay, no extra money for meals, no retirement plan, no company pension, no raises, no parking spot, and I'm not allowed to participate in company events – despite the fact that I am in some respects better qualified for the job. I would rather not speak about the psychological stress, which is terrible – because you always feel like a second-class citizen and are continually made to feel that way. Where will this development lead to next? How am I going to find a way out of it? What advice would you give me? I am completely out of ideas at this point.

This passage from an e-mail written by a temporary worker carries a typical complaint commonly heard throughout the world of work. What it reveals is not physical suffering or neglect in an absolute sense; the experiences depicted are, rather, of an existential nature. At first glance, this person seems to have done everything right. Employed in a modern leading sector,

---

1   For Ulla and Frank Deppe.

2   [Trans. Note] BZA is the abbreviation of Bundesverband Zeitarbeit Personal-Dienstleistungen e.V. This is the employers' and business association of licensed temporary work agencies, consisting of about 700 member businesses and around 2,000 subsidiaries.

the IT industry, he engaged in extended vocational training only to find that, even with an *Abitur* (the German leaving certificate, equivalent to British A-levels) there is no path back into the core workforce. All that is left is painful discrimination and helplessness.

How can, or rather, how must a sociologist react to these sorts of grievances? Certainly there is no shortage of scientific *instrumentarium* capable of transcending the expression of cheap, frivolous sympathy. One could inform the inquiring temporary worker that he has become the victim of a risky decision – frustrating on a personal level, but nevertheless the self-chosen fate of many in an individualised modernity. If trained in hermeneutics, one could make the case that he is absolving himself of personal responsibility via the scapegoat of capitalism, instead of seriously pursuing a university degree so as to avail himself of the statistically proven opportunities offered by higher education. Observers schooled in systems theory may confront the author of the e-mail with the fact that his complaint will result in, at most, a slight rustling in the system, the structures of which he will invariably remain embedded within. But one could also attempt something surprising: take the temporary worker seriously and chart a path from the hints that he has laid out in his e-mail. Is there really a connection between the precarious living conditions of one individual and a particular variety of capitalism? How can this capitalism be criticised and changed? What kinds of alternatives exist?

The following attempt to respond to the inquiring temporary worker rests upon the thesis that, since the 1970s, the contours of a new capitalist formation have begun to emerge, (tentatively) referred to in the present article as *financial market capitalism*. A fundamental trait of this fragile formation is that it has made institutions designed to restrict the activity of the market the object of a new *Landnahme*. By now, this process has produced dramatic crises. The limits of this finance-driven *Landnahme* have become evident and thereby open up space for change. In order to explicate this perspective, we will (1) illuminate the socio-economic structure of capitalism; (2) introduce the concept of *Landnahme*; (3) enumerate the distinctive features of financial market capitalism, as well as its crises; and finally (4) take up the question of how everyday grievances can be translated into a contemporary sociological critique of capitalism (5).

1. WHAT IS CAPITALISM?

Anyone inquiring about the core socio-economic structure of capitalism is commonly directed to the concept of socialisation through markets

(*Marktvergesellschaftung*). For the economic mainstream (referred to as *neo-liberal* for the sake of simplicity), ideal capitalism is identical with a market society regulated by a lean state and held together by nothing more than the ethical self-obligation of its members. Numerous diagnoses of the times in which the transition to a new capitalist formation is dealt with as the 'economisation of the social', 'marketisation', or even 'market totalitarianism',[3] build – albeit critically – upon this model. Whether affine or counter-hegemonic, such paradigms have a common problem: they identify capitalism too strongly with the generalisation of the commodity form and competition. As will be shown, however, neither the postulate nor the critique of 'pure' competitive capitalism suffices for a comprehensive grasp of a new social formation. Thus, we will begin by clarifying that which capitalism is *not*, or at least what it is not *exclusively*.

The paradigm of market orthodoxy

Fundamental to the economic-liberal system of thought and its accompanying methodological individualism is the 'demand for a strict limitation of all coercive or exclusive power'.[4] Freedom is defined primarily as the absence of coercion and regulation. Market relations based upon the pursuit of vested interests and allowing market participants the maximum possible scope of decision-making are considered the ideal case of free interaction. Accordingly, contemporary market orthodoxy views the form of competitive capitalism currently unfolding as a precondition for political freedom. In this ideal capitalism, the pursuit of profit is the driving force of economic activity. Anything that detracts from this drive accordingly leads to distortions of competition and, as a result, to social deformations. The ideal of an entrepreneur with a sense of social responsibility represents an especially problematic distortion – at least to Milton Friedman.[5]

---

3 Cf. N. Rose, 'Tod des Sozialen? Eine Neubestimmung der Grenzen des Regierens', in U. Bröckling, S. Krasmann, T. Lemke (ed.), *Gouvernementalität der Gegenwart*, Frankfurt a.M. 2000, pp. 72–109; D. Sauer, 'Arbeit unter (Markt-)Druck: Ist noch Raum für innovative Arbeitspolitik?', in *WSI-Mitteilungen* 58 (4), 2005, pp. 179–185; K. G. Zinn, Art. 'Neoliberalismus', in H.-J. Urban (ed.), *ABC zum Neoliberalismus*, Hamburg, 2006, pp. 164–66, p. 164.

4 F. Hayek, *Individualism and Economic Order*, London 1976 [c1949], p. 48.

5 'Few trends could so thoroughly undermine the very foundations of our free society as the acceptance by corporate officials of a social responsibility other than to make as much money for their stockholders as possible. This is fundamentally subversive doctrine. If businessmen do have a social responsibility other than making maximum profits for stockholders, how are they to know what it is?' (Friedman,

It must be added, however, that the paradigm of market orthodoxy is itself highly multifaceted and encompasses various schools and systems of thought.[6] Even the paradigm's most radical proponents purport to have learnt their lessons from the failure of *laissez faire*, and acknowledge that there are some limits to market coordination. State and government are regarded, not only by ordoliberals but also by followers of the Chicago School, as a 'forum that determines the "rules of the game"', but also as an 'umpire to interpret and enforce the rules decided on'.[7] Consequently, market orthodoxy is not generally opposed to social associations and organisations as such, but rather insists on the principle of freedom of contract being valid for any and all types of organisations. Its opposition is directed 'only against the use of coercion to bring about organisation or association, and not against association as such'.[8] Under this paradigm, the labour market is simply a market like any other; thus freedom of contract is also (indeed, especially) demanded in dealings with the organisations of the wage-earning population.

The presumption is that a market does not do away with inequalities and asymmetries of power, but rather exploits them with the utmost efficiency. Inequality itself is considered 'highly desirable'[9] as it increases the individual's willingness to perform. For modern market orthodoxy, market activity is (aside from a few vital functions of the state) conducted according to the principle of the survival of the fittest. Her Royal Majesty, that is to say economic efficiency, decides, and only the strongest survive! Of course there are rules of the game that all participants must observe, but these rules are only accepted for one reason: not because they are in some way God-given or rationally founded, but simply because they have already established themselves. Accordingly, capitalism can be translated into the formula 'market plus functioning competition plus freedom of contract equals efficiency (maximum output of goods at the lowest possible cost)'. Particularly in ordoliberalism, however, the formula is amended to include the caveat that markets require a state capable of acting, which in turn can only be strong if it limits itself to a few core functions. Thus, the 'market's great achievement' is the reduction of the number of problems that 'must

---

Milton, *Capitalism and Freedom*, in collaboration with Michael Edwards, unabridged, Chicago 1982 [1962], p. 135.)

6   Cf. J. L. Campbell, O. K. Pedersen, *The Rise of Neoliberalism and Institutional Analysis*, Princeton 2001.

7   Friedman, *Capitalism and Freedom*, p. 15.

8   Hayek, *Individualism and Economic Order*, p. 16.

9   Interview with F. A. v. Hayek, in *Wirtschaftswoche*, 6 March 1981; Cf. L. Gertenbach, *Die Kultivierung des Marktes*, Berlin 2007, p. 141.

be decided through political means'.[10] Though state and government may initially be introduced as guardians, presiding over the market and enforcing its rules, it is ultimately the economy that determines the efficiency and market compatibility of politics.

Economic liberalism also holds an answer for the author of our e-mail. According to market orthodoxy, temporary workers' status as outsiders is generated as a result of over-regulated labour markets. While one part of the workforce is paid above the current market rate and enjoys excessive job security due to the cartel-like power of the trade unions, the outsider groups remain excluded, denied access to well-paid and secure employment.[11] In order to improve these outsiders' position on the labour market it is necessary to reduce the power of the trade unions, lower the overall wage level, weaken job security, introduce flexible forms of employment such as temporary labour, and concede to in-house agreements over sector-wide collective bargaining. The take-away is: the complaining worker can be helped, but only if the 'market for labour' is further deregulated so as to finally resemble the market for apples or pears[12] once again.

...and the critique

The notion that a triad consisting of maximisation of vested interest, competition, and freedom of contract leads to optimal economic performance and thus to more prosperity for all has always been a subject of sociological critique. One version of this critique laments economic liberalism's construction of a supposed *homo economicus* operating within ideal, ever-transparent markets of equilibrium (*Gleichgewichtsmärkte*), frequented by fully informed participants, and leading to complete self-regulation. This critique, however, is only partially valid, since its underlying methodological individualism is based on the very assumption of 'the limitations of individual knowledge'. Further, the supposed superiority of market coordination over other forms of coordination itself derives its justification from the fact 'that no person or small group of persons can know all that is known to somebody'.[13]

Another variant of this critique takes a more fundamental approach, revealing the naïve concept of efficiency market fundamentalism that economic liberalism rests upon. Efficiency may be achieved, for example, through a minimisation of transaction or agency costs (that do not even

10   Friedman, *Capitalism and Freedom*, p. 25.
11   Cf. ibid., p. 145 ff.
12   Cf. H.-W. Sinn, *Ist Deutschland noch zu retten?* Berlin 2005, pp. 143, 148 and 150.
13   Hayek, *Individualism and Economic Order*, p.16.

appear in neoclassical deliberations). Transaction costs are caused by 'frictions during the exchange of performance(s) within markets or within a company's internal cooperation'. Such frictions emerge from 'different knowledges and capacities, diverging interests, limited possibilities of knowledge and potentially opportunistic conduct'[14] on the part of market actors. We learn from these deliberations on transaction costs that efficiency is determined not only at the level of the single enterprise, indeed not even by companies exposed to price competition, but to a large degree by institutions that regulate market-based exchange. Approaches that view institutions as resulting from relatively autonomous political and historical processes, as opposed to efficient solutions for owners of capital who wish to maximise their profits, go even further. According to these variants of critique, economic efficiency is based upon highly complex relational systems between market participants and regulatory institutions, which is why economic performance cannot be adequately analysed without identifying structural asymmetries of power and conflicts of interest.

This is where a fundamental critique of economic liberalism begins, as incomparably formulated by Karl Polanyi. Polanyi shatters the market-fundamentalist notion that labour power, land and money are commodities like any other. Labour power is flexible only to a limited degree for the very reason that it lives in a human body, subjected to biorhythms and requiring integration into family structures and social networks in order to procreate. According to Polanyi, the transformation of finite natural resources into commodities reaches its physical limits. Additionally, the use of the medium of communication called money as an object of speculation will sooner or later lead to economic instabilities. Due to this ignorance concerning the peculiarities of labour power, land and money, the notion of a pure market economy is not 'a crass utopia'. A market capitalism regulating itself could 'not exist for any length of time without annihilating the human and natural substance of society; it would have physically destroyed man and transformed his surroundings into a wilderness'.[15]

Consequently, Polanyi defines the relation between freedom and capitalism in diametrical opposition to the paradigm of market orthodoxy. According to him, positive freedom can only, indeed exclusively, arise from

---

14   O. E. Williamson, *Die ökonomischen Institutionen des Kapitalismus*, Tübingen 1990, p. xiii. (English: *The Economic Institutions of Capitalism*, New York 1985).

[Trans. Note] this quote is part of a foreword that only appeared in the German edition of the book, thus it has been translated back into English here.

15   K. Polanyi, *The Great Transformation: The Political and Economic Origins of our Time*, unabridged, Princeton 2005 p.3

limitations on and regulations of market forces: 'The comfortable classes enjoy the freedom provided by leisure in security; they are naturally less anxious to extend freedom in society'. Elementary civil rights, including a 'right to nonconformity', should also be guaranteed, and 'should be upheld at all costs – even that of efficiency in production, economy in consumption or rationality in administration'. This may involve limiting negative freedoms, which are enjoyed at the cost of the weaker sections of society, to the benefit of positive freedoms. Only the end of the pure market economy may signify 'the beginning of an era of unprecedented freedom'.[16]

To the liberal mainstream of economics, such considerations may seem like outright heresy today. And yet it was precisely these ideas that had a powerful impact on the thinking of economic and political elites post-1945. Economic liberalism appeared to be dead until its resurrection as an ideological weapon against the social gains achieved by the brief wave of worker militancy in the 1970s. As it was aimed primarily at market liberalisation, the state-political dimensions of market fundamentalism could be easily masked. Variants of critique that took the negative utopian view of a 'pure' competitive market literally also contributed to this idea. What market orthodoxy supposedly praised as its guiding principle was turned into the object of the 'anti-market totalitarian' critique. Without a doubt, these variants did manage to grasp prominent aspects of the transformation of modern day capitalism to some degree; particularly because the conceptually embedded concern for the market that pushed Hayek and Friedman to accept limited state intervention is usually reduced to simpler expressions and prescriptions in everyday discussion. But here it is crucial to emphasise that the critique of 'turbo-capitalism' and its 'unchained markets' largely misses the point. Capitalism, including its contemporary form, is not a pure market society – it is not a purely competitive capitalism, nor will it ever become one. Its dynamic and ability to survive through a crisis-prone and partly catastrophic process has its roots in the very fact that, thus far, it has always been able to generate self-stabilisers that ensure its survival. For this reason, capitalism cannot be reduced to competition alone. It is true that capitalism cannot function without market-mediated competition. However, to function within said competition, modes of behaviour based on cooperation – if not solidarity – are needed from both individual and collective actors; thereby postulating the exact opposite of market-mediated competition.

An understanding of capitalism that addresses this contradictoriness will be our point of departure for a few conceptual considerations. It seems appropriate to build on Pierre Bourdieu's early study of Algerian society in

---

16   Ibid. pp. 255–56. Cf. also D. Harvey, *A Brief History of Neoliberalism*, Oxford 2005.

transition.[17] In the vein of Weber[18] and Sombart,[19] Bourdieu links the transition to a capitalist mode of production with the problem of acquiring a rational lifestyle based on a calculated mode of thinking. What market fundamentalism views as a quasi supra-historical, organic trait of *homo economicus* – the development of a rational and calculated mode of thinking detached from basic wants – can only arise in specific historical circumstances. Corresponding patterns of thinking and acting are part of what Bourdieu calls the 'economic habitus'. In contrast to Weber and Sombart, Bourdieu links the chances of appropriating and habitualising calculated modes of thinking to the experience of elementary social stability. The French sociologist considers a minimum level of job and income security as a prerequisite for the conscious conceptualisation of one's own future. Only with this consciousness of the future, presupposing individual planning capacity, is rational-calculated behaviour possible. Even innovative entrepreneurs confronted with uncertainty on a structural level require a minimum of planning security. In their own best interests (i.e., pursuit of profit), they strive to restrict the capriciousness of market competition, albeit temporarily, through deployment of their resources of power. Thus, socialisation through markets (*Marktvergesellschaftung*) is based on contradictory, or even conflicting, underlying logics of behaviour. Any single transaction regulated via prices – as long as not viewed in isolation – requires a social anchor, specifically a time frame that extends beyond the horizon of market-driven transactions. The developed forms of capitalism, with their highly differentiated sub-systems, cannot escape this inevitability.

Indeed, the market-orthodox critics of 'social capitalism'[20] are largely aware of this fact. Their guiding principle of a competitive capitalism that regulates itself within certain confines has remained a fiction even in the most radical attempts at its implementation: in Chile, Mexico, the USA or Great Britain. Everywhere, the reinforcement of socialisation through markets has spawned in its wake a bureaucratic surveillance state that monitors the most basal economic activities in minute detail. Essentially, the universalist assumption of economic liberalism already contains, if not its opposite, at least several diverse particularities. If economic liberalism propagates the openness of markets, civil-rights liberalism requires a functioning body politic capable of issuing legal guarantees. The contemporary (and

---

17   Cf. P. Bourdieu, *Algeria 1960*, Cambridge 1972.

18   M. Weber, *The Protestant Ethic and the Spirit of Capitalism*, 23d printing. London, New York 2001 (Routledge Classics) (orig. *Die protestantische Ethik und der Geist des Kapitalismus* [1904/05]).

19   Cf. W. Sombart, *Der moderne Kapitalismus*, 2 volumes, Munich 1924.

20   R. Sennett, *The Culture of the New Capitalism*, New Haven 2006, p. 27.

not at all minimal) competitive state generates a plethora of rules to rein in market principles. For its advocates, this is precisely what constitutes the cynical charm of the radical free-market paradigm. Market fundamentalists know very well that they are formulating an ideology of attack that will never entirely reach its goal.[21] This way, the message they seek to convey becomes inexhaustible. Wherever the doctrine of free market fundamentalism fails, its proponents can claim that there are still remaining institutions strangling market forces and distorting competition, thus resulting in misallocations. Should state intervention occur for, say, ailing financial institutions, this can be justified by referring to the necessary regulatory functions of government. In this sense, market fundamentalism is always right. Resembling a theodicy, the market orthodoxy paradigm projects an image of itself as a compendium of eternal truths, the challenging of which (at least German) economists still consider sacrilege.

Capitalism as a self-negating market economy

This assessment also implies that fundamentalist economic liberalism conveys a reductive, unrealistic conception of capitalism. In order to avoid such reductionism, it seems appropriate to update a variant of critique that grasps capitalism as a continuously self-negating market economy. According to Marx, we can only speak of capitalism if it has become an economic mode in which accumulated assets are invested in commodity production for the sole purpose of generating more money – a discovery that can be subsumed under the brief formula M-C-M′. The metamorphosis of labour power and natural resources into capital, i.e., the 'constant reintroduction of capital into the economic circuit with a view to deriving a profit – that is to say, increasing the capital, which will in turn be reinvested',[22] is what defines the particular dynamic of capitalist economics.

The caricature of a pure market economy is rejected threefold by Marx. First, hidden behind the relation of exchange in which free commodity owners meet in market spaces to exchange commodities of equal value is a fundamental power asymmetry. In the capitalist economy, human labour power becomes an ordinary commodity, in as much as it is subjected to the principle of 'exchange of equivalents'. Equipped only with the power to create exchange value, it nevertheless has a unique feature: its capacity to produce exchange value can be consumed by users beyond a threshold, as

---

21   Cf. N. Klein, *The Shock Doctrine: The Rise of Disaster Capitalism*, London 2007.

22   L. Boltanski, E. Chiapello, G. C. Elliott, *The New Spirit of Capitalism*, London, New York 2007, p. 5.

defined by the average cost of reproduction of labour power. Human labour power can thus become the source of surplus product, of surplus value. What is constitutive for capitalist economics is, then, that the appropriation and use of this surplus product occurs in the form of particular relations of production. A class of owners of capital that monopolises the ownership of the means of production is in the position to appropriate the produced surplus value. While wage labourers are paid according to the value of their labour power, which oscillates around the cost of its reproduction, depending on the material standards of living and the balance of forces between different social classes, the owners of capital are in a position to consume this labour power beyond its cost in paid wages. After deducting the costs of constant capital (raw materials, energy, machines), they earn a profit, which may then be reinvested with the aim of generating even higher earnings. You do not have to agree with the controversial labour theory of value contained within Marx's diagnosis of exploitation[23] to recognise that therein lies a fundamental power asymmetry behind the exchange of labour power for wages. The owners of capital can rely first and foremost on their own market power to achieve their goals. The relation of capital does not in itself provide any incentive to organise. Wage labourers, on the other hand, only stand a chance of influencing the conditions under which they sell their labour power if they overcome competition and begin to 'form combinations (trade unions) against the bourgeoisie.'[24] Associations such as the trade unions are primarily defensive organisations; as 'price warriors', they ensure that wages correspond to the full value of labour power. According to Marx, they in fact fail at this function to the extent that they merely wage 'guerrilla war against the effects of the existing system, instead of simultaneously trying to change it.'[25]

The class conflict within the capitalist mode of production, which may be pacified but never fully suspended, is not the only structural characteristic that deviates from the market equilibrium ideal – which, if need be, is created by means of state force. No less severe is, *secondly*, the crisis-proneness of capitalism. In order to survive in competition, the capitalists, each producing in isolation from one another, are forced to constantly improve their methods of production. One important motive behind this is the search for extra profits. 'A capitalist working with improved but not as yet

---

23   Cf. M. Berger, K. Marx, *Das Kapital*, Munich 2004, pp. 64–128; M. Heinrich, *Kritik der politischen Ökonomie*, Stuttgart 2004; P. Sraffa, *Warenproduktion mittels Waren*, Frankfurt a.M. 1963.

24   Marx, Engels, 'Manifesto of the Communist Party', *Collected Works*, vol. 6, p. 493.

25   Marx, Engels, 'Value, Price and Profit', *Collected Works*, vol. 20, p. 149.

generally adopted methods of production sells below the market price, but above his individual price of production; his rate of profit rises until competition levels it out'.[26] This motive guarantees ceaseless improvement of the means of production, technical equipment and the organisation of labour, while simultaneously causing a systematic build-up of market imbalances. Individual capitalists expand their production capacity in lucrative business sectors, but sooner or later reach the limits of their turnover. This problem of realisation has the effect that capital accumulation has a tendency toward systemic instability. Market participants, especially the capitalists, exhibit a kind of behaviour that does not, as *doyen* of market speculation George Soros phrased it (with regard to investment strategies in contemporary financial markets), correspond to any ideal of harmonic equilibrium. Rather, the behaviour of these markets resembles a wrecking ball, its pendular movement leading again and again to dramatic exaggerations, crises, devastation and destruction of capital.[27] In Marxist theory, however, periodic economic crises[28] do not feature as an indicator of approaching systemic collapse. On the contrary, the cycle of crisis is to an extent functional since, at a certain point, the destruction of capital necessitates substituting the means of production, triggering solvent demand and stimulating a new dynamic of accumulation.

However, what is essential, *thirdly,* is that economic crises drive forward a process that amounts to a partial restriction of competition and a change in property relations within the capitalist mode of production. To put it bluntly: capitalist competition produces its own counterpart: the suspension of free competition and the socialisation of private property. This 'expropriation is accomplished by the action of the immanent laws of capitalistic production itself, by the centralisation of capital', because 'one capitalist always kills many'[29] of his fellow capitalists. The concentration of the means of production and labour forces, along with the simultaneous centralisation of capital, turn stock corporations, (as Marx anticipated) into monopolistic enterprises. These large corporations can never fully suspend capitalist competition. They can, however, leverage their market power to influence price formation, erect barriers to entry of the market, and delay capital depreciation.

26   Marx, Engels, *Collected Works*, vol. 37 (Capital vol. 3), p. 229.

27   Cf. G. Soros, *Die Krise des globalen Kapitalismus*, Berlin 1998, p. 83 ff. (orig. *The Crisis of Global Capitalism*, New York 1998).

28   Cf. R. Brenner, *Boom and Bubble*, Hamburg 2003 (orig. *The Boom and the Bubble: The US in the World Economy*, London 2002); J. Hoffmann (ed.), Überproduktion, Unterkonsumtion, Depression, Hamburg 1983.

29   Marx, Engels, *Collected Works*, vol. 35 (Capital vol. 1), p. 750.

The emergence of large corporate conglomerates negates the idea of market equilibrium in several ways. That is to say, bureaucratic corporations and even state enterprises are by all means capable of utilising their market power in a positive way. The world would have probably been without railroads for a long time if it 'had to wait until the accumulation of individual capitals had proceeded far enough'[30] to make the necessary investments. Large corporate bureaucracies ensure a certain degree of orderliness and predictability in economic activity. At the same time, though, this 'abolition of the capitalist mode of production within the capitalist mode of production itself' represents a permanent source of economic instability:

> It [the contradictory process of a relative suspension of competition] establishes a monopoly in certain spheres and thereby requires state interference. It reproduces a new financial aristocracy, a new variety of parasites in the shape of promoters, speculators and simply nominal directors; a whole system of swindling and cheating by means of corporation promotion, stock issuance, and stock speculation. It is private production without the control of private property.[31]

Apart from the problematic comparison to 'parasites', Marx anticipates almost clairvoyantly a problem reflected today in, for example, agency theory. Even in the historical stage of capitalist development known to Marx, the specialisation of capital functions – separation of capital ownership and management, the differentiation in the credit sector, and the emergence of a financial oligarchy with specific vested interests – all inevitably created sectional interests, frictions, and nontransparency stripping the ideal of self-regulating markets of any degree of credibility. To be sure, organised capitalism, the existence of which Marx best anticipated, is a specific market economy. However, it can only function as a market economy because it is based upon state intervention, bureaucratisation, the recognition of organised interests and a partial suspension of competitive relations, the latter of which it actually reproduces on an expanded scale.

2. How does capitalism develop?

What can our aforementioned temporary worker learn from the line of argument thus far? Well, he now knows that the market economy and capitalism are not identical. And he is probably somewhat aware of the fact that modern market orthodoxy does not have anything positive to offer him. The more he

---

30   Ibid., p. 693.
31   Marx, Engels, *Collected Works*, vol. 37 (Capital vol. 3), p. 436.

learns, the more he is unable to shake the feeling that he will have to engage with Marx and his analysis of capitalism. Delving into the writings of that old philosopher from Trier, he will come to understand capitalism as an 'absurd system'[32] in which the vast majority of producers have lost ownership over the goods they produce while a comparatively small number of capitalists remain locked into an abstract process that is utterly detached from actual human need or practical value, aimed exclusively at the self-realisation of value and the expansion of capital for its own sake. Indeed, the division into use-value and exchange-value alone carries with it the possibility of crisis. Nevertheless, it manages again and again to motivate not only the capitalists but also the broader masses to participate in said 'absurd system'.

Our temporary worker will have to extend his scholastic efforts beyond Marx if he wants to fully comprehend all of this. It seems to be the case that some special 'spirit of capitalism'[33] endows gainful employment with a sense of meaning, as it does other activities critical to the system's functionality. The spirit of capitalism is an ideological system, but it is not merely false consciousness. A more accurate description would be to say that, under capitalism, individuals or social groups acquire certain motivations, techniques, behaviours and thought patterns which are in turn necessary prerequisites to acquiring agency in concrete life conditions. The integrative effect achieved through this can at times be so strong as to absorb even the most fundamental critiques of capitalism that emerge in times of crisis, transforming them into a conflict-mediated form of legitimacy. This realisation will probably make our inquirer feel even more perplexed. Is it possible that capitalism is simply invulnerable? Attempting to answer this question leads us to another problem. In order to defuse critique, capitalism must legitimise itself, sometimes through actual democratic procedures, and has to respond to said critique at least partially. Thus, to whatever extent critique of capitalism may aid in stabilising the system, it is not without consequence. Indeed, it contributes to, and may even cause changes in capitalism. What this implies is that, if critique seeks to remain influential, it must always refer to specific stages in capitalism's development and adapt its coordinate system to changes in the system itself. So how does capitalism in fact develop? We might find an answer to this question in a theorem devised by David Harvey[34] in reference to Rosa Luxemburg and Hannah Arendt.

---

32   L. Boltanski, E. Chiapello, G. C. Elliott, *The New Spirit of Capitalism*, London, New York 2007, p. 7.

33   That is to say 'the set of beliefs associated with the capitalist order that helps to justify this order and, by legitimating them, to sustain the forms of action and predispositions compatible with it'. (Ibid. p. 10.)

34   Cf. D. Harvey, *Limits to Capital*, London 2006.

According to this theorem, capitalist development can be understood as a succession of *Landnahmen* of previously non-capitalist terrain.

Primitive accumulation

Marx did in fact analyse the basic form of capitalist *Landnahmen*. In his reflections on 'so-called primitive accumulation',[35] he sketches the emergence of capitalism in a non-capitalist environment. The essential feature of this development is the formation of capitalist property and class relations. He views the expropriation of the rural population as a pivotal precondition for the emergence of a new type of producer: a wage labourer who is 'free in a double sense', with no attachments to lands or guilds. Marx depicts this process, complemented by the monopolisation of the means of production in the hands of a small group of owners, as an extremely brutal sequence of events based not on talents or virtues so much as on centuries-old histories of peasant expropriation, violent enclosure of community lands, seizure of church property, colonial oppression, and the slave trade.

Historical research has replaced Marx's sharp polemics with sophisticated analyses. What seems clear is that Marx's conclusions rely far too much on a singular example – Great Britain. Furthermore, he was of course limited to the historical knowledge of his time. Today it is known that the transition from feudalism to capitalism occurred in a far less despotic manner[36] (as, for example, Edward P. Thompson has found in the case of Britain during the industrial revolution), which implies a renunciation of 'catastrophic historiography'. This does not necessarily imply endorsement of an 'anti-catastrophic orthodoxy',[37] however. What is of more interest at this point is not so much differing interpretations over the emergence of capitalism, but rather the basic logic behind the Marxian line of argument. *Landnahme* therefore means the expansion of the capitalist mode of production internally and externally. This way, the separation of large parts of the rural population from its traditional lands created an 'internal market': the landless population was forced to survive by selling its labour power. Production based upon human need was abandoned by means of this process; raw materials and foodstuffs now became commodities. The subsequent elimination of sub-industries and the separation of manufacturing and agriculture caused

---

35   Cf. Marx, Engels, *Collected Works*, vol. 35 (Capital vol. 1), p.705 ff.

36   Cf. E. M. Wood, *The Origin of Capitalism*, New York 1999; F. Braudel, *Sozialgeschichte des 15.–18. Jahrhunderts*, 3 volumes, Munich 1985–1987; M. Mann, *Geschichte der Macht*, vol. 2, Frankfurt a.M., New York 1994, pp. 319–424.

37   E. P. Thompson, *The Making of the English Working Class*, Toronto 1991, p.195.

even more radical restructuring, providing the necessary reserves of potential labour power for an expanding capitalist mode of production.

As Marx impressively demonstrates, this internal *Landnahme* was and is a highly political process that depends on state intervention from the outset. Without state intervention, neither changes in property relations and the expropriation of the rural population, nor the adjustment and disciplining of displaced workers for the new mode of production are possible. This is why laws of feudal origin were used again and again to engender a general social compulsion to work and establish political wage norms suited to the system's needs. The 'agricultural people ... turned into vagabonds' were to some extent 'whipped, branded, and tortured by grotesque and terrible laws – constrained to accept the discipline required by the wage system'.[38] From a systematic perspective, this process is less about the degree of brutality than about the fact that a politically motivated precarity was used to discipline redundant labourers and press them into service of the new mode of production. This disciplining in a manner critical to the system's functionality could nevertheless occur less violently, such as through systemic absorption of pre-capitalist capacities, knowledge and social relations.

Only large industry, with its machines and factory system, provides a 'lasting basis of capitalistic agriculture, expropriates radically the enormous majority of the agricultural population, and completes the separation between agriculture and rural domestic industry', and 'therefore also, for the first time, conquers for industrial capital the entire home market'.[39] Indeed, it was true for the industrial revolution as a whole that it rested upon a long period of political exclusion of the working class. Even in England, freedom of association and the right of workers to form unions was only introduced after a long delay. So, capitalism was never, not even in its beginnings, a self-regulating market economy; rather, the state served as a crucial midwife of the new mode of production. It ensured that market formation occurred under the conditions of structural power asymmetries. The external expansion of the capitalist mode of production, only possible due to the fact that capitalism constituted itself as an international system from its inception (one interconnected above and beyond the borders of nation-states), was also politically facilitated. Market formation during that centuries-long period of primitive accumulation was, then, a process to a large extent politically motivated and marked by power asymmetries. Marx held the view, however, that political coercion, including open violence in its most

---

38   Marx, Engels, *Collected Works*, vol. 35 (Capital vol.1), p.726. Cf. also M. Foucault, *Madness and Civilization*, New York 1965, p. 46f.

39   Marx, Engels, *Collected Works*, vol. 35 (Capital vol.1), p.737 f.

extensive manifestation, would remain a mere episode in the early history of capitalism. Over the course of history, a class of workers that 'by education, tradition, habit, looks upon the conditions of that mode of production as self-evident laws of Nature' would emerge. Violence outside the economic realm would only be deployed in exceptional cases, but usually, the workers could be left to the 'natural laws of production'. 'The dull compulsion of economic relations completes the subjection of the labourer to the capitalist'.[40]

Generalisation of the Landnahme thesis

Marxist heretics[41] are not the only ones who have called the universal validity of this assumption into question. In her studies on imperialism, Hannah Arendt shows that primitive accumulation seems to be repeating itself, albeit under an altered set of historical circumstances.[42] Arendt draws upon an argument developed by Rosa Luxemburg in her major work The Accumulation of Capital, positing that capitalist development is in a sense two-faced. One type of development takes root in the centres of production of surplus value: in the factories, the fully capitalised sectors of agriculture, and the commodity markets. Here, capitalism reproduces itself mainly along its own foundations. The other type of development breaks ground and forges ahead in the relations of exchange between capital accumulation on the one hand, and non-capitalist modes of production and territories on the other.[43] Luxemburg's argument is that only a limited amount of the total social product can be realised in the 'internal movement of goods'. Structurally restricted solvent demand necessitates the realisation of parts of total surplus value 'externally'. This problem becomes more evident and more intense the greater the total value mass, whether in absolute terms or, say, relative to the surplus value being created. For Luxemburg, the tensions arising from this help explain the contradictory phenomenon that 'the old capitalist countries provide ever larger markets for, and become increasingly dependent upon, one another, yet on the other hand compete ever more ruthlessly for trade relations with non-capitalist countries'.[44] Alluding to this remark, Hannah Arendt phrases it slightly more bluntly:

---

40   Ibid. p.726.
41   Cf. R. Luxemburg, The Accumulation of Capital, London 1951 [1913].
42   Cf. H. Arendt, The Origins of Totalitarianism, New York op.1958, pp.137 ff.
43   Luxemburg, The Accumulation of Capital, p. 315.
44   Ibid., p. 367.

The ensuing crises and depressions during the decades preceding the era of imperialism had impressed upon the capitalists the thought that their 'whole economic
system of production depended upon a supply and demand that from now on
must come from outside of capitalist society.' Such supply and demand came from
inside the nation, so long as the capitalist system did not control all its classes ...
When capitalism had pervaded the entire economic structure and all social strata
had come into the orbit of its production and consumption system, capitalists
clearly ... [realised that] the forms and laws of their production system 'from the
beginning had been calculated for the whole earth' [and] had to decide either to
see the whole system collapse or to find new markets, that is, to penetrate new
countries which were not yet subject to capitalism and therefore could provide a
new non-capitalist supply and demand.[45]

Two ideas that resonate with both Luxemburg and Arendt cannot be
maintained in light of recent debates. These pertain firstly to the theory of
under-consumption.[46] Although there are certainly phases or periods of
development in which processes of economic crisis can be traced back to
under-consumption, today most internationally dominant approaches recognise that weak demand can be compensated for by, for example, increased
investment. Therefore more recent theories of crisis, insofar as they relate
to the Marxist critique of political economy, base themselves increasingly
upon the phenomenon of over-accumulation.[47] Particularly problematic in
the *Landnahme* thesis are its implications in terms of a breakdown theory,
as formulated quite explicitly by Arendt and Luxemburg. Surely, capitalist
Landnahmen are in some sense irreversible, i.e., when they completely absorb
traditional modes of production or seriously deplete natural resources. In
this sense, the total capitalisation of external markets appears as a process
that must come to an end at some far off, distant time, for without external
markets, there can be no capitalism.

There exists, however, a very different and intriguing reading of the
Landnahme thesis. According to this interpretation, capitalism is capable
of shedding its skin at certain conjunctures of its development. That is
to say, the *regime of accumulation*[48] and property relations, the *modes of*

---

45   H. Arendt, *The Origins of Totalitarianism*, New York 1966, p.148
46   It remains disputed whether or not Rosa Luxemburg was a proponent of
underconsumptionist theory. Cf. F. Haug, *Rosa Luxemburg und die Kunst der Politik*,
Hamburg 2007.
47   Cf. Brenner, *Boom*; D. Harvey, *The New Imperialism*, Oxford, New York
2005, p.132 ff.
48   A regime of accumulation is defined by the establishment, over
a longer period of time, of a correlative relationship between the means of

regulation[49] and *models of production*[50] are revolutionised and transformed – but only with the aim of preserving capitalism. One of the founders of Western Marxism, Antonio Gramsci, labelled such transformations 'passive revolutions'. He applied the term not only to Italian fascism, but also when discussing the emergence of the Fordist methods of production and mass culture ('Americanism').[51] Such transformations are possible because capitalism, within certain relations of time and space, can always refer to a kind of 'exterior' that it partly produces itself: 'capitalism can either make use of some pre-existing outside … or it can actively manufacture it.'[52] The proactive creation of an 'exterior' means that the chain of potential *Landnahmen* is veritably endless. The 'original sin' of primitive accumulation, i.e., 'a blasting apart of the laws of pure economics through political action',[53] can and must repeat itself continuously on an ever-expanding scale.

David Harvey has expanded this internal-external dialectic into a broader theory of capitalist development.[54] According to this theory, capitalism's dynamic lies in its capacity to produce and destroy space. Through investments in machinery, factories, the labour force, and infrastructure, capital enters into spatial relations it cannot undo without incurring costs and frictions. In this process, investment geared toward the development of spaces – for example, expansion of transportation lines, development of natural resources, investment in basic and further vocational training and occupational safety – assumes particular importance. These sorts of

production, its development, and its social consumption. Cf. M. Aglietta, *Ein neues Akkumulationsregime*, Hamburg 2000, p. 12ff.

49   A mode of regulation signifies the sum total of forms, organisations, explicit and implicit norms which endow society with cohesiveness by reconciling opposing interests and selfish behaviours with the requirements of capital valorisation. The category regulatory *dispositif* expresses the fact that changes in means of regulation should not be understood as a process of total removal of an antiquated mode of regulation and its immediate replacement with a completely new one. Cf. K. Dörre, B. Röttger, *Im Schatten der Globalisierung*, Wiesbaden 2006.

50   Production models are networks of social relations which create links between business organisations, forms of competition, labour relations, and the education system. Cf. R. Boyer, J.-P. Durand, *After Fordism*, London 1997, S. 3.

51   A. Gramsci, *Prison Notebooks*, Vol. 1, New York 1992, p. 136f; Cf. also A. Gramsci, *Selections from the Prison Notebooks*, p. 279f.

52   D. Harvey, *The New Imperialism*, Oxford, New York 2005, p. 141.

53   [Trans. Note] the passage cited, 'eine Sprengung rein ökonomischer Gesetzmäßigkeit durch politisches Handeln', does not appear in the English translation of Arendt, *Origins of Totalitarianism*, and has thus been translated here to retain the original meaning. It can be found in the original German text: Arendt, *Elemente*, 1951, p. 335.

54   Cf. D. Harvey, *Spaces of Global Capitalism*, New York 2006, p. 71ff.

investments only begin to pay off over longer periods of time, i.e., they are temporarily withdrawn from the primary circuit of consumption (immediate consumption) and diverted into the secondary circuit (capital for means of production, or formation of assets for later consumption, e.g., housing) or even the tertiary circuit (funds for research and development, social programmes, etc.). There is, however, no guarantee that these investments will ever actually become profitable. The sort of outlays required to build, for example, a comprehensive railway network shows clearly that the state sometimes must serve as a kind of 'ideational collective capitalist' when long-term, large-scale investment is required.

Long-term cycles of investment within certain spaces and temporal horizons are evidently connected to the 'long waves'[55] of capitalist accumulation that tend to occur between historical crises of transformation, and from which more or less coherent capitalist formations emerge. The precise nature of the links between these 'long waves', themselves mere analytical abstractions that are distilled 'from the ever-present ups and downs of accumulation and the social product', and the internal-external dialectic of capitalism identified by Harvey would doubtless be worth an entire research programme of its own. At this point it must suffice to note the self-stabilising function of this dialectic. Investments in infrastructure, and in education and training, constitute cycles of economic development within their respective spaces, which, at the very least, mitigate the problem of over-accumulation via long-term commitments of capital. Such periods are ideal for limiting market socialisation – that is, closing off potential fields of investment such as the postal service, telecommunications, public transportation, and education from private exploitation, and turning them into public goods with the aid of state intervention. Hence, molecular individual capitalist operations are provided with an 'exterior' which, though inaccessible for private accumulation, can nevertheless be harnessed for the improvement of economic performance.

Such enclosure of market socialisation provokes strategies aimed at the loosening or even suspension of the spatio-temporal commitment of capital as soon as it becomes an obstacle to capital valorisation. In this sense, the various waves of internationalisation among capitalist corporations can be seen as attempts to escape the problems of producing (surplus) value

---

55   Cf. E. Altvater, 'Bruch und Formwandel eines Entwicklungsmodells. Die gegenwärtige Krise ist ein Prozess gesellschaftlicher Transformation', in Hoffmann (ed.), *Überproduktion*, pp. 217–52; E. Mandel, *Long Waves of Capitalist Development*, Cambridge 1980; A. Kleinknecht, 'Innovation, Akkumulation und Krise. Überlegungen zu den ‚langen Wellen' der Konjunktur vor dem Hintergrund neuer Ergebnisse der historischen Innovationsforschung', in *Prokla* 35, 1979, pp. 85–104.

in their home bases.[56] However, this is only one of many strategic options designed to counter the pressures of over-accumulation. Harvey describes a number of these strategies, which include financialisation (stock market flotation, mergers, company takeovers, etc.) as well as conversion of state enterprises or privatisation of public enterprises, as 'accumulation by dispossession.' These dispossessions allow excess capital to acquire liberated assets at a very low (if any) cost.[57] Wherever this leads to de-industrialisation, economic decline, mass unemployment, and poverty, a new 'exterior' develops – devastated, abandoned regions and idle labour forces – which, at a later stage of development, may become the site of long-term reconstruction investment(s).[58]

According to Harvey, 'accumulation by dispossession' represents the functional equivalent to the violent acts of primitive accumulation and imperialist *Landnahmen* as analysed by Luxemburg and Arendt. *Landnahmen*, however, are not confined to 'cannibalistic', 'predatory', or 'fraudulent' practices.[59] As Harvey notes only implicitly, their actual modus operandi rests upon highly divergent forms of state intervention. As shown, the 'blasting apart' of purely economic laws, e.g., the expansion of public services, the production of collective assets, or the strengthening of social safety nets, can also be achieved by means of de-commodification (decoupling from market risks) and long-term commitment of capital in the secondary and tertiary circuits. Those strategies that Harvey subsumes under the phrase 'accumulation by dispossession' harness the privatisation of public entities and the deregulation of labour markets as a lever to re- or de-commodify labour power. Applied to the problematic of economic and social development, this means that capitalism cannot exist without *Landnahmen* – that is, without the harnessing of external asset values (including idle labour power). Nevertheless, the actual goals, forms and means of *Landnahmen* vary sharply. The choice of strategy is always a political process as well, which implies that *Landnahmen*, at least to some extent, can be subject to political influence.

The internal-external dialectic also helps us to better understand the significance of exclusion and precarity for capitalist economic rationality. The 'mechanism of the industrial reserve army',[60] as explicated by Marx in the first volume of *Capital*, in a sense represents a classic case of the pro-active creation of an 'exterior'. In periods of accelerated economic growth,

---

56   Cf. W. Ruigrok, R. van Tulder, *The Logic of International Restructuring*, London 1995.

57   D. Harvey, *The New Imperialism*, Oxford, New York 2005, p. 140.

58   Cf. Dörre, Röttger, *Im Schatten*.

59   Harvey, *The New Imperialism*, p. 148.

60   Cf. Marx, Engels, *Collected Works*, vol. 35 (Capital vol.1), p. 623 f.

the industrial reserve army in its various manifestations, can be used to mobilise additional labour forces.

Especially in times of crisis, those who are excluded from capitalist production represent a potential source of pressure that can be applied in order to keep labour costs as low as possible.[61] So the social question that Marx had in mind has always known an 'interior' and an 'exterior'. Exploitation and the private acquisition of collectively produced surplus value are at the heart of the 'interior', while within the sphere of the 'exterior' we witness the depression of incomes and living standards to a level below the previous standard of a social class, as well as over-exploitation and in extreme cases, the total demobilisation of labour capacity.

The ongoing impact of this internal-external dialectic leaves its mark on social as well as geographical space. The Algerian case analysed by Pierre Bourdieu dealt with a mere repetition of 'primitive accumulation', temporally and spatially displaced to the periphery of a prospering Fordist capitalism, which entails a specific linkage between capitalist *Landnahme* and precarisation. For the newly emerging class of capitalist owners (whom Bourdieu as a matter of course does not investigate), the Algerian subproletariat represents an 'external market' suitable for the mobilisation of additional labour forces as circumstances require, but more than anything serves to discipline the industrial working class emerging in parallel. The decisive aspect of differentiation between the working class and the subproletariat is the integration of those workers considered qualified into a time regime that allows for longer-term life planning. Especially under conditions of high structural unemployment, skilled workers and qualified staff hold a significant advantage over their competitors. The relative security provided by stable employment allows those workers to orient their lives toward future goals and objectives.

For the sub-proletarians, however, 'the whole of their working existence is dominated by arbitrariness'.[62] A reserve 'army of unskilled labourers'[63] prepared to 'accept any conditions in order to escape unemployment'[64] is more or less endlessly exploitable. Unemployment and temporary work impede the development of long-term life plans. The workers 'are sharply divided into two groups', into 'those who are stable and do all they can to remain so', and those 'ready to do anything to escape from instability'.[65]

---

61   Cf. Harvey, *The New Imperialism*, p. 139.
62   Bourdieu, *Algeria 1960*, p. 35.
63   Ibid.
64   Ibid.
65   Ibid. p. 78.

The mixed economy of social-bureaucratic capitalism

Our temporary worker pricks up his ears. Much of what Bourdieu describes sounds awfully familiar to him, since he experiences the contradictory relationship between 'two classes of workers' every day in his own place of employment. Could history be repeating itself? Or are we actually dealing with a form of capitalism whose mechanisms are reminiscent of an earlier stage of capitalism? The answer is a resounding yes and no! Yes, because the forms of processing and the disciplinary impact of precarity, as analysed by Bourdieu, still resonate with present circumstances. No, because the circumstances of a highly skilled IT specialist cannot conceivably be compared to the situation of Algerian sub-proletarians. To be able to understand and criticise the contemporary manifestations of precarity, one must first picture the historical background against which the new capitalist formation emerged. As indicated, *Landnahmen* always involve an interplay between market liberalisation and market delimitation. In the course of this process, the question is never one of state or market,[66] but rather of a specific combination of markets and political-hierarchical power. In one period, the state may act as the protagonist of market liberalisation, while in the subsequent period it may intervene as an agent of market closure. Indeed, Fordist capitalism, which today serves as the background against which new developments are analysed, was the product of a specific *Landnahme*. More precisely, the emergence of this social-bureaucratic capitalism was rooted in a cycle of investments in infrastructure with long-term effects, the absorption of the potential labour power of a traditional, agrarian economic sector organised in small businesses, and a previously unheard-of level of institutionalisation of 'workers' power'.[67] Its genesis can be traced back primarily to certain strategies aimed at the de-commodification of labour power.

Given that the general features of Fordist capitalism have been outlined in numerous texts, here a brief sketch should suffice. Capitalist *Landnahmen* function as if they occurred by historical chance (*historische Fundsachen*); that is, lacking any kind of accompanying historical inevitability, and temporarily yielding stable variants of regimes of accumulation, regulatory *dispositifs* and production models. Fordist capitalism, which emerged in

---

66 Cf. D. S. J. Yergin, *Staat oder Markt*, Frankfurt a.M. 1999.

67 Generally, a distinction can be made between structural organisational power and institutional power of workers. Cf. B. J. Silver, *Forces of Labour*, Berlin 2005, pp. 30–44; E. O. Wright, 'Working Class Power, Capitalist Class Interests, and Class Compromise', in *American Journal of Sociology* 105 (4), 2000, pp. 957–1002; K. Dörre, H. Holst, O. Nachtwey, 'Organizing – A Strategic Option for Trade Union Renewal?', in *International Journal of Action Research* 5 (1), 2009, pp. 1–35, here p. 3ff.

the 1920s and peaked post 1945, represents just one of these formations. The Fordist regime of accumulation was built on specific combinations of mass production and mass consumption, and on a society of wage earners, which in turn was based on these combinations.[68] Internationally, Fordism evolved under the conditions of stable US hegemony across the Western world and a bipolar world system. It owed its success to a system of fixed exchange rates that gave nation-states the power to implement independent, or at least autonomous, financial policies. Within its interior, the regime of accumulation was able to fall back on a demand-oriented economic policy and the institutionalisation of class conflict. All of this was possible due to a model of production and innovation that relied on increased production to integrate the greater part of the wage-earning population via regulated, normalised conflict and collective bargaining.

The Fordist formation represented the completion of the project of an 'organised modernity', combining the 'anarchy of markets' with the military-hierarchical organisational principles of large bureaucracies.[69] Not only large corporations, but also organisations and institutions of the welfare state, functioned according to the bureaucratic pyramid model.[70] A driving force behind such combinations was the attempt to integrate previously property-less sections of the working class into a regime of 'organised time'. The 'idea of being able to plan defined the realm of individual agency and power' of a majority of wage earners.[71] Due to this time regime, corporate bureaucracies and welfare institutions in some ways also became guarantors of social stability and security after 1949. The reason for this was not only, and in fact not even primarily, the internal operating principle of bureaucratic apparatuses, but rather the broader social-integrationist compromise and the institutionalisation of workers' power.

This process of 'incorporation' of organised workers' interests into Fordist regulatory *dispositifs* has been explored in great detail by authors adopting an institutionalist approach. Originally, the implementation of Fordist production models was only rarely accompanied by strengthening the organisational and institutional power of wage earners. This changed after 1945. Differences in individual national paths notwithstanding, the incorporation of organised workers' interests shaped not only national systems of regulation but also market formation itself. In Scandinavian countries, worker-state coalitions dominated the 'architecture of markets'; in the

68   Cf. M. Aglietta, *A Theory of Capitalist Regulation*, London 1979.
69   R. Sennett, *The Culture of the New Capitalism*, New Haven 2006, p. 19.
70   Cf. M. Weber, *Wirtschaft und Gesellschaft*, London, Berkeley, Los Angeles 1968.
71   R. Sennett, *The Culture of the New Capitalism*, New Haven 2006, p. 23.

USA these alliances were much more in capital's favour; while in Germany these coalitions consisted primarily of compromises between organised labour and capital interests.[72] This was one (but not the only) reason for the formation of divergent welfare state models. To put it bluntly: the stronger the organisational power and mobilisational capacity of working class movements, the more comprehensive the welfare state. Working class movements usually pursue agendas based on policies of de-commodification.[73] Although the strength of workers' movements and trade unions alone does not suffice to explain the varying worlds of welfare capitalism or the variation between models of production and regulatory *dispositifs*, they nevertheless illuminate a key specificity of the Fordist *Landnahme*. It is only with the de-commodifying effect of social property – namely, some sort of collective asset guaranteeing social existence and status – that wage labour is transformed into a gigantic apparatus of social integration. Benefiting from an exceptionally long-lasting post-war prosperity, wage labour became an institution granting classes and groups who were previously excluded somewhat respectable social positions within society (despite persisting inequalities).

This was made possible by the emergence of something that Marx had considered unimaginable: a capitalism without any visible national 'industrial reserve army'.[74] This capitalism was able, through guaranteed social rights and the right to participate in society, not only to mitigate the precarious nature of wage labour, but also tame and subdue absolute and relative poverty.[75] These phenomena did not disappear, but were marginalised and largely restricted to those outside of wage labour protected by tariffs and laws. It was a poverty of minorities, located in close proximity to the 'socially despised'[76] (that roughly 5 per cent of the population populating the bottom of the social hierarchy). Though not quite identical to these groups, the poorest of the poor represented those who seemed incapable of securing their own existence and were therefore dependent on the welfare provisions provided by wider society.[77] The 'street urchins' of social capitalism served

---

72   Cf. N. Fligstein, *The Architecture of Markets*, Princeton 2001, p. 67ff.; C. Crouch, *Industrial Relations and European State Traditions*, Oxford 1996.

73   Cf. G. Esping-Andersen, *The Three Worlds of Welfare Capitalism*, Cambridge 1996, p. 44; W. Korpi, *The Democratic Class Struggle*, London 1983.

74   Cf. B. Lutz, *Der kurze Traum immerwährender Prosperität*, Frankfurt a.M., New York 1984, p. 184ff. [*The Short Dream of Everlasting Prosperity*].

75   Cf. S. Paugam, *Die elementarenFormen der Armut*, Hamburg 2008, p. 164ff.

76   R. Dahrendorf, *Society and Democracy in Germany*, New York 1967, p. 88.

77   Cf. G. Simmel, 'Der Arme', in G. Simmel, *Soziologie*, vol. 11, Frankfurt a.M. 1992, pp. 512–55. [*Sociology: Investigations on the Forms of Sociation* – no existing English translation of the referenced chapter].

primarily as planes of projection for negative classifications and allocations of blame. Pauperism was an issue of the past for the majority populations in wage labourer societies, irrelevant for everyone but the relief and welfare institutions.

This idyllic picture begins to crack as soon as we consider the fact that 'social-bureaucratic capitalism' was always a mixed economy. When Burkart Lutz describes the Fordist *Landnahme* as the absorption of traditional, small-scale businesses and the agricultural sector, he neglects countervailing developments. Even during social-bureaucratic capitalism's apogee, the global, profit-oriented economy depended to an increasing extent on sectors, devices and activities that followed other rationality principles than the Fordist corporations. Fordism was in constant dialogue with a sector of heterogenous small and medium-sized enterprises vital and extremely important for incremental innovations, in addition to the public sector (production of public assets), the non-profit sector (welfare rationality), as well as household production and the informal sector (survival rationality).[78] Protective mechanisms functioned most effectively where organised labour interests were relatively assertive: in the public service and in the large corporations with their mostly male full-time employees. Allocation to different sectors also occurred via the constructs of gender and nationality. Women, if economically active despite the dominance of the 'male breadwinner' family model in the first place, ended up in less-protected sectors to a large extent. Besides political-institutional discrimination, fundamental mechanisms of a social order were at work here, 'as an immense symbolic machine tending to ratify the masculine domination'.[79] In this sense, the internal–external dynamic of social problems did not completely disappear in Fordist capitalism. It persisted in many guises: for example, in the functionalisation of reproductive activities of women, the super-exploitation of immigrants, or in the construction of social outsiders by mainstream society. In West Germany, social capitalism was so cohesive and sturdy that critical theory began to see the potential of transcending capitalism, should such potential still exist at all, exclusively among these outsider groups.[80]

---

78   Cf. L. Gubitzer, 'Wirtschaft ist mehr. Sektorenmodell der Gesamtwirtschaft als Grundlage für Geschlechtergerechtigkeit', in *Widerspruch. Beiträge zur sozialistischen Politik* 50, 2006, pp. 17–29.

79   P. Bourdieu, *Masculine Domination*, Cambridge, UK 2001, p. 9

80   Cf. H. Marcuse, 'Versuch über die Befreiung' [1978], in H. Marcuse, *Schriften*, 8, Springe 2004, pp. 237–317, here p. 254ff.

The crisis of Fordism

In historical retrospect, the 'glory years' of metropolitan capitalism have proven to be a very short-lived episode. Toward the end of the 1960s, those forces that had brought Fordism into full bloom began to morph into economic trouble spots.[81] The stark break in economic history that marked the 1970s can be accounted for, at least in the case of West Germany, by the discontinuation of special concessions associated with the period of reconstruction and a noticeable shift in innovative activity caused by the former. Beginning with the economic crisis of 1973–1975, companies attempted to counter the pressure on capital investment returns that had been felt since the 1950s by reorienting primarily towards a rate-of-profit type of accumulation. Instead of an expansion of productive capacities and the total volume of surplus value, increases in the rate of profit now became the primary objective. However, overcapacity and pressure on the rate of profit were not the only flashpoints. In both small-scale enterprises and large corporations, the resources of productivity of the dominant types of rationalisation had been exhausted, as disassembly, standardisation, and bureaucratic control of work increasingly came into conflict with the demands and expectations of the average highly qualified labourer. The individualisation of lifestyles and consumer choices led to collisions with a system of production that was designed for standardised mass production. The breakdown of fixed exchange rates, a re-configured international division of labour caused by transnational expansion of large corporations, and the huge debts incurred by many developing countries during industrialisation created a new international context for national regimes of accumulation. Increasingly concerned about growing national debt and rising inflation, the elites of many countries began to reject the Keynesian economic policies of demand management. This led to a shift in state policies toward more supply-oriented strategies, which combined strict austerity domestically with an aggressive orientation toward the world market and accelerated technological modernisation.

Yet the fault lines within the Fordist formation came about not least as a result of the character of the productive forces themselves. Due to extensive usage, things like potable water, arable land and clean air began to become scarce commodities, even in resource-rich countries. The main reason for this was the destruction of natural self-renewal and regeneration processes through industrial overexploitation and pollution. Systems of production that functioned by means of linear extraction of a resource from

---

81   Cf. Aglietta, Theory; A. J. Hirsch, R. Roth, Das neue Gesicht des Kapitalismus, Hamburg 1986.

(or injection of pollutants into) virtually closed natural circuits treated the non-human natural world as a cost-free resource. Simultaneously, though far more obvious in state-bureaucratic socialisms than in developed capitalisms, the dominant modes of regulation ensured the externalisation of costs and consequences. The state and industrial bureaucracies responsible for waste disposal established coping strategies that never really went beyond the point of 'temporary repair of the damage wrought by industrialism'.[82] The global dimension of ecological hazards, and its accompanying, (partially) irreversible consequences, provoked public suspicion of highly complex, closely linked technological systems (for example, nuclear power plants) that operated under the claim of infallibility without actually being able to rule out the possibility of a breakdown and subsequent catastrophic chain reaction.[83]

All of this began to undermine the hegemony of both Fordist capitalism and its state-bureaucratic twin in the East. A historical form of capitalism based on the expansion of the domestic market and the ruthless exploitation of natural resources had ceased 'to be the source of stable or even increasing profit rates'.[84] The robust regulation of the post-war era that included an extensive institutionalisation of workers' power now seemed to be the main obstacle to capital accumulation. It became the object of a renewed *Landnahme* that, as the product of a specific 'exterior', revived the capitalist reserve army mechanism. Once set in motion, this *Landnahme* did not stop when profit rates for individual capitalists had been restored. Instead, it found additional resources of legitimation in the integration of external markets opening up due to, among other things, the implosion of state socialism.[85] This two-fold paradigm shift was processed intellectually and politically within a societal constellation in which the institutionalisation of industrial class conflict seemed to remain stable in spite of growing unemployment, poverty, and inequality.

The abrupt rise in worker militancy at the end of the 1960s took many European politicians and intellectuals by surprise.[86] But while the movement of 1968 was marked by unprecedented parallels between an anti-authoritarian student movement and a working class upsurge, Fordism's crisis years,

---

82   J. Grün, D. Wiener, *Global denken, vor Ort handeln*, Freiburg 1984, p. 298.
83   Cf. C. Perrow, *Normale Katastrophen*, Frankfurt a.M., New York 1987.
84   R. Hirsch, *Das neue Gesicht*, p. 88.
85   Cf. W. Streeck, 'German Capitalism: Does It Exist? Can It Survive?', in: C. Crouch, W. Streeck (eds), *Political Economy of Modern Capitalism*, London 1997, pp. 33–54.
86   Cf. C. Crouch, A. Pizzorno (ed.), *The Resurgence of Class Conflict in Western Europe Since 1968*, 2 volumes, London 1978.

particularly in West Germany, saw the rise of new, inter-class movements focused primarily on an artistic criticism (*Künstlerkritik*)[87] of capitalism. Instead of economic equality and a more just distribution of wealth, these new movements aimed mostly to push back against heteronomy and to maximise individual autonomy. Particularly pronounced in West Germany, this artistic criticism found its expression within the political system in the form of the Green Party. In the sciences it expressed itself in the form of the anti-productivist turn of large parts of sociology. Formal gainful employment, it was claimed, had lost the subjective quality of 'being the organisational centre of life activity, of external and self-assessment, and of moral orientations'. Thus, the conflict between capital and labour could no longer function as the centre of relations of authority in developed societies, as for example Claus Offe claimed.[88] This current of sociology seemed to anticipate the erosion of socially protected relations of normal employment in an almost clairvoyant manner. Social critique ('discourses of immiseration'), on the other hand, was forced into a defensive stance. As precarity spread within the developed capitalisms, there was no intellectual frame of reference in which, say, a temporary worker could locate him- or herself.

3. WHAT IS NEW ABOUT FINANCIAL MARKET CAPITALISM?

What conclusions can our inquirer draw from these deliberations so far? He has learnt that capitalist development is to be understood as a series of *Landnahmen*. In Fordism, this intricate internal-external dialectic adopted a form that spared well-trained male specialists with no migrant background from precarity. But *tempi passati*! Though he is aware of all these facts, our temporary worker nevertheless suspects that social security alone does not bring happiness. Perhaps our inquirer had viewed his parents' vision of a well-planned life and its crowning achievement, the construction of a family home, as conformism incarnate. And he may, should he have grown up in West Germany, even have joined the ranks of the anti-authoritarian protest movements. If born in East Germany, he would have experienced how state-bureaucratic socialism, supposedly an alternative project of organised modernity, repressed individual and collective freedoms, up to and including the use of military force – and all of this in the name of social security.

---

87   [Trans. Note] artistic criticism implies the variants of critique of capitalism relying primarily on notions of the good life and decrying neoliberal capitalism's perceived cultural emptiness. See Boltanski and Chiapello, *A New Spirit of Capitalism*, London 2005.

88   Cf. C. Offe, *Arbeitsgesellschaft*, Frankfurt a.M., New York 1984, pp. 7 and 37.

But historical relativisation only heightens our inquirer's impatience. What he wants to know is why capitalism today drives even skilled and qualified information workers into a life of precarity.

A new stage of international restructuring

The answer to our inquirer's question is this: precarisation is the result of a finance-driven *Landnahme* that carves out and weakens market-restricting institutions and regulatory systems. The important players in this process are world market-oriented corporations, which, in the course of reacting to the crisis of the Fordist regime of accumulation, begin to search for new markets beyond the borders of their national bases. These companies' international operations are often misrepresented as the globalisation of the economy. Some authors regard the transnational opening of internal markets as being so advanced that the concept of a national economy has become practically meaningless.[89] Critics have rightfully noted in response that a global economy in which 'anything can be made anywhere and sold everywhere'[90] has always been a fiction and remains one to this very day. It is still the case for the overwhelming majority of internationally operating corporations that economic strength in their domestic bases is an essential precondition for expanding into transnational activity. It is therefore unhelpful to insinuate some sort of a 'globalisation imperative'. It seems much more accurate to describe what is occurring as a new phase of international restructuring in a long history of globalisation.[91] This stage is characterised by geo-economic shifts: the rise of Japan as a major foreign investor; the conversion of the USA into an enormous market for foreign direct investment; the economic liberalisation of eastern and central Europe; the growth of large international corporations based in the Newly Industrialising Countries; the rapid development of large, heavily populated countries (the so-called BRICS); and the increasing weight of macro-regional trade blocks (EU, NAFTA, Mercosur) in the international economy.[92] The most important changes are taking place within relations between corporations, states and financial markets. Here, globalisation means the increasing interdependence and

---

89   R. Reich, *The Work of Nations: Preparing Ourselves for 21st Century Capitalism*, New York 2010 [1992], p. 8.

90   L. C. Thurow, *The Future of Capitalism. How Today's Economic Forces Shape Tomorrow's World*, 1st ed., New York 1996, p. 113.

91   Cf. J. Osterhammel, N. P. Pettersson, *Geschichte der Globalisierung*, Munich 2007; P. Dicken, *Global Shift*, London 2007.

92   Cf. J. H. Dunning, *Multinational Enterprises and the Global Economy*, Wokingham 1992, p. 601ff.

information-technological penetration of different segments of the financial markets. From the 1990s to the outbreak of the crisis in 2008, financial markets represented *the* economic segment with the highest growth rates. Having at first been a mere phenomenon of the advancing internationalisation of trade, production and corporations, the financial sphere has become more or less independent of real, actual economic activity. The volume of daily transactions on the foreign exchange markets was already over 1,400 billion US dollars as early as 1998. This amounted to a sum a hundredfold larger than that required for all transactions involving goods and services. Between 1980 and 2005 alone, assets invested by the big financial firms increased from three trillion to a staggering 55 trillion US dollars.[93]

There are essentially three main causal complexes for the relative decoupling of the financial sphere from the real economy: (1) increasing vertical inequalities in assets and income, leading to a concentration of surplus finance in the hands of already affluent social strata, thereby tendentially withdrawing it from consumption; (2) delayed economic growth in the traditional centres, accompanied by a continuously widening gap between rising rates of profit and declining rates of investment; as well as (3) the ongoing privatisation of pension schemes and the resulting increased significance of institutional investors, such as pension funds.[94] Excess liquidity is the topsoil upon which the transformation of financial capital into fictitious capital can thrive. Fostered by deregulation of financial markets, and further accelerated by modern information and communication technology, the risks associated with financial transactions are broken up into their basic elements and restructured into financial instruments, which can be traded. So M, expressed in stocks, securities or bonds, goes from being a means of payment and credit to becoming a purely speculative object invested with the goal of realising M'. It is important to emphasise that none of the operations mentioned above produce any adequate replacement value, since it is only possible to distribute that which has been produced *in the real economy*. The fetishised notion of monetary capital that can somehow multiply itself in the form of securities and derivatives disconnected from the real economy represents the origin of a bubble economy.

Actors in the central markets of finance capital have long since ceased to deal only in foreign currencies. Today they exchange risk profiles and swap maturing securities. In this process, even micro-economic activities can have spectacular macro-economic impacts. Due to their extensive leverage – financial assets prior to the global economic crisis could be moved in figures that were many times that of their owners' equity – the trade in

---

93   Cf. Le Monde Diplomatique(ed.), *Atlas der Globalisierung*, Berlin, p. 32.

94   Huffschmid, *Politische Ökonomie der Finanzmärkte*, Hamburg 2002.

derivatives entails substantial, significant risks. The size of assets dealt with by financial actors is immense. The case of Long Term Capital Management L.P. (LTCM) is exemplary for the industry as a whole: prior to its collapse in 1998, LTCM moved assets of 125 billion US dollars – with actual equity capital of only 4.5 billion US dollars. As a result of interest arbitrage, foreign exchange speculation, and debtor/creditor positions, a fragile system of mutual interdependence – not only of financial market actors and financial institutions but also of nation-states – has emerged. Institutional investors, which in the Anglo-Saxon countries usually consist of pension funds, hedge funds, and private equity funds, collect individuals' savings and invest them on financial markets. They gain influence over companies and their shares or loans via the pooling of assets, as well as over governments whose debt titles they acquire. In Europe and Germany, institutional investors often function as investment branches of large financial institutions, whose influence over market activities grows even further.[95]

The finance-dominated regime of accumulation

Until recently, the mainstream of economic science assumed that the logic of financial market capitalism not only optimised risk distribution and capital allocation, but could also potentially put an end to the thirst for power exhibited by some top managers. The almost matter-of-course application of this doctrine led to numerous critical reactions, and an argument emerged accusing the doctrine of creating a growth regime of the wealthy that was beginning to generalise itself in the developed countries. The new regime of accumulation was allegedly adopting 'the dominance of competition, corporate management via institutional investors, the decisive criterion of profit as well as capitalisation through the stock markets as found in Anglo-Saxon capitalism'.[96] Indeed, the new type of accumulation in Europe may have still suffered from a lack of regulation, but, as it was argued, it should be possible to program it for social progress by making the benefits of stock capital more accessible to employees. Due to an all-too-optimistic assessment of the so-called New Economy boom (and particularly the claim that the regime of capital owners could only be democratised *from within*), Michael Aglietta's reflections triggered intense disagreement even before the global financial crisis broke. Economists such as Robert Brenner argued that the boom years of the New Economy had merely prolonged the developmental patterns of structural over-accumulation.[97] Critics argued that the credit-based boom

---

95   Cf. B. Eichengreen, *Globalizing Capital*, Princeton 1997.
96   Aglietta, *Ein neues Akkumulationsregime*, p. 66.
97   Cf. Brenner, 'Boom'.

period of the US economy had further exacerbated the structural problems of the world economy, as enormous over-capacities had now been created in new sectors like IT, telecommunications and media.

One explanation is offered by those authors who speak of a finance-dominated regime of accumulation but who do not necessarily identify this regime with constellations of prosperity.[98] In a rather original recourse to Marx's term of 'fictitious capital',[99] Francois Chesnais reasons that the transition to relative independence of finance capital does not necessarily reduce itself to 'parasitic' effects. According to this view, accumulation consists not only of the growth of the means of investment and productive capacities, but can also be realised through the expansion of private capitalist relations of production into previously unexplored areas; through the absorption of surplus value based on the power that focal enterprises wield over their supplier networks; or through flexibilisation and precarisation of labour. In other words, the finance capitalist dynamic can act as a long-term engine of *Landnahmen* aiming at a re-commodification of living labour. This is possible because finance capital, although in many aspects 'fictitious', is fundamentally an expression of social power. This social power can be utilised to stabilise financial market-driven accumulation over longer periods of time.

This is precisely what has occurred in the capitalist centres. The social power of finance capital is finding expression in institutions and organisational forms which, seemingly paradoxically, stabilise the new regime of accumulation on the one hand, while on the other opening it up to misallocation, speculation and corruption; thereby contributing to the crisis-prone tendencies of the entire system. Beyond the stock markets (which serve as functions of capitalisation), the institutions that can temporarily produce a relative stabilisation of the system include investment funds (as proprietors), analyst and rating agencies (in boundary roles, ensuring reliability of expectations), and transfer mechanisms such as hostile takeovers in the market of corporate control. Within the more or less institutionally secured financial markets, different financial market actors carefully watch each other's *expected* expectations, 'which form on the basis of a constant flow of information.' In this sense, financial markets function as 'efficient machines

---

98   Cf. F. Chesnais, 'Das finanzdominierte Akkumulationsregime: Theoretische Begründung und Reichweite', in C. Zeller (ed.), *Die globale Enteignungsökonomie*, Münster 2004, pp. 217–54; F. Lordon, 'La «création de valeur» comme rhétorique et comme pratique. Généalogie etsociologie de la «valeur actionnariale», in *L' Anneé de la Régulation*4, 2000, pp. 117–68; A. Orléan, *Le Pouvoirde la Finance*, Paris 1999.

99   Cf. Marx, *Capital* vol. 3, pp. 397 ff. and 506 ff.

for information processing'.[100] Unfortunately, this is only one side of the coin; the systemic crisis-proneness is the other.

Indeed, there are a great number of solid arguments that would, in terms of economic efficiency, speak against the notion of a financialised regime. These arguments posit that financial market capitalism's emergence was not the result of a superior or particularly efficient model of production. In contrast to the emergence of Fordism, the hegemony of finance capitalist rationality does not originate primarily on the shop floor, or in the interplay between superior conceptions of rationalisation and mass consumption. Ultimately, that which can be efficiently *enforced* is what becomes real. Transnationally, the new regime has transferred essential economic functions concerning the commitment, volume and direction of investment to the financial markets. It has led to far-reaching changes in the system of corporate governance, influencing corporate mergers and reorganisations just as it does the regulation of levels of consumption and consumer behaviour. The numerous tensions produced by the financialised regime, then, impact 'wage earners in a concentrated way'.[101]

In the following, these impacts will be examined on the basis of three different transfer mechanisms.

(1) Shareholder value and market-centred governance. In order to protect themselves from hostile takeovers and preserve their own capacity for acquisition, world market-oriented corporations – including those in Germany and continental Europe – have adopted capital market-oriented forms of governance.[102] The outcome has been a planned economy in the name of returns and profit. Profit margins appear less and less as the result of economic performance but instead are assumed to be the entitlement of the owners, thereby becoming the central planning factor in corporate governance. Management (endowed with the authority to make strategic decisions) is thus no longer interested in profit as such, but much more in equity returns (ROE) and, importantly, equity returns as they compare to industry leaders in each respective market segment. So, to the management of Deutsche Bank, 20 per cent returns seem inadequate as long as competing

---

100   Cf. Windolf, 'What is Financial-market Capitalism?' Original article, 'Was ist Finanzmarkt-Kapitalismus?', in P. Windolf (ed.), *Finanzmarkt-Kapitalismus*, Wiesbaden 2005, pp. 20–57, ed. and trans. for Glasshouse Forum 2008, at https://www.uni-trier.de/fileadmin/fb4/prof/SOZ/APO/FinancialMarketCapitalism.pdf.

101   F. Lordon, *Aktionärsdemokratie' als soziale Utopie?*, Hamburg 2003, p. 60.

102   Cf. M. Höpner, *Wer beherrscht die Unternehmen?*, Frankfurt a.M., New York 2003.

institutions are realising returns of up to 40 per cent. Corporate govern-ance based upon shareholder values, which has become dominant even in such flagship enterprises of social capitalism as the Siemens corporation, acts as a link between insecure, volatile financial and sales markets on one side, and flexible corporate organisation on the other. Capital market-oriented governance is said to sustainably ensure the long-term profitability of corporations.[103] In reality, however, something quite different is happen-ing. Corporate decision-making systems and organisational structures are subordinated to a tight management of profit, which replaces the 'regime of organised time' and its long-term planning time frames with a one-sided profit orientation and a management regime of the short term.

The most important instruments of tight profit management are per-formance evaluations and profit targets oriented toward maximum capital productivity, which are then broken down by top corporate management into the various sectors of business, e.g., factories, centres of excellence, profit centres and even individual work groups. What lies at the heart of this form of management is an economic quantifier (economic value added, EVA) composed of assets and liabilities; the current capital interest as banks would grant it; and, finally, a premium for potential investors. The sum total of these processes amounts to a margin of profit that is then set as the stand-ard for all management personnel of the individual operating units. In order to create incentives for reaching these goals, a competitive culture is fos-tered, featuring tools such as benchmarking, scorecards, and best practice sharing. This approach to corporate governance becomes effective through further acquisitions and the 'forceful rectification' of problem areas. Entire areas of a business, whether factories, centres, or segments must reckon with corrective measures (staff reductions, outsourcing), or even closures should they fail to achieve their prescribed profit margins.

Internal financialisation can in fact lead to greater transparency within factories and production centres. Misallocations of resources and ineffi-ciency become easier to identify. What matters more, however, is that the recourse to (financial) market-compatible norms profoundly transforms vertically integrated corporate bureaucracies. The Fordist primacy of a productive economy vis-à-vis the market economy is reversed. Corporate and factory organisation are guided by buyer markets as well as financial markets and adopt corresponding structures. On the one hand, production is determined by solvent customer demand. Thus, in modern car plants, cars are only manufactured that have actually been ordered. On the other hand, these operations are liable to strict fiscal controlling. As a result, a

---

103   Cf. A. Rappaport, *Creating Shareholder Value*, New York 1986.

standardised multitude of organisational forms has emerged which are characterised by the gradual transformation from *intra-organisational* to *inter-organisational* relations. Key enterprises focus on core competencies, company-related services are outsourced, plants divided up, production and management functions are re-distributed along the supply chain and partially relocated (offshoring). The vertically integrated enterprise is fragmented; the principle of cross-subsidisation is done away with both in the corporations and the factories. Through this process, sales cycles directly impact the organisational units. The result, then, is not a uniform organisational type, but perpetual restructuring.

Tight profit management and a management regime of short-term cycles exercise influence through a certain type of hegemony, which replaces the combination of participation and hierarchical control common in Fordist corporate organisation with a market-centred mode of control. The hierarchies and bureaucratic organisational forms of Fordism do not disappear, but executive management uses the 'diffuse power' of the market[104] to discipline workforces and the organised representation of their interests. Enterprises and workforces are expected to breathe according to the condition of the market, and to mitigate cyclical fluctuations and eruptions of crisis by sacrificing their own assets. The crucial lever for creating market-compatible flexibility is the consolidation of competition among the working population. Strategic and operational decentralisation allows for keeping some partly autonomous segments, such as profit or cost centres, in a permanent state of competition. The insecurity this engenders becomes the source of power for management rule by means of budgeting, investment allocation, and resource allocation. The functioning of the market-centred mode of governance includes the reification of coercion and the anonymisation of dominance. Where 'the market' prescribes the targets, the responsibility of managers and owners seems marginal. The career-boosting rotation common among managerial elites means that corporate rule literally ceases to have a face. It is not, as Boltanski and Chiapello claim, a network-like form of corporate governance that represents the essence of capitalist transformation, but rather the enforcement of market-centred control.

Unlike authoritarian power, the diffuse power of the market does not work according to a master-servant principle; its effect is founded upon indeterminacy. It articulates itself in abstract and anonymous forms. It frequently appears as a constraint that seems inescapable, as a *fait accompli*. The management hierarchy does not vanish but harnesses the abstract

---

104   Cf. Mann, *The Sources of Social Power: Volume 1. A History of Power from the Beginning to A.D. 1760*, 2nd ed 2012, pp. 6–14.

power of the market in order to disguise its own influence. This 'faceless' mode of rule is extremely difficult to perceive by those being ruled. It does not always function perfectly – after all, it ultimately depends on social integration to minimise disturbances, as well as on target agreements, and thus on communication with those dominated. In this sense, the pressure from world-market competition cannot be seamlessly transferred to the bottom ranks of individual corporations. However, real or simulated competitive situations can be used by top management over and over to exert pressure on workforces and organised interest representation in the name of securing particular sites of production.

(2) *The competition-based regulatory dispositif.* This label already points to changes within the regulatory *dispositif* as a central component of the transition to financial market capitalism. The driving force behind this is a new spirit of capitalism which, in the same sense of market orthodoxy as described above, proclaims the primacy of market socialisation to the detriment of hierarchical governance and bureaucratic rigidity. This new spirit of capitalism is only capable of exerting hegemony because it presents itself as a project of liberation. Market orthodoxy has managed to absorb the critique of capitalism as articulated by social movements against the dominant regime of the late Fordist stage. Industrial sociology's classical critique of Taylorism, and the humanising policies based on this critique, is only one example of this absorption. Conceptualised as a form of artistic criticism of the disassembling, standardisation, monotony, and authoritative control of labour activity, it formulated alternatives along the lines of autonomy, self-determination, and self-responsibility. In its feminist variants, similar patterns of critique were directed against the pervasiveness of male-dominated 'normal' work over other, reproductive forms of labour activity. Indeed, neither Taylorism nor male dominance have vanished from our *Arbeitsgesellschaft*[105] (work-centred society), but the Fordist era's patterns of critique nevertheless seem to be kicking at an open door. In a regime in which many essential sectors are based on the disruption of routines, on flexible work and employment, on trust-based working hours and rationalisation with limited employee initiative, they grow increasingly out of touch with their subject. Instead, critics are confronted with discourses in which, for example, the stars of the 'digital *bohéme*', to

---

105   [Trans. Note] *Arbeitsgesellschaft*, literally 'work(-based) society', is a term pioneered by German sociologist Claus Offe that describes a society in which the lives of the majority of individuals, and thus social life itself, is defined by wage-labour relations; the term could also be translated as 'employment society'. Due to the lack of a precise, widely-accepted translation, the original has been retained in this text.

paraphrase Brecht ('what is the murder of a man compared to his permanent employment?'), sing hymns of praise to flexible labour and modern job-nomadism.[106] In this light, flexible capitalism becomes a project of personal self-realisation. However, that which presents itself as the spirit of liberation often morphs into polemic against what it deems to be restrictions on personal freedom, such as collective bargaining, workers' co-management, and social safety nets.

The new spirit of capitalism, with its accompanying credo of flexibility, velocity and activation, simultaneously represents the medium that manages the transfer of financial market-compatible norms to other areas previously inaccessible to private-profit rationality. In competition for state development funds, different micro-regions act as 'collective entrepreneurs' and fight among one another in an attempt to mitigate the costs of economic restructuring. Once-public enterprises, such as post and rail services, have long been (partially) privatised, are run as profit-oriented enterprises and, if not already on the stock market, seem destined to land there. Public administrations privatise certain services and are themselves restructured according to the principles of New Public Management. For labour administration, the unemployed become clients who are then, under the continuous pressure of strict rules of conditionality (*Zumutbarkeit*),[107] pushed to develop an entrepreneurial relationship to their labour capacity.[108] Not even the universities are spared. For quite some time now, the guiding image of the 'entrepreneurial university',[109] which is supposed to be run according to target specifications and evaluated on its output efficiency, has been the established benchmark of academic reforms in the higher education sector.

All these manifestations of a *Landnahme* aiming at re- and de-commodification shift the boundaries between competing forms of coordination in

---

106   Cf. H. Friebe, S. Lobo, *Wir nennen es Arbeit*, München 2007.

107   [Trans. Note] The term *Zumutbarkeit* translates into reasonableness, appropriateness, or acceptableness. In the context of the German labour market *Zumutbarkeit* is to be understood in a broader sense: it more generally entails the interpretation of what can be deemed reasonable work (or reasonable activity, reasonable schemes), and thus, what can be reasonably expected from benefit claimants as obligatory requirement for receiving provisions ('workfare') – hence, the term 'conditionality' is used.

108   Cf. P. Bescherer, S. Röbenack, K. Schierhorn, 'Nach Hartz IV: Erwerbsorientierungen von Arbeitslosen', in *Aus Politik und Zeitgeschichte* (33–4), 2008, pp. 19–24.

109   Cf. S. Maasen, P. Weingart, 'Unternehmerische Universität und neue Wissenschaftskultur', in H. Matthies, D. Simon (ed.), *Wissenschaft unter Beobachtung*, Wiesbaden 2008, pp. 141–60.

favour of the market. This way, the logic of financial market capitalism seeps deep into the pores of the broader social organism. When this occurs, there is usually no direct challenge to the regulatory institutions involved. Thus marketisation is not something that occurs automatically. Policies aimed at a strengthening of market coordination come into conflict with bulky institutional filters just as they do with competing rationalities. Yet they still rearrange society's regulatory *dispositifs*. Good examples of this are industrial relations and systems of collective bargaining. Although forays into radical decentralisation at a company level have so far remained the exception, organised industrial relations are increasingly coming under the pressure of competitive restructuring. This is due not only to the fact that zones free of tariffs and co-management expand in the wake of economic restructuring; the erosion of the system of collective bargaining is a multi-layered process. Employers' federations introduce membership without commitment to collective bargaining agreements, thereby ensuring that the trade unions are stripped of their negotiating partners. Throughout the world market-oriented sector, policy packages promoting in-house competition have become the standard form of regulation. They regularly establish strongly asymmetric compromises between opposing interests and ensure that actual wages differ severely from tariff wages, even in such highly organised sectors as the metal and electronics industries.[110] In poorly organised sectors such as temporary work, this undercutting of small unions is creating a balkani-sation of the collective bargaining landscape. Groups occupying jobs with unique social power, such as doctors or train engineers, reverse this rela-tion, exploiting their occupational position to enforce exceptionally high wage agreements in their sector, and adding to the erosion of the collective bargaining system. The times of industry-wide multi-employer agreements that regulated labour and wage conditions on the basis of binding standards 'belong to the past'.[111]

(3) Precarisation. The erosion of collective bargaining stands as a stark reminder of the decline in institutional workers' power, which in turn was preceded by a decade-long, partially self-inflicted weakening of the organi-sational power of trade unions. As a consequence, labour organisation and forms of employment are equally subject to the increasing pressure of flexi-bilisation. Market control over gainful employment produces a structured but polarising multiplicity of labour forms.[112] Due to external flexibilisation

---

110   Cf. C. Massa-Wirth, *Zugeständnisse für Arbeitsplätze*, Berlin 2007.

111   Wirtschafts- und Sozialwissenschaftliches Institut in der Hans-Böckler-Stiftung (ed.), *WSI-Tarifhandbuch 2006*, Frankfurt a.M. 2006, p. 64.

112   Cf. M. Schumann, 'Kampf um Rationalisierung – Suche nach neuer

and the abandonment of the social welfare state, as well as the increased legitimacy of low-wage employment and temporary labour, Germany is also witnessing a precarisation of the *Arbeitsgesellschaft*, which crystallises around (at least) three focal points. At the lower end of the social hierarchy are those excluded from regular gainful employment, whom Marx in his time had already termed the 'surplus population' of the capitalist *Arbeitsgesellschaft*.[113] The actual, true *precarians* can be distinguished from this group. The term 'precarian' pertains to those expanding groups of people – among them the bulk of the at-times more than one million temporary workers who are forced to rely on employment in insecure, low-paid and socially ill-regarded jobs for extended periods of time. The increase in 'atypical' forms of employment from 17.5 per cent (1997) to 25.5 per cent (2007) of all employed persons represents only one very unreliable figure of the trend towards precarisation, as it does not encompass precarious self-employment, nor, more importantly, the rapid proliferation of low-wage full-time employment. Meanwhile, more than 6.5 million people earn less than two thirds of the median wage. In 2006 this was true of one in seven full-time employees. The largest group among them were women (30.5 per cent) and low-skill workers (45.6 per cent). Nevertheless, about three quarters of low-paid workers have professional training or qualifications, and even hold academic degrees. The fact that upward mobility in Germany's low-wage sector is on the decline despite such job qualifications signalises a generalised stabilisation of precarious living conditions.[114]

A more hidden point of precarity's crystallisation exists within formally protected employment. By this we mean the fear of losing one's status that haunts large sections of the working class. Such fears are not necessarily expressions of objective threats, but they are more than just an indicator of unrealistic expectations of security. Competition between sites of production (*Standortkonkurrenz*),[115] losses in real wages, and the creeping erosion

---

Übersichtlichkeit', in *WSI-Mitteilungen* 61 (7), 2008, pp. 379–86.

113   Cf. Marx, Engels, *Collected Works*, vol. 35 (Capital vol. 1), p. 623.

114   Cf. G. Bosch, T. Kalina, 'Niedriglöhne in Deutschland – Zahlen, Fakten, Ursachen', in G. Bosch, C. Weinkopf (ed.), *Arbeiten für wenig Geld*, Frankfurt a.M. 2007, pp. 20–105, here p. 42ff.; T. Kalina, A. Vanselow, C. Weinkopf, 'Niedriglöhne in Deutschland', in *Zeitschrift für Sozialistische Politik und Wirtschaft* 164, 2008, pp. 20–4.

115   [Trans. Note] The meaning of the German word *Standort* is difficult to translate. Its literal translation may be 'location', 'position' or 'site'. However, *Standort* is an expression that, although it may simply refer to a specific geographical locus or a particular production facility (or suchlike), in the economic context refers to the totality of the economic and political setting, including e.g., labour laws, quality of infrastructure, level of taxation, etc.; that is to say, the conditions for business. In turn,

of collective bargaining agreements produce fears of drifting out of the middle class, even, the unionised core of the workforce. Indeed, there are numerous indicators that there is still considerable stability at the heart of society. However, in light of the increases in precarious forms of employment relations 'particularly at the fringes of mainstream society', declining income advantages, and growing risks on the labour market, existential fears are hardly surprising in the secluded 'core'.[116] What is new about these developments is that the 'return of social insecurity'[117] increasingly reaches groups that enjoyed relative security under the previous regime. For the time being, capitalism without a reserve army remains a thing of the past in Germany. Instead, what we are witnessing is a transition from marginal to discriminatory precarity. To a large extent, the mere presence of precarious and irregular employment, as well as precarious living conditions well below the standard of their class, is enough to discipline the permanently employed. Functioning as a sort of boomerang effect, the competition that precarians experience on a daily basis causes the core workforce to perceive their permanent employment as a privilege to be fought for tooth and nail. In this regard, 'discriminatory precarity' represents more than just a socio-structural shift; the term actually depicts a system of governance and control that subtly disciplines even permanent workers.

Of course, the market-centred mode of control does not descend upon people as an economic *fait accompli*. As in its original variant, the new *Landnahme* is a deeply political process. Whether discussing the deregulation of financial markets, the privatisation of enterprises, or activating labour policy, politics and the state are always involved. By privileging the shareholder and dismantling the social citizen (*Sozialbürger*), the new *Landnahme* changes property relations. The ideological motor behind this transformation is market orthodoxy (albeit sometimes integrated into a softer variant of the 'Third Way'[118] or competitive corporatism). Although the discourses revolving around the 'entrepreneurial self'[119] do not even remotely capture the empirical reality of this new subjectivity, they still (at least in their more critical variants) convey guiding images and norms

---

Standtortkonkurrenz refers to competition between (potential) sites of production in attracting new businesses and potential investors.

116   Cf. M. Werding, M. Müller, 'Globalisierung und gesellschaftliche Mitte. Beobachtungen aus ökonomischer Sicht', in *Herbert-Quandt-Stiftung* (ed.), *Zwischen Erosion und Erneuerung*, Frankfurt a.M. 2007, pp. 103–61, here p. 157.

117   Cf. R. Castel, 'Die Wiederkehr der sozialen Unsicherheit', in R. Castel, K. Dörre, (eds), *Prekarität, Abstieg, Ausgrenzung*, Frankfurt a.M., New York 2009, pp. 21–34.

118   Cf. A. Giddens, *The Third Way*, Cambridge 1998.

119   Cf. U. Bröckling, *Das unternehmerische Selbst*, Frankfurt a.M. 2007.

which connect with institutional practices in a contradictory way and thus become a challenge for groups and individuals. Where market liberalism's promise of liberation fails it is complemented by a disciplinary regime. Hartz IV,[120] for example, increases the willingness to make concessions particularly among those who still have a job. Viewed systematically, strict rules of conditionality in financial market capitalism can reasonably be expected to fulfil a similar function to that of legal relics inherited from feudalism during the phase of primitive accumulation. What they do is activate and discipline wage earners for a new, flexible mode of production. This system can only function because it *cannot* be completely and comprehensively enforced. The myth of the market[121] still has such an impact *precisely because* attempts at micro-social implementation always contain mistakes and generate counter-movements. It corresponds to the basic interests of social groups participating in the mode of flexible accumulation. These groups – in the developed capitalisms they entail the majority of economic and political elites, but at least periodically extend to relevant parts of the middle classes, expert professionals and skilled workers – have provided the backbone of market culture in society's core. Pushed forward by powerful interest blocs, Fordism's foundational welfare-state compromise is being irreversibly dismantled. Still seemingly enveloped by the cover of stable institutions, the regime of accumulation, production models, and social regulatory *dispositifs* have undergone changes which, when viewed in total, indicate a new aggregate physical condition of society.

4. The crisis (or crises) of financial market capitalism

Our temporary worker now recognises that functioning financial market capitalism and discriminatory precarity are two sides of the same coin. But why all this talk of a capitalist formation, when the global casino that is financial market capitalism is being torn asunder anyway? The global crisis of finance and over-accumulation has indeed laid bare the limitations of financial market capitalism for all to see. What began as a subprime mortgage crisis in the USA has morphed into a full-blown collapse of even the

---

120 Translators' note: 'Hartz IV' refers to the series of welfare and labour market reforms implemented by the German government in 2004. The name is a reference to commission chairperson Peter Hartz, while the IV refers to the fourth stage of the reform which combined welfare and unemployment assistance into one provision, effecting a significant cut in state welfare benefits.

121 Cf. C. Deutschmann, *Postindustrielle Industriesoziologie*, Weinheim 2002, p. 8off.

real economy, the dimensions of which have been compared to the beginnings of the Great Depression of the 1930s.[122] One should of course be careful when presenting a final analysis, since events are still unfolding. We can, however, definitively state that the widely held belief that large crises can be 'prevented these days'[123] is built on sand. Financial crises are an organic part of the new *Landnahme* modus operandi. Crisis management corresponds to strategies of de-commodification, such as the reserve army mechanism discussed previously. In the case of financial crises, the modus operandi of the new *Landnahme* directly impacts property relations. Assets are depreciated, only to be re-introduced into the cycle of capital at dramatically reduced prices and under altered conditions of ownership. According to David Harvey, this variant of 'accumulation by dispossession' can be effectively directed and rationalised.[124] Following this line of argument, financial crises have always produced 'transfer of ownership and power to those who keep their own assets intact'. In retrospect, the crisis management as conducted by the International Monetary Fund amounts to the greatest 'transfer of assets from domestic to foreign owners in the past fifty years'.[125] The social implications of the crisis mechanism are, once again, devastating. Take for example the Argentinian debt crisis of 2001, in which half the population was pushed down to or below the poverty threshold. An estimated 15 million people were no longer able to afford the most basic daily necessities; one million lived on less than one US dollar per day.[126]

Market orthodoxy refuses to label such crises as 'severe' simply because the capitalist centres have found ways to shield themselves from the most dire impacts. That said, the financial markets have harshly punished economies such as those of Mexico or the Asian Tigers (of all countries!) who for so long served as poster children of the Washington Consensus. For years now, the widely held belief that the Great Depression was a historically unique 'work accident'[127] that could be prevented has reinforced and encouraged financial actors' and politicians' faith that the rationalisation of crisis mechanisms could be prolonged endlessly. This faith has been

---

122   Cf. J. K. Galbraith, *Der große Crash 1929*, 2008, pp. 7–19.

123   Cf. H.-W. Sinn, '1929 traf es die Juden – heute die Manager', in *Tagespiegel*, 27 October 2008.

124   D. Harvey, *The New Imperialism*, Oxford, New York 2005, p. 145.

125   Ibid. pp. 150–51. Cf. also R. Wade, F. Veneroso, 'The Asian Crisis: The High Debt Model vs. the Wall Street-Treasury-IMF-Complex', in *New Left Review* (228),1998, pp. 3–23.

126   Cf. N. D'Alessio, 'In Argentinien ist etwas schief gegangen', in *SOFI-Mitteilungen*(30), 2002, pp. 47–53.

127   For a critical approach, cf. P. Krugman, *The Return of Depression Economics and the Crisis of 2008*, New York 2009, p. 3.

crushed by the global collapse of the financial markets. The modus operandi of finance capitalist *Landnahmen* has only been able to regionalise and
control its crises by measures through which, as Marx predicted, the larger
contradictions will intensify and eventually erupt. By observing the history
of the crisis thus far, four causal complexes that lead to a greater crisis of
transformation can be identified.

(1) *State intervention and moral hazard*: Although the dynamic of the new
Landnahme was based mainly on the liberalisation of financial markets as
mandated by international institutions and executed by national governments, there was always a need for permanent state intervention to keep
the system running. The precepts of market fundamentalism once again
came into conflict with their actual realisation. Whenever push came to the
shove, as during the collapse of LTCM, the state did not hesitate to step in
to stop the worst from happening. Wall Street and the City could assume
with confidence that the state would not be able to ignore their economic
weight and social power in the event of a crisis. This 'moral hazard' only
increases managers' willingness to take more risks, thus contributing to the
current major crisis. Admittedly, the phenomenon of 'moral hazard' is not
found solely among the manager caste. Governments like those of Britain or
Spain, which implement financial market capitalism according to doctrine,
rely – along the lines of a kind of bastardised Keynesianism – on being able
to channel the profits earned from finance into loans for the domestic real
estate market. Here we find one of the major reasons why the political and
managerial class, but also the managers of public credit institutions, are so
willing to take large risks.

(2) *Global economic imbalances and the limits of monetary policy.* The
temporary success of cheap money policies, as introduced by the Federal
Reserve (the Fed) in reaction to the bursting of the New Economy bubble,
evidently encouraged the relevant protagonists to operate as if the financial
sector could be decoupled from the real economy. This tendency has been
expedited by structural imbalances within the global economy. Major financial crises always occur at times when hegemonic powers in decline attempt
to maintain their dominant position through the manipulation of foreign
exchange policies. This is precisely what the USA has been trying to achieve
for decades now. Counter-measures such as the buying up of US dollars,
as carried out by the financially powerful Asian countries (China, Japan),
have repeatedly thwarted the US's monetary policy measures and further
cemented global economic imbalances. Here we find another factor that
contributed to the onset of today's crisis. When the Fed lowered the Federal

Funds Rate at the beginning of the past decade, US real estate and mortgage banks used this to begin selling loans with variable interest rates. These low interest rates in turn drove up prices in the real estate market. Homeowners were able to capitalise on the increased value of their residential properties by taking out second mortgages and using the additional cash for increased consumption. Excess liquidity on the financial markets was thus redirected and injected back into the primary circuit of capital. The real estate boom was able to continue even after the Fed began to raise interest rates in 2004, as Asian economies seeking to secure their exports (and thus to increase their domestic prosperity and consumption) bought up more US dollars and kept the currency artificially overvalued. The overvalued dollar pushed real estate prices even higher. In order to afford the dream of home ownership in the face of a booming real estate market, many Americans resorted to cheap home loans. Between 2005 and 2006 alone 3,200 billion US dollars were invested, of which 20 per cent were subprime mortgages – that is, loans given to buyers lacking sufficient credit-worthiness. About 2.3 million US citizens were taken in by this borderline-illegal lending practice.[128] Subprime mortgages are made so problematic by the fact that their initially low interest rates start rising after a few years, leaving debtors often unable to make the increased payments.

(3) Nontransparency of financial products. In search of a way to refinance the booming loan industry, banks bundled together subprime mortgages into portfolios and sold them to international investors in the form of tranches. These toxic assets then, through 'securitisation', became objects of speculation. Since losses flowed to the lowest segment of the tranche, and further losses had to be carried by the next respective segment, the bulk of the bonds seemed secure. Astoundingly, 75 per cent of these bad loans received the best possible rating: AAA. Seeking ever more lucrative investment opportunities, more and more institutional investors and hedge funds joined the fray. Since the managers of real estate banks and funds were receiving their share of the profits while losses were transferred to shareholders and investors, their willingness to take further risk knew no bounds. Hedge funds and American real estate banks were not the only ones participating in this game, however – many erstwhile reputable lending institutions also took part. German banks circumvented regulatory measures as laid out in Basel II by founding special-purpose entities to engage in securitisation. These entities siphoned off profit by buying up cheap loans, bundling them together, and re-selling them as securities. The margin between the loan interest that had

---

128 Cf. C. Tigges, 'Amerikas neue Geisterstädte', in G. Braunberger, B. Fehr (ed.), *Crash*, Frankfurt a.M. 2008, pp. 118–24.

to be paid to the homeowner in the USA and the repayments going to financial investors represented additional profit.

(4) Nontransparent risk: These business practices further fuelled the loan-
financed hunt for maximum rates of return and, as a consequence, financial
market actors' willingness to take risks. The bubble grew bigger and bigger,
as did the prices of virtually all asset values. It was only a matter of time,
however, until a situation in the US would arise in which more and more
home owners could no longer afford to service their toxic loans and the
real economy would make itself felt once more. Insiders like Warren Buffet
had long considered the new types of derivatives used to shift credit risks as
'financial weapons of mass destruction'. The events of 2007 and 2008 proved
them right. In April 2007 the market leader in subprime loans, New Century
Financial, went into crisis. What followed was a series of economic shock
waves. Moreover, a general retreat from the security and bond markets set
in. The market suffered from a lack of buyers and investor equity capital to
satisfy the demand for liquidity. Unlike previous crises, in 2007 the economic
web of interdependencies and mutual liabilities had grown so tightly woven
that the crisis entered a global phase almost immediately. By July 2007, the
subprime crisis had reached Germany. The Deutsche Industriebank (IKB
– German Industrial Bank) had to be rescued from insolvency by a trio
of the Federal Financial Supervisory Authority, the Bundesbank (German
Federal Bank), and the Ministry of Finance. But these were only hints of
the collapse that would be kicked off by the bankruptcies of the mortgage
banks Fannie Mae and Freddie Mac and large institutions like Lehman
Brothers. As financial institutions outside of the Fed's immediate sphere
of activity went into a tailspin, seeds of suspicion and mistrust began to
spread through the entire banking system. Because banks no longer trusted
each other, what began as mere excess liquidity turned into a collapse of
transaction payments. In the US, not a single investment bank survived
the crash, while countries like Iceland were pushed to the brink of national
bankruptcy.

Ever since, governments have been conducting financial rescue operations on an absolutely unprecedented scale. The first wave of responses
alone saw the developed states spend around 2,400 billion Euros to stabilise
the mortgage lending system. Other countries undertook 'nationalisation' of
their banks, while others such as Germany assembled their rescue packages
through a voluntary process in which most banks chose to participate. But
steep losses on the stock markets and delayed impacts of the crisis on a real
economy already burdened with over-capacities in several key sectors could
no longer be avoided. In late autumn 2008, the world economy tumbled

into a deep recession, the extent, duration and social consequences of which remain to be seen.

From financial crisis to social crisis

Confronted with the prospect of global disaster, market orthodoxy is doing all it can to conceal its failure. The causes of the crisis are made out to be 'bad policies' and the conduct of specific individual actors. These include: a Fed which clung to low interest rates for far too long; greedy Wall Street investors[129] who, thanks to a ratio leverage of one US dollar of actual capital to thirty or more dollars of borrowed capital, were willing to take almost any conceivable risk; ineffective banking supervision that permitted high-risk financial products and insufficient rules regarding transparency of hedge funds; and institutional investors who, driven by growing competition in narrow market segments, were also willing to take greater and greater risks. Indeed, all of these factors contributed to the collapse of the financial system. However, these explanations tend to ignore a particular 'anonymous system error' that Hans-Werner Sinn (of all people!) pointed out when comparing criticism of bank managers to the persecution of Germany's Jews.[130] Of course, this 'system error' that Sinn speaks of is a direct result of the concepts that economists like him have preached for years. These economists endorse the notion that financial markets tend toward a state of equilibrium, as (supposedly) all markets do.[131] This alleged tendency toward equilibrium is then dogmatically applied to a reality that frequently diverges from that model. Even the ordoliberal credo of government-defined rules along which speculators ought to speculate[132] studiously avoids the fact that the entire game is based on constant infringement of the rules. This is precisely what is reflected in the *Landnahme* theorem. The parallelism between rationalisation of subsystems on the one hand and the permanence of manipulation, fraud, rule violations, and repressive acts on the other are cast into institutional forms in the finance capitalist formation. At the zenith of expansion, institutions and actors who have temporarily stabilised the system then

---

129   Cf. D. Henwood, *Wall Street*, London 1997.

130   [Trans. Note] German economist Hans-Werner Sinn spurred public controversy in 2008 by comparing popular anger at financial elites with the anti-Semitism of Nazi Germany. The comparison was intended to illustrate that bankers were not to blame for capitalist crisis, but rather 'system errors' within capitalism itself.

131   Cf. Sinn, *Ist Deutschland noch zu retten?*, pp. 102f. and 533.

132   Cf. M. Bloss, D. Ernst, inter alia, *Von der Subprime-Krise zur Finanzkrise*, Munich 2009, p. 229ff.

contribute to intensifying crisis-prone contradictions. To illustrate how this works, let us use the example of capital market-oriented corporate management. Though nominally at the top of the hierarchy, the owners of capital remain outside the actual activities of their managers. Effectively, the relative success or failure of an executive manager can only be judged by shareholders *ex post facto*. The same is true for those institutions originally designed to rectify this dilemma. When analysts and rating agencies decouple their assessments from verifiable factual knowledge, they operate by projecting current trends into the future, by relying on expectations and, as it were, on expectations of expectations – all of which obviously have a highly speculative character. In doing so, they internalise ignorance as a resource and exploit public trust in their expertise in order to offer owners of capital their commercial consulting services.[133]

An analyst's job is to distil the complexity of future market processes down to a single figure, the 'expected value of future earnings'. There are extensive opportunity structures permitting corruption in the process, as analysts are paid by investment banks who themselves have a substantial interest in the prognoses being offered.[134] Areas of uncertainty that make it past rating agencies and analysts can then be used by top management who, having access to exclusive insider knowledge, obtain powerful advantages over their shareholders. Personal stock options shift these managers' interests toward the stock market. The corporation's internal perspective loses ground to the external market perspective. This shift does not reinforce manager loyalty to the shareholders, but instead inhibits the commitment of managers to their own company. To the same extent that the collective will of the enterprise is ignored, the influence of competing insiders who could perhaps rectify this autonomisation of management interests slips away. Despite claims to the contrary, the application of the doctrine of shareholder value further extends the autonomy of a management capable of making strategic choices. This control deficit has clearly aided the breakthrough of a new generation of management elites who place the pursuit of short-term profit maximisation at the heart of their actions. The control and guidance promised by efficient shareholder governance is in reality a falsehood, with systemic instabilities being the logical consequence.[135]

Relying on an insider's perspective, the experienced speculator George Soros defines these sorts of mechanisms as the 'reflexivity' of financial

---

133   Cf. T. Strulik, *Nichtwissen und Vertrauen in der Wissensökonomie*, Frankfurt a.M. 2004.

134   Cf. Windolf, *What is Financial-market Capitalism?*

135   Cf. N. Fligstein, *The Architecture of Markets*, Princeton 2001, p. 168f.; A. Berle, *The American Economic Republic*, New York 1963, p. 28.

markets. By this he simply means that markets do not function as passive coordination mechanisms of processes of exchange. Instead, market participants actively seek to influence events.[136] However, investment funds do not stop at buying company shares. By threatening to take advantage of their exit option, major investors can stoke fears of stock market losses or hostile takeovers and use them to exert permanent pressure on businesses. Hedge funds, which disclose neither their investors nor their investment strategies, have tried time and time again to influence the outcomes of the real-world events upon which they speculate. Private equity funds are forced to draw on their companies' liquid assets in order to satisfy shareholders' demands. Wherever this leads to cannibalisation of plants and the shuttering of profitable production facilities, their effect is the opposite of innovation. In short, financial market capitalism as a system is based on institutions and organisational forms with an intrinsic tendency toward manipulation, exaggeration, speculation, misallocation, fraud and thus imbalance and, ultimately, crisis.

The financial crisis finally reached the real economy over the course of 2009. More specifically, it carried the effects of the (relative) autonomisation of the financial sector, which itself began as a sort of escape from the difficulties posed by low profitability in the real economy, back onto the production of goods and services in a powerful and destructive manner. Faced with the most severe global recession since 1945, once zealous partisans of market orthodoxy quickly changed their stripes and reverted to being professed Keynesians. The crisis responses of economic and political elites seem to be dictated by circumstance more than anything else. Shortly after declaring himself in opposition to any form of 'nationalisation', a German Minister of Finance is forced to push the buying-out of crippled banks' shareholders through parliament. His advisers, economic wise men who spent years calling for greater and greater cuts in public spending, are now telling him that his government's stimulus packages are far too small. Keeping this sudden re-evaluation of values in mind, critical theory must not allow itself to be misled by the new euphoria surrounding state intervention. The sinking of billions into a failing banking system does indeed discredit the notion that austerity is unavoidable and inevitable. And of course we agree that the aforementioned stimulus packages carry with them more than just a hint of Keynesianism. But that does not mean that financial market capitalism has been defeated. For, at least to some degree, the new state intervention carries on the process of 'accumulation by dispossession' seamlessly. This is all the more true when considering those groups

---

136   Cf. G. Soros, *The New Paradigm for Financial Markets: The Credit Crisis of 2008 and What It Means*, New York 2008.

of society who bore the brunt of the alleged 'globalisation imperative' in the form of wage restraint, pension cuts, precarisation and poverty in the first place – as precisely these groups are now expected to pay up again, this time as taxpayers. The redistribution of social property now occurs in the name of rescuing banks, financial institutions and corporations that are allegedly 'too big to fail'. Funnily enough, the seal of systemic relevancy is bestowed by the very same economic experts whose 'expertise' led us down the path of financial disaster only a few years before.

Such continuities give cause for concern. Top managers like Josef Ackermann have already made it clear what outcome of the crisis they would prefer. Although he helped to draw up the plans for the 'umbrella' of state subsidies for German banks, the head of Deutsche Bank did not hesitate to publicly disassociate himself from the plan once it became public. His claim that only weak lenders were in need of government assistance illustrates what at least some members of his class hope will occur. There will of course be winners and losers, but financial market capitalism itself will, they hope, recuperate from the current turbulence and flourish anew. And although it may be sensible and necessary to enact new rules pertaining to the transparency of institutional investors and hedge funds or the prohibition of some highly speculative operations, they will ultimately change very little.[137]

Focusing exclusively on the nontransparencies of finance-driven accumulation furthermore leads to a failure to recognise that the financial crisis has long since grown into a social crisis. In more or less all social sectors, a generalised competitive logic which takes from one group what it gives to another is coming into conflict with unwieldy social realities. The precarisation of the *Arbeitsgesellschaft* will increase to the same degree that the buffers (e.g., short-term employment), which were at first able to mitigate the impacts of the crisis, cease to be effective. We are already witnessing a consequence of precarisation, that which Richard Sennett has described as the 'exhaustion' of work identities due to constant personal and institutional re-invention. Financial market capitalism is an engine of acceleration[138] and activation[139] that feeds primarily on people's fears of downward social mobility. Fear motivates individuals to come to terms with the existing status quo again and again. The uncertainty experienced by the precariously employed illustrates how this engine works quite vividly. Motivated by dreams of becoming part of the core workforce, precarians mobilise all of their energies

---

137   Cf. J. K. Galbraith, 'Die Weltfinanzkrise – und was der neue US-Präsident tun sollte', in *Blätter für deutsche und internationale Politik* 11, 2008, pp. 41–57, here: p. 52.

138   Cf. H. Rosa, *Social Acceleration: A New Theory of Modernity*, 2013.

139   Cf. S. Lessenich, *Die Neuerfindung des Sozialen*, Bielefeld 2008.

to achieve this social leap. If ever they wane in their efforts, they risk plunging into a zone of complete disconnection from regular employment. Those who live and work under precarity sooner or later adapt to it. What remaining energy they have is devoted to making ends meet; only rarely can they be mobilised for protest and resistance.

A system that replaces participation with market discipline has no political problem with resignation and exhaustion. It does, however, have a problem with the consequences of diminishing activity within the system of innovation. Here, in the heart of capitalist productivity, we find a rather peculiar variation of the opposition between market-mediated competition and creative activity. Quite unlike Schumpeter's classic image of an assertive and powerful 'Führer',[140] innovation today rests on collective, reciprocal processes organised in the form of networks. Besides expert knowledge, 'tacit knowledge' is also of vital significance. Informality, subjectivity, cooperation, and often the active participation of employees play essential roles in the mobilisation of such implicit bodies of knowledge.[141] Because the quantifying logic of finance capitalist rationality continuously disregards these requirements, it systematically produces *innovation blockages*. New best practices are rapidly exhausted by permanent restructuring. During innovations of process, management oriented around short-term cycles carries out a form of negative selection, as elaborate projects involving further qualification or group work appear risky. Moreover, the ongoing (pseudo-) entrepreneurial appeal to employees to constantly innovate their own work processes, combined with never-ending competition between sites of production (*Standortkonkurrenz*), leads to strategies of avoidance, evasive behaviour, or simply abstinence.

Just how poorly the dominant principle of rationality is suited for the specificity of creative processes can be seen in the universities, where the logic of competition has so far taken root in only a mediated and modified form. Economically quantifiable innovations, such as academic spin-offs (business start-ups launched out of the university), are undertaken primarily by 'invisible entrepreneurs' who tend to belong to the precariously employed (non-professional) academic staff. Wherever such spin-offs are realised, they rely heavily on the support of outside networks and, more specifically, on professors who provide potential start-up founders with the free spaces and resources necessary for creative labour. As this example proves, innovations emerge for the most part from unplanned processes in institutional niches that elude direct managerial control. They are based on

---

140   Cf. J. A. Schumpeter, *Theorie der wirtschaftlichen Entwicklung*, Berlin 1997.
141   Cf. C. Deutschmann, 'Finanzmarkt-Kapitalismus und Wachstumskrise', in Windolf (ed.), *Finanzmarkt-Kapitalismus*, pp. 58–84, here: p. 77.

collective learning and require trust and mutual recognition.[142] The 'entrepreneurial university' model of governance being introduced worldwide, in the form of target specifications, stricter specifications regarding resource allocation, and a strict focus on 'excellence', also mandates optimising the university's economic performance. However, the opposite is often the case. As university courses of study are re-structured into school-like arrangements and efficiency becomes the central focus, it is the very associative forms of labour, free spaces, and relations of trust which represent essential preconditions for successful spin-offs and economically quantifiable innovations that come under pressure.[143]

If the rationality of financial market capitalism and its transfer mechanisms have truly failed in their claim to efficiency, problems of political legitimacy seem only logical. The question remains, however, whether democratic institutions are still capable of dealing with such developments productively. The regulatory *dispositifs* of modern mass democracies have longsince come to represent an indicator of the 'tension between the expansive force of capital and the democratic principle'.[144] Capitalism has proven over the course of its development (at least in its centres) that it is capable of coexisting with democratic principles, since they successfully mediate between the coercion to compete and the latent need for social cohesion. The state-bureaucratic socialisms never achieved anything of the sort; indeed, up until recently this was precisely what made social capitalism so attractive. For the time being, financial market capitalism is squandering this advantage. Where decisions of vital importance are made outside of parliament (by a managerial elite lacking all democratic legitimacy), the state outsources essential functions, and the political parties sever their links to civil society. It therefore makes sense to speak of *post-democracy*. One central characteristic of the post-democratic era is that the 'shareholding and "executive" classes' have found it increasingly difficult to 'perceive themselves ... as clearly defined social groups'.[145] In other words, the generalised logic of competition's destruction of collective identities robs the citizens it encourages to participate of the very resources necessary for democratic engagement. By accepting, and even promoting, the physical and mental exhaustion of large social groups, the finance capitalist *Landnahme* results

---

142 Cf. W. Lazonick, 'The Theory of Market Economy and the Social Foundations of Innovative Enterprise', in *Economic and Industrial Democracy* (24), 2003, pp. 9–44.

143 Cf. M. Neis, K. Dörre, 'Visible Scientists' und 'unsichtbare Entrepreneurs', Jena 2008 (Ms.).

144 Aglietta, *Ein neues Akkumulationsregime*, p. 25f.

145 C. Crouch, *Post-Democracy*, Cambridge 2004, p. 53.

in a profound crisis of not only social cohesion, but also of society's capacity to innovate – and of democratic principles themselves. The *Landnahme* (i.e., the expansion of the logic of competition) becomes dysfunctional not only for the economic system, but indeed for democracy itself.

5. ARE THERE ALTERNATIVES?

What, if anything, does this insight mean for our inquirer? He is, after all, confronted with the impacts of the crisis in a very practical sense. As a temporary worker, he is among the first to be fired. We have no knowledge of how he will cope with that. All we can do is speculate: since he is a die-hard democrat, he definitely will not look to the far right to articulate his anger and indignation. On the other hand, he is no longer willing to put up with the status quo. He spends many sleepless nights overcome with worry. He continually wonders how, and with whom, any change to this system could be achieved.

So – are there alternatives? Global financial crisis, fatigue, innovation blockages, and post-democracy all seem to indicate that the financial capitalist *Landnahme* is nearing its intrinsic limits. These limits were not created by protest movements, but rather are central functional mechanisms of the system itself. To the extent that subaltern groups become conscious and aware of this fact, avenues for change will emerge. Aside from exhaustion and resignation, certain events can also trigger critique, resistance, and opposition. Even precarised groups are capable of staging protest and revolt from time to time. Innovation blockages can cause economic decline, but they may also strengthen the motives for political reorientation. Incidentally, the tendency toward post-democracy occasionally produces remarkable counter-movements, as the mass political participation unleashed by Barack Obama's 2008 presidential campaign evidenced.

The possibility of resistance, or even of recalcitrant behaviour, touches on a point the sociologist should take notice of in order to learn something from our inquirer. Whether or not our exemplary temporary worker becomes involved, whether he searches for political alternatives, or whether he even makes an effort to translate his implicit critique of capitalism into action remains outside of the bounds of scientific prognosis. We are ultimately talking about decisions every individual makes for him- or herself after weighing all possible courses of action. The question for us is whether or not intellectuals can provide frames of reference that encourage resistance and collective engagement. Despite the crisis, this space has yet to be filled satisfactorily. Critical theory in all of its modern variants finds itself confronted with a 'post-socialist situation'. Although there may be many fronts of struggle, there is 'an absence of any credible overarching emancipatory project'[146] which could provide political perspective to the initiatives and movements that today are so abundant, yet so fragmented. If this situation is ever to change, the range of alternatives available to oppositional movements must first be assessed. James Fulcher takes an unambiguous stance on this question: 'The search for an alternative *to* capitalism is fruitless ... Those who wish to reform the world should focus on the potential for change *within* capitalism'.[147] In other words: financial market capitalism can be defeated, but only insofar as it is replaced with another form of capitalism.

A renewed, inbuilt transformation of capitalism is indeed possible. It is even possible that one of financial market capitalism's major trouble spots could become a lifeline that has thus far been ignored. The finance capitalist logic of competition has displaced the ecological question, or at least dealt with it only via market mechanisms, for quite some time. But ecology, long ignored by the new *Landnahme*, is now returning with more force than ever.[148] Climate change and the looming transition to renewable energy exert tremendous pressure (not only) on the Western nations to innovate and develop. In order to meet the most important climate goals, the industrial nations alone would have to reduce CO_2 emissions by 30 per cent; since 1990, the EU has managed a reduction of just 1.5 per cent. To get anywhere even remotely close to the stipulated targets would require 'the greatest, most profound structural change that an economy has ever had to undertake'.[149]

Ideally, an ecological New Deal could invoke the 'state as pioneer' to set the course for gigantic investment programmes (expanding solar energy, increasing usage efficiency) and as a result channel surplus capital into the tertiary cycle, i.e., into urgently needed infrastructural projects. Developed countries would have to provide technology and expertise, while the emerging economies would be granted improved opportunities to develop resource-efficient economic modes compatible with the planet's climate.[150] All of this could be possible within a multilateral world order in which

146   N. Fraser, *Justice Interruptus. Critical Reflections on the 'Postsocialist' Condition*, New York 1997, p. 3.

147   J. Fulcher, *Capitalism. A Very Short Introduction*, Oxford, New York 2004, p. 127

148   Cf. U. Beck, *Die Risikogesellschaft*, Frankfurt a.M. 1986.

149   M. Machnig, 'Der Staat als Pionier im 21. Jahrhundert', in *Zeitschrift für sozialistische Politik und Wirtschaft* 158, 2007, pp. 14–18, here: p. 14f. For critical treatment cf.the contributions in*Widerspruch. Beiträge zu sozialistischer Politik* 54, 2008.

150   Cf. *Bundesministerium für Umwelt, Naturschutz und Reaktorsicherheit, Ökologische Industriepolitik*, Berlin 2006.

the USA were to peacefully accept the loss of their erstwhile hegemonic position. At this point, the possibilities for an ecological cycle of capitalist growth cannot be elaborated in any detail. All the same, some of the more insightful US economists such as James K. Galbraith are calling for precisely this strategy. And they add what the rather technocratically minded suggestions of German brain trusts tend to overlook: an ecological *Kondratiev* wave would have to take pressure off of the weakest groups in society. It would have to invest in social security, in public goods, and in employment programmes, thereby applying a social corrective to the 'exterior' generated by the finance-capitalist *Landnahme*.[151]

Perhaps the path toward eco-social capitalism can in fact rescue the system, at least temporarily. With a view to the sheer enormity of current global challenges, however, there is no guarantee whatsoever that the problem-solving capacity of the capitalist economy will be sufficient to overcome pivotal challenges in the future. As one of the first to do so, Immanuel Wallerstein has articulated the possibility of a transformation of the system in light of these facts. According to Wallerstein, the decades ahead will belong to a new reign of protectionism, which may assume a markedly democratic or authoritarian, right-wing populist form. It may be 'confidently' assumed, however, 'that the present system cannot survive':

> What we cannot predict is which new order will be chosen to replace it, because it will be the result of an infinity of individual pressures. But sooner or later, a new system will be installed. This will not be a capitalist system but it may be far worse (even more polarizing and hierarchical) or much better (relatively democratic and relatively egalitarian) than such a system. The choice of a new system is the major worldwide political struggle of our times.[152]

Wallerstein's argument is founded upon the extraordinary successes of the capitalist world system, which allegedly eroded the basis for further accumulation. This argument is not new; we have heard it before. Nevertheless, Wallerstein's hypothesis is not without plausibility. Assuming the global crisis of finance and over-accumulation is to result in lasting stagnation, then the question of how system-stabilising resources will be produced and distributed remains unanswered. Should unemployment and precarity continue to grow, battles around social distribution will increasingly carry explosive potential. The outcome will be problems of legitimacy for the system as they already manifest in the everyday consciousness of individuals. In this

---

151   Cf. Galbraith, 'Weltfinanzkrise,' p. 47f.

152   I. Wallerstein, 'The Depression: A Long-Term View', *Agence Global*, 10 Oct 2008, at http://www.agenceglobal.com/index.php?show=article&Tid=1766.

constellation, critical sociology cannot and must not exclude the possibility of a transformation of the system from the spectrum of potential social development paths. Such a taboo would also be unscientific, since no historical social formation has a monopoly on eternity. After all, the example of state-bureaucratic socialism has shown rather clearly how quickly scientifically veiled guarantees can be embarrassed by reality.

Thus, sociological critique should explore – soberly and without illusions – alternatives *within* but also alternatives *to* capitalism. In the context of a 'post-socialist situation', however, four fundamental premises must be adhered to. Firstly, critique requires a hermeneutic examination connecting it to the everyday, empirically ascertainable grievances of all those who otherwise have no voice. Secondly, critique must embody the imperative of a critical plurality. In a democratic society, critique cannot stake a claim to universality or generality. Instead, it is indispensable that even critics acknowledge the intrinsic value of democratic procedures and position themselves within them.[153] Any critique must take into consideration that it may be wrong. Thirdly, a radical critique of society requires a moral community.[154] Having said that, it should by no means refrain from going beyond its moral foundations and the communities within which these are communicated. It should delimit a framework in which arguments can be theoretically and empirically reviewed. This framework requires a threefold critical distance: with respect to the society being criticised; to those complaining and protesting; and to the constraints of originality, the struggles for recognition, and various other rituals of the academic field. *Fourthly*, and finally, radical social critique requires social subjects whom it addresses; otherwise, it remains inconsequential.

This is currently the greatest challenge for contemporary critical theory. For classical social critique, but also for the classic critiques of alienation, the pivotal social subject was the working class movement. This subject has been weakened and must, now more than ever, be defined in the plural as working class *movements*. From a global perspective, however, these working class movements are anything but absent. Particularly in emerging economies like those of South Korea, Brazil, South Africa, and even China, working class movements have often stood at the forefront of democracy movements and alliances for reform. Delicate green shoots of trade union revitalisation can even be observed in the capitalist centres.[155] An influential critique of the new world of labour and the necessary counter-expertise that it entails will hardly be possible without reference to these social

---

153 Cf. E. Hobsbawm, *Age of Extremes*, London 1994 p. 135.
154 Cf. M. Walzer, *Zweifel und Einmischung*, Frankfurt a.M. 1991.
155 Cf. U. Brinkmann, R. Detje u.a., *Strategic Unionism*, Wiesbaden 2008.

subjects.[156] At the same time, the prospect of reconstructing workers' power as an exclusive force is not feasible either. The task at hand is to broaden our horizons. The *Landnahme* theorem implies that critical theory must overcome its disregard for seemingly peripheral, non-commodified forms of production and activity. The same is true with regard to social movements that do not neatly correspond to the norms of a modernised concept of 'working class socialism'. The still-to-be-realised project of an egalitarian democracy encompassing the economic system requires different and additional forms of heterodox power. For the purpose of scientific inquiry, these forms shall be preliminarily termed *associative power*. This entails new combinations of political perspectives, synthesising both producer- and consumer-based approaches.[157] The protagonists of associative power aspire to strengthen the many principles of rationality which the internal imperialism of the finance-capitalist system seeks to advance. This is something that cannot be achieved through protest and resistance alone. What is needed is the exploration of alternatives, the expansion of sectors, whether in the form of a solidarity economy or the public recovery of a privatised sector, wrested from the profit-oriented private sector. If there is a conceptual answer to the questions of our oft-quoted temporary worker, then in my view it is best subsumed under the term *economic democracy*. Recent sociological thought has at best diversified our understanding of the variants of capitalism, but economic democracy means thinking in terms of overcoming it entirely.

---

156   Cf. F. Deppe, *Politisches Denken im 20. Jahrhundert,* 4 volumes, Hamburg 1999–2008.
157   Cf. H. Geiselberger (ed.), *Und Jetzt?,* Frankfurt a.M. 2007.

CHAPTER 2

Capitalism as a Spiral of Dynamisation: Sociology as Social Critique

HARTMUT ROSA

> Modernity was born under the stars of acceleration and land conquest, and these stars form a constellation which contains all the information about its character, conduct and fate.
>
> – Z. Bauman, *Liquid Modernity*

1. SOCIOLOGY AS CRITIQUE OF SOCIETY

Whether we choose to believe it or not, the ultimate object of sociology, though rarely articulated (at least not consciously), is *the question of the good life*, or more precisely: the analysis of the social conditions under which a successful life is possible. That is why sociology takes an interest in the world of work, the family, political relations or the development of the family; in doing so it assumes, as it always has (though not always explicitly so, but mostly tacitly and often only intuitively) that family relations, educational processes, work, and a degree of political influence are relevant factors as far as a decent chance at a successful human life is concerned; that is to say, that variations in the respective forms of these aforementioned spheres of life or their realisation have an impact on the life choices made by individuals. Phenomena which are not, at least on principle, related to these fundamental questions are not considered to be worthwhile objects of sociological study.[1] This is, in the final analysis, the more profound core of the Weberian insight: namely, that the 'cultural significance' of phenomena is what becomes the object of study, and that these cultural significations are determined by the extent to which active subjects ascribe them positive or negative relevance within the context of their ways of life.

---

1 For a more detailed treatment cf. C. Taylor, *Philosophical Papers*, vol. 2, Cambridge 1985; H. Rosa, *Identität und kulturelle Praxis*, Frankfurt a.M., New York 1998, pp. 240–303.

Therefore, this relation can often no longer be detected in respective contemporary research: researchers looking at, for example, the development of the number of single households in cities, changes in the duration of employment relationships, or the distribution of voter volatility or educational mobility, may deny outright that their analyses have *anything* to do with the question of the good life. And yet such studies are ultimately motivated and legitimised by nothing else than this very question: it is for this reason alone that they are considered significant and meaningful, whereas research on the question of whether there are more blades of grass in the Allianz-Arena in Munich or in Dortmund's *Westfalenstadion*[2] will surely not be awarded any research funds.

Indeed, the impulse for social-theoretical reflection usually arises from the often-vague sense that subjects' 'relationship to the world', and thus their opportunities for successful lives, is *affected* or even *threatened* by changes in social relations. In my view, sociology is born out of the diffuse but probably universal basic human perception that 'something is wrong here'.[3] It is no coincidence that sociology as a scientific discipline emerges only in those places and times in which processes of modernisation visibly and palpably engulf people's immediate conditions of life. At the end of the nineteenth and the beginning of the twentieth centuries, when in the course of industrialisation and urbanisation the underlying tendencies of rationalisation, differentiation, domestication and individualisation – in short, social 'acceleration'[4] – manifested beyond the level of the discursive and altered the modern form of life entirely.[5]

2   [Trans. Note] the commercial sponsor's naming rights to call the *West-falenstadion* the Signal Iduna Park, which were granted in 2005, are only in effect through 2021; the author therefore chooses to hang on to its real, that is to say, non-commercial name.

3   According to Michael Walzer, the basic impulse for social critique therefore lies at the same time in 'anthropological' human nature itself: whenever two or three people are together they start complaining about the state of social relations. Similarly, the French authors Boltanski, Chiapello and Thévenot share the view that social critique represents a component equally constitutive as indissoluble of any form of socialisation. Cf. M. Walzer, *The Company of Critics*, London 1989; L. Boltanski, È. Chiapello, *Der neue Geist des Kapitalismus [The New Spirit of Capitalism]*, Konstanz 2003; L. Boltanski, L. Thévenot, 'The Sociology of Critical Capacity', in: *European Journal of Social Theory* 2(3), 1999, pp. 359–77.

4   Cf. e.g., H. Rosa, 'Modernisierung als soziale Beschleunigung: Kontinuierliche Steigerungsdynamik und kulturelle Diskontinuität', in A. Reckwitz, T. Bonacker (ed.), *Kulturen der Moderne*, Frankfurt a.M., New York 2007, pp. 140–72.

5   Cf. H. Rosa, D. Strecker, A. Kottmann, *Soziologische Theorien*, Konstanz 2007, pp. 12–28.

What the analyses of the sociological classics, from Marx to Durkheim and from Weber to Simmel or Tönnies, have in common is that they all proceed from the observation of massive *changes in the conditions of life* – leading to the classical juxtaposition of 'archaic' versus 'modern' societies described by all the founding fathers of sociology – and that they all exhibit great concern for the consequences these changes may have for the human condition. These include, for example, alienation and demystification in Marx and Weber; anomie, loss of a sense of community, and the disappearance of individuality in Durkheim, Simmel and Tönnies. Underlying this socio-critical dimension of the sociological classics we find always the fear of both an almost 'invisible' *loss of freedom* which lurks behind modernity's manifest liberalism – or rather, under its 'steely shell' – as well as a *loss of meaning* (as the downside of the possibility for individual self-determination).[6]

Though it may appear obvious that the early, classical sketches of sociology were not only, and not from the outset, intended as critiques of society, it is nevertheless just as conspicuous that they invariably *also contained* this critical dimension; that it was concern about the development of the conditions of life which pushed these drafts forward in the first place. This may be the reason that these classics never lose their actuality: every generation of sociologists seems to return to them anew, seizing upon them as sources of inspiration and motivation for their own work; whereas much of what sociology has produced since then has seemed to slip into oblivion rather quickly.[7] This is obviously where the ongoing appeal of *critical theory* for successive generations of young sociologists is derived from: its programme and name promise to address that fundamental sociological impulse: the perception that something is not quite right in social relations. At the same time, many competing schools deliberately attempt to deny this motivational origin and legitimising anchor of sociology, as it seems to collide with claims of 'scientificity' and 'neutrality' with regard to questions of values. By contrast, I wish to advance in a straightforward manner the hypothesis that sociology is only appealing and justified when it addresses its inquiries, at least indirectly, to the aforementioned point of departure, the successful way of life; and moreover, that sociology can only honour its own foundations if it is capable of explicitly accounting for

---

6   Cf. e.g., J. Habermas, *Der philosophische Diskurs der Moderne*, Frankfurt a.M. 1988.

7   Cf. H.-J. Dahme, O. Rammstedt, 'Die zeitlose Modernität der soziologischen Klassiker. Überlegungen zur Theoriekonstruktion von Emile Durkheim, Ferdinand Tönnies, Max Weber und besonders Georg Simmel', in: H.-J. Dahme, O. Rammstedt (ed.), *Georg Simmel und die Moderne*, Frankfurt a.M. 1984, pp. 449–78.

those very 'cultural significations' that implicitly drive research and study forward.

In my view, sociological 'enlightenment' that lives up to the theoretical conceptions of a Bourdieu or a Luhmann or rational choice theory must mean the acquisition and development of insights into those (social) relations and processes that hinder, or foster, successful ways of life.

2. CRITERIA FOR A CONTEMPORARY CRITIQUE OF SOCIETY

This unexpectedly presents a severe problem: how should the sociologist know what the standards and criteria *are* for measuring a 'successful way of life'? Against what benchmark does he or she measure potential 'pathologies', i.e., social conditions which unavoidably cause human suffering? To make a long answer short: the history of normative theory, or rather of social philosophy over the past 150 years – or perhaps even since antiquity – has made one thing clear: the sociologist does not know. Sociology possesses no ahistorical, universal, or transcultural standards upon which it could base its work. All attempts by critical social theory to distinguish 'true' from 'false' needs and to identify an objectively true as opposed to a 'false' consciousness have ultimately failed. To the extent that theories of alienation or 'ideology-critical' (*ideologiekritisch*) approaches rely conceptually on the definition of an 'essential nature' of humanity or an 'ideal mode of existence', they have been de-legitimised by the plasticity (i.e., the historico-cultural changeability) of this definition, and by the inevitable contingency of all essentialist and idealist concepts. As the sociological critique of power and post-structuralist-inspired *Sprachkritik* (language criticism) have shown, any sociology that formulates such a 'core human essence' should itself be suspected of ideology and reification; it inevitably becomes paternalistic as soon as it considers itself to possess knowledge of the 'true nature' or 'true needs' of humanity, as opposed to the active subject.

Leading social philosophers – including those standing in the tradition of critical theory[8] – have drawn the conclusion that, instead of the good life, (distributive) justice should be established as the guiding standard of social critique. I regard this response to be inadequate for two reasons: firstly, a social analysis which only addresses (individual) rights and allocations systematically neglects a large proportion of the same potential pathologies already addressed by the sociological classics: a society may maintain comprehensive distributional justice yet still be characterised by the withering

---

8   This includes Jürgen Habermas, Rainer Forst, and to some extent Nancy Fraser.

away of its resources of meaning and the overwhelming, structurally induced experience of alienation. Under such conditions, successful life is rendered structurally impossible, or at least very difficult, by social relations – and yet no straightforward diagnosis of injustice is made. As I intend to show, the capitalist regime of acceleration in late modernity causes (in addition to the injustices it produces) precisely such pathologies. Secondly, in my view standards of justice cannot – irrespective of their individual justifications, whether substantial or procedural – be considered trans-historically valid: their foundation and reliance on the notion of the individual is itself culturally contingent. To my mind, the arguments of communitarian critics on the one hand and post-structuralist authors on the other seem convincing in this regard.

This, however, is not the right forum to reconstruct disputes over the universality of standards of justice in detail. There is a far more obvious, easier path open to sociology which also helps to overcome the aforementioned problem: the standards of sociological 'enlightenment' – of social critique – can and should be rooted in the society that is studied. It is the affected subjects' experience of suffering that – when and if they systematically result from social relations – can provide the criteria for the sociologists' diagnosis.

The basic pattern of sociological critique of society thus appears as follows: in an 'idea-logical' analysis, sociology reconstructs the guiding normative concepts, or rather conceptions of a successful way of life to which individuals adhere, either explicitly or (far more often and to a much higher degree) implicitly in their day-to-day activities, their decisions and their routine practices. At the same time, sociology unearths the 'constitutive ideas of value', which implicitly (and, in many legitimatory texts, explicitly) substantiate central societal institutions. The institutions of the market economy, the academy or democracy, for example, rest on specific concepts of actors and values, on (implicit) conceptions of a successful way of life, and on notions of 'the good', without all of which they could not deploy the powers of legitimatory coherence.[9] The task of social critique is, then, to conduct an analysis of the (structural) causes of the *collective* (or group-specific) *failure to lead a successful life* as defined by the socially powerful conceptions of a successful way of life that guide the subjects' actions.[10]

---

9   Cf. Taylor, *Philosophical Papers*, vol. 2, or H. Rosa, 'Four Levels of Self-Interpretation: A Paradigm for Social Philosophy and Political Criticism', in: *Philosophy and Social Criticism* 30 (5/6), 2004, pp. 691–720.

10   For a similar take on social critique cf. M. Walzer, *Interpretation and Social Criticism*, Cambridge 1987, or Walzer, *The Company of Critics*.

Of course, sociology can also mean to present evidence of potential incompatibilities of those potent ideals and conceptions. Incompatibility may mean that the institutional 'leading ideas' (*Leitideen*), such as efficiency in the economic sphere and equality in justice and in politics, are irreconcilable and thus lead to inevitable suffering due to the friction between them; however, it can also be demonstrated in a deconstructionist or genealogical manner, in which the historical dubiousness of certain ideals are clarified and subjects made aware of the coercion or violence that those ideals enact upon them.[11] Such ideals can then be identified as the reason why subjects find themselves unable to lead successful lives, whether because they are unfree, alienated, or otherwise.

As I intend to explicate in the following, a sociological critique of society can, on the basis of such a programme, convey with convincing argumentative force *if* it adheres to the 'fundamental promise of modernity'; to its *cultural and political project of autonomy*[12] in the face of the processes of (capitalist) modernisation that have taken on a life of their own; and if it makes it clear in the course of doing so that the conditions of late modernity make a successful life on the basis of the as-yet culturally valid standards of modernity, that is to say, of this very society itself, increasingly difficult, or even impossible. Thus, a sociological critique of society ultimately always assumes an 'if … then…' form: *if* we adhere to the standards of autonomy (and authenticity) so fundamental to the modern market economy and modern democracy, *then* the capitalist economic regime of acceleration causes significant pathologies of ever-increasing proportions. That is the core argument that will be developed here.

3. CAPITALISM AND THE ANALYSIS OF SOCIETY

If the central task of sociological 'enlightenment', or rather, social critique, consists of reconstructing the leading conceptions of a *successful way of life* on the one hand – i.e., the hidden as well as manifest goals, desires and value standards of subjects – and the *social conditions* under which these subjects

---

11   Such as the 'terror of authenticity' identified by Foucault. Cf. M. Foucault, *Dispositive der Macht*, Berlin 1978 (*Dispositifs of Power* – no English translation available).

12   The claim that the notion of autonomy lies at the normative and cultural centre of modernity is also endorsed today – following Castoriadis – by J.P Árnason 'Autonomy and Axiality', in J. P. Árnason, P. Murphy (ed.), *Agon, Logos, Polis*, Stuttgart 2001, pp. 155–206; cf. also P. Wagner, *Soziologie der Moderne*, Frankfurt a.M., New York 1997.

pursue these conceptions; on the other hand there can be no doubt that modern sociology needs to take as its point of departure with regard to both aspects the promises and modes of operation of *capitalist relations.*

Capitalism represents the 'most fateful force in our modern life'[13] – so says not Karl Marx (although he may surely have agreed), but Max Weber in the preface to *The Protestant Ethic.* This type of economic organisation is 'fateful' not only because it determines society's form of production and thus the social conditions under which subjects lead their lives, but because it dominates their 'spirits': 'The capitalism of today … educates and selects the economic subjects which it needs',[14] writes Weber; resembling a kind of 'training', it virtually forces subjects into a specific lifestyle in the service of capitalism; this pertains to subjects' approach to employment, their competitiveness, their concept of individuality, their standards of recognition and, what must be added in late modernity, their consumer behaviour.

That the way of life is driven by fear on one side, and promises (hopes) which come to define conceptions of a successful versus an unsuccessful life on the other, is by no means specific to modernity. But that fear and expectation are related to the extent of success in economic activity is a specific outcome of the capitalist economic form. As Weber attempts to establish in *The Protestant Ethic,* fear and promise have been the cultural driving forces behind the 'capitalist ethos' from the outset. Indeed, over the course of the modernisation process they changed form, as their surface of projection shifted from the realm of an extra-social transcendence (*eternal salvation vs. damnation*) to the system-immanent arena of social competition (*fear of the loss of competitiveness and social connectedness,* and consequently, of unemployment, *vs. the promise of everlasting prosperity*[15] *and growing power in the sense of a continual growth of autonomy*[16]). And yet they nevertheless retained their function with regard to their, as Weber would call it, 'unnatural' culture-specific effect: the creation of a capitalist producer's ethos focused on profit maximisation and thus on growth and acceleration, but without the real, individual, consumptive indulgence in the returns featuring as a constitutive element of the conception of a successful life.

The aspect of promise within capitalism, however, can only be fully understood if its relation to the fundamental pledge of modernity is

---

13   M. Weber, *The Protestant Ethic and the Spirit of Capitalism,* London, New York, xxxi.

14   Ibid. p. 20.

15   Cf. B. Lutz, *Der kurze Traum immerwährender Prosperität,* Frankfurt a.M., New York 1984.

16   Cf. C. Deutschmann, *Die Verheißung des absoluten Reichtums,* Frankfurt a.M., New York 1999.

considered. This pledge, in which the ideas of the Enlightenment converge with the desire for democracy and fantasies of technical possibility, is the notion of individual (and collective) autonomy: the promise of being able to lead a self-determined life according to one's own standards without having to bend to the heteronomous *diktat* of church, king or tradition, of poverty or resource scarcity, of ignorance or lack of alternatives; or even to the forces of nature.[17] This ideal of autonomy is necessarily complemented by a second defining cultural ideal: the modern conception of individual and/ or collective authenticity, according to which the task at hand is not only to determine oneself, but more importantly: to determine oneself 'correctly', or rather, to do oneself 'justice' or 'stay true to' oneself. In other words, authenticity entails the idea that a good life is determined by the progressive development of our own respective individual talents and capacities, and we therefore need to 'listen to our inner voice' in order to find out what our 'true' needs really are. For the subjects of modernity a good life consists, to a large extent, of the notion of discovering and realising – in the words of Herder – their own 'measure', their individual mode of being human.[18] Indeed, even though the romanticised ideal of an internal essence that must be materialised is called into question these days, the idea that the form of life we each choose (or are subordinated to) must 'fit' our individual dispositions and needs nevertheless remains highly culturally effective. This can be observed in all cases where actors (through their action as well as their self-legitimisation) express their desire to 'remain true' to themselves, that they no longer want to 'bend or break', that they wish to 'stick to their principles', that they need to find out 'who they really are'.[19]

If, in this sense, autonomy and authenticity represent the cornerstones of the modern conception of a successful life,[20] then capitalism and democracy constitute the equally essential means to their realisation: only the efficiency of the capitalist economic system – as runs the succinct legitimatory formula employed by defenders and proponents of the market economy from Adam Smith to Ludwig Erhard – provides the material resources

---

17   In this sense, the desire to (freely) decide one's gender (or the physical and mental traits of one's offspring) ultimately represents further evidence of this promise of and demand for autonomy constitutive of modernity.

18   'Each man has his own measure, as it were an accord peculiar to him of all his feelings to each other'. J. G. v. Herder, 1877–1913, *Vom Erkennen und Empfinden der Menschlichen Seele, von Bernhard Suphan*, Volume 8, pg. 199, Berlin 1892.

19   Cf. also A. Ferrara, 'Authenticity and the Project of Modernity', in *European Journal of Philosophy* 2(3), 1994, pp. 241–73; and especially P. Vannini, J. P. Williams (ed.), *Authenticity in Culture, Self and Society*, Burlington 2009.

20   Cf. C. Taylor, *Quellen des Selbst*, Frankfurt a.M. 1994; also Rosa, *Identität*, pp. 181–211.

that allow for leading a self-determined life, for overcoming constraints and limitations and for establishing just distribution and political partici-pation in the shaping of living conditions. By contributing to solving the problem of material scarcity once and for all, the success and innovative force of capitalism *releases subjects from conducting lives concentrated on the economic sphere, the daily struggle for existence, and more generally, on the material dimension of life.* Only then is there a chance of a genuine cultural autonomy – this is what constitutes the faith in progress that has always been implicitly and explicitly tied to capitalism; it can still be found in Marcuse's idea of a truly 'pacified existence.'[21] If today – as I intend to show – the oppo-site occurs, if human life conduct is increasingly determined by competition in the economic sphere, if the scope for leading a self-determined life and for political organisation of society similarly fall prey to the boundless imperatives related to the maintenance and growth of individual and col-lective competitiveness, then this is an expression not only of the perversion of the leading cultural idea of capitalism, but also of a constitutive betrayal of the project and fundamental promise of modernity. Sociology does not require any trans-historical or anthropological criteria in order to reveal this pathological contradiction.

Once we direct our attention not to the 'spirit' of a modern way of life, but instead to the social conditions under which subjects pursue their individual conceptions of a successful life, we quickly realise that these (individual conceptions) are thoroughly determined by the capitalist logic of production (and consumption). Essentially, this logic is *dynamic*: it effects a perpetual change (or 'revolution') in the material and social structures of society.

That 'capitalism' as such even exists in the sense of a unitary social formation has been contested often and heavily, in particular after 1989 (especially by disillusioned veteran leftists). As the argument goes, the term 'capitalism' – which suggests some sort of uniformity – in reality conceals highly divergent historico-cultural forms of production and thus regimes of social provision and political participation, and therefore, in turn, differ-ent conflicts between corresponding classes or strata, or between economic, political and cultural systems. According to the argument, then, it is obvious that Manchester Capitalism and social market economy; early capitalism; Fordism and flexible post-Fordism; as well as Anglo-Saxon, Rhenish and Southeast Asian Capitalism lie worlds apart from one another.[22]

---

21   H. Marcuse, *One Dimensional Man*, London 1968, p. 246.
22   On this cf. e.g., E. Altvater, 'Kapitalismus – Zur Bestimmung, Abgrenzung und Dynamik einer geschichtlichen Formation', in *Erwägen Wissen Ethik* 13 (3), 2002, pp. 281–92.

This, which I believe to be a blatant misdiagnosis, seems to be the result of decades-long overemphasis of the *internal* contradictions of capitalism. This includes the divisions, tensions, and separations between classes and strata, between economic and political systems, and between the more developed and the 'backward' states. Such fault lines may indeed vary sharply throughout history. Yet as a consequence of this focus on contradictions, analyses of capitalism became blind to the sweeping 'fateful force of modern life'[23] *behind* these tensions so important to Weber; that is to say, a force which imposes, beyond all lines of division, a common trajectory of development not only on subjects, but on social relations themselves, and which recasts both according to the unrelenting logic and dynamic of capital accumulation.

If we then inquire about the ways in which the fundamental principles of capital accumulation and circulation shape the social conditions and the systematic and constant transformation of social relations, we find two mutually interrelated principles of dynamisation guiding the whole process, the culturally and structurally defining influence of which cannot be overestimated: the *principle of growth*, on the one hand, and the *logic of acceleration* on the other. I would like to briefly explain what I mean by this.

a) Growth: there can be no doubt whatsoever that capitalist societies – throughout different stages of development and beyond all cultural or geographical differences – have always been societies of growth. They continuously increase their aggregate national output and productivity unless they fall into crisis. These societies' crises are always and have always been *crises of growth*. Beyond all the differences between the leading industrial nations, e.g., at the G8 summits, and ultimately irrespective of differences between modern states or even between almost all the political parties in said states, there is one common objective – the universal *telos* of the stimulation of economic growth. The idea that *everything conceivable must be done to boost economic growth* is disavowed neither by Republicans nor Democrats in the USA; neither by socialists nor liberals nor conservatives in Italy, France, England or Germany. Usually there is no disagreement regarding the unconditional priority of growth over ecological concerns. What is remarkable about this is that such a one-sided growth totalitarianism would have been inconceivable in virtually all known previous social formations. By contrast, the capitalist system – the cultural legitimatory basis of which rests on the promise of overcoming all material constraints – produces this growth totalitarianism, and in such a way that the growth

---

23 Weber, *Protestant Ethic*, p. xxxi.

imperative disengages from any real material needs. Thus, regardless of the actual volume of national output, it *can never reach a conclusion*. Although this may seem self-evident to us today, it carries serious implications, as growth must always be obtained on the basis of previous growth, which manifests itself in a virtually exponential upward curve in terms of productive capacity. Thus, those who claim that capitalism as such does not exist do not sufficiently account for the fact that as actors within such societies we are all forced to produce more every year, and to circulate and consume more than the previous year, regardless of the precise form the realisation of this 'more' assumes. This systemic imperative inevitably has an effect on the self-conception and self-definition of actors who in turn must always unconsciously adapt their individual definitions of a successful life to a mode that makes them compatible with the ethos of the successful producer as well as that of the consumer addicted to, or at least willing to participate in, accumulation.[24]

b) Acceleration: in capitalist societies there is not only *more and more* of most things, but also more and more things happen *faster* – as a matter of fact, even serious analysts of capitalism such as Elmar Altvater are fooled into believing that more or less 'everything' does so. Economic growth and social acceleration are tightly interwoven in a reciprocal logic of escalation. *Time is money*: such is the basic temporal formula of capitalism, and in the same way that money is *per se* scarce under competitive economic conditions, so time is equally scarce, because time – in the form of working hours – is an immediate production factor. Hence, productivity increases always represent a competitive advantage achieved through savings in necessary labour time; in other words, *more output per unit of time*. However, not least owing to the *principle of interest rates*, to the problem of *moral depreciation* of machines, and particularly to the opportunity to make quick *extra profits* through the introduction of new products or technologies to the market, capitalist economic activity in its very essence rests on the detection and utilisation of temporal advantages. The increasing velocity of the rate of capital turnover, and thus the pace of production, circulation and consumption, therefore represents a characteristic feature of all capitalist economies that is just as irresolvable as economic growth.

In this sense, the one characteristic that has existed as an unchanging 'essence' or 'formation trait' throughout all historical epochs and cultural appearances of capitalism and which therefore should be included in its

---

24   For a more elaborate treatment of this cf. H. Rosa, 'Kapitalismus und Lebensführung. Perspektiven einer ethischen Kritik der liberalen Marktwirtschaft', in *Deutsche Zeitschrift für Philosophie* 47(5), 1999, pp. 735–58.

definition is *that specific, peculiar, fatal connection of growth and accelera-tion, that 'bicycle principle' of capital accumulation*: either the process of circulation occurs at high and increasing speeds, or the system 'falls over' (Claus Offe). It is that general condition of society in which there can no longer be any static, lasting equilibrium, no stable, idle state; one in which any kind of rest or halt causes an immediate backslide. It is this implacability that marks Weber's 'iron cage' as well as Jameson's TINA principle.[25] It is the principle of escalation found in both of these concepts that lets modernity appear to us as 'total mobilisation' (Paul Virilio,[26] Peter Sloterdijk[27]) and has the effect that 'all that is solid melts into air', as Marx and Engels already pointed out. It is in this constant 'melting into air' that Marshall Berman discovers the fundamental principle of modernisation itself.[28] Growth and acceleration thus appear as the central *culture-shaping* and *structure-forming* forces of a capitalist social order.

4. CHANGING TRENDS IN CAPITALISM – A DIAGNOSIS OF THE TIMES

It is the socially formative, unrelenting compulsion of the capitalist logic of growth and acceleration that enables and enforces the revolutionising of capitalist production regimes and political modes of governance, as well as the forms of subjectivity and identity formation. For example, in a certain epoch and at a certain state of development in capitalism, the strict spatial and temporal differentiation of production, i.e., the separation of work and recreation, and later the standardisation of (workplace) processes and movements (in the sense of Fordism and particularly Taylorism), allowed for enormous productivity increases. Today, by contrast, these are achieved in precisely the opposite way – that is to say, the potential for gains is sought largely in *de-standardisation* and *de-differentiation*. As a consequence of the corresponding 're-education of subjects' necessitated by this de-standardisation, people today work faster and harder when they are *not* tied to strict working hours; for instance when work processes are adapted to

---

25   TINA: There Is No Alternative – One of Margaret Thatcher's key slogans, the almost indisputable validity of which, in terms of the continued existence of the liberal-capitalist order of governance, the American cultural philosopher Fredric Jameson identifies to be the one remarkable feature of late modernity: Cf. F. Jameson, *The Cultural Turn*, London, New York 1998.

26   Cf. P. Virilio, *Geschwindigkeit und Politik*, Berlin 1980.

27   Cf. P. Sloterdijk, *Eurotaoismus*, Frankfurt a.M. 1989.

28   Cf. M. Berman, *All That Is Solid Melts Into Air*, New York 1988; also D. Harvey, *The Condition of Postmodernity*, Cambridge, Mass., Oxford, 1990.

individual routines or can be worked on from home. Following the comprehensive internalisation and habitualisation of standards of competition and performance, individuals turn out to be more productive and creative if they are not controlled via attendance checks and time clocks, but exclusively through deadlines for turning in results – via the 'power of the deadline' (what a telling expression!). The 'purification' of the sphere of work, in terms of being isolated from all other issues of the lifeworld as ensured by spatial separation, is no longer necessary; rather, the dissolution of this separation facilitates the utilisation of other lifeworld resources (from non-work-related spheres of life) in order to achieve additional productivity gains. Once again, one must be particularly stubborn to not see that a simple logic lies behind the changes to the mode of production; and one must be more or less 'deaf' to the important questions of individual as well as collective life conduct and lifestyle not to recognise that this logic exerts a great deal of determining influence on both the mode of production and on ways of life.

Elmar Altvater is thus correct to point out that those phenomena which are discussed today under the catch-all label of 'globalisation' are actually nothing more than the preliminary spatial, temporal and social end products of expansive and intensive growth as well as maximum acceleration, which when viewed together border on global *synchronicity* as far as processes of proliferation and circulation are concerned.[29] He also notes that on the one hand, it was a 'consequence of growth' that 'in capitalist economic and social life radical changes occur at such a high tempo and thus in such short historical periods of time as never before in the economic or social history of humankind',[30] while on the other hand he equates his central concept of the 'disembedding' of the economy from 'natural and social ligatures' as an essential characteristic of this economic mode with acceleration: 'Disembedding is therefore synonymous with the acceleration of all social processes'.[31] Nowhere does that which Altvater describes become clearer than when evaluated in light of the social function of economic growth: not a single percentage point of growth rates – forcefully imposed under mobilisation of all social forces and celebrated by politicians of all stripes – serves the purpose of responding to specific material needs. Instead, growth becomes an end unto itself; or rather, it *creates work*. From the perspective of any other social formation such a condition must undoubtedly appear as perversion, as an expression of genuinely pathological *pleonexia*.

If the endless spiral of growth and acceleration characterises the capitalist social formation as a whole, the substantial, i.e., structural and cultural,

29   Cf. Altvater, *Kapitalismus*, p. 290.

30   Ibid. p. 284f.

31   Ibid. p. 285.

constitution of society nevertheless changes its substance and appearance over the course of capitalist modernisation; this change can be observed at two critical transition points. These points, however, can only be accurately defined by drawing upon a theory of acceleration.

My diagnosis departs from the assumption that manifestations of disjunctive cultural upheavals appear throughout the more or less structurally continuous process of social acceleration in the same way that the steadily accelerating movement of molecules changes the aggregate state of substances (frozen, liquid, gaseous) at certain critical tipping points. If one accepts the hypothesis that the pace of societal change throughout the trajectory of modernity increases – that patterns of association, bodies of knowledge and forms of praxis are accelerated– then it seems likely that qualitative changes in the perception of social reality are triggered at certain critical points in this process, and that these transitions are linked to changes in respective influential spatio-temporal regimes, forms of subjectivity, and the ways in which individuals relate to themselves politically. As I now intend to show, these tipping points are closely related to the (unchanging) pace of generational exchange.

Authors like Jan Assman and Reinhart Koselleck have demonstrated that communicative social memory, and with it a communicatively imparted consciousness of the past and present, is limited in its temporal span to roughly eighty to one hundred years.[32] This means that the phenomenon so characteristic of modernity – the widening gulf between the realm of experience and the horizon of expectation – and thus the experience of a 'shrinking of the present', can have a cultural impact only when drastic processes of change take place *within the life span of three to four succeeding generations who can potentially be contemporaries.* If, however, societal change (i.e., the transformation of structural and cultural certainties) reaches a higher velocity than the *simple succession of generations*, it seems likely that, as Karl Mannheim anticipated,[33] it will result in grave consequences for intergenerational relations, and the erosion of lifeworld reliability and continuity will reach a qualitatively new level – a circumstance that undoubtedly has an impact on cultural reproduction as well as on subjects' forms of identity. The appeal of postmodern ideas today could therefore potentially signal the approach of such a threshold, beyond which certain forms of narrative, cumulative and linear appropriation of the world can no longer function properly. After all, beyond a certain high (however ill-defined) threshold,

---

32   Cf. J. Assmann, *Das kulturelle Gedächtnis*, München 1992; R. Koselleck, *Vergangene Zukunft*, Frankfurt a.M. 1989, p. 328ff. and 366ff.

33   Cf. K. Mannheim, 'Das Problem der Generationen', in K. Mannheim, *Wissenssoziologie*, Berlin, Neuwied 1964, p. 509–65.

change is no longer perceived as a change within solid structures but as a profound and potentially chaotic *indeterminacy*.

Our thesis, the argument for an ongoing *acceleration* of societal change over the course of the modernisation process, could also be expressed in a more pointed manner; namely, that the tempo has shifted from an *inter*-generational pace of change in early modernity, through a phase of approximate synchronisation with generational succession during classical modernity, to a speed that has become virtually *intra*-generational by late modernity.

Despite the difficulties in empirically measuring such a change of tempo, in the following I will attempt to make this claim at least plausible with reference to the structural transitional dynamic of those foundational social institutions which organise the essential processes of production and reproduction. In western societies these have been the institutions of the family as well as the capitalist employment system, more or less immutably – this is why analyses of societal change very often focus on precisely these areas.[34] In spite of numerous contradictions and ambiguities in the empirical findings concerning these two social dimensions, such a shift in the pace of change from an *inter*-generational, via a *generational*, to a potentially *intra*-generational velocity can only be postulated if socially endogenous causes (the self-inflicted causes of change that really matter in this context, as opposed to exogenous occurrences like hostile attacks, natural disasters, and so on) are taken into consideration. Thus, the ideal-typical family structures in agrarian societies – as far as the life cycles of families as economic entities or 'households' are concerned – tended to remain stable for many generations: generational transition did not touch upon basic structures as it only replaced individual position holders.

The author Arthur Imhof describes this family structural preservation of stability over generations as such: 'Not the individual Johannes Hoos, born in one year and deceased in another, was the deciding factor. Far more important was that there was always another Johannes Hoos standing by to assume his role and take charge of the farm during his physically most pro-ductive and socially most integrated years. This way, a farm was not only the property of one Johannes Hoos for ten or twenty or thirty years, but instead it remained so continuously for four and a half centuries. A truly astonish-ing stability despite uncertain life spans.'[35] That many members of society,

---

34   For a more elaborate treatment cf. H. Rosa, *Social Acceleration: A New Theory of Modernity*, 2013, pp. 108–19.

35   A. E. Imhof, 'Von der sicheren zur unsicheren Lebenszeit. Ein folgens-chwerer Wandel im Verlaufe der Neuzeit', in *Vierteljahresschrift für Sozial- und Wirtschaftsgeschichte* 71, 1984, p. 175–98, here p. 188.

such as servants and maids, were deprived of establishing their own families by no means contradicts this finding; as their social position was determined by their relations to the core family structures, they would simply function as part of the family household. Structurally (and culturally) normative family structures were therefore designed to last a long time. During classical modernity, then, the core family – which is ideal-typically designed for one generation and centred around one married couple, dissolving after the death of said couple – replaces the extended family and along with it the cross-generational family group and its corresponding stable permanent structure. It becomes an indispensable identity-forming and autonomy-securing task of the modern middle-class individual (but increasingly the 'proletarian' as well) to *start his own family* which, in theory, ceases to exist as an economic entity once the two partners die. In late modernity, finally, family cycles exhibit a clear tendency toward an *infra*-generational life span, of which rising rates of divorce and remarriage as well as household restructuring or dissolution are the clearest evidence.[36] The temporary significant other tends to replace the life partner today – this argument by no means declares the decline of the *ideal* of the bourgeois family as such, in fact quite to the contrary: it is absolutely compatible with empirical findings that this form of life increasingly constitutes the social ideal once again, and that individuals today continue to enter into new family ties and arrangements. The model of lifelong monogamy is thus more and more often replaced by a new form of 'serial monogamy', or of having temporary lovers.[37]

Despite valid empirical objections to such a simplified and schematised depiction of the changes in family structures, it is undeniable that a general *awareness of the contingency* of family structures is increasing, including among those who decide to remain together for the rest of their lives. The awareness that arrangements *could be otherwise*, whether through one's own decision or someone else's, and the resulting *uncertainties,* as well as the pressure to justify holding on to the existing arrangement, are surely increasing. Sighard Neckel quite aptly remarks in this regard, that 'This creates a symbolic reality, from which there is no turning back. This alone already changes society, regardless of whether the changes are really as comprehensive compared to the times in which it still consisted of a few major groups'.[38] Furthermore – in contrast to 'exogenous' contingencies and such

---

36   Cf. e.g., U. Beck, E. Beck-Gernsheim (eds), *Riskante Freiheiten,* Frankfurt a.M. 1994.

37   Cf. G. Burkart, B. Fietze, M. Kohli, *Liebe, Ehe, Elternschaft,* Wiesbaden 1989, p. 244ff.

38   S. Neckel, 'Identität als Ware. Die Marktwirtschaft im Sozialen', in S. Neckel, *Die Macht der Unterscheidung,* Frankfurt a.M., New York 2000, pp. 37–47, here p. 40.

vagaries as diseases, natural disasters, the repercussions of violent relations of dominance, etc., which often rendered pre-modern family structures unstable and susceptible to decay – the contingencies of late modern family structures are of a more self-inflicted, more family-endogenous and more individualised nature.

These dynamisation-related findings are particularly valid for assessing the development of forms of employment relations. Here the argument can be made with typifying emphasis that professions in pre- and early modernity tended to be handed down from father to son, resulting in a cross-generational stability in occupational and employment structures. The free, but usually one-time choice of one's own, lifelong and identity-forming occupation then became an outright constitutive characteristic of classical modernity in which occupational structures displayed a 'generational' stability.[39] *Find your calling!* became, alongside *Start your own family!*, the second identity-forming task in modernising societies – initially addressed to young men, but increasingly also to young women. In late modernity, by contrast, it seems to become less and less common that professions and employment relationships last an entire working life: according to the overwhelming majority of empirical data, multiple changes in profession and employment *within* an individual's working life (often accompanied by varying periods of unemployment) seem to have gradually shifted from being an exception to becoming the rule.

Today, a young American with at least two years of college can expect to change jobs at least eleven times in the course of working, and change his or her skill base at least three times during those forty years of labour',[40] as Richard Sennett confirms in his deeply relevant study on the 'corroded character' (or, in the German translation, the 'flexible human') of 'turbocapitalism'. As Daniel Cohen summarises this transition, 'Whoever begins a career at Microsoft has not the slightest idea where it will end. Whoever started it at Ford or Renault, could be well nigh certain that it will finish in the same place'.[41]

An additional factor in this process is how the de-regulation of forms of labour produces new forms of employment, such as temporary work and

39   Cf. e.g., Z. Bauman, *Liquid Modernity*, Cambridge 2000, p. 116.

40   R. Sennett, *The Corrosion of Character*, 1998, p.22

41   D. Cohen, quoted in: Bauman, *Liquid Modernity*, p. 116. On the empirical findings cf. M. Grotheer, O. Struck, 'Beschäftigungsstabilität: Entwicklung und Arbeitszufriedenheit. Ergebnisse aus der IAB-Beschäftigtenstichprobe 1975–1997 und der BIBB/IAB-Erhebung', in*Mitteilungen aus der Arbeitsmarkt- und Berufsforschung* 36(3), 2003, pp. 300–28; C. Köhler, O. Struck i.a. (eds), *Offene und geschlossene Beschäftigungssysteme*, Wiesbaden 2008.

various forms of part-time work. The information technology industry in particular created completely new occupational sectors altogether, coinciding with the disappearance of numerous traditional professions. Here again we have a case where the dynamic of change is *endogenous* to society, where changes can be brought about by internal or external decisions and where contingency awareness, i.e., uncertainty concerning the short-, mid-, and long-term employment situation, increases even in those areas where professions and forms of employment relations do *not* change.

As I argue, the acceleration of social transformation can therefore be gauged generally by the relationship between generations: from a premodern situation in which structural and cultural resources were mainly handed down for generations, this acceleration leads into a modernity in which, as Ansgar Weyman points out, 'generations' act 'as collective actors and in an innovative way'[42] (that is to say, changes can be identified by the generational change) and finally to a late modernity in which the relations change fundamentally even within the timespan associated with only one generation. Under the conditions of an *intra*-generational pace of social transformation, then, both politics and forms of subjectivity lose their claim to participation and development, and thus to autonomy, as acquired in classical modernity. Bearing the marks of 'temporalised time', in which the sequence, duration, and pace of events (in life as well as politics) no longer corresponds to specific plans and patterns but instead occurs at the moment of realisation, they assume a 'situational character'. What *situational politics* means in this context is that democratic politics, precisely because it can hardly be accelerated – on the contrary, democratic processes of opinion-formation and decision-making in fact cause deceleration under the highly dynamic conditions of globalised modernity[43] – loses its role as the pacemaker of social development and is forced to limit itself to a strategy of 'muddling through' current events as well as *adjustment programmes*. Progressive politics today, to the extent that such a thing still exists, no longer pursues the controlled *acceleration of societal change* in the sense of a notion of progress, but rather its *deceleration* in order to safeguard a claim to political steering, while (liberal-)*conservative* politics seems to be characterised by a straightforward inversion of classical-modernist relations in its willingness to remove all impediments to acceleration posed by these claims. State bureaucracies (and democratic decision-making) as instruments of governance are today no longer considered the embodiment of

---

42   A. Weymann, 'Sozialer Wandel, Generationsverhältnisse und Technikgenerationen', in M. Kohli, M. Szydlik (ed.), *Generationen in Familie und Gesellschaft*, Opladen 2000, pp. 36–58, here p. 44.

43   For a more detailed explanation cf. Rosa, *Social Acceleration*, pp. 259–76.

efficiency, but instead as paradigmatic examples of sclerotic decay. The era of modern democratic politics (i.e., of a collective autonomy) has it would seem come to an end, replaced by talk of 'post-democracy' and 'output legitimation'.[44]

Situational identity, by contrast, describes the self-relation corresponding to the *temporalised* time of late modernity. Under the conditions of an *intra*-generational pace of societal change, one's own life is no longer perceived as a progressively unfolding (and predictable) project, but instead as an open 'game',[45] or 'drift',[46] in which all attributes of one's identity must be complemented by a temporal indicator: one is married to X *at the moment*, one is *currently* working as a graphic designer, one voted Green *during the last election*. Consequently, *situationality* means, firstly, that the claim to diachronous continuity and synchronous coherence – and thus the capacity for long-term life planning – is surrendered. Secondly, however, it also means that those changes, partially through one's own choosing and partially imposed from outside, are no longer perceived to be in any way *directed*; despite – or maybe precisely because of – the high velocity with which they are enacted, they stand in no noticeable relation to one another. Politically, as well as with regard to life in the everyday practical sense, this late modern form of *temporalised* time, marked by high, unpredictable and only slightly controllable rates of change, gives the impression of what can best be described as a *frenetic standstill*: things change, but they do not develop; there is an innumerable scope of options, but as they continually change their form there are no long-term strategies to harness them cumulatively. Movement becomes aimless and contingent, even erratic; it loses its temporal, factual and political compass.

This change has long since affected the institutional arrangement of modern societies: the nation state and its bureaucracies, welfare state institutions, relations of labour and employment and the associated 'life course regime', even the strict institutional separation of the spheres of recreation and work, and thus of *public* and *private* as such. Under the conditions of globalisation, they all are confronted with erosional pressures; and their restructuring in turn accelerates social transformation, the emergence of social uncertainty and the erosion of the classical-modernist paths of development.

If we are to ask, using the sociological terms defined at the outset of this

---

44   Cf. C. Crouch, *Post-Democracy*, Cambridge, UK 2004.

45   Cf. K. H. Hörning, D. Ahrens, A. Gerhard, *Zeitpraktiken*, Frankfurt a.M. 1997.

46   Cf. Sennett, Richard, *The Corrosion of Character: The Personal Consequences of Work in the New Capitalism*, 1st ed., New York 1998.

text, how the chances of realising the modern conception of a successful life – of the attainment of late modernity's promise of autonomy – are subject to change, then a sceptical diagnosis seems inevitable. This can be seen rather clearly in the shifting balance between this social formation's motivational driving forces: the system's ability to induce fear is gaining in importance (competitive constraints are becoming more intense, the danger of social decline or even exclusion is mounting, the social 'drop height', so to speak, is increasing), while the aspect of promise seems to be fading away. The hope of achieving a position of security and material prosperity that allows for a self-determined, independent life is gradually disappearing.

This is mainly owed to the fact that the transition to an *intra*-generational pace of change is accompanied by a shift from 'positional' to 'performative' relations of competition and recognition. Under the generational pace of change found in 'classical modernity', it was quite promising for subjects to pursue a positional strategy: to reach a certain professional position (this may have included, on one end of the social spectrum, the position of executive manager, chief editor, or professor, or – closer to the other end of the spectrum – that of a shift foreman, overseer, or permanently employed cleaner), to assume a certain family position (that of husband, family father or home owner), or to find a position in volunteer community work. Such positions used to ensure a decent standard of living, but also status, recognition, security and, in particular, spaces of autonomy. They represented the basis upon which people could perceive life as their own personal project (albeit within certain limits). In late modernity, by contrast, the struggles revolving around competition and recognition have shifted from a struggle of position, which allowed for the achievement of certain stepped levels of competition and recognition, to an endless performative struggle: recognition, status and often income are now no longer determined according to what level is reached (e.g., the position of executive manager, professor, chief editor, cleaner, foreman, etc.), but instead are continuously re-negotiated on the basis of performance criteria: sales figures, circulation and ratings figures, numbers of publications and volume of third-party funding are evaluated and redefined quarterly or biannually. For the less privileged, temporary work, precarious forms of employment and fixed-term labour contracts both indicate and enforce this accommodation to performance criteria and thus to permanent competition and existential uncertainty. Interestingly enough, this shift from position to performance can also be found in family relations and, for example, in the field of volunteer work: long-term relationships derive their legitimation less and less from entering into contracts (marriage) and more and more from a mutual performative satisfaction repeatedly put to the test, while volunteer social work is increasingly losing its 'office-holding' character. The question of how long and how intensively someone wishes to and is allowed to fulfil a specific responsibility is subject to a permanent and process-related re-evaluation.[47] The compulsion to prove oneself over and over in all spheres of life – given that there is no certainty that status, once achieved, will be maintained – undermines any confidence that one is 'in charge' of one's own life and thus able to lead it in a self-determined way. Surprisingly, this loss of autonomous room for manoeuvre can be detected not only in the main spheres of social life (workplace, family, politics, volunteering, etc.), but also in the more peripheral areas, with similarly dire consequences: today, there are just as few 'secure positions' in one's choice of telephone or electricity providers, health insurance, or financial investment. Instead we find growing pressure for permanent performance monitoring and re-evaluation, as that which today may lead to first-class service (and thus spaces of autonomy) may become the source of a serious competitive disadvantage tomorrow.

If and to the extent to which autonomy, then, comes to mean the *power, the freedom and the security to shape and build one's life (Gestaltungsmacht, Gestaltungsfreiheit und Gestaltungssicherheit)*, the loss of autonomy is particularly noticeable with view to the material and technical structures integral to our daily lives. By acquiring functioning telephones, cameras, stereo systems and computers we also acquire the chance to accomplish even the most ambitious goals swiftly and efficiently: to listen to the music that means something to us, to capture the scenes we wish to preserve, to establish the personal connections that are important to us. Throughout the process of modernisation we have reached certain positional levels of action and power to shape our own lives through technical efficiency. However, this positional autonomy threatens to disappear at any time in late modernity: *ever since we bought a new mobile phone, we can no longer call our most important family members on short dial because the memory was lost; we do not know where the redial button is, how to adjust the voicemail settings, etc.* We may own hundreds of records, allowing us to listen to almost any piece of music that we cherish – but unfortunately, no one can fix our old record player and many of our most treasured classics do not exist on CD (at least not in our collection). We have descended from the positional level that we once had achieved. Essentially, we now have less to listen to, we have

---

47 This represents the essence of what Rolf Heinze and Thomas Olk have recognised to be the transition from the 'old' to the 'new' (form of) volunteering. Cf. R. Heinze, T. Olk, 'Vom Ehrenamt zum bürgerschaftlichen Engagement. Trends des begrifflichen und gesellschaftlichen Strukturwandels', in E. Kistler, H.-H. Noll, E. Priller (ed.), *Perspektiven gesellschaftlichen Zusammenhalts*, Berlin 1999, pp. 77–100.

less immediately accessible music at our disposal than we used to.[48] Because the new computer is running Vista instead of XP, we even have to relearn how to save files, how to open them – indeed, even how to shut down the computer. Surely, these devices can do all sorts of things and more, but if we never find the time to adapt ourselves, we have less power to shape our lives than we previously did; we are forced to 'performatively' re-appropriate the agency to create what we used to simply possess in the first place. This way we surrender our spaces of autonomy over and over again: with view to ensuring leeway for autonomous behaviour, we must *keep running faster in order to stay informed*. The thought of a targeted, time-resistant, long-term – or in a word: autonomous – utilisation (of these spaces) is out of the question. Then again, in most recent times it has seemed as if the cultural elites are taking notice of this imbalance between the acquisition of technical devices promising capacity increases and continuous capacity losses due to rates of innovation that exceed the pace of cultural learning: it is not the purchase of a product that establishes our opportunity for gaining prestige, but the mastering and application of this product. After all, the 'bargain hunt' for ever newer technical capacity seems to have increasingly become an underclass phenomenon from which the elites are beginning to distance themselves quite decidedly. An interesting question, (but one I cannot deal with in depth at this point) is what the implications of all this may be for the chances of future growth (and for the reproduction of social inequality). Beyond dispute is that the fundamental promise of modernity – the increase in and securing of autonomy (through growth and acceleration) – has taken on a life of its own on the technical side of civilisation to such an extent that although the technical possibilities for shaping one's life constantly increase, the rate of exhaustion of these possibilities progressively decreases. The transition of competition and recognition criteria from position to performance may in fact also serve as an explanation for the significant rise in illnesses related to anxiety, depression and burnout in late modernity; even the rising number of cancer cases may be related. Recent research indicates that the most effective factor to protect against cancer is a strong sense of self-efficacy (or autonomy). The rate of cancer correlates – far more so than with factors such as smoking, alcohol consumption, body weight and nutritional habits – with the feeling of being unable to control, make decisions about, or be in charge of one's own life. In short, cancer correlates heavily with lacking

---

48   Whoever may insinuate that this is an exceptional case is mistaken: while many (members of the cultural elite in particular) are attempting to be autonomous with respect to a personal film collection and are amassing rapidly growing DVD collections, the industry has already announced the definitive end of DVD production as such; not to mention the many times it has declared the end of the CD era.

a sense of autonomy. If, as Walter Benjamin and Alain Ehrenberg suspect, every era has its own illnesses, then it comes as no surprise that cancer rates correlate with the fulfilment or non-fulfilment of the essential value beliefs of this age.

5. ON THE CRITIQUE OF CONTEMPORARY SOCIETY

If we are to pursue the sociological agenda in terms of a social critique as stated above, i.e., if we are to compare and contrast the culturally effective conceptions of a successful life with the social conditions under which they are pursued, then the direction that a contemporary social critique must take is fairly self-evident. The aspiration to autonomy so characteristic of modernity, the ideal of a way of life independent of material and economic constraints, is being continually and ever more intensively frustrated – at a collective level of political organisation of society (a) as well as at the level of individual life conduct (b). At the same time, this leads to experiences of alienation (c) and, moreover, is linked to dysfunctional effects (d) which endanger the reproduction of the system *independently* of the cultural ideals that serve as its base.

a) The decline of collective autonomy

As I have (I hope) adequately demonstrated, capitalism's fundamental promise lies in the prospect that poverty and material scarcity (and thereby existential economic conflict as a whole) can be overcome (what Marcuse calls 'pacified existence'[49]), allowing the configuration of the way of life as a whole to become a democratic political project along self-defined normative standards. In late modernity it has become obvious that this programme has failed on all levels: not only have poverty, material destitution and extreme inequality *not* been fundamentally overcome, in western societies they are even in ascendancy once again. More people than before are threatened by this prospect, and levels of prosperity are once again declining as a result of welfare state reforms (e.g., Hartz IV). Simultaneously, physical violence in the form of war and terror has returned as a daily reality. The hope that the struggle to survive could be marginalised is rapidly fading. On the contrary, the ecological crisis caused by the capitalist economic system has meant that existential dangers are not only persisting, but indeed intensifying.

---

49 H. Marcuse, *One Dimensional Man*, p. 246.

Even more serious, meanwhile, is the undeniable fact that modern societies – as political subjects – are completely powerless in the face of both the pressures of growth and acceleration they themselves engender as well as the intensifying innovation and competition-induced compulsions accompanying them: as if by force of nature (TINA!), the societies of late modernity are brought under their *diktat*; democratic governments no longer appear as shape-giving actors, but instead as reactive agents (of capital). Even the 'zero option' has become an unattainable utopia.[50] 'We can no longer afford to follow our ideals of social organisation because it puts our competitive edge at risk', is a standard argument deployed in all parts of the world to deflect non-economic claims to shape society. We can no longer afford to wait to send our children to school until they are six or to leave them in school for thirteen years (as was the norm in Germany until quite recently); we cannot afford to implement redistributive policies in accordance with our notions of fairness, to adopt effective environmental protection standards, or to maintain high standards of care in the health sector; indeed, in the eyes of many politicians and influential publications of record we cannot even afford to follow what is probably the strongest and most fundamental shared value in the Federal Republic of Germany, *'Nie wieder Krieg!'* (No more war!) any longer, as this could call into question whether Germany is able to meet the expectations of its allies. Efforts to maintain competitiveness in the struggle between different locations (e.g., regions, production centres, etc.) concentrate and occupy all collective resources and political strategies; policy shaping today means providing the social, political, economic, educational and infrastructural resources for lucrative capital investment. Experiences of political powerlessness have therefore replaced the early modernist fantasies of shaping or re-shaping society and the political promises of progress.

b) Liberal ideology and the totalitarianism of acceleration:
the colonisation of everyday life conduct

The most astonishing aspect of societies in late modernity is how their subjects feel completely free (and thus: autonomous) while *at the same time* feeling bound by existential constraints to a degree virtually unprecedented in history. This sense of freedom is owed to a far-reaching *ethical autonomy* as realised by liberal political policies. Indeed, the ethical code of late modernity entails only minimal restrictions: there are hardly any ethical-collective compulsions to do or believe or like anything specific – or *not* to do so: we can 'become' who or what we want, live where we want, choose what we

---

50   Cf. C. Offe, 'The Utopia of the Zero Option: Modernity and Modernisation as Normative Political Criteria', in *PRAXIS International* 1, 1987, pp. 1–24.

like, wear (or take off) clothes as we please, love whom we want, believe what we want, and so on. This freedom legitimises late-modern social formations by meeting them on their own terms, i.e., it satisfies the expressed desire for autonomy. Given this reality, it is all the more remarkable that the extent, number and depth of interrelations between action and interaction and thus society's need for coordination, regulation and synchronisation is greater than it has ever been in any other social formation. This immediately raises the question of how modern society, with its minimally restrictive ethical code, is to meet such a staggeringly large demand for coordination. In my view, the answer to this seems rather simple: it employs governance via fixed terms and deadlines, via appointments and filing deadlines, and especially through increasingly unbridled competition (not only for jobs, money and positions, but also for respect, friends and acquaintances, fitness and beauty), in which competitors 'never sleep', thereby forcing us to invest more and more time and energy in the maintenance of our competitiveness without being able or even willing to ask ourselves what our quest in life should be, what goal(s) in life we should pursue beyond economic competition and the struggle for existence. If a totalitarian regime is characterised by the fact that its subjects wake up in the middle of the night drenched in sweat, their pulses racing, haunted by what feels like a ton of pressure weighing on them – indeed, what can only be described as existential fear – then we in fact live under a totalitarian *time regime*: this aforementioned feeling is probably more familiar to citizens of late modern capitalist societies than to the subjects of most dictatorships. Late modernist anxiety is not caused by the intelligence services, or the henchmen of some tyrant. Subjects wake up every morning in fear of not keeping up, of losing touch, of not being able to cope with the workload, of being left behind – in some cases, they wake up because of the crushing certainty (e.g., in the case of an unemployed person or a dropout) that they already *have* been left behind. However, if heteronomy means having one's life determined by external compulsions and contingencies, then the subjects of late modern societies most certainly live under an historically unprecedented form of 'foreign rule', regardless of the liberal promise of freedom and the minimal requirements of its ethical code.

In principle, this claim can be empirically proven by analysing the relation between economic competition and life conduct. No one would consider a life dictated exclusively by the struggle for survival to be a self-determined life. Fortunately, there is hardly any culture in which there is no room for manoeuvre or participation whatsoever; moreover, these spaces are used to define a culturally determined 'sphere of freedom' unburdened by any form of struggle, in which a 'successful life' can be pursued according to culturally defined (and often collectively binding) standards of 'the good'. It was precisely in this sense that Aristotle distinguished between a life determined by work, and one relieved of work and instead determined by philosophical and cultural criteria. Modernity's fundamental promise consists of continuously expanding this sphere and ceding it to *individual self-determination*. Economic efficiency should enable subjects to define and live a life beyond the sphere of scarcity and struggle to an ever-increasing extent. Individual and collective economic success serves (at least in theory) to expand spaces of autonomy. In this sense, work time and recreation ('free time') – or work and life – in classical modernity were mutually opposed to one another temporally, spatially, socially, and ideationally: during working hours subjects were 'heteronomous', yet it was through work that they acquired the resources to compose their 'life sphere' autonomously. Indeed, up until the 1980s it actually appeared as if the autonomous sphere of life was continuously expanding in relation to the heteronomous sphere of work.[51]

In late modernity, however – as is easily demonstrated with the aid of identity-theoretical and biography-sociological analyses – the inverse is occurring: life conduct is now tailored to heighten economic competitiveness. The aforementioned temporal, spatial, social and ideational suspension of the distinction between 'work' and 'life', as well as the neo-liberal intensification of social competition, have enabled and accelerated this process. All aspects of life – health, appearance, clothes, fitness, education, knowledge, skills, relationships, and so on – come under pressure from this unfettered competition; all these aspects' constant individual (and combined) improvement is therefore indispensable for maintaining one's competitiveness in all social spheres. *Subjectification of labour* is therefore nothing more than a euphemism for the colonisation of the 'free sphere' by the 'competitive sphere'. This can be observed in the fact that young people in particular (as e.g., the findings of the *Shell Jugendstudie* [Shell Youth Survey] show) refrain from defining substantial life goals: the motivation behind choosing their university, completing an internship, learning a foreign language, completing some vocational training, or spending time abroad is that all these factors further enhance their range of options and chances of keeping in touch and networking successfully – in short, their competitiveness. Social conditions force them – as Kenneth Gergen or Richard Sennett, but also Hörning, Ahrens and Gerhard point out[52] – to abandon the idea of an autonomous life and instead become flexible 'wave riders' who are open to situational changes and seize opportunities where and whenever they

---

51   For more detail cf. C. Taylor, 'Legitimation Crisis?', in Taylor, *Philosophical Papers*, vol. 2, pp. 248–88.

52   Cf. K. Gergen, *The Saturated Self*, New York 2000; Sennett, *The Corrosion of Character*; Hörning, Ahrens, Gerhard, *Zeitpraktiken*.

emerge, without expecting control of the general direction of their lives. In a passage titled 'Out of Control' in the introduction to the new edition of his book on the 'saturated self', Gergen describes his own experience on the path to 'multiphrenia' as follows: 'I am also struggling against my modernist training for constant improvement, advancement, development, and accumulation. Slowly I am learning the pleasures of relinquishing the desire to gain control of all that surrounds me. *It is the difference between swimming with deliberation to a point in the ocean – mastering the waves to reach a goal – and floating harmoniously with the unpredictable movements of the waves*'.[53] To be sure, this form of 'floating' should by no means be misunderstood as a lifestyle of *passivity*: depending on context, the situational self may exert great efforts in order to reach its goals and/or live up to social expectations, but it refrains from committing itself to overarching 'life goals' that would incur long-term obligations. Curiously, this kind of 'wave riding' is not only a relatively successful way of *leading one's life* under late modern conditions, but also an increasingly necessary form of *day-to-day behaviour*. Time management consultants report being confronted with the overwhelming task of convincing management executives that the pile of work on their desk no longer (as was the case in classical modernity) needs to be finished completely; instead it is normal, good, and desirable that the pile grow faster than they could ever hope to work through it. Loss of control and thus of autonomy are inevitable, and are therefore to be re-evaluated.[54]

c) Experiences of alienation as disruption of subjects' relation to the world

The concept of alienation is very controversial in sociology and has nearly been abandoned, even in critical theory. Its detractors claim that it presupposes the notion of a 'core essence' – or at least some sort of ideal form of life which can then either be realised or not.[55] In contrast to this, I would like to propose the use of 'alienation' as a general term describing subjects' dysfunctional relation to the world. This relation to the world may encompass various dimensions which have both individual and collective implications: it can refer to the relation to our fellow humans, to society as a whole, to work, to nature, to the world of things or – in the sense of self-estrangement – to one's own body, desires, or personal beliefs. The term denotes the absence of constitutive, 'responsive' relationships, of

---

53   Gergen, *The Saturated Self*, pp. 150 and xviii (emphasis by the author, H.R.).

54   Cf. Hörning, Ahrens, Gerhard, *Zeitpraktiken*.

55   Cf. R. Schacht, *Alienation*, New York 1971. Rahel Jaeggi has recently made an attempt at re-appropriating this concept for critical theory: R. Jaeggi, *Entfremdung*, Frankfurt a.M., New York 2005.

self-efficacious and controlling convictions, as well as of positive ties to the subjective, objective, or social world to orient one's actions. Indeed, though I am unable to provide detailed evidence, I would like to put forward the thesis that the late modern regime of acceleration prevents these 'processes of adaptation' from taking place. It is, after all, these processes which allow us to rapidly acclimate to the things that surround us, the people with whom we interact, the desires and beliefs we develop, and the experiences we live through in the first place – so that, ultimately, the experience of the world (including the subjective world) 'becoming alien' turns into an inevitable phenomenon of late modernity: late modern subjects' approach or relation to the world becomes profoundly disturbed.[56]

d) Dysfunctional reproduction of the system

Surely, one likely objection to this sort of critique of late modern conditions is that normative standards, or rather the culturally dominant conceptions of a successful life, are not immutable. If it is in fact true that modernity's promise of autonomy necessarily falls prey to the forces of acceleration and growth through modernisation – that is to say, if the 'project of modernity' cannot be maintained in the face of capitalist modernisation – then this may (and should) result in a change in the *conceptions of a successful life*. A social critique that directs its attention to the discrepancy between the 'lived' notions of the good life and the institutionalised social reality could at least – in principle – seek out solutions, perhaps even in terms of a gradual change of the former, or rather in a process of mutual accommodation. After all, such a change in normative conceptions is also postulated by authors like Kenneth Gergen or Hörning, Ahrens and Gerhard in the company of many followers of post-structuralist or deconstructionist approaches, who consider surrendering the claim to autonomy as more of a gain than a loss. Indeed, though it may strike me as cynical and totally unacceptable from a normative and political perspective to advise subjects to change their conception of a successful life in order to become compatible with the 'hardened' structures of the social world, I do not wish at this point to engage in a dispute with positions that are not only willing to abandon the 'project

---

56   I developed some initial considerations in this direction in H. Rosa, *Identität* as well as H. Rosa, 'Kritik der Zeitverhältnisse. Beschleunigung und Entfremdung als Schlüsselbegriffe der Sozialkritik', in R. Jaeggi, T. Wesche (ed.), *Was ist Kritik?* Frankfurt a.M. 2009, pp. 23–54. Currently, I am working on a definition of alienation within the theoretical framework of a 'sociology of the relation to the world', so as to revitalise the term as the paradigmatic form for a disrupted (or absent) relation to the world.

of modernity', but even claim to have already found empirical evidence for this *de facto* capitulation in the subjects' way of life. In my view, it is evident that – even beyond the normative approach suggested here – modern accelerated capitalism is necessarily accompanied by inevitable dysfunctional side effects which threaten to undermine its own conditions of reproduction, regardless of whether the subjects' *subjective* conceptions do in fact shift in its favour or not. Evidence of this is not hard to find. Firstly, the fast pace of production and reproduction overburdens ecosystems in terms of both the reproduction of raw materials and in the processing of pollutants. Secondly, the late capitalist production regime may well produce a growing group of the excluded who then, as it were, threaten the system's reproduction 'from without' (for example through acts of violence or revolutionary aspirations). Thirdly, modern society is a highly complex entity consisting of numerous interlocking, yet highly differentiated sub-systems: the educational system, judicial system, political system, financial markets, welfare state institutions, etc. all operate at least partially along their own standards and time structures. These systems are subordinated to complex synchronisation requirements. The hyper-acceleration of late modernity profoundly overextends the synchronisation capacities of some of these sub-systems: the education system (and thereby cultural reproduction), the judicial system and the political system, for example, are all markedly less 'accelerable' than financial markets or scientific-technological development. This may in fact lead to *severe problems of de-synchronisation.*

Fourthly: the unfettered acceleration at its late modern level undermines the conditions of long-term stability essential to the system's reproduction and is thereby self-destructive: the successes of acceleration throughout modernity can be attributed to the shutting down and stabilisation of some areas of social functions (e.g., law, the education system or the 'life course regime'), which created broad horizons of calculability and thus allowed for (and ultimately facilitated) long-term education, infrastructure and capital investments. It becomes obvious that 'flexibilisation' and 'dynamic developments' can only endure conceptually and practically if they take place against solid background structures; after all, movement is only noticeable against a stationary background. Flexible elites confronted with stubborn institutions, managers who sail from project to project, or football coaches who coach a different club every year may all be successful; if, however, the corporations and football clubs begin to dissolve and reconstruct themselves just as rapidly as these individuals do, then dynamic and development disappear, and instead a situation of a 'frenetic standstill' or of 'organisational heart flutter' sets in. This actually seems to be happening, as can be seen in the reorganisation of universities, agencies and companies (and sometimes football clubs). A rather similar situation can be observed in some fields of the goods market: new plugs, connections and ports, for example, become useless if the products they are supposed to connect to one another have already become obsolete by the time the former are introduced.

Fifthly and finally: the preservation of certain qualitative levels of rationality in (individual and collective) decisions rests on temporal preconditions that increasingly can no longer be met, resulting in a decreasing level of collective rationality. If we are to measure a decision's level of rationality (and thus the resulting level of quality of an action or product) purely by its objective adequacy, it becomes obvious that this level of rationality progressively declines the less time our complex world allows for a decision (or an action). If, beyond that, the background conditions relevant to a decision (or action) change ever faster and/or become increasingly complex, then the preservation of a certain level of quality requires *more and more time*. If these processes represent contradictory processes – the available time (for writing a grant application, developing a new product, drafting a new law) *decreases*, whereas the level of complexity of the background conditions (or rather, their instability) *increases* – then the effects multiply: the rationality of decisions (and the quality of actions and products) rapidly declines. Anyone who writes or reads research grant applications will surely recognise what I am describing.

6. Conclusion

As I hope to have shown in the preceding deliberations, sociology can be both an exciting and rewarding field of social self-reflection if it does not, in the sense of a critique of society, cease to address (and pursue an answer to) the question of 'the good life'. Although, as a social science, it cannot provide an answer to the philosophical or even theological question of what a good life actually *is*, it can critically contrast and compare conceptions of a successful life implicitly or explicitly pursued by individuals and anchored in institutions and practices with the social conditions under which they are actually pursued. Furthermore, it can gauge the observable changes in society against 'operative' conceptions of the good, and is therefore able to determine society's potential for pathology. In this way, socially critical sociology can not only assume an important function in terms of societal self-observation and self-reflection, but it can at the same time become a constitutive corrective instance, especially with respect to those social developments that take on a life of their own.

Should sociology take this task seriously, it will have to recognise and come to terms with the fact that the capitalist form of social order found in contemporary societies (not only) of the West represents the basic determining factor forming, shaping, and transforming the conditions under which subjects individually and collectively pursue their own life plans. And, what is more, sociological analysis is likely to reveal that the logic of escalation engrained in this economic order is tightly linked to those life plans; or even that the socially effective fears and promise implicit in the social formation of modernity intrinsically feed on the latter's promises (and compulsions) of acceleration and growth. Nevertheless, as I have attempted to illustrate, such a 'blindly running' (i.e., remaining ethically-politically non-reflective) dynamic of escalation in the late modern phase undermines (foundational) conceptions of a successful life, and in particular the promise of autonomy so constitutive of modernity.

Of course, this is but another diagnosis of the crisis, and sociologists produce diagnoses of crisis almost incessantly. One quite influential theoretical tradition locates the causes of crisis in modernity's capitalist economic system. In that respect, while my diagnosis may be neither new nor original, this by no means renders it false or irrelevant. In fact, the time may well have come for a re-adoption of that theoretical tradition. Deviating from this theory's mainstream interpretation, however, I would like to propose that a critique of capitalism should focus not on evidence of inherent economic contradictions or functional problems, nor on the hardly deniable shortcomings with regard to distribution and thus justice as such, but instead should grasp capitalism at its ethical root: even if capitalism runs smoothly, by logical inevitability it leads to a limitless game of escalation that eventually throws even the profiteers and winners into misery, for it commits all their individual and collective energies to that single, blind, instrumental *telos* – the struggle to maintain competitiveness.

CHAPTER 3

Mobility and Control: On the Dialectic of the 'Active Society'

STEPHAN LESSENICH

> Capitalism, that old rogue,
> has lived off of us long enough
> over overoverover
> now, it's finally over
> it has been here long enough
>
> P. Licht, 'Lied vom Ende des Kapitalismus'
> (Song of the End of Capitalism)

1. POLITICAL SOCIOLOGY: SOCIAL CRITIQUE IN TIMES OF 'ACTIVATION'

Sociology has been haunted by complaints about its limited public profile for quite some time now. At the biennially held German Sociological Congress – hosted, incidentally, by the University of Jena in 2008 – observers regularly derided sociology for its self-referentiality and detachment from reality. The discipline itself is baffled as to why it remains so marginalised, dwarfed by the definitions of reality put forward by academic economics, demand for which has been growing for decades. The problem is not, however, that sociological knowledge is unable to find its way into the process of political-medial self-understanding taking place in society. On the contrary, reference to sociological concepts and arguments (often implicit, yet often also explicit) – for example to the expertise and opinions of professional sociologists – is a daily occurrence in many areas of policymaking, as well as in all segments of the media landscape. Furthermore, in some cases (although by no means often enough) the profession distinguishes itself through the findings it produces and the stances it takes on current issues and structural problem areas that depart noticeably from the economic mainstream. Thus, sociology is by all means present in the public eye as a scientifically and professionally established, empirical and analytically grounded, highly differentiated, 'normal science' which assembles its knowledge based on a division of labour. One thing sociology does not accomplish (or accomplishes just barely) is what it may have stood for in better times, and what, in a strict sense, has characterised it as a discipline: the extraordinary task known as 'social critique'.

The decline of social critique – which, though perhaps still found in the sociologically adept review sections of newspapers, no longer has a place within the professional academic sociological milieu – is an indicator of profound intellectual and social impoverishment, at least in the case of German-speaking sociology. Such a damning indictment, however – at least when issued by representatives of the profession itself – would amount to little more than a repetition of the aforementioned complaints directed from outside *at* the discipline if it was not simultaneously seized upon as an opportunity to make efforts towards its improvement – i.e., for the *intra-disciplinary* effort towards a revitalisation and re-appropriation of sociology's potential for social critique. As stated in the introduction, this present volume is dedicated to that very aim.

But what *is* social critique? What are its aims and how does it operate? The purpose of social critique is defined, according to Axel Honneth, in opposition to the democratic public relations work of the 'normalised intellectual'.[1] While the latter engages in the everyday business of critically observing and evaluating political decision-making processes, social critique questions the normal as such – the socially produced forms of normality. The social critic is not particularly interested in 'individual events … particular mistakes or relative injustices',[2] but rather in the whole, the principle, the absolute. He or she aspires to 'a form of criticism that inquires behind the premises of publicly accepted problem descriptions and tries to see through their construction'.[3] The matter at hand, then, is the critique of social self-descriptions and self-conceptions, of that which appears self-evident – a critique that shatters 'normalities', contests 'necessities' and subverts 'truths'.

The sociologist as social critic is, in this sense, a 'myth hunter',[4] hunting for social myths and mystification processes. He or she unearths the social *dispositifs* – of which social sciences and indeed sociology are a part – which

1   A. Honneth, *Pathologies of Reason: On the Legacy of Critical Theory*, New York, Chichester 2009, p. 179.

2   Honneth, *Pathologies of Reason*, p. 185.

3   Ibid., p. 182.

4   Cf. N. Elias, *What is Sociology?*, London 1978, pp. 50–70.

anchor the 'self-evident' in our knowledge of society, thereby holding us hostage in the sense that 'owing to our fixed descriptions, certain procedures seem to us like parts of nature from which we can no longer detach ourselves'.[5] He or she becomes the agent of a critique that reveals the existing to be something that was not always so (something that is socially constructed, rather than natural), a critique 'which brings to light that the given is always a construct and that the object emerges from the very forms of its problematisation'.[6] In this sense, the social critic authors a 'problematisation of social problematisations'; one of, if you will, the second order – that targets the structure as a whole. In contrast to the normal intellectual, he or she questions 'not the dominant reading of any particular practical problem, public ignorance towards deviant opinions, or merely the selective perception of the matter to be decided upon, … but rather the structural properties of a social sphere's constitution as a whole'.[7]

If the following critique of a politics of 'activation' – the gradual implementation of which we have witnessed both in this country and elsewhere – does not deal with individual occurrences (such as Hartz IV), particular mistakes (such as Hartz IV), or relative injustices (such as Hartz IV), then it is because it conforms to the spirit and form of a critique of the structural properties of the societal constitution. Social critique in times of activation – or rather the reconstruction of the welfare state in pursuit of an 'activating' agenda – must go beyond the classical form of critical social-political science which, however morally upright that may be, ties the analysis of the 'dismantling of the welfare state' to the demand for its restitution. It must problematise the normalities, imperatives, and truths on the basis of which the politics of activation operates. Its task is to reveal the paradoxes contained within a set of objectives that reflect the current internal structure of democratic-capitalist social formations. A social policy that operates under the guise of activation can thus only be approached – insofar as the analytical depth of focus and diagnostic reach of a socially critical intervention is not to be systematically undercut – with an historico-critical sociology of the active society.

As will be shown in the following (at least implicitly), Marx and Foucault acted as a (neo-)classical impetus for this kind of sociology in at least two respects. On the one hand, both social theoreticians share 'a mistrust in

---

5   Honneth, *Pathologies of Reason*, p. 184.

6   F. Ewald, *Der Vorsorgestaat*, Frankfurt a.M. 1993, p. 31; cf. S. Krasmann, 'Gouvernementalität: Zur Kontinuität d der Foucaultschen Analytik der Oberfläche', in J. Martschukat (ed.), *Geschichte schreiben mit Foucault*, Frankfurt a.M., New York 2002, pp. 79–95.

7   Honneth, *Pathologies of Reason*, p. 185.

the obvious, the given, the compliant'.[8] Marx analyses the reproduction of social rule 'in ideological forms which do not disclose their functionality or historicity',[9] while Foucault reconstructs the modern history of the social – to a large extent scientifically mediated – validity of contingent 'truths'. Thus, in a way they share a common methodological and political objective, upon the foundation of which the following study of the activated social formation is based. 'One must peer beyond the surface of what is commonly said and thought in order to identify the driving forces.'[10] On the other hand, this study builds upon Marx and Foucault in that the works of both authors deal with the analysis and critique of the (historically contingent) constitution of social subjects. 'Marx witnessed the emergence of "large industry" and the correspondingly appropriate labour subjects. Foucault was a contemporary witness of the transition from the industrial to the post-industrial mode of production and the crisis of the postmodern subject.'[11] Their descriptions, explanations and interpretations of the genesis, reproduction and (potential) transformation of capitalism refer to the process of social production (and productivity) of adaptable subjects, whereby each exhibits his own distinct method of comprehending the respective contemporary conditions. This tradition (which adopts Marx indirectly, Foucault directly) represents the point of departure for the following analysis and critique of contemporary democratic-capitalist society, shedding light on the specific welfare-state mode of production of functional, 'active citizens' tailored to suit market needs on the one hand, while illuminating the 'neo-social' within the so-called 'neo-liberal' on the other, i.e., the novel forms of subjectification of the social.[12]

As this already indicates, the critical focus on the active society must simultaneously and necessarily fall back onto the state of that active society. The following analysis will illustrate how the welfare state establishes itself historically as a socio-structural formation, located 'between' capitalism and democracy, that generates and resolves problems equally, thus placing it in permanent crisis; the way in which, in its historically changing form, it constitutes (or attempts to constitute) subjects 'fitted' to the respective functional condition of the democratic-capitalist social formation; and

---

8   U. Brieler, ' "Erfahrungstiere" und "Industriesoldaten": Marx und Foucault über das historische Denken, das Subjekt und die Geschichte der Gegenwart', in Martschukat (ed.), *Geschichte*, pp. 42–76, here p. 68.

9   Ibid. p. 69

10   Ibid.

11   Ibid. p. 76.

12   For more elaboration on this cf. S. Lessenich, *Die Neuerfindung des Sozialen*, Bielefeld 2008.

how the current welfare-state agenda of activation transfers (or seeks to transfer) flexible capitalism's problems of sustainability and crises of reproduction onto the individual subjects themselves. A substantial portion of this analysis will be dedicated to problematising socially accepted knowledge concerning the welfare state and its developmental dynamic, its current functional problems and the objectives of political steering. With view to the dimension of the formation of welfare-state structures, socially critical knowledge production must attempt to grasp the secular expansion ('hypertrophy') of the welfare state, and its institutions and interventions, not as a mere effect of the special interests of politicians desperate for re-election, but as a development-related, systemic requirement for the further development of capitalist socialisation (*Vergesellschaftung*). Correspondingly, the possible 'crisis' of the welfare state, and its institutions and interventions, should not be regarded as a temporary distortion rectifiable through policy, but as an irresolvable structural problem – as the ineluctable, permanent 'normal state' of democratic-capitalist societies. Concerning the dimension of subject formation in welfare states, on the other hand, the task is to convey that behind the much complained about 'passivity' and 'lethargy' of society's individuals, behind their subjective need for security and interest in the preservation of personal assets, lies nothing more than the (in fact quite 'normal') dead weight and momentum of once-dominant orientations for social conduct. Hence, all variants of subject-centred, behaviour- and disposition-related deficit diagnoses, that are currently problematised in the public arena as supposed causes of the crisis, actually require problematisation themselves. Moreover – as the vanishing point of this analysis, so to speak – the paradoxical nature of the politics of activation currently being introduced will be highlighted. This paradoxical nature arises from the fact that this political agenda tends to undermine itself by jeopardising those very resources of social productivity that it seeks to politically mobilise.

In the process of hunting for welfare state myths and pointing to the paradoxes of the active society's socio-political constitution, political sociology – as a sociology of the political, of political intervention in social relations, of the (historically specific) mode of social inclusion in the field of politics[13] – itself becomes political. This observation should not and need not provoke disdain from critical-rationalist 'normal scientists' suspecting value judgement, if and as long as the standards of a political-sociological social critique, along with its value references and criteria of problematisation, are clearly stated as such by the individual responsible for the critique. The social critic, as myth hunter and 'problematiser' of problematisations, is

---

13   Cf. N. Luhmann, *Political Theory in the Welfare State*, Berlin 1990.

at the same time a border crosser, systematically going beyond 'the intellectual horizon of his or her contemporaries who tend toward conservativism – including that of intellectual "normal critique" – in which the limits of the conceivable are identical with the limits of the familiar'.[14] The border crossing in the present contribution permutes two different logics of critique: on the one hand (and primarily) along a critique of the functional logic of capitalism in the contemporary constitution of active society and activating state representing nothing but the contemporary version of a deeply contradictory, even paradoxical mode of socialisation. Analytically, this variant of critical social analysis leads, as will be shown, to a point at which it converges with a second genealogical strain of critique[15] aiming to document those 'social shifts of meaning',[16] implicit in the concept of activation, that accompany its utilitarian-functional, neo-social instrumentalisation. By including this kind of 'metacritical standpoint',[17] the present analysis positions itself in the context of meaning of a critical theory of society that thinks not only in terms of contradictions, ambivalences, and paradoxes,[18] but also in terms of the very categories of change, triumph and resistance.

2. POLITICS AT THE INTERSECTION OF CAPITALISM, DEMOCRACY AND THE WELFARE STATE

Mobility, control and the dialectic of capitalist socialisation (Vergesellschaftung)

What is capitalism? According to James Fulcher, there is a plain answer to this simple question: it is 'the investment of money in order to make a profit'.[19] To be more precise, the guiding principle of capitalist economic

---

14   V. H. Schmidt, 'Gerechtigkeit als Ordnungsprinzip', in *Soziologische Revue* 31(1), 2008, pp. 3–9, here p. 8.

15   Cf. A. Honneth, 'Rekonstruktive Gesellschaftskritik unter genealogischem Vorbehalt. Zur Idee der ‚Kritik' in der Frankfurter Schule", in Honneth, *Pathologien*, pp. 57–69. Also: A. Honneth, 'Organisierte Selbstverwirklichung. Paradoxien der Individualisierung', in A. Honneth (ed.), *Befreiung aus der Mündigkeit*, Frankfurt a.M., New York 2002, pp. 141–58.

16   Honneth, 'Rekonstruktive Gesellschaftskritik', p. 69.

17   Ibid. p. 68.

18   Cf. M. Hartmann, 'Widersprüche, Ambivalenzen, Paradoxien – Begriffliche Wandlungen in der neueren Gesellschaftstheorie', in Honneth (ed.), *Befreiung*, pp. 221–51.

19   J. Fulcher, *Capitalism. A Very Short Introduction*, Oxford, NY 2004, p. 13–14.

activity consists of 'the investment of money to make more money.'[20] – and, in turn, to re-invest this money in anticipation of reaping even more profits. Behind this basic concept and its condensation in the classical Marxian formula M-C-M' lies, quite conspicuously, the fundamental constitutive and functional principle of the social formation characterised by the capitalist economic mode: the principle of movement. 'Indeed, it is typical of a capitalist society that virtually all economic activities that go on within it are driven by the opportunity to make profit out of capital invested in them.'[21] Marx had set out on a search for just this – historically novel – driving force of economic behaviour: or, more precisely and comprehensively, he set out on a search for the laws of movement concerning the specifically capitalist development of society, as 'economic' considerations tied to the pursuit of profitability and rates of return do not (by any means) remain restricted only to the production and exchange of economic commodities (in the strict sense of the word). Rather, the capitalist logic of action exhibits a historical tendency to encompass ever more areas of life (in the sense of their 'economisation'), and the specific rationality of capitalist economic activity increasingly determines the way of life of ever-expanding groups of individuals in an increasingly comprehensive way. If capitalism is thus necessarily and in principle a social formation of permanent movement – of expansion and accumulation, of *Landnahme* and 'Acceleration' – then this movement and, in particular, its permanence, stem from the indispensable functional requirement of structure-forming measures.

> Capital is money that is invested in order to make more money. By extension the term capital is often used to refer to money that is available for investment or, indeed, any asset that can be readily turned into money for it. ... It is, however, only possible to turn property into capital if its ownership is clearly established, its value can be measured, its title can be transferred, and a market exists for it. A characteristic feature of the development of capitalist societies is the emergence of institutions that enable the conversion of assets of all kinds into capital.[22]

And what is true for capital, for the economic and social exchange of and between the owners of money and material assets, applies just as much to labour – that is to say, to the non-propertied and their economic and social interaction with the owners of capital: yet there is no chance that this could function without the installation of institutions to promote, guide, oversee and regulate this exchange. These institutions set capitalism into motion by

---

20   Ibid. p. 29.

21   Ibid. p. 14.

22   Ibid. p. 14 (emphasis in the original, S.L.).

guaranteeing the transformation of 'commodities of all kinds' into capital – and are thus the necessary precondition for capitalist socialisation of work as wage labour, by allowing potential 'workers' to turn their labour capacity into their own 'capital' (or rather, into the object of utilisation by owners of capital).

At this point, two aspects should be noted: firstly, the observation that functionally required supporting institutions of capitalist development emerge historically should not be understood as strengthening the position of a crude functionalism. The claim here is not that these institutions were created because the capitalist economic mode required them. Instead, it is a strictly empirical argument stressing the semantics of possibility: only where the necessary structural formation has been successful – in terms of developing institutional arrangements that facilitate capital formation and the transformation of work into wage labour – can the dynamic of capitalist socialisation be set in lasting motion (it is no surprise, then, that the World Bank demands more institutional 'reformative fervour' wherever this is not already the case, from Azerbaijan to Zimbabwe). Secondly, it is clear that only *one* institution can adequately play the role of third party in a confederation of potential market actors, the institution-forming effects of which modern capitalism's sustainability and capacity to develop is based upon: the state. It is precisely the state that acts – in ways that shift and change over time – as the enabling agent of capitalist movement. This includes the form of *Rechtsstaat*[23] which (according to the liberal self-understanding) attempts to 'guarantee the freedom and predictability of bourgeois relations of transaction';[24] the form of the welfare state, which in the context of such guaranteed statutory freedom of action of citizens (and in its social democratic self-description) tries to '*correct* or *compensate* for the unwanted side effects of the resulting momentum';[25] or – in its current self-manifestation, which in the following shall be subjected to analysis and problematisation – as the guiding and controlling state which, quite aware of the discursively produced and enforced knowledge of the limitations of the welfare state's problem-solving capacity, creates new forms of responsibilities for itself. The 'more or less periodic or local interventions to correct infringements

---

23   [Trans. Note] the German word *Rechtsstaat* can be understood to mean the 'state under the rule of law (and justice)', 'legal state', or 'constitutional state'. Generally regarded to have originated in the enlightenment philosophy of Immanuel Kant, it is a central doctrine of European legal thinking. For reasons of precision, the German term is used.

24   F.-X. Kaufmann, 'Diskurse über Staatsaufgaben', 1994, in F.-X. Kaufmann, *Soziologie und Sozialstaat*,Wiesbaden 2005, pp. 335–59, here p. 343.

25   Ibid. p. 346 (emphases in the original, S.L.).

on the law ... or to the betterment of certain groups in society',[26] by the classical *Rechtsstaat* and welfare state, are increasingly being replaced by a political programme of control over social conduct which no longer 'departs from sanctions at the level of the actions of individual actors, but instead their very premises of these actions',[27] thereby operating more and more in a pre-emptive manner.

What has been said thus far, however, fails – beyond this transformation of state agency – to make clear the dialectic of movement that characterises the state-organised process of capitalist institution formation. After all, state activity under capitalism by no means limits itself to the one-dimensionality of a positive agenda of enabling possibilities: to the constitution of free legal subjects formally capable of market participation; to the material compensation of the owners of effectively unmarketable commodities (or for those that are no longer so) and the assurance of their market participation at least as consumers; or to the 'empowerment' of citizens to adopt the role of market-competent, entrepreneurial agents. Regardless of whether it takes the form of a *Rechtsstaat*, welfare state, or guiding and controlling state, the state-organised structure formation of capitalist societies has (almost as if taken directly from a sociology textbook) both 'enabling' *and* 'constraining' effects.[28] It is not only an instrument for facilitating capitalist movement, but also – simultaneously and contradictorily – for the curtailment of such movement. In the modern state, action movement is enabled, yet at the same time limited; mobility is systematically combined with and countervailed by control. The history of state-sponsorship of wage-labour society (through, for instance, public housing or wage standards) illustrates this with remarkable clarity.

At closer glance, modern capitalism has since its beginnings – and equally fundamentally – been a political and social regime of both liberation and (re-)enclosure of human labour power; the mobilisation and regulation of 'free' labour – or rather the subjectivity of its bearers – has its origins in capitalism itself.[29] 'Marx is the first theoretician attempting to develop a systematic understanding of the impact of the forces capital unleashes unto people, the way they form, fetter, and fixate them. ... And if Marx in fact espouses a utopia, then it is the idea that these unleashed forces produce a subject that suits them.'[30] The phenomenon referred to by Marx as labour in early capitalism being 'free in the double sense' – the process of its

---

26   Ibid. p. 350f.

27   Ibid. p. 351.

28   Cf. A. Giddens, *The Constitution of Society*, Cambridge 1984.

29   Cf. Y. Moulier Boutang, *De l'esclavage au salariat*, Paris 1998.

30   Brieler, '"Erfahrungstiere" und "Industriesoldaten"', p. 61.

'disembedding'[31] from local habitats and hegemonic structures, its decoupling from traditional rights and duties followed immediately by its integration into and interlinking with the emerging system of capitalist production and reproduction – already hints that this detachment, and the accompanying opportunity structures, simultaneously comprise forms of reintegration, of fixation and thus of limitation of freedom: movement and its impediment go hand in hand. By articulating an analysis of this fundamental interrelation, theoretical talk about the liberal-capitalist 'rule of freedom'[32] begins to take on a social form. Even this twofold historical process would have been inconceivable without a socio-political foundation and accompanying support, for this process was not only mediated by the *Rechtsstaat*, but – *avant la lettre* – by the welfare state. 'Power is exercised only over free subjects, and only insofar as they are free.'[33] The bosses' historically new operational power of command over their employees rested on the discretionary and, more precisely, contractual freedom of *both* parties, i.e., on a wage-labour relationship entered into voluntarily. However, the functional prerequisites for this capitalist constellation – namely, the initial 'commodification' of its (future) workers, who lost, or rather, were robbed of their agrarian means of subsistence, and the permanent transformation of non-wage workers into wage-earners – were only met due to socio-political measures (as numerous as they were comprehensive) of negative and positive, active and passive 'proletarianisation' – from the emancipation of the serfs and the Prussian Civil Code (*allgemeines Landrecht* – 1794) to the ban on begging, the workhouse, public hygiene and factory inspections.[34] Additionally, the at least temporary fixation of labour power as related to the establishment and reproduction of the wage labour relation, its integration into production organisation and workplace hierarchy, epitomises rather palpably the capitalist movement of fixating the emancipated: it is an expression of the dialectic of mobility and control, movement and enclosure, freedom and discipline, which is constitutive of capitalist modernity and which time and again is furthered and reproduced in the process of welfare state development.[35]

---

31   Cf. K. Polanyi, *The Great Transformation*, Frankfurt a.M. 2004 [1944].

32   Cf. M. Saar, 'Macht, Staat, Subjektivität. Foucault's Geschichte der Gouvernementalität im Werkkontext', in S. Krasmann, M. Volkmer (eds), *Michel Foucault's 'Geschichte der Gouvernementalität' in den Sozialwissenschaften*,Bielefeld 2007, pp. 23–45.

33   M. Foucault, 'The Subject and Power', in *Critical Inquiry* 8(4), 1982, pp. 777–95, here p. 790.

34   Cf. G. Lenhardt, C. Offe, 'Staatstheorie und Sozialpolitik. Funktionen und Innovationsprozesse der Sozialpolitik' [1977], in C. Offe, *Strukturprobleme des kapitalistischen Staates*, Frankfurt a.M., New York 2006, pp. 153–80.

35   Cf. P. Wagner, *A Sociology of Modernity*, London, New York 1994.

To trigger, promote and utilise mobility while at the same time channelling it, curbing excessive mobility and impeding unwanted mobility – that is the 'eternal' run of events in (the increasingly welfare-state regulated) capitalist wage labour society. This dialectic of capitalist socialisation (*Vergesellschaftung*) is symbolised by and materialises as historically changing social typologies: from the unwanted vagabond in early modernity, still fully exposed to public disciplinary power; via the employee (*Arbeitnehmer*) of wage labour society's boom years[36] taken care of in terms of labour rights, social rights, as well as public and private freedoms; and to the undocumented immigrant of our day who is left to his or her self-discipline, invisible to society.[37] In industrial high-capitalism the main objectives include (and indeed always have included) encouraging (i.e., mobilising) people to productively exert their labour power, to keep them at the workplace for as long as possible, or rather, as long as necessary (that is to say, to immobilise them at least spatially for the purpose of a sustained local activity); to selectively remove ('detach') them from the workplace if need be, or rather, if they are no longer needed (in other words: redundancy); and to potentially remove them from the labour market altogether (and, if you will, demobilise them into 'inactivity'); to increase employability in return (for the purpose of starting a new cycle of mobilisation); to avoid counterproductive (over-)exhaustion and excessive use of labour power (in the past this included issues such as child labour, today phenomena such as the burnout syndrome) through selective or temporary deactivation; to prevent or sanction unproductive under- or misuse of labour power resources (in the form of dawdling, strikes, work in the shop committee, or the like) through motivating, controlling and disciplining practices – and so on and so forth. Incidentally, the current, late modern dialectic of mobility and control, appropriately differentiated and flexibilised, has an equally 'internal' and 'external' impact:[38] with view to the external frontiers of the body politic defined in national-territorial terms (which remain functional as such in the era of 'globalisation'[39]), constant parallel- and counter-movements of mobilisation and demobilisation of labour can also be observed. 'Foreign' labour forces are recruited, their recruitment is then halted and they are either encouraged to return home or

---

36   Cf. R. Castel, *Die Metamorphosen der sozialen Frage*, Konstanz 2000.
37   Cf. S. Karakayali, *Blinde Passagen*, Bielefeld 2008.
38   Cf. S. Lessenich, 'Beweglich – Unbeweglich', in: S. Lessenich, F. Nullmeier (eds), *Deutschland – eine gespaltene Gesellschaft*, Frankfurt a.M., New York 2006, pp. 336–52.
39   Cf. H. Gerstenberger, 'Fixierung und Entgrenzung. Theoretische Annäherungen an die politische Form des Kapitalismus', in *Prokla* 37(147), 2007, pp. 173–97.

forcibly repatriated. Alternatively, they are admitted (depending on country of origin, qualification or other economically and/or politically determined criteria), spatially fixated in case of 'illegal' entry (in dormitories, camps, or prisons), subsequently deported or tolerated, illegalised in case of unnoticed entry, then picked up by police (and expelled) or informally socialised and exploited – to name only a few, more obvious aspects of the phenomenon.

Foucault contrasts (or complements[40]) Marx's great narrative of the combined unfettering and (in his view: historically transient) re-fettering of humans and their productive capacities on the path to their capitalist socialisation as industrial subject (*Vergesellschaftung*) with his own lengthy narrative of how control over individuals – including extra-economic – is established, along with the attendant technologies. Foucault notes how 'economic utility and political deference as an effect of these technologies'[41] converge and coexist in humans, that is to say, how the modern, nowadays 'neo-liberal' subject is produced and formed by guidance and governance – which may also (though by no means exclusively) be political, or rather state-led. Foucault also (at least in his later works) focuses on that very same dialectic of freedom and coercion, liberation and capture: 'According to Foucault's central historical and political hypothesis, governmentalities since the 18th century have been concentrated around the governance of freedom, or rather, through freedom.'[42] Both grand critics of society – each in his own way – base themselves upon the historically productive effects of early, high and late industrial subject formation, respectively: 'The industrial soldiers and the subjects of discipline (of Marx and Foucault, respectively, S.L.) represent two facets of a modern genealogy carried by the theoretical impulse to recognise subjective forces as historically formative potential(s).'[43]

Instead of presenting a mere one-sided history of the exploitation, alienation and repression found in capitalist social formations, both Marx and Foucault identify the dialectic of that history's movement, its contradictions and ambivalences, counter-currents and ambiguities, and thus the structural possibilities for development and opportunities for progress, subjective scopes of action and potential(s) for resistance that are contained and preserved – but may remain concealed as such – therein. The vanishing point of that critique is where this contribution intends to arrive. Before doing so, however, the further development of structural analysis of the

---

40   Cf. The essays on social theory according to Marx und Foucault, in: *Prokla* 38(151), 2008.

41   Brieler, "'Erfahrungstiere" und "Industriesoldaten"', p. 67.

42   Saar, "Macht, Staat, Subjektivität", p. 37; Cf. T. Lemke, *Eine Kritik der politischen Vernunft*, Berlin 1997.

43   Brieler, "'Erfahrungstiere" und "Industriesoldaten"', p. 67.

capitalist form of socialisation (*Vergesellschaftung*) and its contemporary manifestation – or rather, the manifestation currently emerging – must be taken into account. The task is to continue, in light of all that has been said so far, the analysis of that institutional arrangement without which – *avant* as well as especially *après la lettre* – capitalism as we know it would never have taken form, let alone been capable of surviving: the configuration of the modern (depending on one's terminological preference) interventionist, social, welfare state. The *bonmot* of neo-institutionalist political science of 'bringing the state back in',[44] cited ad nauseam and modified in every conceivable way, does in fact make (perfect) sense: after all, *bringing the state back* into a critical theory of society truly represents a veritable desideratum of social critique. Not only the historico-empirical meaning of the broader labour- and socio-political institutional regime of advanced capitalist societies, but also the social-theoretical relevance of the momentum, independent existence and obstinacy of the modern welfare state, coupled with both capitalism *and* democracy, remains largely unrecognised or at least underreflected. This is the case despite highly instructive and pertinent efforts which – though dating back an entire generation of critical social theory at this point – will be taken up and made analytically fruitful here. These efforts not only reveal that the theoretical 'game of "imagining the welfare state out"'[45] of society – still a favoured pastime of liberal economists to this day – is no longer an option. What is more, they reveal the blatant structural problem and 'embarrassing secret'[46] of modern capitalism: the fact that it can neither live without the welfare state nor live *with* it.

The welfare state in 'late capitalism'

It is the theory of 'late capitalism', or rather of the structural problems of the late capitalist state as developed by Claus Offe in the early 1970s, which, in an attempt at an adequate time diagnosis, places its focus on the contradictions and ambiguities of state intervention into social relations. Offe's objective was to (re-)adopt and update Marx's question about the logic of development in existing social formations, thereby adhering to Marx's theoretical point of departure of making 'the inherent self-contradictoriness both the terminological constituent of "capitalism" as well as the starting point of an

44   Cf. P. B. Evans, D. Rueschemeyer, T. Skocpol (ed.), *Bringing the State Back In*, Cambridge 1985.
45   H. Achinger, *Sozialpolitik als Gesellschaftspolitik*, Frankfurt a.M. 1971, p. 138.
46   C. Offe, 'Zu einigen Widersprüchen des modernen Sozialstaates', in: C. Offe, *Arbeitsgesellschaft*, Frankfurt a.M., New York 1984, pp. 323–39, here p. 330.

analysis of capitalist systems.[47] The model of contradictions found in the social dynamic in (or rather of) capitalism represents the core of a neo-Marxist analysis of society – including the present one.

In Offe's view the capitalist social formation's structural contradiction is composed of a fundamental 'non-correspondence'[48] of systemic problem-producing mechanisms on the one hand, and institutionalised programmes to solve those problems on the other: 'Capitalism subordinates all sectors and aspects of society to its own movement, that is to say, to its own profit-driven valorisation' – but 'in an "anarchical", "primordial", uncomprehended manner that intentionally lacks control, as a by-product of capital's momentum.[49] In its movement, capital, or, more appropriate in sociological terms, the *capitalist* as 'empirical subject of actions'[50] systematically abstracts from the actual social impacts of capital valorisation in that he (or she) follows the system's intrinsic logic independently, regardless of the consequences (apart from those directly impacting him or her). The fundamental problem of this 'problem production' inherent in the system lies in the fact that the unrecognised and uncontrolled long-term effects of the process(es) of capital valorisation 'question the continued existence of capital as well as the social formation structured by it as a whole,'[51] that is to say: if and as long as they remain uncontrolled, these effects irreversibly intensify and become increasingly self-destructive.

It is the aspect of the 'ineluctability of the self-negating tendencies embedded in the *private* production process,'[52] the concept of 'factual systemic self-contradictoriness'[53] that represents the linchpin of Offe's analysis of capitalism, as well as the point of contact with his state-theoretical deliberations. The capitalist formation exhibits an enormous rationality deficit, an inherent problem of governance, which historically has brought the state into play. The state counters the 'anarchic' mechanisms of capital movement with a programme of conscious regulation and targeted control – so far, so good. A problem of the second order now arises, however; in this very act

---

47   Offe, *Strukturprobleme*, p. 62.
[Trans. Note] The German text *Strukturprobleme des kapitalistischen Staates* has only partially been translated into English and has appeared in the two indicated volumes of *Kapitalstate*. All the quotes by Offe from the text *Strukturprobleme* indicated here have not previously been published in English and represent direct translation from the original.
48   Offe, Ibid. p. 57
49   Offe, Ibid. p. 54
50   Ibid.
51   Ibid.
52   Ibid. (emphasis in the original, S.L.)
53   Ibid. p. 62

(or rather in ongoing acts of resolving the system's problems, as it were) it adopts, internalises, and reproduces in its institutions the intrinsic contradictoriness of capitalist movement – thereby generating new problems (now of the third order). The state itself (and again, in precise sociological terms it would have to read: the nexus of activities performed by state administrators) now becomes the bearer and executor of that very structural contradiction contained in the capitalist form of socialisation 'between the unlimited *consequences* that the institutionalised capital valorisation process entails, and the limitations of system-compatible *means* with the aid of which said consequences may be controlled, processed, or overcome altogether'.[54]

Indeed, the emphasis here must be on the question – or rather the problem – of the system-compatibility of the measures to which state policy resorts in order to resolve the (self-destructive, because ultimately bouncing back on itself) 'external effects' of the process of capital accumulation. Offe distinguishes 'three broad categories of "containment mechanisms", through the successive institutionalisation of which the self-negating consequences of the basic capitalist structure can each be intercepted, cushioned, or diverted – at any rate prevented from materialising in the form of crisis',[55] which pertain to small capital units' ability to survive (e.g., through the elimination of ruinous competition), as well as that of total capital (e.g., through the production of collective goods instrumental to valorisation) and of the entire structure of capitalism (for example, via the institutionalisation of class conflict). Each one of these 'containment mechanisms' – and particularly their accumulation – requires the activity of an (at least halfway) external 'interceptor' which takes into account, quasi-externally, the need for a 'permanent self-adaptation'[56] of the inherently contradictory capitalist system. At this point it is again necessary to clarify that Offe's analysis does not treat the state as a mere functionalist 'derivative' of the necessities of capital accumulation. Instead, the emphasis of the functional necessity for 'external' processing of the effects of capital movement is on the retrospective insight that capitalism as a mode of socialisation could only establish and consolidate itself (in those places) where successful adaptive structure formation(s) of social governance in the sense of the three aforementioned mechanisms had been put into place, and in turn have over time caused an 'objective deceleration and interruption of the development of contradictions'.[57] The historical waves of institutionalisation of legal, social,

54   Ibid. p. 58 (emphases in the original, S.L.).
55   Ibid. p. 62.
56   Ibid. p. 59.
57   Ibid. p. 56.

and welfare-state intervention outlined above must then be understood, in terms of a political sociology, as essential building blocks and milestones of such adaptive structure formation in capitalist societies.

Nevertheless – and this is the essence of both Offe's analysis as well as my own – the success of state-mediated self-adjustment in capitalist systems certainly has its limits, theoretically as well as empirically. The 'borderline character' of system-compatible state intervention in capitalist societies has several systemic causes. First, there are of course limits to the rationality of state control – state action can never be aware of or even guess, let alone implement or enforce (but more on that later), everything that could be considered system-compatible intervention. Further, since every state intervention relies on social implementation[58] – whatever system-compatible intervention is carried out, not only sporadically but indeed as the rule, causes unintended consequences. This ought to be taken into account along with the not only plausible but historically demonstrated fact that state actors are more than mere automatons of the (alleged or real) interests 'of capital'. Rather, state administration develops an institutional momentum[59] and intrinsic dynamic over the course of its political-regulatory activities, which threatens to remain uncomprehended (by relevant actors) and thus uncontrolled.

Second, it is central to the question of the limits of state-mediated 'border stabilisation'[60] of the capitalist system – and thus essential for the subsequent argument to be developed here – that the capitalist state, irrespective of how 'external' it ultimately remains and can remain to the process of capital valorisation, essentially represents an alien element in this process, the interventions of which must be understood as 'results which are alien to the system but are caused by movement(s) within the system itself'.[61] It is not for nothing that the 'market' of capitalist societies reflexively calls for 'less state' (even if it does not always really mean it), for at first glance more state intervention implies, *ceteris paribus,* less formal entrepreneurial freedom – as well as more public spending, which in turn can be equated with a decrease in material entrepreneurial freedom. Offe subsumes this interrelation in the concept of the 'formation of systemic elements that are alien to the structure but functionally necessary for the maintenance of the system',[62] or rather the 'necessary *dualism* of capitalist and non-capitalist forms',[63] and refers in

58   Cf. Lenhardt, Offe, *Staatstheorie und Sozialpolitik*, p. 174ff.
59   Cf. Offe, *Strukturprobleme*, p. 127ff.
60   Offe, Ibid. p. 57.
61   Offe, Ibid. p. 68.
62   Offe, Ibid. p. 75.
63   C. Offe, 'The Abolition of Market Control and the Problem of Legitimacy',

particular to all those welfare-state interventions which – from the expansion of the public or semi-public economic and employments sector(s) to the socio-political 'de-commodification' of labour power – represent 'specific *deviations* from the capitalist modes of social life forms which "abstract" labour power into "commodity" with view to the production and expansion of surplus value'.[64] In a way they necessarily become the object of resistance for agents of capital and thus of political conflict – the hitch, however, is that welfare-state interference, structurally alien as it may be, is nevertheless indispensable; that is to say, it is essential for the continued existence of the structure – and vice versa. 'In this sense, the politicisation of functions designed to maintain the capitalist order, which the market-controlled economy no longer generated by itself, represents an inevitable, yet ambivalent and self-contradictory solution to the problem':[65] in order to stabilise the system, the state resorts to measures that are essentially incompatible with that system – that this arrangement cannot function smoothly over a longer period of time, or at least does not do so automatically, is rather obvious.

No 'higher insight' can a priori guarantee that recourse to the state-as-steering-mechanism will not simultaneously reinforce the state's capacity to act as a relatively self-autonomous 'alien element'. The question that remains unanswered, left open solely to contingencies, is whether the intervention of any 'separate' sector of the state, to counteract the functional gaps arising in the market-controlled capital accumulation process, will in the long term serve to stabilise or jeopardise this process.[66]

Lastly, the uncertainty regarding the actual functionality of interventionist state action is accompanied by an additional moment of potential crisis-proneness, which in turn explains why Offe had already adopted, 'by no means as a casual turn of phrase',[67] the concept of 'late capitalism' at the beginning of the 1970s – prior to the world-economic caesura of the 'oil crisis': the regulative instrumentarium that the capitalist-, state- (and, more recently, welfare state-)constituted social formation has at its disposal to neutralise the effects of its self-contradiction are 'categorically exhausted' by these three containment mechanisms. 'What remains is the variation and refinement of the triad of self-adaptive mechanisms that has thus far been

---

64   Offe, *Kapitalistate* 2, p. 73 (emphasis in the original, S.L.).
65   Offe, *Kapitalistate* 1, p. 111.
66   Ibid.
67   Offe, *Strukturprobleme*, p. 65.

at least more or less commonly used in all advanced industrial nations'[68]: a politics of permanent 'muddling through' on the edges of systemic and social integration; that is to say, on the line between system compatibility of state intervention on one side, and the social compatibility of capitalist economic activity on the other. Indeed, as a result of the historical waves of institution- alisation of state activity and of the transformation from the *Rechtsstaat* to the welfare state, that fine politico-economic line between compatibility and incompatibility, between functionality and dysfunctionality, between latent and manifest crisis-proneness has become even narrower.

> The less the state apparatus can limit its activities to merely sanctioning the trans-
> actions among commodity owners and the greater the complexity and continuity
> of the sector of its concrete, goal-directed activities, the more difficult it becomes
> to maintain the balance between the economic system of capitalist domination
> and its politically provided preconditions.[69]

In the following, I will take a closer look at the nature of this balancing act of welfare(-state) capitalism, or rather the capitalist welfare state today – over the course and under the banner of its morphogenesis into the reg- ulatory state of the active society. Before this question can be tackled, however, a third macro-social structure beside state and capitalism needs to be included in our considerations – one that tends to be neglected in most politico-economic analyses (and not only in Marx and Foucault); yet the systematic consideration of which is actually the precondition to fully comprehending the structural constraint of capitalist state activity – we are talking, of course, about democracy. Offe's theory of late capitalism is also instructive to the extent that it takes into account the democratic constitu- tion of the late capitalist state, albeit from the latter's own perspective (but consistent in theoretical terms), as one of the 'organisational means' of its social regulatory activity. After all – as its (systemically required) concern for the social compatibility of the capitalist mode of production hinted at earlier already indicates – the state is compelled to respond politically not only to economic demands resulting from the maintenance of the capital valorisation process, but also to the social demands arising from the pro- cesses of social interest formation. The expanding interventionist state is therefore – as is typical for late modernity – confronted with structural 'problems of compatibility'[70] caused by the twofold functional point of reference of its actions: economic requirements and social demands; and

---

68   Ibid.
69   Offe, *Kapitalistate* 1, p. 111.
70   Lenhardt, Offe, *Staatstheorie und Sozialpolitik*, p. 177.

accumulation and legitimation (or, in terms of a wage earners' society: capital's requirements and labour's needs). This 'system of organisational means' of the capitalist social formation includes more than just the guarantees of private freedom for all market actors provided by the *Rechtsstaat* and the preservation of labour in its commodity form through the welfare state. It furthermore refers to the regulatory state's instrumentarium of taxation, which creates the state's scope for material action in the first place, but at the same time binds it to a stable functional dynamic of the process of accumulation. Finally, then, this includes an ensemble of democratic processes and procedures through which the state consistently secures its formal agency in order to perform (any potentially necessary) interventions into the process of capital valorisation – an organisational means which nevertheless has its downside, too, as it 'renders any specific government force's capacity to act dependent on legitimation attained through periodic, general and representative elections'.[71]

The situation of the late modern state, as a capitalist *and* democratic welfare state, is then – as should be obvious at this point – anything but comfortable. It is an agent (or rather a complex interrelation of social actions) of the systemically required political containment of capitalist societies' self-destructive dynamic. However, it engages in this activity utilising an instrumentarium alien to the process of private valorisation, using material resources that it necessarily must withdraw from that process – that is to say, in such a manner that conflict with the respective actors of the process of private valorisation is inevitable. On the other hand, the state operates on the basis of the legitimatory resources which it has to constantly 'earn' anew, as well as through the guaranteed accommodation of certain claims to social provisions, the dynamic of which it cannot effectively control – which in turn raises the probability of conflicts with the subjects of these entitlement rights. In this context the democratic-capitalist state makes an effort – in the sense of an ultimately futile attempt at meta-coordination – to 'actually find and preserve a system of organisational means of social life that is both free of contradictions and sustainable'.[72] In the end, however, it transfers the intrinsic contradictoriness of capitalism into its own action programme – and is thus incapable of solving problems of social regulation without simultaneously producing new functional problems.

Taking this into account, state activity in late capitalism is not heteronomously determined, at least not exclusively; for in its attempts to resolve the capitalist-democratic compatibility problematic, the welfare state constituting itself in this manner attains its – historically and nationally – specific

---

71   Offe, *Strukturprobleme*, p. 144.
72   Ibid. p. 131 (emphasis in the original, S.L.).

logic. Conversely, however, the agents of the welfare state are by no means free in their action rationality, but rather are bound in (at least) a twofold sense. We have before us the theory of late capitalism as a political theory of a doubly bound character, which allows us to borrow from a reading of psychology's double-bind theory: the late capitalist state – as democratic-capitalist welfare state – is in a situation of ambivalent, communicative dilemma in which it becomes the 'victim' of competing, indeed even contradictory, calls to action if it is to accommodate both capitalist requirements *and* democratic demands equally in its interventionist activities. As is the case in a psychological double-bind constellation, these dual invocations must in a sense tear the state apart. Due to the close material and formal relation to both of its structures of reference, capitalism and democracy, and to the looming threat of (potentially double) resource deprivation, the state has no chance of escaping those profoundly contradictory action prescriptions: it is neither in the position to withdraw from the relation, nor can it criticise both demands, so to speak, in a meta-communicative manner (even though it sometimes does launch cautious attempts in this direction, such as Nokia in Bochum or General Motors in Detroit, as well as, more regularly, towards certain groups of welfare benefit recipients) – let alone address the contradiction that exists between the two. Essentially, it can only attempt to shoulder this contradiction – and to make the 'best' of it through ever new adaptive self-transformations of its political agenda and its regulatory instrumentarium.

By now, we are nearing an analysis not only of the welfare state, but also of its current transformation into the state of the 'active society'. We come even closer to the fundamental objective of this contribution if we reformulate the welfare-state dilemma of systemic double-bindedness in the terminology of the capitalist dialectic of mobility and control introduced at the beginning of this chapter. After all, if the point of observing the process of capitalist accumulation and its institutional structure – as has been shown – is in fact to reveal the double political intervention of liberation *and* containment of labour power, in the sense of its capitalist socialisation (*Vergesellschaftung*) as wage labour, then the structurally analogous functional problem of an equally fundamental control of the social movement mobilised by the opening up of opportunities for social participation also arises during the process of democratic legitimation. Ultimately, this is part and parcel of the search for a happy medium: a degree of democracy that is compatible with the functionality of the capitalist economy and associated with the capitalist system's ability to regulate. Correspondingly, it is no coincidence that claims to democratic-participatory rights, as soon as they extend beyond the functional field of politics to that of the economy and begin to demand the comprehensive participation and decision-making rights 'of labour' in the organisation and investment processes of capital, always trigger determined rejection by business elites and partisans of political liberalism. But it is not only hardened statists who consider direct-democratic dilutions of the processes of representative democracy to be potential gateways to an unpredictable, potentially democracy-threatening political populism. Thinking (and even practising) through the dynamic of capitalist-democratic freedom, the free voter, just like the free wage earner, as it were, represents in the final analysis an element of uncertainty for the reproduction of social relations, crying out for systematic control.

In this sense, the social and economic productive resources of the democratic-capitalist social formation simultaneously represent a source of destructive risks: a structural dilemma confronting the welfare state, which mediates between the dynamics of accumulation and legitimation, economic productivity and social participation. For uncontrolled capitalist and democratic dynamisation processes remain problematic not only within their respective functional domains, but also with regard to their systemic interactions. The democratic mobilisation of subjects, if taken too seriously by the subjects themselves, jeopardises the capitalist process of private-autonomous production-related decision-making: having been asked their opinion and invited to make a decision, they may vote against child labour, low wages or monopolies in the energy sector. By contrast, capitalist mobilisation, if prolonged indefinitely, places the democratic process of political participation at risk: individual and collective rights to object to the over-exploitation of labour power, life time or natural resources are then essentially little more than smoke and mirrors, an annoying background noise in the effectively uninterrupted systemic operations of the economy.

In both respects – for the economic as well as the social order of late capitalist social formations – it is valid to say that the welfare state acts as political regulator of capitalist and democratic movement, and that it constantly (re-)defines the limits of that movement's compatibility. The fact that this represents a balancing act to avoid the one-sided increase of one logic or the other, is what constitutes the 'permanent crisis' of late capitalism; that is to say, the sustained crisis of democratic-capitalist society as institutionalised in the welfare state. The task of a critical political sociology, as Offe already had in mind in the 1970s and as is to be developed and renewed here, is a theoretical rehabilitation of the concept of capitalism and the establishment of a sort of 'contradiction model'[73] of capitalist movement without advancing a theory of economic breakdown rooted more in dogmatic faith than

---

73   Ibid. p. 67.

scientific rationality. Rather, the prime objective of such a sociology must be the 'analysis and critique of the system's adaptive self-transformations',[74] in combination with the follow-up question of 'the possibilities of the system' – in plain language: of the democratic-capitalist welfare state – 'to self-adaptively extend its own limits even further'.[75] The 'activating' reconstruction of the welfare state currently under way may be seen as a contemporary form of such a politics at the limits of system adaptation – and it represents the centrepiece of the subsequent deliberations, which in this regard are considered a contribution to the adaptive self-transformation of welfare state research into a critical analysis of capitalism.[76]

3. Activation, or the adaptive self-transformation of the welfare state

The interventionist welfare state and its crises

The historic breakthrough of the industrial-capitalist, representative-democratic and welfare-statist social formation and its long-term consolidation is – at least in Germany and western Europe – primarily a consequence of the two most disastrous crises of the 20th century: the two wars of mass annihilation during the first half of the century. The rapid historic double cycle of war preparations, warfare and the ensuing consequences was accompanied by extraordinary, downright extreme demands for economic accumulation and social legitimation for the 'total' role of government (to some extent in World War I, but especially in World War II). Both wars can be considered 'midwives' of the Fordist regime[77] of accumulation and regulation that materialised institutionally in the Keynesian welfare state of the post-war long boom. It need not be elaborated here as to how gigantic the fiscal, technological and infrastructural efforts in both Great Wars indeed were. Moreover, the mobilisation of all – literally *all* – social resources and reserves for the war effort generated ineluctable functional necessities in terms of, e.g., the institutionalisation of political and social conflict and the regulation of gender relations. Even after the war, state capacities – that is, its material, bureaucratic and personnel capacities – which had been vastly expanded during the war, were at least partially retained as a tool of long-term public intervention. What also survived were those socio-political

---

74   Ibid. p. 65 ff.

75   Ibid., p. 66.

76   Cf. also J. Borchert, S. Lessenich, '"Spätkapitalismus" revisited: Claus Offes Theorie und die adaptive Selbsttransformation der Wohlfahrtsstaatsanalyse', in *Zeitschrift für Sozialreform* 50 (2004), pp. 563–83.

77   Cf. J. Hirsch, R. Roth, *Das neue Gesicht des Kapitalismus*, Hamburg 1986.

ideologemes instrumental to welfare-state interventionism which, though perhaps not born out of the two 'people's wars' as such, nevertheless became politically potent on a massive scale. This pertains in particular to the notion of a shared national destiny as a site and source of collective solidarity.

The historically specific constellation of the European post-World War II era was particularly conducive to the successful cultivation of the idea of a national 'social community' (*Sozialgemeinschaft*) integrated through the welfare state. In West Germany and large parts of western Europe, the 1950s and 1960s witnessed a golden age of unprecedented, sustained rates of high economic growth.[78] The conditions were rather advantageous for developing a qualitatively new level of social affluence, unlike anything previously known:[79] the effects of catching-up in reconstruction and copying imported innovation, a labour supply (initially domestic, later imported) as reliable as it was flexible, and consistently undervalued currencies in the context of an open world economy 'embedded' via international financial and trade regimes, allowed for numerous smaller and larger national-economic success stories across the European continent. This was further reinforced, quite significantly, by the more or less politically directed coordination of relevant market actors and their respective economic strategies as was practised throughout Europe for some time, yet which manifested as greatly varying instruments and institutions in different countries.[80] Up until the 1970s, the model of coordinated capitalism[81] predominant throughout western Europe was widely regarded as guarantor of economic prosperity and social stability – whereas Great Britain, under-equipped as it was with similar coordination mechanisms, was labelled 'the sick man of Europe.'[82]

European post-war prosperity was thus was not only the result of favourable conditions, but also owed a great deal to massive political intervention. The so-called 'Keynesian welfare state' that was established in European societies – in some earlier than in others, some with more and others with less explicit reference to the theoretical structure of its British namesake, sometimes in a more and sometimes in a less controversial manner, and (in terms of macro-economic indicators) sometimes more and sometimes less successfully – was (contrary to the indignant retrospective critique offered by

---

78   Cf. K. Voy, W. Polster, C. Thomasberger (ed.), *Beiträge zur Wirtschafts – und Gesellschaftsgeschichte der Bundesrepublik Deutschland (1949–1989)*, 2 Volumes, Marburg 1990/91; H. Kaelble, *Der Boom 1948–1973*, Opladen 1992.

79   Cf. B. Eichengreen, *The European Economy since 1945*, Princeton 2006.

80   Cf. A. Shonfield, *Modern Capitalism*, London 1994 [1965].

81   Cf. P. A. Hall, D. Soskice (eds), *Varieties of Capitalism*, Oxford 2001.

82   Cf. F. W. Scharpf, *Sozialdemokratische Krisenpolitik in Europa*, Frankfurt a.M., New York 1987.

some liberal thinkers) not only a generous and redistribution-obsessed profiteer, but also the political architect of the European economic resurgence.
The grand systemic feat of the Keynesian welfare state was to neutralise,
through mediation, the tendency toward antagonistic and thus potentially
conflicting logics of the organisation of the social process of production – as
represented by the organisations of capital and labour, respectively – or at
least to render the two seemingly compatible. The 'golden age' of capitalism
rested, to a significant extent, on a balance between the logics of capitalism
and democracy as established (or at least successfully insinuated) through
the welfare state; that is to say, its functional mode and operational logic
were founded on the historic compromise 'between the economic and
the social':[83] between the economic rationality of production on one side,
and the social rationality of participation on the other. The social welfare
state of the post-war era let the Keynesian theory of the circular (or rather
cyclical-sequential) balance between economic interest and social expectations become a political reality, or so it seemed. According to this logic, 'the
social' as created by political intervention, i.e., 'artificially' created demand
for commodities, services and labour forces (as far as necessary and possible) supports 'the economic' (i.e., the long-term profitability of the process
of capital valorisation), which in turn sustains the social (public protection
of and provisions for wage earners and their families), which then again
underpins the economic (through making available an employable supply
of labourers and establishing a safety net to cushion the social impact of
decreases in demand for labour power): a veritable *circulus virtuosus*, maintained by means of permanent and methodical state intervention.

The consolidated welfare state thus assumes a twofold institutional
responsibility: while regulating the economic for social purposes, it simultaneously regulates the social to economic ends. On both counts it becomes
the *social* state: by elevating wage demands to the same status (in terms of
their compatibility with the general economic good) as capital interests it *de
facto* sides with 'labour', and – though by no means unilaterally, but nevertheless repeatedly – promotes overall social welfare. In doing so, however,
it always and consistently acts on a national scale: throughout the international post-war regime of 'embedded liberalism',[84] state interventionism
was always about the regulation of the *national* economy in the interest of
maximising *national* welfare. The welfare state's promotion of the social also

---

83   J. Donzelot, 'The Promotion of the Social', in *Economy and Society* 17, 1988,
pp. 395–427, here p. 421.

84   Cf. J. G. Ruggie, 'International Regimes, Transactions, and Change:
Embedded Liberalism in the Postwar Economic Order', in S. D. Krasner (Hg.),
International Regimes, Ithaca, London 1983, pp. 195–231.

systematically sides with the national, as it creates a national social space which – to this day – not only internally, but necessarily also externally, creates new structures of the social, i.e., structures of social inequality and social exclusion. For the sake of clarity it should be stressed at this point that talk of a 'golden age' of the welfare-statist social formation – in contrast to what often seems to be the case in many left critiques of the current transformation – by no means implies any kind of nostalgia for the 'good (or at least better) old days', nor the retroactive glorification of the welfare-capitalist post war arrangement. In opposition to creating any sort of myth, all that is being said here is that the institutions of the so-called 'Keynesian' welfare state in a specific historical stage of development contributed significantly to the stable reproduction of the industrial capitalist mode of socialisation, and thus – in the words of Offe – were able to succeed in preventing the self-negating consequences of the basic capitalist structure from becoming manifest as crises. They thereby helped to bring about that constellation of socio-economic prosperity in the advanced industrial societies[85] which for three decades now has been superseded by an age of 'crises' in which the welfare-state arrangement has been fundamentally transformed.

The temporary success of the welfare state's mediation between economic and social rationality, capitalist requirements and democratic demands, during industrial society's 'golden age' can still be remembered today. In the three decades following World War II the welfare state launched a seemingly never-ending movement of expansion: social spending, in absolute as well as in relative terms, constantly increased; this was by all means regarded as positive proof of solid state policy. Continual growth of new social policy programmes and ever more welfare-state institutions encompassed an increasingly broad swath of people and mitigated against more and more social risks. Western capitalism was booming, and with it the welfare state. Since at least the mid-1970s, however, its expansive, stable trajectory has been accompanied by critical diagnoses of an 'inflation of expectations' and of a 'government overload' in which the state is portrayed as a rampant, greedy, insatiable leviathan that in its thirst for control morphs into a welfare state (in the pejorative sense) which in turn throttles all individual proactivity in economic as well as in social life. These invectives against an all-powerful 'nanny state', often in the form of polemic, have found and continue to find an authoritative sociological foundation in the social theory of Niklas Luhmann.[86] In the context of Luhmann's theoretical structure, the

---

85   Cf. B. Lutz, *Der kurze Traum immerwährender Prosperität*, Frankfurt a.M., New York 1984.

86   Cf. N. Luhmann, *Political Theory in the Welfare State*, Munich, Wien 1981; N. Luhmann, *Die Politik der Gesellschaft*, Frankfurt a.M. 2000; J. Kaube, 'Das

emergence of welfare statehood represents a sideeffect of the evolutionary transition towards the structural type of functionally differentiated society. According to his theory, the differentiation of the political system and the historical tendency towards democratisation of political decision-making lead to the role of government becoming the object of societal disposition. Adhering to the basic principle of inclusion that pertains (essentially) to all social functional systems, the political (sub-)system, in system-theoretical analysis, is found to similarly exhibit an in-built tendency towards the inclusion of evermore groups of people, as well as their needs and interests, into the realm of political jurisdiction and protection. The consequence of this inclusionary movement is a new form of statehood: 'The welfare state is the realisation of political inclusion.'[87]

This movement of political inclusion of social issues and needs, if we are to believe Luhmann, possesses an uncontrollable momentum of quasi-endless expansion: nothing and no one can halt the interaction between the semantics of social expectations and the logic of political compensation. Thus, the system-theoretical account paints an image of an uncontrolled and uncontrollable, 'self-propelled, self-driven welfare state',[88] which in its movement spares nothing and no one and therefore eventually overextends itself, indeed even 'consumes itself'.[89] Here, politics in a democratic state appears as a self-referential system, and social welfare an arbitrarily resilient 'wishful thinking'.[90] It is fair to say that – for Luhmann – if the state was still an innocent child at the start of its evolution toward the social state, then the extended welfare state has morphed into the evil uncle with a penchant for 'self-satisfaction'.[91] To locate the driving force of the paternalistic welfare-state vehicle exclusively in the functional area of politics (as is implied), and to dismiss out of hand any other impetuses or decelerating forces affecting the development of the welfare state – such as, say, the functional system of the economy – presents itself as a patently absurd move with respect to arriving at a more profound understanding of the democratic-capitalist welfare state and its evolutionary dynamic – regardless of how successful and necessary it may be in a systems theoretical context.

Rather, as I believe to have demonstrated extensively thus far, it is

---

Reflexionsdefizit des Wohlfahrtsstaates', in S. Lessenich (Hg.), *Wohlfahrtsstaatliche Grundbegriffe*, Frankfurt a.M., New York 2003, pp. 41–54.

87   N. Luhmann, *Political Theory in the Welfare State*. Berlin, New York 1990, here p. 35.

88   Ibid. p. 27.

89   Ibid. p. 9.

90   Luhmann, *Die Politik der Gesellschaft*, p. 365.

91   N. Luhmann, *Political Theory in the Welfare State*, p. 87.

precisely the contradictory entanglements and interactions of social *and* economic action rationalities of political actors in parliament, government and administration, which explain the triumph – as precarious as it is paradoxical – of the welfare state. It is the assumption of a twofold economic and social responsibility by the Keynesian-inspired interventionist state that leads to a permanent expansion of the role of state activity, and, still more, renders this expansion necessary, and in fact even enforces it. The (partly voluntary, partly imposed) role of serving as mediator between the interests of capital and labour, and between the functional logics of capitalism and democracy, places the Keynesian welfare state between fronts in society, rendering it the addressee of economic as well as social demands. To the extent that it constitutes and legitimises itself through its very ability to accommodate and balance *both*, it almost inevitably comes under fire (not only fiscally). 'There is a considerable price to be paid then for this clever move':[92] that is to say, a price to be paid for the welfare state's claim to be *everybody's darling*, to operate as a mediator between the worlds of capitalist imperatives and democratic expectations.

The mobilisation of capitalist and democratic social dynamic on the one hand, and the control of the economic for social aims and control of the social for economic gains on the other, represented an extremely ambitious agenda for the 'heroic welfare state', one evidently more than it could handle. At any rate, we have been witnessing its gradual abdication since the mid-1970s. Its regime is headed for – at first imperceptibly, but lately increasingly accelerated – its end. The welfare state as we used to know it, seen by some to have reached the 'afternoon'[93] of its life, is by no means disappearing from the scene, but is instead changing its form in a profound manner. Its new face remains rather shadowy for the time being. Nevertheless, the main features of its transformational movement can already be discerned – as well as contradictory, dilemmatic, and dialectic aspects stemming not least from its new role as the state of the active society.

The 'neo-social' transformation of the welfare state.

Without falling back into the retrospective liberal-conservative rhetoric of damnation in our analysis, we may nonetheless speak carefully of an 'aging'[94] of the welfare-state arrangement over the course and under the banner of

---

92   Donzelot, *The Promotion of the Social*, p. 425.

93   Cf. B. Vogel, 'Der Nachmittag des Wohlfahrtsstaats. Zur politischen Ordnung gesellschaftlicher Ungleichheit', in: *Mittelweg 36* 13(4), 2004, no. 4, pp. 36–55.

94   Cf. F.-X. Kaufmann, *Herausforderungen des Sozialstaates*, Frankfurt a.M. 1997.

the political, economic and social sea change of the 1970s and 1980s. As a result of the two oil crisis-related economic slumps, the 'automobile welfare state' (*automobiler Sozialstaat*) ran out of fuel both literally and figuratively, making it impossible to continue the old game of national win-win distribution, of 'welfare for all'. What began to challenge the welfare state in its role as mediator were conflicts revolving around the relative share of national income that had now ceased to appear as if it could grow endlessly; the state became increasingly less able to meet the competing demands for performance and distribution by business management and employees (*Arbeitnehmer*), respectively (and increasingly by the unemployed among them). Both the economy and the state began a systematic search for cost reduction potential and relief from certain responsibilities. Economic and social policies increasingly propagated and implemented supply oriented strategies; since the Reagan/Thatcher era, the improvement of the overall conditions for business operations rose to – and in fact still stands at – the very top of state agendas across the entire western economic world.[95] The greatest possible extent of discretionary freedom for 'economic subjects', as the supply-side credo runs (and which remains essentially undisputed by any empirical counter evidence whatsoever), ensures maximum growth in terms of value creation, prosperity and employment by means of stabilising companies' profit expectations. Ever since, the magic word in economic and labour market policy (applied ad nauseam) has been 'flexibility'. From flexible exchange rates to flexible location selection, from the flexible organisation of work and production, flexible working hours and flexible forms of employment all the way to flexible prices, flexible wages and flexible rights, and ultimately, as it were, the flexible human.[96] Against the backdrop of globalised markets, a culture of economic success and the collapse of state socialism, flexibility has become the quintessence of the 'post-Fordist' era's capitalist *zeitgeist*, whereas any kind of rigidity whatsoever is confidently ascribed to the social Evil Empire.

It is clear is that the 'old' welfare state, institutionally charged with the task of, and bound to, the socio-political normalisation of the wage earners' society and the standardisation of the corresponding forms of work and life, was expected to be and in fact was shaken to its very core as a consequence of the shift to flexible capitalism (and the corresponding forms of work and life). The aforementioned 'golden circle' of political support for the process

---

95   Cf. C. Offe, 'Die Aufgabe von staatlichen Aufgaben: "Thatcherismus" und die populistische Kritik der Staatstätigkeit', in D. Grimm (ed.), *Staatsaufgaben*, Frankfurt a.M. 1996, pp. 317–52.

96   Cf. R. Sennett, *The Corrosion of Character: The Personal Consequences of Work in the New Capitalism*, New York 1998.

of economic accumulation by the state and social consumption has been broken, its base in terms of interest group politics – namely the trade unions – has dried up (or their 'countervailing power' (*Gegenmacht*) has at least been severely weakened), the stable Fordist relations of work, life and gender were profoundly shaken, and the 'heroic' welfare state, as the institutional bearer of overall political control, has been subjected to public obituaries consistently portraying the former hero as a villain ever since. The fact that the Federal Republic of (West) Germany in a specific world-economic and geopolitical constellation still managed – thanks to an expanding welfare state that was not only active in terms of social policy in the strict sense but also in terms of economic, fiscal, infrastructural and subsidies-related policies – to become one of the world's leading industrial nations is obscured by a negative retrospective myth-making designed to politically discredit the antiquated welfare-state agenda of political regulation, social protection and economic redistribution (however limited the latter may be). The relevant institutional mechanism is well-known to sociology: the 'old' is portrayed to be obviously unsustainable, indeed even mischievous and reprehensible, so as to then let the 'new'(a different welfare state, an altered regime of state activity) appear all the more plausible and inevitable; to turn it into 'the conclusion of a long chain of imperative "necessities".[97] As we know, such a view of the old versus the new – if repeated and heard often enough – will begin to seem perfectly plausible; positive and negative readings are gradually perceived as self-evident, indeed as 'true'.

But what, then, constitutes this 'new' welfare state? What distinguishes it from its predecessor, in terms of its role as mediator between economic requirements and social demands? How does it respond to the emergence and proliferation of the forms of work and life found in flexible capitalism? How does it relate to the ongoing capitalist *Landnahme*[98] extending to spheres of social life previously untouched by the price mechanism and the logic of profit; to the constant revolution of the way of life in the 'new capitalism'; and what is its relation to the new 'spirit' of the latter? The French sociologists Luc Boltanski and Ève Chiapello[99] rightly identify this

---

97   K.-S. Rehberg, 'Die stabilisierende Fiktionalität' von Präsenz und Dauer. Institutionelle Analyse und historische Forschung', in: R. Blänkner, B. Jussen (ed.), *Institutionen und Ereignis*, Göttingen 1998, pp. 381–407, here p. 401.

98   Cf. K. Dörre, 'Einführung. Gewerkschaften und die kapitalistische Landnahme: Niedergang oder strategische Wahl?', in: H. Geiselberger (ed.), *Und jetzt?*, Frankfurt a.M. 2007, pp. 53–78.

99   Cf. L. Boltanski, È. Chiapello, 'Die Rolle der Kritik in der Dynamik des Kapitalismus und der normative Wandel', in *Berliner Journal für Soziologie* 11(4), 2001, pp. 459–77; K. Boltanski, E. Chiapello, *The New Spirit of Capitalism*, London 2007.

'new spirit of capitalism' as the underlying 'project' character of economic activity, of work and of life itself. Flexible capitalism follows a project-based legitimatory order that merges all social relations into a network-like structure, which relies on adaptability and the short-term as such, celebrating life in a 'connectionist world'.[100] In this world – and this is the first crucial link for an analysis of the contemporary transformation of the welfare state – the degree of activity, the *more* or *less* of individual mobility and movement, tends to acquire more relevance than all other social distinctions or, more precisely: essentially all other social distinctions tend to become subsumed under the social meta-distinction between activity or inactivity, mobility versus immobility.[101] According to Boltanski and Chiapello's analysis, one cannot succeed in this new active-activist narrative of justification of social life and behaviour[102] merely as an effective, self-interested egotist; rather 'one can only be considered "great"if he or she acts as more than a "network opportunist", on behalf of the common good – this is one of the normative restrictions'.[103]

It is this normative restriction which then marks our second point of reference for an understanding of the current transformation of the welfare-state social formation: individual activity, mobility, and movement only 'count' if – and only if – they can be considered and recognised as beneficial to the common good, if they are carried out with a social aim, or if such socially compatible action rationality can at least be discerned in their self-understanding or insinuated in an external ascription.

The 'culture of the project' described by Boltanski and Chiapello – and its inscribed normative determinacy, through a sociality that goes beyond simple individualist action orientations – is located by them primarily in the realm of economy, of management, of business activity in the narrower sense. Nevertheless, as a culture of activity, of the acceleration of social conduct in life[104] and of the 'entrepreneurial self',[105] it extends far beyond business activity (in the actual sense of the term) in its social relevance; in fact, it represents 'a general pattern which has begun to encompass countless other areas',[106] increasingly becoming a general concept of life and of

100 L. Boltanski, 'Leben als Projekt. Prekarität in der schönen neuen Netzwerkwelt', in *Polar* 2, 2007, pp. 7–13, here p. 11.

101 Cf. Lessenich, 'Beweglich – Unbeweglich'.

102 Cf. Boltanski, Chiapello, *The New Spirit of Capitalism*, p. 152ff.

103 Boltanski, 'Leben als Projekt', p. 11.

104 Cf. H. Rosa, *Social Acceleration: A New Theory of Modernity*, 2013.

105 Cf. U. Bröckling, 'Jeder könnte, aber nicht alle können. Konturen des unternehmerischen Selbst', in *Mittelweg 36* 11(4), 2002, pp. 6–26; U. Bröckling, *Das unternehmerische Selbst*, Frankfurt a.M. 2007.

106 Boltanski, 'Leben als Projekt', p. 10.

social – and socially responsible – behaviour. Yet this dynamic of social universalisation and normalisation of activity also brings politics into play; that is to say, it includes the welfare state as an institutional mechanism of political inclusion and social regulation. The 'activating' turn of welfare-state policy, under way in all late industrial societies for at least a decade, perfectly toes the line of the new, flexible capitalism's legitimatory order. What is more: the 'activating welfare state' is not only the victim of the general social mobilisation, but also a driving force behind it. Taking up the functional requirements of flexible capitalism and transmitting them, enhanced through their social charge, to social subjects, the welfare state – in its new, 'activating' guise – represents the central institutional transmission belt of a society-wide movement aimed at the movement of society.

At the core of the welfare state's activation policy agenda lies the tendency to shift from 'state provision' to self-provision; from public to private responsibility for safety and security; from collective to individual risk management. The issue here is never just activity as such and for itself, but individual movement in pursuit of a 'higher' cause – that is to say, with a social aim. The new rationality of welfare state activity is realised through the socio-political construction of *doubly* responsible subjects, who not only assume responsibility for themselves but also are committed to 'society' as a whole. Responsible subjects – i.e., people who are aware of their responsibility and act accordingly – compare certain alternative courses of action by their individual as well as social costs and benefits. In their actions, economic-rational and moral-social orientations are successfully combined – even though this may not occur automatically. Rather, as we learn from 'studies in governmentality' building on the later work of Foucault,[107] this individual self-governance, which adheres to both economic and social rationality, simultaneously requires external direction. This is precisely the principle on which a political governance agenda rests, finding its socio-regulatory point of reference in the subjectivised figure of the 'entrepreneurial self'; a governmentality which '"invents" a new (autonomous) subjectivity and aims to equip this subjectivity with political imperatives';[108] a socio-political configuration which drives people to proactivity in the interest of the social community. Within the framework of this agenda, active self-help, private provisioning, proactive preventative medical care – all of which represent possible varieties of the activation of self-responsibility – are at the same time indicators of personal autonomy and evidence of social responsibility, as they follow both an individual *and* social logic, a subjective *and* social

---

107   Cf. G. Burchell, C. Gordon, P. Miller (ed.), *The Foucault Effect*, London 1991; Krasmann, Volkmer (ed.), *Foucault's 'Geschichte der Gouvernementalität'*.

108   Lemke, *Kritik*, p. 256.

rationality equally. Conversely, any individual's failure to render assistance to him- or herself must be seen, in this configuration, not only as irrational, but as unethical behaviour, as any sign of absent or insufficient willingness to be active is regarded not only as inefficient, but indeed as anti-social – as proof of individual failure or personal unwillingness to make economically sensible and socially responsible use of the scope of action provided by society. Either way, such behavioural deficiencies in light of activation politics testify to an obvious inadequacy in terms of self-governance, which in turn just as obviously requires external direction.

The empirical-political 'visual aids' for the activating state's programme of social utilisation of individual independent activity are extensive – and are constantly growing in number.[109] The unemployed who are fit to work are admonished to make greater efforts towards their re-employment – promoted through qualification measures and enforced via a reduction of the *Lohnersatzleistung* ('wage substitution provision', unemployment benefits) and stricter administrative controls – in the interest of the community of contributors and taxpayers. Women are identified as the bearers of the burden of the 'compatibility problem' (*Vereinbarkeitsproblematik*[110]) and their integration into the job market declared a political priority – to prevent their labour power potential from laying idle, thereby losing returns on the investment that went into their human capital. The 'baby boomers' are expected to prolong their working life and privately arrange for their retirement – on behalf of the financial feasibility of pension funds and out of concern for the subsequent generations' opportunities in life. Praise of the family is enjoying a genuine renaissance, with fondness for children becoming a social obligation – to ensure that there are any subsequent generations in the first place, and so that Germany (or rather the Germans) will not die out; children are to receive all sorts of educational opportunities from early on – for they represent not only our security in old age, but (considering the work their brains are expected to perform) also the actual capital of this society. Even the elderly, who are no longer fit to work, are still encouraged to be productive in one way or another, to actively participate, to commit themselves, to make themselves useful in the service of the common good. Proactivity and self-governance, retirement plans and movement in service of the bigger picture: that is the political agenda of a welfare state in which the subject with its needs, desires, and goals increasingly disappears behind the objectives of a new politics of (and with) the social, behind the

---

109   Cf. Lessenich, *Neuerfindung*, pp. 85–128.

110   [Trans. Note] The 'compatibility problematic' refers to the problematic arising in terms of the compatibility of rearing children while working fulltime (*Vereinbarkeit von Beruf und Familie*).

intentions and compulsions of abstract, anonymous collective social entities
– behind the community of solidarity (*Solidargemeinschaft*) which must not
be milked dry by the individual; the social state, which is to be preserved
through intervention; the *Standort*, which must not be burdened by excessive demands; or the nation, the continued existence of which must not be
jeopardised through selfish abstinence from domestic happiness, but, *au
contraire*, must be supported with active parenthood.

Characterising the regulatory content of this activation programme of
the welfare state as 'economisation of the social',[111] as neo-liberal proliferation of the economic system's rationality for austerity, calculations and profit
interests into all spheres of life is, however, only semi-accurate. Indeed, the
triumph of just such a logic of economisation in all late industrial welfare
capitalisms is undeniable, while it is equally clear that, within them, the
regulation of the economic is conducted less and less out of social concern –
as had been a characteristic feature of the 'old' welfare state. However, this
alone does not sufficiently grasp the functional logic of the politics of activation; that is to say, the social idea behind the activating welfare state. After
all, the progressive *economisation* is complemented by a parallel *subjectification* of the social: concern for the social, its protection and consolidation, is
transferred to the sphere of individual responsibility – and no longer to the
'public hand' of state institutions, nor the 'invisible hand' of market mechanisms and price signals, but instead primarily to the active hands of each
and every one of 'us'. The welfare state of the 20th century, which incorporated the ceaseless proactive mediation between capitalism and democracy,
between an economic and a social rationality, into its operational logic, is
now trying to shift this task onto the subjects, as it is to be internalised by the
latter and serve as the twofold motivation behind their actions. Talk of the
'privatisation' of the welfare state thus acquires another, more far-reaching
significance: by becoming proactive in terms of taking care of their own
personal well-being, as is increasingly expected, subjects themselves – personally, locally, on a small scale – assume the functions of the welfare state
in terms of economic and social regulation. As a result, the private (though
in a very different sense than was attached to this expression at the time)
indeed becomes political.

With view to the regulatory content of the 'new' welfare state it would
therefore be far more appropriate to speak of a *neo-social* instead of a neo-
liberal political governmentality: of a new form of governing society (in the
double sense), which is simultaneously a government of the self.[112] In the

---

111   Cf. U. Bröckling, S. Krasmann, T. Lemke (eds), *Gouvernementalität der
Gegenwart*, Frankfurt a.M. 2000.

112   Cf. S. Lessenich, 'Soziale Subjektivität. Die neue Regierung der Gesellschaft',

activating welfare state, society constitutes itself as a subject that aims for a socially compatible behaviour of its subjects – as it attempts to inscribe the social as their point of reference for action. The activation of individuals' socially responsible proactivity marks the establishment of a new pattern of welfare-state socialisation, which, as it were, refers subjects *uno acto* to the responsibility for themselves as well as for the wider social community. In the structural dilemma of the late capitalist welfare state, namely its economic-social double-bind character, the neo-social programme of activation offers a new opportunity for an at least temporarily successful crisis management, for it at the same time creates – if it is successful – economically *and* socially rational subjects, market compatible *and* socially competent subjects. Nevertheless, it also creates – how could it be otherwise? – new contradictions and paradoxes of welfare-state action resulting from the subjectification of the social.

4. THE LIMITS OF POLITICS: THE CONTRADICTIONS OF THE ACTIVE SOCIETY

The late- or post- (according to preference) industrial, flexible capitalism is also in existential need of the (in this case 'activating') state; it cannot constitute and reproduce itself solely from within, but only through state-provided care work. First and foremost, the programme of activation appears as a seemingly perfect solution to the double-bind problematic of welfare state activity: it aims to adapt the mode of state regulation to the changing requirements of the post-Fordist accumulation regime – while (so it seems) simultaneously accommodating the citizens' demands for social participation.[113] The interventions of the activating welfare state are discussed politically (and scientifically) largely under the label of social participation (and participatory justice[114]). Over the past few years, 'inclusion' has been established as a scientific-political magic formula for conceptualising the social order which – rather compatible with accumulation as such – is not primarily about the redistribution of material resources with the aim of equalising the conditions of social life, but instead seeks to enable participation in the process of producing material opportunities in life.[115] It

---

in *Mittelweg 36* 12(4), 2003, pp. 80–93.

113   E.g. G. Esping-Andersen, 'Towards the Good Society, Once Again?', in G. Esping-Andersen, *Why We Need a New Welfare State*, Oxford 2002, pp. 1–25.

114   Cf. L. Leisering, 'Paradigmen sozialer Gerechtigkeit. Normative Diskurse im Umbau des Sozialstaats', in S. Liebig, H. Lengfeld, S. Mau (eds), *Verteilungsprobleme und Gerechtigkeit in modernen Gesellschaften*, Frankfurt a.M., New York 2004, pp. 29–69.

115   Cf. e.g., H. Bude, *Die Ausgeschlossenen*, München 2008.

is no longer the classical structures of social inequality, but rather phenomena of social 'exclusion'[116] threatening 'anyone and everyone' that is regarded as *the* major social problem of the present, and which in turn can only be remedied with a politics that seeks to universalise market opportunities: according to the activating social state's agenda of inclusion, no one is to be excluded from market citizenship – all people become brothers and sisters on the labour market! Embedded in such a way, activation policy indeed appears as the square in the welfare state's interventionist circle, so to speak, in which economic requirements of an expanded and accelerated market conformity enter into a congenial pairing with social demands for participation in public life. Yet, upon closer inspection, we find that new structural problems of the democratic-capitalist state are produced – once again the welfare state's dilemma of mobility and control is reproduced, albeit at a different level and in a different form.

First of all, the 'active self', which integrates – in place of the welfare state, so to speak – the functional mediation between economic and social action rationalities into the everyday praxis of its way of life, represents a highly contradictory social character. For this figure can only come into existence by means of political intervention in the first place: the implementation of the activation agenda, after all, is by definition executed against the narrative backdrop that the average subject in post-industrial society is *not* sufficiently active, mobile or flexible. Simultaneously, however, this agenda assumes the construct of an 'as-if-anthropology'[117] and depicts people as if they were already the mobile, economically and socially rational subjects that it in fact expects them to become only subsequently; that is to say, *after* activation. Therefore, the paradox constitutive of governing the active society lies in the fact that 'it creates a reality which it at the same time presupposes as already existing'[118] – but at the same time as one that has yet to be constructed. The agenda of activation as such is therefore (in principle) interminable not only for the subjects themselves who are to be – or rather who are – activated, but also for the activating state: the active society's subject requires being endlessly, 'permanently taken care of'[119] by a welfare state, the self-conception of which is based on its activation-ensuring (social) care work. The activating

116 Cf. H. Bude, A. Willisch (eds), *Das Problem der Exklusion*, Hamburg 2006; H. Bude, A. Willisch (eds), *Exklusion*, Frankfurt a.M. 2008.

117 U. Bröckling, 'Menschenökonomie, Humankapital. Eine Kritik der biopolitischen Ökonomie', in: *Mittelweg 36* 12(1), 2003, pp. 3–22, here p. 17.

118 T. Lemke, S. Krasmann, U. Bröckling, 'Gouvernementalität, Neoliberalismus und Selbsttechnologien. Eine Einführung', in Bröckling, Krasmann, Lemke (eds), *Gouvernementalität*, pp. 7–40, here p. 9.

119 L. Gertenbach, *Die Kultivierung des Marktes*, Berlin 2007, p. 124.

state thus becomes a *perpetuum mobile,* as does the active self, which is to be and is constructed by the former.

The key functional precondition of this society-encompassing mobility interrelation is the political production of a corresponding order of social knowledge. The political governance of the active society represents an act of, as it were, governing in the realm of possibility: the primary objective is not to actually make the subject *be* active at all times and in all places, but rather to make them *think* of and develop *knowledge* of themselves as potentially active. Indeed, in the nascent active society existence is – quite nonmaterialistically – determined by consciousness: the success of the agenda of activation rests on the process of the expansion of social consciousness – on the realisation and awareness of being active, being able to be active and wanting to be active, on the effective embedding of a social knowledge of the desirability and necessity of activity on the one hand, and its feasibility and naturalness on the other hand. The subjects who act in accordance with the active society's spirit of the social thus constitute themselves as active citizens who are aware of, think of, want and live the normality of movement.

However, this shows only one side of the active society's production of normality and is valid only in a repeatedly and contradictorily refracted sense. After all, in their fixation on the subjects' mobilisation, state activation programmes do in fact apply multiple standards, they essentially operate on the basis of political constructions of 'good' and 'bad' movement (and thus at the same time, and in contrast to the agenda, of patterns of political interpretation of 'good' immobility[120]), the former to be fostered and unleashed, while the latter is to be controlled – or better yet, halted entirely. And so it is that the social character of the immigrant, who in fact truly *is* equipped with all the trappings of activity and mobility, is precisely *not* the model subject of the active society, but is instead considered a free rider on the national community of solidarity (*Solidargemeinschaft*) whose interest is focused solely on increasing his or her own individual prosperity – except if he (or, more rarely, she) belongs to the group of highly qualified immigrants defined as politically desirable. These immigrants are supposed to compensate for the shortage of skilled labour and contribute financially to the social security systems (preferably without ever redeeming their entitlement to benefits by returning home immediately after the demand for skilled labour has been met). Just like undesirably mobile immigrants, those belonging to the 'indigenous' underclass who – even if absolutely willing to become mobile – in turn founder on the assumptions of normality, job requirement profiles

---

120   Cf. Lessenich, 'Beweglich – Unbeweglich'.

and opportunity structures of the active society, become personifications of the paradoxes of activating socialisation all the same: as the embodiment of the tragic social character of the 'active loser'.[121]

The active society's and activating state's contradictions, however, by no means end here. The permanent political idealisation of 'the active', the obtrusive discursive celebration of 'the flexible', leads to social cleavages – as a standard of life conduct which constantly produces, and necessarily must produce, the social abnormality of those insufficiently mobile groups. It therefore results in a structural excess of political mobilisation, carrying within it the danger of activation overproduction crises which may undermine the actual objectives of regulation, and in which the subjects are not able to live up to the 'naturalness' of total flexibility discursively insinuated by the active society. Mobilisation through activation policies can, however, at the same time lead to an overall excess of mobility in society – of politically undesired movement – and to subjective reinterpretations and 'misinterpretations' of the welfare state's demand for activity, which must be answered with regulatory control – a political surveillance that may produce new consequences running counter to the activation agenda (for this activity may just as well tend to overshoot and overly impede and fetter the active subjects).

All these deliberations on the inherent contradictions of activation policy converge in the recognition of the real secret to its success – or failure: that is to say, the fact that the welfare state's activation agenda always (and always anew) remains dependent on the extent to which its implementation is socially accepted. In the determination of purpose of its political regulation of the social, the activating state relies fundamentally on social participation. Indeed, this may be true for any kind of welfare-state programme whatsoever. However, what makes or breaks a mode of political governance – which in the process of transition to active society attempts to transfer its logic of economic and social regulation onto the subjects and relies on the internalisation of the requirements of economic productivity and social participation by the latter – is the extent to which the collectively individual, quotidian-practical programme is reliably executed. It is no coincidence that the political protagonists of the activating welfare state expend such vast propagandistic energies on the public invitation to and instruction on how to be active, on their 'education toward market adequacy'[122] and service toward the common good, on a 'new political

---

121   Cf. S. Neckel, 'Gewinner – Verlierer', in Lessenich, Nullmeier (eds), *Deutschland*, pp. 353–71.

122   F. Nullmeier, 'Vermarktlichung des Sozialstaats', in: *WSI-Mitteilungen* 57(9), 2004, pp. 495–500, here p. 497.

pedagogy of leadership over people',[123] which, in its control-oriented intentions to promote all governance, will do anything, up to and including a legal
obligation to participate in the active society. All these activation-political
efforts demonstrate one particular – even if merely pre-reflective – insight
on the part of bearers of state action: the social reality of the active society
must and *can only* be constructed in forms of socio-political co-production
of a movement-promoting *public-private partnership*.

The complexity and contradictoriness of the active society's agenda,
its socially demanding as well as precarious character, the dialectic of its
functional and implementational mode can nowhere be seen as clearly as
in the construction and configuration of the social character of the 'illegals'.[124] Here, the highly ambivalent regime of controlled mobility (and
mobilised control) becomes especially palpable; unlike anywhere else, here
it is materially, even physically (in the literal sense of the word: in its inherent limitations as such) experienceable. The image of the *illegal alien* reveals
the welfare state's dilemma of political control at its finest, and moreover,
the paradox that lies especially in its morphogenesis; correspondingly, the
sociological myth hunt for the self-descriptions of the activating state and
active society's accepted truths is particularly fertile in the field of migration
(prevention) policy. After all, the national welfare states in Europe – each
in accordance with its respective economic structures, legal traditions and
institutional constructions – not least for reasons of cheap sources of legitimation (in the double sense) in one of the last remaining fields of at least
symbolic displays of state sovereignty – offensively opt for the control card:
for the defence against unwanted immigration beginning at the EU's outer
borders (*Schengen*); for a denial of statutory social entitlements for immigrants who are *de facto* successful (yet *de jure* illegal); and, finally, for the
public display of combat readiness on behalf of those already included in the
realm of national solidarity, in the form of workplace inspections, minimum
wage regulations and discourses of benefit fraud (such as the statement that
'illicit work is no trivial offence'). On the other hand, however, the European
welfare states benefit greatly from the economy of illegality and the mobility of the 'illegals', as (especially in southeastern Europe) a new agrarian, or
rather (primarily in northwestern Europe) service proletariat has emerged
here, which due to its status (or rather lack thereof) dwarfs all domestic
standards of flexibility (or, more precisely: exploitability) in terms of work
hours, wages and social security. Finally, one can, without drawing any
suspicion of excessive cynicism, establish that even in this extreme case
the (here informal) logic of active society is not simply prescribed and

---

123   Brieler, "'Erfahrungstiere" und "Industriesoldaten"', p. 74.
124   Cf. Karakayali, *Blinde Passagen*.

implemented 'from above', i.e., through the social state's agencies of mobili-sation and control. Rather, even here the active society constitutes itself – as it does in other, less politically disgraceful cases, albeit in very different ways – as a social co-production; that is to say, with active participation (however it may have been achieved) by the illegalised, who ultimately attempt to and know how to productively and actively utilise the restrictions on their legal status (however deplorable these may be).

What may seem like a game of interpretation by sociologists with regard to the *sans papiers* and associated debates about the 'autonomy of migration',[125] is in fact rather obvious with view to the 'normal', fully 'legal' socio-political constellations of activation: activation is not a mere power *dispositif*, not an expression of purely legal and political disciplining power. Activation relies on the participation of individuals, their own will and their own knowledge. The activating welfare state gambles on – even assumes – the subjects' autonomy; it enters into its equation as a subjectivity that is no longer to be subdued, but instead to be harnessed, utilised in controlled mobilisation. Mobilisation and control, the opposing yet complementary functional attributions of political intervention in the democratic-capital-ist welfare state, are subjectivised under the banner of flexible capitalism, i.e., transferred onto the subjects themselves. In exercising political rule that is 'neither openly confrontational nor intrinsically negative',[126] the contradictory logics of welfare-state activity – if successful – morph into a 'private politics' of subjectivised regulation, into a double movement of self-mobilisation and self-governance within the context of the active society.

The emphasis here is on: *if successful*. After all, the dependence of politi-cal governance of activation on the structural compatibility and continuous willingness to participate on the part of the subjects also represents the Achilles' heel of its otherwise (somewhat) stable reproduction. 'New dis-courses pertaining to the responsibilities of the state reflect changes in the perception of the relation between the state and its sphere of activity',[127] between political actors and the addressees of their policies, altered notions which – to the extent that they establish themselves discursively – become part of the socially shared body of knowledge. Discourses are hubs of social knowledge; and the subjects' knowledge of society, or rather socie-ty's knowledge of itself, its self-understanding manifested and materialised in discourses, represents the basis of its constitution as nexus of social

---

125   Cf. S. Karakayali, V. Tsianos, 'Mapping the Order of New Migration: Undokumentierte Arbeit und die Autonomie der Migration', in *Peripherie* 97/98, 2005, pp. 35–64.

126   Saar, *Macht, Staat, Subjektivität*, p. 37.

127   Kaufmann, *Diskurse*, p. 353f.

interaction and meaning – as well as its potential transformation. The order of knowledge of the active society – the knowledge that subjects (conceived as active citizens) have of and about society and about themselves – is its greatest capital asset, which must be preserved and expanded as such in the interest of its (self-)stabilisation, yet which may also disappear and depreciate at any time. At this precise point we find the gateway for forms not only of critical social analysis, but also of practical social critique: the gateway for social processes of 'active' and 'passive' resistance (terms which have never been as relevant as they are in times of activation) against the active society and its regime of knowledge production.

5. SOCIOLOGY ON POLITICAL TERMS: THE RETURN OF A SOCIAL CRITIQUE TO SOCIETY

'Activation' is the contemporary expression of the unresolved – and irresolvable within the system, as it must perpetually be contained and processed anew – fundamental contradiction of the democratic-capitalist social formation between requirements of economic productivity and demands for social participation. In contrast to that suggested by its self-description as an instance of promotion of social inclusion, the activating welfare state processes this contradiction so as to re-assert 'activity' as a subjective value reference for individual claims to social participation, and as a formula of control to be applied in harnessing the social and economic productivity of those it addresses. Such social shifts of meaning within the normative ideals of social development are the point of departure for a genealogical mode of critique,[128] which places the social costs of modern subject formation at the heart of its considerations.

Genealogical critique emerges as the result of 'processing an experience of difference',[129] which '[appears] as an experience of loss compared to a past … and as a blocked potentiality with regard to a future'.[130] It is precisely in this sense that Marx criticises the industrial-capitalist labour regime not only as a source of the subjects' exploitation, but also as a form of socialisation in which 'the possible does not become reality because the form of the organisation of labour does not unleash living labour power, but instead systemically binds it'. In a structurally similar way, the activation-political efforts of the post-industrial, late-capitalist welfare state (its mobilisation always tied to an element of control) in pursuit of the formation of the 'active self' ensures a social configuration in which the possible never becomes real.

---

128   Cf. Honneth, 'Rekonstruktive Gesellschaftskritik'.
129   Brieler, '"Erfahrungstiere" und "Industriesoldaten"', p. 75.
130   Ibid.

'Today, as the "individual capitalist" (*Kapitalindividuum*) (Marx) threatens to become, as subject of its self-realisation, a natural fact of society – as "entrepreneur", as "labour force contractor", or, in its raw state, as "marketing expert" – It might make sense to point out the genesis of this massive subject formation':[131] the genealogy of the wage labour society and the welfare state enabling its constitution, the trajectory of the subject's political liberation and renewed capture, and of the most recent form of its political governance by the programme of welfare-state activation.

If, however, we follow the genealogical trail back a bit further, we stumble across traces of the functional-logical critique of the active social formation. Indeed, the welfare state as activating state achieves, through an ostensible retreat, a new quality of governance, a withdrawal to a 'soft' control mode of political governance by means of the subjects' self-governance, which inevitably reminds the observer of Alexis de Tocqueville's classic aphorism on the character of modern statehood: 'at no other period in our history has [state power] appeared so weak or strong.'[132] Not even the initiation of its programme of activation, then, can help the capitalist-democratic welfare state escape its double-bind dilemma of competing economic and social action rationalities. It is still – as is evidenced by the numerous contradictions of the active social formation – the prisoner of a politics on the fringes of social controllability. What the activating welfare state ultimately does is resort to new variations and elaborations on the particularities of self-adaptive mechanisms, which are nonetheless insufficient to escape the systemic limitations of its capacity to intervene. For whether the subjects 'play along', whether they dance to the tune of active society, remains to be empirically determined – the 'success' of the agenda of activation policy must be proven in social practice. At least one thing seems safe to assume: not even activation is (necessarily) always as socially despicable as it appears politically.

In the active society, a sociology committed to its legacy of social critique assumes a practical role, the significance of which should be neither under- nor overestimated: that of active participation in the deconstruction of active society's knowledge order. A political sociology of the active society must seek to expose the contradictions of welfare-state intervention in (and into) flexible capitalism, to articulate the paradoxes of the political production of active subjects, to map out those sites of potential (at least initially more so than real) rupture of the political agenda and social praxis.[133] Political sociology therefore operates in a manner that would best

---

131   Ibid. p. 76.

132   A. de Tocqueville, *Democracy in America*, 7th printing, 2 vols., New York 1990, p. 313.

133   Cf. S. Opitz, *Gouvernementalität im Postfordismus*, Hamburg 2004.

be described as distrusting the art of political governance over people – and that instead places faith in their own obstinacy and everyday praxis.[134] This already indicates the limitations of critique as scientific critique: while it may attempt to shake up the supposed self-evident implications of the activation-political movement, to develop a knowledge of problematisation capable of unsettling the former's self-understanding, and with this knowledge, speak to active society's subjects, it cannot make a claim to speak *for* them truthfully, effectively, or influentially. 'If the critic, at the "twilight" of the classical work-centred society, can no longer speak on behalf of the excluded, if it turns out to have been a mistake to speak out on behalf of others in the first place, if there is no subject of critique, then critique falls to pieces – or in fact falls back on itself.'[135]

Hence, within the framework of a socially critical programme of sociology as a discipline and profession, a fair degree of self-critical modesty seems appropriate. This includes a realistic picture of the social effectiveness of a social critique which sees it as its task to 'step out of the horizon of the publicly apportioned self-understanding':[136] 'Social criticism does not aim at rapid success in the democratic exchange of opinions but at the distant effect of gradually growing doubt'[137] on the part of the people regarding the politically manufactured assumptions on which this exchange of opinions is based. The topic at hand, then, is not the action of a socially critical proxy, but in a rather empathic sense, enlightenment – enlightenment of society or, more precisely, enlightenment of this society about its own nature and its future possibilities. For it is precisely in not-yet-realised possibilities, in the potentiality that 'things could be different' and in the awareness thereof, that even (and particularly) in capitalism's current social formation of the active society the inherently subversive lies.

No matter how utopian it may sound: the possibility of that which is completely different, the conceivability of the fundamentally alternative is still what social critique must aim for today – the emancipation from hegemonic knowledge, the subversion of the active society, the end of capitalism. The latter has indeed been draining our pockets – and, apropos of knowledge production, our very minds – for long enough.

134   Cf. M. Foucault, 'What is Critique?', in M. Foucault, S Lotringer, ed., *The Politics of Truth*, New Edition.Los Angeles 2007, pp. 41–82.

135   Brieler, '"Erfahrungstiere" und "Industriesoldaten"', p.74.

136   Honneth, *Pathologies of Reason*, p. 184.

137   Honneth, *Pathologies of Reason*, p. 188.

Section II

CRITICISMS

CHAPTER 4

Capitalism, Acceleration, Activation: A Criticism

KLAUS DÖRRE

My concern is that we may see social tensions increase in a number of countries. That's why it's important for us to work together to find solutions that lead us out of the crisis now. We're all sitting in the same boat.
 – J. Ackermann (CEO of Deutsche Bank), in *Bild*, 6 April 2009.

'I was at the demonstration on Saturday ... I had a one-Euro job for a week, the earnings from which were then even deducted from my Hartz IV ... It was my sixth one-Euro job. I studied business, became a mid-level civil servant, then took a course of study in social work – I completed everything and passed all of the tests. A single mother of two children (both study at the university), I have worked countless jobs: telephoning, clerical work ... And then, at 59, you're no more than an *Abwrackprämie*[1] for the labour market, and you get sent to employers who actually *do* provide proper jobs, except these jobs don't pay. I can't do it any longer, and I don't want to. Capitalism has got to go'.
 Letter to the editor, in *Frankfurter Rundschau*, 3 April 2009.

Capitalism is probably in its deepest crisis since 1929–1933. Leading representatives of the economic elite worry about the system's continued existence, and in people's everyday consciousness – manifested in letters to the editor such as the one above – the profit economy as a whole is being disavowed. One would think that this presents an ideal constellation for a sociologically grounded critique of capitalism. Yet the matter is not quite that simple. Critique of capitalism is as old as the system itself; it has existed in different

---

1 The so-called *Abwrackprämie* was introduced in Germany in 2009 as part of the economic stimulus package. It prescribed a 2,500 Euro subsidy for anyone who scrapped his or her (at least ten-year-old) car and bought a new one. It is in fact similar to what is referred to as the Car Allowance Rebate Scheme or 'cash for clunkers' in the USA.

variants ever since, some of which, according to their own self-descriptions, are downright antagonistic toward one another. The Enlightenment and the French Revolution were in this sense midwives of a conservative critique of capitalism, which counter-posed bourgeois society and its contradictions with a romanticised image of feudal-aristocratic relations. In variants resistant to anti-democratic usurpation (mostly socialist), the critique of capitalism has often amounted to little more than a driving force of capitalist modernisation. Its far more dangerous fundamentalist variants (fascistic or Stalinist) have produced systems, both of which liquidated democratic civil societies their differences notwithstanding.[2]

Contemporary sociological critique of capitalism is thus not without historical baggage. Its forefathers, Marx and Weber, can only be cited as critics of capitalism if the history of errors, misdiagnoses, unintended effects and counter-modernisations which were and are entangled with these various programmes of critique in various ways are taken into consideration and reflected upon at least to some rudimentary extent. In this sense, sociological critique of capitalism not only operates in a 'post-socialist situation', but must also be able to give a reflected account of what it has learnt from its own past. This is all the more true if it not only asserts a claim to improve capitalism, but also calls the system as a whole into question. Particularly in times of crisis, the so-called *Systemfrage* (the 'system question') separates the 'good' (because useful) from the 'bad' (because dysfunctional) critiques of capitalism. In the current systemic crisis, as an article in *Die Zeit* accurately remarks, the 'decay of the world of communist states and thought ... represents the true guarantor of survival for the ailing capitalism of our day.' 'However, it would be disastrous', it reads further, 'if that were to remain the only guarantor. Historical memory fades; and if the situation worsens, socialism may end up appearing as the more humane alternative'.[3]

Moderate critique(s) of capitalism, as a metaphorical 're-insurance' against the feared rebirth of socialism, usually culminate in denunciations of the 'neo-feudal mindset' of greedy managers and call for regulatory state measures to restore lost faith in the system. If the more radical critique of capitalism appears in bourgeois publications at all – and it does so especially if it celebrates the supposed ineffectiveness of protests, or the absence of alternatives presented by social movements and organisations critical of capitalism – it remains mostly confined to the reviews section.[4] In

---

2 Cf. U. Rödel, G. Frankenberg, H. Dubiel, *Die demokratische Frage*, Frankfurt 1989.

3 J. Jessen, 'Wut ohne Empfänger', in *Die Zeit*, 2 April 2009, p. 1.

4 Indeed, even a critic as thoughtful as Robert Misik actually believes to have found evidence of an alleged 'end of history' even during the system's crisis due to

a public sphere structured in such a manner, sociological critique of capitalism must operate carefully and, more important still, self-reflexively. It must bow neither to the taboos set by the newspaper columnists nor to the pseudo-radicalism of some feature writers. In short, what a social-scientific critique of capitalism requires is more than the immanent standard of the corresponding capitalist order of legitimation; it requires its own *cité* (or theoretical 'polis'[5]), which renders the coordinates of the respective programmes of critique transparent to the addressees. Without being able to live up to such a claim systematically, I would nevertheless like to at least elucidate the perspective from which I approach Hartmut Rosa's and Stephan Lessenich's critiques of capitalism.

Both authors claim – Rosa explicitly, Lessenich more subtly – to be transcending the confines of an immanent critique of capitalism. What is noticeable is that both contributions presuppose a core capitalist structure, which is nevertheless mostly obscured from analysis over the course of their subsequent argumentation. In one sense this seems to be perfectly logical for a reflexive critique of capitalism, as many attempts at a reconstruction of a critique of political economy in the style of Marx (as had indeed briefly become an academic fashion following the movements of 1968) got lost in economic dead ends. In times in which Marxian orthodoxy has been replaced by 'blind flying' as far as a capacity for critical economic analysis is concerned, the abandonment of a more detailed inspection of socio-economic structures becomes a theoretical problem.

Owing to the fact that economic processes, forms of work and production, and property and ownership relations no longer feature in Rosa's and Lessenich's programmes of critique – or when they do, only as evidence of the respective core theorem – this 'presupposed' capitalism appears as an 'engine of activation and acceleration', yet it remains unclear why, how, for what purpose and by whom this acceleration and activation takes place, or, for that matter, who is in fact being accelerated and activated. Accordingly, the critiques are in this sense less radical than the authors themselves claim. Should the limitations of both theoretical programmes be illuminated in the following, then it is my own willingness to learn that serves as the primary motivation for any critical remarks. For in contrast to the market orthodoxy responsible to a large extent for the finance-capitalist disaster of our time, the theorems of acceleration and activation represent approaches that

---

a lack of major system alternatives, i.e., the lack of alternatives *proves* the end of history.

5 [Trans. Note] To Boltanski, the term *polis* (in French: *cité*) comprises a specific logic of justification in order to justify, so to speak, the hierarchies of humans or objects.

partly compete with, yet in their central objectives are nevertheless compatible with, the *Landnahme* thesis I espouse. Any remarks by my co-authors concerning their conceptualisation of capitalism, diagnosis of the times, and possible alternatives are thus evaluated with the aim of exploring overlapping elements and commonalities with a project aiming at a revitalisation – and above all a sociological grounding and expansion – of critical political economy.

1. Capitalism in the Spiral of Acceleration

In his remarkable theory of acceleration, Hartmut Rosa combines a communitarian motive with a quite original critique of alienation. Capital's system-immanent drive toward acceleration, so claims the hypothesis, has surpassed a critical threshold beyond which it begins to collide with the standards of a 'good life' so entrenched in individuals. In fact, the contemporary regime of capitalist acceleration calls the notion of a successful life into question in such a fundamental way that the former becomes increasingly dysfunctional for late modern capitalism as a whole. Capital's 'dromological drive toward acceleration' (Elmar Altvater) undermines the rationality of a system grounded in competition and the pursuit of profit, as it is no longer capable of ensuring the fulfilment of the 'fundamental promise of modernity': the individual and collective increase in autonomy. Since it becomes more and more difficult to realise one's plans for a successful life in late modernity, what emerges is a kind of mega-social pathology which we are all exposed to in one way or another. Not only has capitalism finally become an end in itself, but the resources of meaning which for a long time served to motivate people to participate in this 'absurd system' (Boltanski and Chiapello) are drying up. With respect to our daily lives, the system's failure becomes obvious even before we begin to identify specific injustices. It is therefore the essential task of a sociological critique of capitalism to expose the structural causes for the collective absence of a successful life (as promised by capitalist modernity). This can begin by addressing the discrepancies and frictions that emerge between institutionalised principles and the actual praxis of everyday life.

As he sets out on his endeavour, Rosa the theoretician of acceleration becomes a kind of hunter and gatherer, so to speak. Each and every theoretical building block and empirical phenomenon that can 'somehow' be incorporated into his diagnosis of acceleration is deployed. This creates the impression of a universal theory to which all of us can relate. Whether it be the purchase of CDs one will not even listen for lack of time, or the 'flexible wave riding' of young people who seize opportunities wherever and whenever they emerge without expecting control of the general direction of their lives[6] – just about anything appears as an expression of the single great pathology generated by a capitalist acceleration that has spiralled out of control.

Without doubt, the idea as such is magnificent and by all means has something subversive about it. In its quest for empirical evidence in proximity to the everyday world, critique of capitalism seems to require neither any particular subject nor any specific objects, as the consequences of the overarching social pathology appear omnipresent. Indeed, even in the CD section of a department store does the consumer find traces of his or her alienated life.

But does this alone make him or her a critic of capitalism? As much as Hartmut Rosa may wish for this to be the case, the reader's force of reason clearly overwhelms the force of his or her romantic hopes. Upon closer inspection, what is supposedly the greatest strength of Rosa's acceleration theorem – the ability to interpret and, where appropriate, criticise just about any everyday phenomenon – turns out to be its greatest weakness as well. The reasons for this are to be found in the theory itself. With view to the construction of its terminological logic, the acceleration theorem is based on a reductionist – in fact severely limited – understanding of capitalism. Building on Max Weber, Hartmut Rosa defines capitalism as a 'fateful force' that creates its own economic subjects.[7] Capitalism, he continues, is therefore a specific regime of rational life conduct which concentrates its internal driving forces, namely fear and promise, on economic activity, which is why it is 'thoroughly determined by the capitalist logic of production (and consumption)'. Hartmut Rosa believes he can dispense with a more detailed analysis of structures of production and capital accumulation because he has (allegedly) identified two universal principles of dynamisation that stand 'behind' internal capitalist tensions and ultimately constitute that 'fateful force' (capitalism) in the first place. This force 'imposes ... a common trajectory of development' on social relations as well as on social subjects, whether a one-Euro jobber or the head of *Deutsche Bank*. These are 'the *principle of growth*, on the one hand, and the *logic of acceleration* on the other'.[8] Interlinked through the 'bicycle principle' of capital accumulation, they are subject to a culture, and structure, defining the logic of escalation, which in turn produces the social pathologies so typical of our times.[9]

6   Rosa, pp. 92–3 in this volume.
7   See chapter 3 in this volume.
8   Rosa, p. 76 in this volume.
9   Rosa, p. 78 in this volume.

Of course, one can hardly dispute that the acceleration of economic and social processes represents a constitutive feature of capitalist developmental dynamic. But as soon as we approach the principle of growth, we must specify what should grow: goods and services, surplus value, profits, or earnings? None of these are identical, as, for instance, the financial oligarchies often achieve their greatest earnings in phases of weak growth in the real economy. Nevertheless, such complications, to which many more could be added, are not decisive in this context. Far more relevant in terms of a theoretical strategy is how Hartmut Rosa seeks to decouple the two 'principles of dynamisation' of an under-analysed capital accumulation from capitalism's contradictory, crisis-prone, concrete historical development. To Rosa, principles of acceleration and growth appear as formative features that remain intact throughout all historical phases of development and manifestations of capitalism. From this point of departure Hartmut Rosa – in an abrupt *volte-face* – sets out to jettison the larger part of what twentieth-century critical analysis of capitalism has achieved. This theoretician of acceleration considers the notion that there are 'worlds' between Manchester Capitalism, Fordism and flexible post-Fordism to be a 'blatant misdiagnosis' as far as the continuity of the formative principles of dynamisation is concerned. He sees the origin of this misdiagnosis in a decades-long 'overemphasis' of capitalism's internal contradictions, that is to say, 'the divisions, tensions, and separations between classes and strata, between economic and political systems, or between the more developed and the "backward" states'.[10]

With this device Hartmut Rosa intentionally abandons all analyses, diagnoses, strengths and errors of a theoretical type that interpret capitalist development as inherently contradictory, as well as socially and politically contested. In lieu of antagonistic or at least opposing logics of socialisation as is common in the Marxian type of theory (the political economy of capital versus the political economy of labour), we find the one-dimensionality of a trans-historical spiral of acceleration, which 'we all' are ultimately at the mercy of – regardless of class, strata, status or gender. Though this one-dimensionality of analysis and critique by all means adheres to the tradition of a critical theory which – confronted with fascism as well as authoritarian influences within the working classes themselves – emerged as a kind of Lukácsian Marxism without a proletariat,[11] Rosa – without considering the strengths and weaknesses of his forebears – now follows this principle of construction in a way that ends up throwing the baby out with the bathwater not once, but several times.

The basic assumption that the 'fateful force' called capitalism is based

---

10   Rosa, p. 76 in this volume.
11   Cf. R. Wiggershaus, *Die Frankfurter Schule*, München 1989.

on principles of rational life conduct, the dynamisation of which results in the spiral of acceleration, already shows the *aporiae* of this one-dimensional principle of construction. As I have attempted to convey with reference to Bourdieu, the appropriation of those calculative patterns of behaviour and thought that enable market-appropriate conduct in the first place require certain historical preconditions. The practice of, for example, strategies for mastering competition, can only take place if the competitors have sufficient resources and planning security at their disposal to actually develop an awareness of the future that renders it worthwhile to engage in competitive activity in the first place. On this rather basic level we already find an inherent contradictoriness in the rational life conduct of capitalist economic subjects, which, in contrast to what Marx had believed, actually pre-dates the form-specific contradiction between collective production and private-capitalist appropriation. Functioning competition in a way always presupposes its opposite. On the flipside, the expansion and generalisation of commodity relations and competition creates a systemic need for non-market-tailored yet simultaneously market-stabilising institutions and modes of behaviour – an opposition which, mediated through crises, social struggles and political compromises, develops into an essential form of movement in capitalist formations. Rosa's principles of dynamisation, growth and acceleration do not at all exist 'behind' this form of movement; neither do they possess any kind of materiality beyond this contradictoriness.

Acceleration, as we would say with respect to processes of innovation driven by the hunt for extra profits, for example, can only function because in other respects – say, in the production of knowledge relevant to innovation – there are spaces of autonomy which are at least temporarily exempt from the spiral of acceleration. By ignoring this competition between different rationalities that has always existed in capitalism, in favour of a supposed one-dimensionality, Rosa deprives himself of the opportunity to analytically reflect upon the sequence of qualitatively different time regimes, as well as the struggles around shorter working hours[12] that are fought out within these regimes.[13] Just as all cats are grey by night, so is capitalism always capitalism. As an aside, this claim (which surely has some truth to it) rests on a reductionist concept of efficiency ('output per time unit') that lies in unsettling proximity to concepts of efficiency found in market orthodoxy. Simplified understandings of what passes as economically viable, however, collide with the fact that those capitalisms which possess 'decelerating' institutions that

---

12   Still worth reading: O. Negt, *Lebendige Arbeit, enteignete Zeit*, Frankfurt a.M., New York 1986.

13   This deviates slightly from the comprehensive acceleration study (cf. H. Rosa, *Social Acceleration: A New Theory of Modernity*, New York 2013).

limit profits and are based on tedious compromise-building (co-determination, collective bargaining, etc.) have proven to be particularly economically and socially productive for decades.

By casting aside institutional differences, Hartmut Rosa surrenders, in terms of theory, the search for scopes of action within capitalism as well as the system's mechanisms of self-stabilisation. His analysis thus becomes increasingly blurred, as time is no longer defined as the measure of value creation and productivity, but as a 'factor of production'. To me, this categorical error does not appear to be coincidental. Once time becomes the actual substance and materiality of capitalist development, one no longer has to deal analytically with the world of work in any greater detail – the social question, struggles around distribution, the de-privileging, the inequalities or the injustices. Admittedly, Hartmut Rosa does concede: 'not only have poverty, material destitution and extreme inequality *not* been fundamentally overcome' (Why have they not, by the way? K.D.), 'in the western societies they are even in the ascendancy once again'.[14] The author at least deems this 'important', yet the actual meaning of the word 'importance' stands in stark contrast to the status the phenomena are granted in Rosa's theoretical structure. Though they are present and must be taken into consideration, what weighs much 'heavier', at least according to his main trivialising argument, is the loss of sovereignty resulting from the hypertrophic pressure of acceleration and growth.

The irritating aspect about this argument is its exclusivity. To use Boltanski's and Chiapello's terminology, Hartmut Rosa one-sidedly and needlessly casts in his lot with an artistic critique – moreover, one that is quite constricted. As a result, the limited understanding of capitalism in its temporal substantiation exhibits an odd imbalance in favour of an allegedly universal problematic of alienation, and ultimately results in a self-restriction of critical intervention. The eminently inspirational and astute analysis of the 'attack of the present on all remaining time' (Alexander Kluge) and on, as one feels compelled to add, the remaining social space, suffers from the fact that it tends to consciously sacrifice all terminology with the aid of which the crises, relations of exploitation, inequalities and power asymmetries that are inherent to contemporary capitalism could really be expressed in the first place. Accordingly, that modern social pathology produced by the late modern spiral of acceleration in Rosa's understanding culminates in something Ulrich Beck has termed 'democratic *Allbetroffenheit*'[15] with view to the

---

14   Rosa, p. 89 in this volume.

15   [Trans. Note] *Allbetroffenheit* is a term that is not easily translated, hence the German term is used throughout the text. It literally means the 'affectedness of all', the 'impact on everyone', or something that concerns us all.

global ecological danger.[16] All of us, whether banker or one-Euro jobber, are 'somehow' victims of the *diktat* of growth and acceleration. But since we all – the Ackermanns of the world, as well as those who criticise capitalism in letters to the editor – also 'somehow' participate in that dynamic of growth and acceleration, Rosa's critique of capitalism ultimately leaves us perplexed and, worse, lacking a grasp of the practical consequences. The programme of critique seems radical because it claims to have identified a destructive dynamic of escalation 'behind' the internal contradictions and social cleavages of the capitalist formation itself. Meanwhile, detached as it is from the sphere of power asymmetries, conflicting interests and political conflicts, this supposedly fundamental critique of capitalism threatens to morph into a mere uneasiness concerning the culture of acceleration as it has surfaced in numerous conservative social analyses in a similar fashion. The intriguing idea that progressive politics must challenge the conservatives in the field of anti-progressive deceleration and attack economic liberalism as acceleration totalitarianism thus receives an essentially affirmative character. The only adequate counter-measure against acceleration totalitarianism may be, as one could deduce from Rosa's text, a binding normative framework for a 'good life'. But how is sociological deliberation to discover such a framework? If interests and concepts of justice are already culturally preinformed, then what can we say about the variants of a good, successful life? And who is to not only put forward such a framework, but also enforce it? Could this be the sociological headmaster, as accomplice to and pontiff of an authoritarian politico-economic value-imposing elite (*Wertelite*[17])? I am neither able nor willing to believe that such a theoretician as brilliant Hartmut Rosa would truly adopt such a standpoint.

2. CAPITALISM AS AN ENGINE OF ACTIVATION

In order to deflect any conservative-authoritarian cooptation, Hartmut Rosa could, for instance, productively explore a logic of contradiction in reference to Claus Offe's early theory of late capitalism, as suggested by Stephan Lessenich. My colleague and co-author analyses capitalism as an engine of

---

16   Cf. U. Beck, *Risk Society: Towards a New Modernity*, London 2005 [1992], p. 36.

17   [Trans. Note] in economic sociology, the term *Wertelite* (value elite) denotes a minority group which due to special social, intellectual or political qualities distinguishes itself from the majority of a society based on a generally accepted set of values, and whose decisions and conduct are perceived to be value-asserting or even value-imposing, and thus structurally influence the society's development.

activation. Over the course of his analysis, he develops an understanding of capitalism that – particularly with regard to the idea of how elements 'alien to the system' are adapted – exhibits parallels to the *Landnahme* thesis. However, Lessenich's analysis places its emphasis beyond the realms of economy and labour, focusing instead on the welfare state and state activity. In terms of clarity and originality, the basic pattern of the argument resembles that of Rosa's. To begin with, Lessenich reconstructs Claus Offe's theorem of late capitalism, which states that capitalism can only develop because expanding market socialisation is simultaneously facilitated and reined in by an institutional order produced by the state. In the late capitalist stage of development this institutional order has assumed the form of the welfare state. This welfare state responds to 'the 'anarchic' mechanisms of capital movement with a programme of conscious regulation and targeted control'.[18] As the state, in its problem-processing capacity, absorbs the self-contradictoriness of capitalist movement (problems of the second order), it produces new problems (of the third order), which in turn require further processing.

Stephan Lessenich therefore locates the fundamental problematic of the welfare state in a kind of oscillating movement between requirements of economic competition and democratic legitimacy. If the demands on the welfare state grow too great – as do the amount of resources withdrawn from private capital valorisation (*Verwertung*) in order to meet these demands – the familiar criticisms of the expansive, bureaucratic and performance-diminishing welfare state are triggered. If, however, the promises of the welfare state fail to meet the expectations of its addressees over a longer period of time, the welfare state's legitimacy in the democratic arena comes under threat. This fundamental contradictoriness constitutes late capitalism's specificity: on the one hand, it cannot do without those 'measures that are essentially incompatible with the system' of welfare-state integration; neither can it live with them (at least not without noticeable turbulence). In this sense, the crisis of welfare-state capitalism becomes a permanent condition. Unable to solve the problems of control associated with the capitalist economy, the state, in its interventions, repeatedly resorts to measures that in turn create new problems of control and functionality. Since it is more or less undisputed that that which Claus Offe had in mind in terms of structural problem-solving – a transformation of state and society leading to the dominance of non-capitalist principles of rationality – is more or less out of the question, the only remaining 'system-immanent' strategy is an ongoing 'muddling through', the 'search for a happy medium: a degree of democracy

---

18   Lessenich, p. 111 in this volume.

that is compatible with the functionality of the capitalist economy and, by association, the capitalist system's ability to regulate'.[19]

To be clear: I consider Lessenich's and Offe's basic idea of capitalist movement – as interplay between the requirements of capitalist valorisation, welfare-state intervention and democratic legitimation – to be analytically fruitful. To me it seems perfectly suited for developing at least a partial explanation of changes in the modus operandi of capitalist *Landnahmen*; that is to say, of the transitions from predominantly market-opening to primarily market-restricting state interventions. What renders the two of us somewhat 'kindred spirits' is our aspiration to attain a 'critique of the functional logic of capitalism'[20] that takes its cues from Marx. Yet I nevertheless remain sceptical of the attempt to combine the theorem of late capitalism with an analysis and critique of the active society as found in Foucault. For it is only at the cost of inconsistencies that a functional analysis of capitalism oriented along systemic contradictions can be combined with a theoretical agenda that considers these very systemic contradictions to have been pacified through certain modes of subjectification. In light of this contradiction, in the following I shall defend Lessenich, the theoretician of contradiction against Lessenich, the representative of governmentality studies.

To this end, we should point out beforehand several aspects in need of clarification in the context of a (re-)actualisation of the theorem of late capitalism. To begin with, it is striking that, in Lessenich's minimal definition, the conceptualisation of capitalism also remains oddly reductionist. Building on Marx's formula of simple circulation, the 'principle of movement' is identified as the fundamental constitutive and functional principle of the capitalist economic mode. 'Capitalism is thus necessarily and in principle a social formation of permanent movement.'[21] Without explicitly being defined as such, movement is presented here as being essentially some trans-historical underlying principle of the capitalist order. What is still conceded at the outset – the movement's direction towards the goal of M' – is then gradually abandoned over the course of the subsequent argument. The constitutive relations of power and class, which according to Marx define the extent of the formal determinacy of capitalist movement, do not even appear in Lessenich's basic definition of capitalism. Furthermore, the political economy of capital, as a structurally crisis-prone form of movement, class division and exploitation of labour power, is not addressed in any detail. The self-contradictoriness of capitalism appears at best as a process of 'liberation' and '(re-)enclosure' of labour power.

---

19   Lessenich, p. 117 in this volume.
20   Lessenich, p. 103 in this volume.
21   Lessenich, p. 104 in this volume.

Presumably this occurs because Stephan Lessenich wishes to build his thesis of an emerging 'active social formation'[22] terminologically. However, in the section of his argument that deals with late capitalism, the equation of capitalism with the rather vague principle of 'permanent movement' has the effect of shifting the contradictoriness of the capitalist formation more or less exclusively to the functional domain of the state and politics. Owing perhaps not least to the specific research focus of each of this book's authors, it is henceforth the problems of the 'second' and 'third' order that are relevant to the critic of activation. The price one has to pay for this initially innovative shift in meaning is the restriction of the object of analysis. Contradictions in the capitalist accumulation regime can only be perceived as contradictions within state activities; the subject matter at hand is ineluctably – also – that of politically constructed contradictions. And although this basic idea does indeed exhibit parallels to the *Landnahme* theorem, what again is irritating here is the gesture of exclusivity – although somewhat more discrete in contrast to Rosa – with which Lessenich presents his argument. Where capitalist contradictions are always already 'statist' and 'political', there is no real need to ask questions about which social interests lie behind the political forms of processing these contradictions, for these interests are – like their corresponding positions of social status – themselves politically predetermined.

This over-politicisation of capitalist contradictions is both grave and highly consequential, for in Lessenich's analysis the welfare state appears as a more or less neutral instance, which in its activities oscillates back and forth between the horizons of legitimation of both the economy and democracy. At this point we can discern the downside of dismissing a socio-structural determination and localisation of collective interests (even if in opposition to one another) – the accommodation of which becomes part and parcel of the state's activity. The author does concede that the self-contradictoriness of capital accumulation is incorporated into the state's activity, yet one would have been keen to find out more about how exactly this happens and what its outcomes are. The same is true with view to 'state actors' and the nexus of action they constitute. What exactly is the state in its materiality, which aspects about it are 'capitalist', and which are 'alien to the system'? For the sake of precision, the author could have, for example, expanded on the debate around the state that has been the subject of intense exchanges in western Marxism. Antonio Gramsci's concept of the 'integral state', which grasps the consensus-building of civil society as a process of hegemony-creation beyond the repressive state, or even the approach of a Nicos

---

22   Lessenich, p. 138 in this volume.

Poulantzas, who analyses capitalist state apparatuses as fiercely contested arenas and as distillations of power relations, may represent suitable points of departure.

The advantage of a material definition of the state and state activity would be an opportunity to analytically systematise the simple insight that asymmetries of social power influence state activity, even and particularly in western democracies. After all, the economic elites or, more precisely: the owners of the means of production and top managers, still represent highly influential groups, in the mass democracies as well; thanks to their capital resources they are in a position to effectively subvert or even prevent any curtailments of their (economic) freedom. They are able, for instance, to 'relocate means of production, to abstain from investment, to divest monetary capital, to commit tax evasion'[23] and thereby create problems of legitimacy for the welfare state, precisely at the latter's interface with the economy. Moreover, they are capable of 'harnessing the media and advertising' for their agendas, and of 'besieging the population and the public with propaganda for their positions', they are able, in short, to influence the political class – even if this is accomplished primarily through legal omissions and non-decisions,[24] as was practised for a long time in the case of the yet-to-be-established regulation of financial markets. In this sense, the economic elites usually influence the – autonomous, because bureaucratically mediated – activity of the state far more than the interests of subaltern groups ever could. This observation, however, is not only valid for the interface between state and economic lobbying, but can also be applied to arenas of direct democratic decision-making.

Nevertheless, and on this I fully agree with Stephan Lessenich, the state – let alone the democratic welfare state – can by no means be regarded as a mere executive committee in the hands of the ruling class; neither is it entirely at odds with capitalism. The welfare-state elements that are 'alien to the system' have been forced upon capitalism, over the course of a long history of social conflicts, by (workers') movements 'from below' and by pre-emptive social reforms 'from above'. What appears in retrospect, as Lessenich himself admits, as a functional necessity – that is to say, the development of an institutional order which also has a de-commodifying effect – is a real product of social struggles and the political regulation of social interests, which can be traced back to social regularities and structures, but which under no circumstances can be treated as historical inevitabilities. In

---

23 A. Demirović, 'Wirtschaftsdemokratie, Rätedemokratie und freie Kooperation. Einigevorläufige Überlegungen', in *Widerspruch: Beiträge zur sozialistischen Politik* 55, 2008, pp. 55–67, here: p. 58.
24 Ibid.

this context, it is surprising that Lessenich dismisses an analysis of heterodox sources of power almost entirely; in other words, he eludes the tedious
and contradictory process of incorporating collective labour interests – a
process which underlies not only welfare state formation as such, but also
the divergent manifestations of its different models.

Consequently, the welfare state's two figures of reference, namely the
capitalist economy and democracy, remain relatively abstract; their respective specific forms of movement are effectively left unanalysed. At this point
we stumble across another weakness: explicitly stating an orientation along
the Marxian critique of capitalism, Stephan Lessenich claims to go beyond
'the intellectual horizon of ... contemporaries who tend toward conservativism – including that of intellectual "normal critique" and, in terms of
functional logic as well as genealogy, to develop categories of change, of
overcoming and of resistance.[25] Notwithstanding, and in contrast to earlier
works, Lessenich already falls behind this claim in his definition of the
welfare state and its crises. The basic principle of antagonistic socialisation is
not elucidated. This basic principle stems to a large extent from the process
of turning what has been wrested from economic and political elites – frequently in fierce conflicts – into a functional component of the system. Yet
capitalism also has to pay a price for successful integration, as is illustrated,
for instance, by the institutionalisation of workers' power. Since the contradictoriness and fragility of integration processes remains categorically
underexposed, it remains unclear what in fact constitutes the conservatism
of sociological 'normal critique'. Is it the underestimation of progressive
potentials ultimately inherent to capitalist development? And if so, what is
the measure of such supposed progress? The development of the technical forces of production? 'Social progress', as regulation theory calls it? Or
could it perhaps be the expansion of the capitalist promise of freedom? The
author leaves these questions unanswered. Consequently, capitalist movement appears as an attempt to 'square the circle'; the welfare state remains
permanently trapped in its oscillating movement between the accommodation of functional requirements of capital accumulation on one side, and the
need for democratic legitimacy on the other.

If this sounds like an (perhaps somewhat modified) 'eternal recurrence',
one cannot help but wonder how something new is supposed to result from
this circular movement. At this point, Stephan Lessenich takes a decisive
theoretical step. What is new to him is not the welfare state's oscillating
movement 'on the edges of systemic and social integration.[26] Within the
paradigm of late capitalism, the breaking apart of the Keynesian state can

---

25 Lessenich, p. 103 in this volume.
26 Lessenich, p. 115 in this volume.

most certainly be read as the end of a 'heroic welfare state', with an agenda that contained 'more than it could handle'.[27] What really are new are the forms of processing or dealing with this process, which Lessenich refers to as the 'subjectification of the social'.[28] If Offe had a more or less functioning, organised capitalism in mind, which exhibited a seemingly inherent perspective of socialist transformation due to functional elements 'incompatible with the system' and the irreversible politicisation of contradictions, the 'subjectification of the social' is now designed to describe and explain the reconstruction of welfare-state regulation as it set in during the crisis of Fordist capitalism. Theoretically, Lessenich bases himself on Foucault and governmentality studies in this aspect. His core argument is that the 'active social formation' bases itself on a capitalist 'rule of freedom' (Foucault)[29]: that state responsibility is replaced by individual self-reliance, public responsibility for security by private responsibility, and collective risk management by private risk management. Yet the activities of a self that is heroicised in such a way, which certain guiding images call for and which certain social publics celebrate, all represent activities on behalf of a 'higher cause', in the spirit of the common good, which is in turn why Lessenich wishes to call the new regime not *neo-liberal*, but – in my view not particularly convincingly – *neo-social*.

It is not least the success of this pattern of argument that proves it possesses substantial potential for a diagnosis of the times. However, I cannot help but doubt that it is capable of a comprehensive analytical penetration and radical criticism of the new capitalist formation's mode of domination and control. I would like to summarise my main objections in several points. To begin with, I dispute that the new regime is in fact built on a network-based *polis*. What is far more likely, in theoretical and empirical terms, is that we are witnessing a shift of borders between market control and hierarchical coordination.[30] Network participation may well be an important component of the new regime; however, it does not restrict mobility and is not capable of constituting a 'rule of freedom'. This is achieved primarily through the

---

27   Lessenich, p. 124 in this volume. Of course, it would have to be clarified as to what this 'too much' to handle consists of. After all, the austerity programmes that were implemented over the past years, as 'inevitable' practical constraints imposed by globalisation, appear downright ridiculous in the light of government rescue packages for ailing banks and private companies that followed them.

28   Lessenich, p. 131 in this volume.

29   Lessenich, p. 107 in this volume.

30   Cf. G. Wagner, 'Ein neuer Geist des Kapitalismus? Paradoxien der Selbstverantwortung', in Österreichische Zeitschrift für Soziologie32, 2007, pp. 3–24; K. Dörre, B. Röttger, *Das neue Marktregime*, Hamburg 2003; D. Sauer, *Arbeit im Übergang*, Hamburg 2005.

internalisation of market mechanisms within companies, welfare-state institutions, schools and universities. Even though these markets are often only fictional or staged, the competition-based mode of control still takes effect *qua* abstraction. The diffuse power of the market seems anonymous, impersonal, impalpable. It is precisely this – in the words of Hartmut Rosa – supposed 'fateful force' of competition which exerts, as a subjective pendant, a peculiarly radicalised 'coercion toward self-constraint' (Elias), the ideological evocation of which may indeed be perceived as liberation, since it provides justification for self-assertion in the processes of competition. In other words, the ideological reinforcement of market coercion may have a subjectively relieving effect because it frees the individual subject from any excessive consideration of others. After all, anyone who disregards the compulsion to be free constantly runs the risk of one day finding themselves on the losing side of the equation.

If this objection is still compatible with Lessenich's activation thesis, then the second point of criticism touches upon the substance of the argument itself. As a consequence of his orientation towards governmentality studies, my colleague is essentially asking for all the problems of a theoretical method whose endpoints are precisely not what it professes to achieve: an adequate analysis of subjectivities in post-Fordist capitalism. The reasons for this are for the most part intrinsic to the theory itself. Interested primarily in the reconstruction of an almost perfect-seeming disciplinary mechanism, governmentality studies systematically overestimate the new regime's promise of freedom. What is indeed and without a doubt an analytical step forward compared to, say, the formula of hegemony deployed almost indiscriminately these days, is that these studies do elucidate, in part even convincingly, consensus-building within the market regime and partially even its discursive breakpoints – via the re- and deconstruction of guiding images such as the 'entrepreneurial self'. Nevertheless, governmentality studies remain one-sided and over-simplified with a view to the proclaimed goal of an analysis of modes of subjectification. This is due not only to the fact that the relevant protagonists refrain from an empirical verification of their theses on subjectification[31] – which instead is extracted from self-help literature, management studies, or from blueprints for welfare-state reform – but because the entire approach is based on a theoretically problematic concept of the subject.

Individual and – at a different level of analysis – collective subjects can be depicted as 'historical blocs' in accordance with Gramsci. In their

---

31 Cf. T. Reitz, S. Draheim, 'Schattenboxen im Neoliberalismus. Kritik und Perspektiven der deutschen Foucault-Rezeption', in C. Kaindl (ed.), *Subjekte im Neoliberalismus*, Marburg 2007, pp. 109–22.

common forms of thought, not only the dynamic promises of freedom of an activating market regime are constantly present; the requirements of dynamisation encounter action and thought patterns which Bourdieu quite fittingly described as forms of habitus, as a 'structuring structure' which affects class consciousness. The habitus, in the sense of an incorporated history, incessantly adjusts individuals' and social groups' modes of action to the requirements of respective social fields. This preserving and somewhat bulky aspect of habitus can have an impact far beyond its own conditions of emergence, yet is systematically neglected in post-structuralist concepts of the subject that build on Foucault. Despite all relativisations and interesting insights, Stephan Lessenich does not rectify this shortcoming.

This categorical weakness – with its over-emphasis on the dynamic moment supposedly found in ideologies of legitimation – distorts the diagnosis of the times. What is postulated as novel in the guiding images of the market-based justificatory regime, as well as in its ideology-critical deconstruction, then, is presented in circular argumentation as the 'total reality' of flexible capitalism. The problematic of such theorisation has already been revealed and criticised in sociological debates numerous times. Let us take one prominent example: the ideal type of the 'labour force entrepreneur'[32] may have at one point been profoundly eye-opening as a critical reconstruction of the guiding image of capitalist rationalisation; the empirical proof of this supposedly new 'basic form of labour force usage', however, turns out to be quite disappointing. This does not stop the creators of this ideal type from explaining away the limited empirical relevance of the labour force entrepreneur with (a merely) rudimentary enforcement of the new mode of production. Having become immune to any kind of empirical criticism as a result, it is then fairly easy to attack the demands for job security of employees and their organisations as traditionalist and backwards, as they are (so runs the argument) cleaving to a capitalist formation that is ultimately doomed. Numerous critiques have addressed the inconsistencies of such patterns of argument, the appeal of which rests on little more than an inadmissible theoretical generalisation of empirical observations.[33]

The crux of Stephan Lessenich's welfare state–tailored diagnosis of subjectification is that, by adapting and applying the outlined pattern of argument,

---

32 G. G. Voß, H. J. Pongratz, 'Der Arbeitskraftunternehmer. Eine neue Grundform der "Ware Arbeitskraft"?', in *Kölner Zeitschrift für Soziologie und Sozialpsychologie*50(1),1998, pp. 131–51.

33 Cf. B. Aulenbacher, 'Subjektivierung von Arbeit. Ein hegemonialer industriesoziologischer Topos und was die feministische Arbeitsforschung und Gesellschaftsanalyse dazu zu sagen haben', in K. Lohr, H. M. Nickel (eds), *Subjektivierung von Arbeit*, Münster 2005, pp. 34–64.

it inevitably adopts its immanent weaknesses as well. With respect to the self-immunisation of his theorem, however, Lessenich does venture beyond similar analyses in one very important aspect. He believes he can confront the discrepancies between guiding image and empirically comprehensible reality by pointing out an 'order of knowledge', in which thinking about and developing knowledge of themselves as potentially active becomes a permanent challenge for individual subjects[34] – a challenge they can ultimately only fail at. In a similar vein to Hartmut Rosa, the critic thus grasps a central pathology – or rather, a contradictoriness – of the late capitalist regime. He elaborates quite elegantly how the regime proclaims a general mobilisation in the name of a higher cause while simultaneously depriving subjects of the resources that would be (and are) vital to meeting those mobility demands. In my view, the analysis and critique could have been significantly more radical in this aspect. At this point, however, I would like to avoid countering theoretical arguments with empirical findings. I will permit myself only one brief remark: to this day, subject-oriented research on precarisation has provided a plethora of evidence casting doubt on the notion that the integrative achievement of the post-Fordist activation regime can really be primarily attributed to an internalisation of the promise of freedom, to the 'compulsion to be free'. If anything, this may only be the case for groups endowed with abundant cultural and/or financial resources. Thus for large parts of the population (and not only the precarised and excluded) the silent compulsion – to some extent politically constructed – posed by market risks is bound to dominate perspectives on freedom.[35] One comes to terms with the regime – begrudgingly, reluctantly, due more than anything to a lack of subjectively realistic alternatives – which, as in the case of the labour market, increasingly employs the 'visible hand' of political coercion in order to 'motivate' subjects to activity under the flexible mode of production. This simple fact is reflected in Lessenich's 'subjectification of the social', albeit insufficiently. In his attempt to distinguish his own critique from over-simplified criticisms of neo-liberal spending cuts, Lessenich fails to depict clearly and precisely the political changes in direction which have – as exemplified in the case of labour market policy, but visible throughout society – instigated a veritable paradigm shift. This new course accomplishes the abandonment of a mode of control based more on the sharing of productivity increases and the search for socially integrative compromises, and shifts to a disciplinary regime of a market girded with the armour of political compulsion. From the perspective of a political economy of labour, phenomena such as the

---

34 See chapter 4 in this volume.
35 On this cf. R. Castel, K. Dörre, (eds), *Prekarität, Abstieg, Ausgrenzung*, Frankfurt a.M., New York 2009.

above-average (in Europe) expansion of a precarious and low-wage sector, and the dramatic erosion of wage and security standards for large groups of 'ordinary' wage earners in Germany, can be definitively identified as a backward step for workers' interests, without falling into trivial nostalgia. This is the result of (at least in the German case) a competitive-corporatist agenda that has defined this step backwards as a necessary adjustment of national economies to the – alleged – practical constraints of global financial market capitalism. As we now know, the consequences of this shift include not only the devastation of economic structures but also, as Lessenich has correctly pointed out, grotesque *aporiae* of a politically created regime of activation.

The actual process that has lead to these corresponding changes in direction is left unexamined, let alone criticised, despite the proximity of Lessenich's approach to the state. In this sense, the object of critique remains vague. Since the Foucauldian inspection of the subject remains, despite all reassurances, categorically blind to everyday compromises made by real subjects, an endogenous explanation for resistance cannot be provided. Accordingly, Lessenich's critique of the capitalist regime of activation ultimately remains rather tame. This is unintentionally expressed by a categorical indeterminacy. Quite characteristically, Lessenich uses the terms 'contradiction' and 'paradox' almost interchangeably right from the start in the introduction of his contribution. Yet, while the category of *contradiction* always has a determining aspect to it that drives toward resolution, a *paradox* (by contrast, terminology-wise) means that a phenomenon, a movement or a development causes an effect in one particular aspect, which in another aspect involves its exact opposite. In contrast to contradictions, paradoxes do not, or at least not necessarily, push beyond the status quo. It is perhaps no coincidence that a line of argument beginning from an analysis of the contradictory functional logic of capitalist socialisation eventually ends with the paradoxes of the contemporary regime of activation. A perspective 'beyond capitalism' must, as it were, be appended from without. This results from the postulate of being able to think about the 'completely different', which is surely a noble aspiration. For a sociological critique that claims to surpass the borders of system-immanence, however, I still consider the project to be rather vague.

3. PERSPECTIVES OF CRITIQUE

That said, none of my expressed objections discount the value of the critiques of activation and acceleration, respectively. Both programmes of analysis (when taken by themselves) are important, for both identify some surface level phenomena[36] of financial market capitalism quite precisely. Both the bank CEO and the one-Euro jobber would be able to locate themselves within the engine of acceleration and activation. If he were to follow the deeply humanist approach of Hartmut Rosa, even Josef Ackermann, who has long become (through much fault of his own) Germany's populist whipping boy, could consider himself a victim of the system, a subject who has subordinated his life to the *diktat* of an appointments book. Ackermann the human being and citizen may very well be appalled to learn what sorts of behaviour Ackermann the manager deems necessary in leading his company to success. But even then it is hard to imagine that the top banker will decide, perhaps driven by a lingering sense of self-doubt, to team up with the one-Euro jobber to smash capitalism together. In the vein of Stephan Lessenich, one might add that, yes, there are both activators and activated in the active social formation. Lessenich would remind the activating banker that his profit economy simply cannot go on without the much-reviled welfare state. He would also have to turn to the one-Euro jobber and say that a more generous regulation of social transfer payments would quickly overwhelm the system's capacities, as has now been confirmed by even the OECD.

But does that mean we are all sitting in the same boat? Having been pressed through the grindstones of acceleration and activation, at least the author of the letter to the editor has not yet taken the step from illusion engendered by the state to illusion engendered by the self. The passage 'I can't do it any longer, and I don't want to. Capitalism has got to go.' sums up, in a nightmarish way, the essence of the finance-capitalist *Landnahme*. Functioning financial market capitalism has already generated a new form of precarity that provokes radical critique, but also exhausts its critics. Whoever attempts to change, interrupt, or even 'abolish' the engine of acceleration and activation will not be able to ignore this relation. Though analyses centred on culture or the state may be brilliant, they cannot dispense with a theoretical and empirically informed critique of political economy. Numerous late modern or postmodern phenomena – technologically induced 'spatio-temporal compression', the 'liquefaction' of social structures, or the replacement of permanent institutions by the 'fixed-term contract' (Lyotard) as manifested not only in relation to one's occupation but also emotionally, sexually, and culturally – are organically intertwined with a flexible type of capital accumulation. Only the analysis of this leads to the centre of capitalist domination. Conversely, theoretical endeavours which start from the core socio-economic structure of capitalism and take into account the reconstruction of networks of finance-capitalist 'class

---

36   This does not refer to 'superstructural phenomena'. The surface of capitalism is just as relevant as its deep structure; both develop in correlation to one another.

power'[37] will only be able to escape the confines posed by orthodox critique of the economy if they involve the analytical processing of dislocations, contradictions, paradoxes and pathologies created by the engine of acceleration and activation. This assessment implies seeking out commonalities, intersecting and overlapping elements as well as points of connection in the respective theoretical programmes. As indicated earlier, such intersections, reciprocal complementation and specialised critiques exist in large numbers. Spatio-temporal compression, the activating state, flexible accumulation and finance-capitalist *Landnahme* comprise a nexus within which every structuring principle implicates the others and vice versa.

I do not wish to forestall a theoretical *rapprochement*; there is nevertheless one particular aspect in urgent need of clarification. Particularly in times of crisis, the co-optive and downright totalising identification with the 'we' must be forcefully rejected and attacked. However, as even the poststructuralist Chantal Mouffe[38] (of all people!) has pointed out, all those 'third ways' into a 'different modernity' that were regarded as being 'beyond left and right'[39] have failed miserably due to the surrender of distinctions of 'us versus them' and the resulting 'negation of antagonism'. The bank CEOs and one-Euro jobbers of this world are nowhere near being 'in the same boat'. Even a 'we' that is given sociological blessing frequently ends in embarrassment, as it ignores real social antagonisms. A living democracy takes root where antagonisms are rendered visible and fought out. Fulfilling this purpose is a self-evident, yet for a long time grossly neglected, task of both sociological research and critique of capitalism.

---

37   D. Harvey, *A Brief History of Neoliberalism*, 3rd reprint, Oxford, New York 2005, p.74.

38   C. Mouffe, *On the Political*. 1st publ., reprinted, London, New York 2005, p.2.

39   Cf. A. Giddens, *Beyond Left and Right: The Future of Radical Politics*, 1994.

CHAPTER 5

Temporary Workers and Active Citizens: What Is Wrong with Late Modern Capitalism?

HARTMUT ROSA

The authors of this volume unanimously agree on three points: firstly, social critique represents both a vital impulse and an indispensable component of sociology; secondly, such a social critique requires a careful diagnosis of the times; and thirdly, neither in modernity nor in the present day can such a diagnosis of the times do without an analysis of capitalism.

Klaus Dörre and Stephan Lessenich have, each in his own way, attempted to prove that something is fundamentally wrong with our contemporary liberal-capitalist regime. So let us get straight to the point: in my view, it remains unclear in both cases what exactly is *wrong* about the present politico-economic formation. Ever since critique of capitalism has existed, it has adopted one of two forms: either it follows a functionalist line of argument, (as did the later Marx), attempting to show that the system *cannot* continue to function over the long term (at least not without incurring massive dysfunction in other areas of society) due to the crises it produces but is incapable of solving; or the line of argument is normative, making the point that the respective politico-economic regime creates a social reality that can under no circumstances be considered desirable, or rather, ethically defensible. The normative critique can in turn be divided into two subforms. The first employs a *moralistic* argument, that the regime is unjust because it produces winners and losers, opportunities and risks, positions, privileges and goods, as well as status and prestige, thus leading to an unequal and unjust distribution of life opportunities. This moral critique – termed 'social critique' (*Sozialkritik*) by Boltanski and Chiapello[1] – inescapably tends to position different layers, classes or groups in society in opposition to one another; it is often linked to interest-driven positions and emphasises that

---

1 Cf. L. Boltanski, È. Chiapello, 'Die Rolle der Kritik für die Dynamik des Kapitalismus: Sozialkritik versus Künstlerkritik', in M. Miller (ed.), *Welten des Kapitalismus*, Frankfurt a.M., New York 2005, pp. 285–322.

the regime operates to the benefit of one group at the cost of others. These 'others' may include workers, the unemployed, migrants, women, or the countries of the so-called 'Third World'. That said, normative critique may also argue along ethical lines. In this form it focuses less on the lines of social differentiation, opting instead to concentrate on the general character and direction of development of the capitalist social formation, to which it ascribes tendencies toward alienation, reification, the destruction of value and community, the depletion of resources of meaning and even the production of collective 'irrationalities' in relation to individual and collective life conduct. This ethical 'artistic critique' postulates that all people share a kind of collective interest in overcoming this social formation; it views all subjects as being 'affected' by the system and thus places them all, as it were, 'in the same boat'.

What strikes me as problematic in both Dörre's and Lessenich's approaches is that they appear unable to decide which form of critique they wish to pursue. Of course, it is theoretically possible to combine them; the argument against the contemporary capitalist social formation then would read: *firstly*, the formation is not sustainable over the long term, and *secondly*, the formation is unjust. I see nothing stopping us from adding to these two points that, *thirdly*, it systematically makes us unhappy. Indeed, I presume (and hope) that the three authors of this book all harbour and share such radical doubts about the present social formation. Nevertheless, it is crucial to distinguish, in an analytically sound and precise manner, the three forms of critique from one another: what is the respective functional problem, what are the moral criteria and the conditions being subjected to criticism, and what does ethical critique base itself on? Establishing the standards and phenomenological foundations of the latter has always been (and continues to be) notoriously difficult; it is no coincidence that Marx, at least to a certain extent, progressed from the ethical critique of the *Paris Manuscripts* to the moral critique of the *Communist Manifesto* before ultimately arriving at the functional critique found in *Das Kapital*.

Thus, the charge I raise against my co-authors is as follows: both of their critiques are motivated normatively and gain their persuasive power not least from the normative subtext of their respective approaches; yet out of fear of not being able to define their moral (and ethical) criteria, both rely on arguments that are predominantly functional – but, astonishingly, without actually managing to substantiate the dysfunctionality of late modern capitalism in detail. By oscillating between the two possible forms of critique throughout their chapters without ever reconciling said oscillation, they ultimately leave the essential question unanswered: what is wrong with (contemporary) capitalism?

I would now like to lay out the reasons for my objection by engaging with my co-authors' contributions; I will begin with Klaus Dörre's text. Dörre, in a brilliant opening move (and repeatedly at crucial points of his argument), invokes the voice of the unhappy and helpless temporary worker, thereby elevating the suffering of subjects and their implicit indictment to his text's leitmotif, through which he insinuates the perspective of a normative critique of actual existing conditions. This critique strikes me as being of a primarily moral nature; for what the temporary worker in particular laments is his unjust treatment compared to that of permanent employees. But is this really what we are trying to convey: that late modern capitalism is unjust because it creates two distinct classes of wage earners defined not by performance but instead arbitrarily? Could the problem then be solved through some kind of de facto levelling or equalising out of temporary workers and permanent employees as far as wages and legal status are concerned (which, of course, could also be achieved by simply relegating *all* employees to the status of temporary workers)? Does that mean that Fordist capitalism was in fact 'just'? Is Dörre's critique based solely on the fate of those precious few per cent of workers affected by temporary employment? Though he may encourage such a misinterpretation by identifying the essential issue for temporary workers to be the question of 'why capitalism today drives even skilled and qualified information workers into a life of precarity',[2] it would obviously be ludicrous to ascribe such a point of view to him.

Indeed, Dörre supplements the 'social critique' perspective with another facet of 'artistic critique' reminiscent of Richard Sennett's diagnosis of the *corroded character*[3] and of Neckel's and Dröge's critique of the conflation of performance and success[4] in his opening remarks: individual prospects concerning career and income have become unpredictable in the age of late modernity, (job) performance no longer serves as a distinguishing trait, life planning becomes difficult or even impossible. Dörre's protagonist, so it seems, is thus not – at least not primarily – treated unfairly because he earns less than others, but because there is no obvious reason why he earns less and because he has no guarantees or security whatsoever in his long-term life planning. Having said that, such a possibility of ethical critique – which Dörre suggests when he writes about the connection between happiness and security and the dominant concepts of happiness throughout the Fordist

---

2   Dörre, p. 39 in this volume

3   Cf. R. Sennett, *The Corrosion of Character: The Personal Consequences of Work in the New Capitalism*, London, New York 1998.

4   Cf. S. Neckel, K. Dröge, 'Die Verdienste und ihr Preis: Leistung in der Marktgesellschaft', in A. Honneth (ed.), *Befreiung aus der Mündigkeit*, Frankfurt a.M., New York 2002, pp. 93–116.

era – is at most implicitly hinted at; nowhere is it systematically elaborated, and nowhere are its normative standards made explicit. Therefore, in my view Dörre's line of argument gains its persuasive power from the ethical and moral problems of the late modern social formation as they become perceptible and tangible in the figure of the temporary worker; nevertheless, because Dörre does not inspect these problems systematically and does not explain his criteria and standards of measurement, his approach ultimately remains fruitless for a normative critique of (neo-)liberal capitalism.

Yet this need not trouble Dörre, for his main interest doubtlessly lies in revealing the core operational principles of capitalism. By attempting to grasp this economic mode's dynamic through the use of the term *Landnahme*, a concept originally developed by Marx and Luxemburg and recently re-discovered and re-introduced by David Harvey, he believes to hold an essential key to understanding the transition from Fordist capitalism to financial market-driven capitalism and the internal logic of its further development. I find the resulting reconstruction of historical phases of capitalist regimes of production as phases of *Landnahme* to be in equal parts fascinating and convincing. The metaphor of *Landnahme* – that is to say, of territorial conquest – renders the perspective and direction of a functionalist critique more or less self-evident: if capitalism can only operate through the ongoing conquest of new territories, then it cannot be sustainable, for at some point there will be no territories left to conquer. 'Land' is always finite. This statement is not diminished by the fact that, as we have seen, the spaces to be conquered need not necessarily be geographically defined: as we all know, expansive imperialism was followed by several phases of 'internal *Landnahmen*' during which spheres of social life that had not yet been exposed to the market economy were 'commodified'. As the metaphor implies, once every single manifestation of life (from Rent-A-Friend agencies and speed-dating events to the entertainment and pornography industries, to care services and the funeral industry) is fully integrated into the capitalist economy, the system itself becomes dysfunctional; its operations come to a standstill. Does this represent the key point of Dörre's critique? Unfortunately, this remains systematically unclear in his contribution.

First of all, as Dörre (rightly) points out in his discussion and criticism of Marx's depiction of the problem of realisation, of Luxemburg's and Arendt's 'underconsumptionist' thesis, and eventually of the thesis of overaccumulation, the interpretations of the *Landnahme* thesis based on a breakdown theory have thus far been rather over-simplified: this economic form seems almost inexhaustibly resourceful in the identification of new 'territories'; time and again it manages to develop even its own 'by-products' (e.g., the production of waste materials or lifestyle diseases) into new 'territories'.

At this point Dörre performs a systematically significant turn in his argument, as he suggests that capitalism always produces its own 'exterior' which it can then, in a subsequent step, conquer; and that, secondly, the commodification of a social sphere (e.g., banks, train services or care services), or rather the capitalist development of an entire region (say, in Sierra Leone) may always be followed by its de-commodification, or rather, its economic abandonment. In this sense, capitalist processing can be understood as an endless spiral: certain areas are subject to *Landnahme*, they are then economically utilised (or 'exploited'), and finally abandoned.

'The proactive creation of an "exterior" means that the chain of potential *Landnahmen* is veritably endless'.[5] This argument appears particularly convincing given that the Fordist-corporatist and welfare-statist phase of capitalism can be described as a period of relatively extensive de-commodification,[6] which was then followed by an at least equally extensive phase of commodification or *Landnahmen* (in the educational sector, insurance sector, financial markets, social services, etc.) during the two decades before and after the year 2000 – and which may well be, since the collapse of the financial markets in 2008, heading for a new phase of de-commodification or nationalisation once again. Yet one may also conceive of this iterative chain in a different way (indeed, Dörre's interpretation seems to be closer to this second reading than to the former): *Landnahme* and 'land surrender' (*Landpreisgabe*) can always occur simultaneously; each capitalist formation would then be marked by a specific principle of *Landnahme*, as well as an opposing tendency toward 'de-commodification'. This might even lead to the discovery of a complex interplay in which the *Landnahme* of external markets correlates with the 'surrender of land' in internal markets and vice versa.

However, if one conceives of *Landnahme* as a kind of endless process of commodification and de-commodification – or of 'land-conquering' and 'devastation', and, subsequently, of the 'surrender of land', or of privatisation, nationalisation and re-privatisation – then the analysis of the capitalist operational mode loses its anchor of functional critique: the system could go on operating like that forever. So what is then 'wrong with capitalism', if not its normative implications – seen, for example, in the 'devastation of land' – yet which Dörre does not explicate?

---

5   Dörre, p. 28 in this volume.

6   This runs counter to Dörre's interpretation of Fordism to some extent, for he considers it to be primarily a phase of internal *Landnahme*; what remains unclear in his depiction, however, concerns the question of what is actually being conquered. In my view his inclusion of agrarian-agricultural or small-scale artisan sectors belongs more accurately to the previous historical formation.

To his credit, he does at least recognise these possible functional problems by himself: on the one hand, the transition from one *Landnahme* regime to another turns out to be rather difficult – it almost inevitably leads to 'crises of transformation',[7] over the course of which a new order of *Landnahme* must be institutionalised within altered regimes of production, accumulation and regulation. If, by contrast, one assumes that transformational crises (in the sense of processes of adaptation and adjustment) represent an ineluctable feature of all living systems, then this alone cannot suffice as a basis for a fundamental critique, and even less so if resolutions of such crises, as impressively demonstrated by Dörre's historical reconstruction, invariably display a considerable level of adaptability, openness to innovation and enormous amounts of creativity. Yet these phases of transformation are problematic not least because of how they threaten social integration and cohesion – which seems to be a second system-threatening functional problem: as a consequence of the 'production' of disintegrated classes – currently Dörre's repeatedly invoked 'precariat' as symbolised by the temporary worker – the capitalist social formation runs the risk, at least during times of transition, of experiencing severe social tensions which could potentially threaten reproduction itself. Even though Dörre's analysis of financial market-driven capitalism does suggest that the 'latent need for social cohesion'[8] cannot be met under this regime – in contrast to the Fordist mode of production and accumulation – he unfortunately fails to elaborate on this functional problem in a systematic way at any point in the chapter: what amount and what kind of social integration is necessary for the system to function, and how is this provided for? Here it is particularly odd that Dörre emphasises Fordism's tremendous levels of social integration in his reconstruction of capitalism's historical formative phases, while at the same time not devoting a single word to the role of the 'actually existing' historical rivalry between political systems (i.e., that of 'The East' versus 'The West') in this process. As Dörre himself remarks, it is 'only with the de-commodifying effect of social property – namely, some sort of collective asset guaranteeing social existence and status – that wage labour is transformed into a gigantic apparatus of social integration'.[9] Whether the 'land surrender' or de-commodification contained within it can really be considered capitalism's 'own' achievement (and thereby repeatable), or whether it is more accurately interpreted as a reaction to the 'external' threat of the socialist system alternative (and thus a unique, non-recurring historical development), is in my view hard to tell at this historical stage. Late modern

---

7   Dörre, p. 53 in this volume.
8   Dörre, p. 61 in this volume.
9   Dörre, p. 34 in this volume.

capitalism's problems of integration and cohesion, as observed by Dörre, in turn seem to be related to a third and final functional problematic, which Dörre (in reference to, *inter alia*, David Harvey) hints at numerous times, but does not expand upon systematically. Capitalism (at least in all of its known formations thus far) requires the existence of *long-term, stable background conditions* that allow for planning security and reliable horizons of predictability, which are in turn crucial prerequisites for long-term investment in the first place. Such stability requirements pertain to, for instance, education systems, infrastructure, and legal certainty, but also those immaterial social conditions instrumental to developing a 'habitus' that corresponds to the respective formation.[10] Especially in its late modern, financial market-driven phase, however, this economic system tends to undermine and erode those conditions of stability because it is propelled forward by increasingly short-term yield expectations, exacting a kind of 'permanent restructuring'[11] in the process. Although the fear that capitalism may wear out the very ('non-market-conforming') preconditions of its own existence, which it cannot (re-)produce itself, is an ancient motif of critique of capitalism and may also serve to account for the plausibility of the *Landnahme* metaphor, it remains unclear in Dörre's depiction where exactly he locates the problem: if Fordism was capable of guaranteeing long-term stability, whereas financial market-driven capitalism is not, does this merely indicate that even the current capitalist formation will only endure for a limited period and have to be replaced in the foreseeable future by a new *Landnahme* principle?

The fundamental question that must be raised at this point is thus: is the erosion of conditions for integration and stability a constitutive functional problem of capitalism, or a contingent phenomenon of the late modern formation? Interestingly, this issue (perhaps) marks a possible structural divergence between Dörre's analysis and David Harvey's conception, even though they do in fact agree on the *Landnahme* thesis, as well as on the diagnosis of the erosion of long-term stability conditions.[12] For David Harvey, the phases of capitalist formation adhere to the logic of a gradually intensifying 'time-space-compression', i.e., of a prolonged 'compression' of spatio-temporal regimes as a consequence of the increasing 'speed-up in the pace of life, while so overcoming spatial barriers'.[13] Accordingly, he interprets the processes and phenomena throughout what is referred to as 'globalisation' merely as 'another round' in this ongoing process of time-space compression, which, upon closer inspection, signifies nothing more

---

10   Dörre, p. 18 in this volume.
11   Dörre, p. 60 in this volume.
12   Cf. D. Harvey, *Spaces of Hope*, Edinburgh 2000, p. 59.
13   Cf. D. Harvey, *The Condition of Postmodernity*, Oxford 1990, p. 240.

than the 'acceleration' of production, circulation and consumption, or rather of social and economic processes in general:

> As space appears to shrink to a 'global village' … and *as time horizons shorten to the point where the present is all there is* … so we have to learn how to cope with an overwhelming sense of compression of our spatial and temporal worlds.[14]

Thus, the potentially fatal tendency toward the contraction of time horizons, becomes a constitutive functional problem of capitalism. For David Harvey, this tendency also includes a logic of development that determines the sequence of formative phases and defines the 'general direction' of the capitalist reconfiguration of world and social relations. As I have attempted to demonstrate in my book, this general direction spanning all of the shifts and polymorphisms found in different 'capitalisms' can be most precisely grasped by employing the concept of social *acceleration*. Since Klaus Dörre refrains from identifying such an overarching 'general tendency' in his reconstruction of capitalism's trajectory (which for Marx appeared in the guise of the steadily increasing productive forces obliterating the system's limits, and in the assumption of an inevitable decline of the rate of profit), in my view he incurs a number of problems that do not pertain to the standards of critique in his argument, but instead to its discriminatory power and analytical capacity. An analysis of the sequence of transformations of capitalist accumulation regimes must be capable of indicating 1) at which point, or rather for what reasons, a historical formation reaches its limits and requires transformation, 2) what determines the selection, or rather the emergence of a new formation, and 3) whether the sequence of formations is to be understood as an aimless and potentially repetitive circle (eternal recurrence), or instead as a 'sequence of steps'. If it opts for the latter model, it must then be capable of determining what constitutes each of these 'steps', and what constitutes the model's dynamic of escalation.

Though Dörre's proposed *Landnahme* model may well be capable of answering the first question – a formation reaches its limits when a specific *Landnahme* model is depleted because all conquerable 'land' has been consumed – it leaves the subsequent two questions unanswered; that is, unless it is supplemented by a concept such as the one I have attempted to outline in my thesis of acceleration. What I have attempted to do by employing the term 'acceleration' is to determine the principle of escalation (question 3) and thus the attendant sequence of formations as a sequence of steps.

---

14   Ibid. (Emphasis by the author, H.R.). For more elaboration on this cf. H. Rosa, *Social Acceleration: A New Theory of Modernity* 2013, pp. 40ff. and 214ff.

And – as I have shown elsewhere[15] – it is the logic of acceleration that determines the transition from early to industrial capitalism, to Fordism, and finally to post-Fordism. Each transformation allowed for the realisation of new levels of velocity, and each formation unleashes forces of acceleration which the formation itself sooner or later becomes incapable of managing. However, this does not mean that the direction of development is irreversible, or that the acceleration thesis and the *Landnahme* thesis are irreconcilable in this regard: when taken together, the former seems to depict the direction of the process, while the latter analyses the substantive dimension thereof. Stephan Lessenich's concept of an 'activation regime', then, may address the subjective 'ethical' dimension of capitalism's general development. Yet before I start elaborating on this idea in more detail, let me first take a closer look at Stephan Lessenich's analysis.

Lessenich emphasises the critical aspiration of sociology he strives toward – far more so than Dörre, who places the analysis of the complex and dynamic process of *Landnahme* at the centre of his deliberations. To him, the reason for the decline in public significance and recognition of sociological interpretative approaches (not only vis-à-vis economic approaches but also, for example, in the face of socio-biological approaches) is not least sociology's 'domestication' into a more or less toothless 'normal science'.[16] In reaction to this he aims to re-establish a form of social critique which – in reference to early critical theory and to Axel Honneth – concerns itself with 'the whole, the principle, the absolute',[17] that is to say, one that does not seek to analyse and solve individual functional problems, but which questions the dominant social formation as a whole. He deems this critical impetus to be so essential that he even conceives of the political sociology he pursues as *political* as such; he considers it a political-normative intervention, so much so that it sometimes sounds as if he would like to formulate the knowledge and insights obtained analytically or, as it were, sociologically-scientifically, in a series of political prescriptions: 'socially critical knowledge production must attempt to grasp the secular expansion (hypertrophy) of the welfare state, its institutions and interventions … as a development-related systemic requirement for the further development of capitalist socialisation (*Vergesellschaftung*). Correspondingly, then, the possible "crisis" of the welfare state … should … be regarded … as an irresolvable structural

---

15 Cf. Rosa, *Social Acceleration*, p. 161ff.; also in H. Rosa, 'Schrankenloses Steigerungsspiel. Die strukturbildende Einheit hinter der Vielfalt der Kapitalismen', in S. A. Jansen, E. Schröter, N. Stehr (eds), *Mehrwertiger Kapitalismus*, Wiesbaden 2008, pp. 33–54.
16 Lessenich, p. 90 in this volume.
17 Lessenich, p. 90 in this volume.

problem …'[18] And as long as the 'standards … value references and criteria of "problematisation"' of critique are explicitly disclosed,[19] Lessenich sees no problem as far as scientific theory is concerned. So what exactly are the standards and value references of his critique? Which variant of critique does he pursue? What are its theoretical foundations? In this respect, the approach Lessenich adopts is marked by a rather interesting twofold perspective: he attempts to develop a model of contradiction for the analysis of capitalism, as popularised by the (neo-)Marxist tradition. Following Offe, Lessenich sees his task as not only identifying inherent self-contradictoriness as a constitutive principle of capitalism itself, but also rendering it the actual point of departure for an analysis of capitalist systems in general. 'The model of contradictions found in the social dynamic in (or rather of) capitalism represents the core of a neo-Marxist analysis of society – including the present one.'[20] Particularly in the introductory and concluding passages, Lessenich also draws on a second, quite different, critique and figure of critique: Michel Foucault. Lessenich points out quite consistently that his contribution follows not one but two logics of critique: on the one hand, informed by Marx and the model of contradiction, he engages in a 'critique of the functional logic [or functionalist critique, H.R.] of capitalism';[21] on the other, he pursues a 'genealogical strain of critique'[22] (in the spirit of Foucault and Honneth) that seeks to reveal the existing social formation's contingencies, i.e., the arbitrary and power-drenched construction of its normalities, naturalisations, forms of problematisation, institutions, and self-definition, through which he makes alternatives *thinkable* in the first place. I suspect that these two models are not only less compatible than Lessenich suggests, but that they are ultimately fundamentally irreconcilable. After all, while the Marxist line of argument seeks to expose the insurmountable, constitutive 'contradictions, paradoxes, dilemmas and tensions' which Lessenich invokes repeatedly, ultimately concluding that the capitalist social formation is greatly unstable, fragile, and crisis-prone, Foucault's genealogy, by contrast, aims precisely at rendering visible the firm, almost monolithic shape of social formations or *dispositifs*: because the axes of power, knowledge and subjectivity are so tightly interwoven and form a cohesive whole, seemingly coherent spaces and figures can emerge which allow historically contingent conditions to seem 'normal', 'naturalised' and 'unquestionable'. Whereas, for neo-Marxists, explaining why the capitalist social formation has not only

---

18 Lessenich, p. 102 in this volume.
19 Lessenich, p. 102 in this volume.
20 Lessenich, p. 111 in this volume.
21 Lessenich, p. 103 in this volume.
22 Lessenich, p. 103 in this volume.

endured for centuries but also proven to be robust and stable despite (supposedly) being shaped by fundamental contradictions, paradoxes and fault lines remains a major problem, Foucault is, as we know, confronted with the reverse difficulty, namely that he is unable to explain why social formations or *dispositifs* could or would change at all if both the production and functioning of knowledge, power and social subjects act complementarily within them. He is mostly concerned with making alternatives to the existing reality conceivable again in the first place, and thus keeping the idea of 'transgression' alive.

However, since Lessenich attempts to pursue both variants of critique simultaneously, both the analytical foundation and the normative claim of his diagnosis become, in my view, curiously vague.

I would like to flesh out this assertion in the following. My argument is that Lessenich's genealogical critique of the activation regime is far more convincing than his critique of late capitalism's functional logic based on Offe (and Habermas), for, in the course of executing the latter, Lessenich commits a superb performative self-contradiction, so to speak: by genealogically revealing the activation regime's efficiency and efficacy, he renders the contradiction model implausible. Yet, as I intend to show, the genealogical critique does not justify the claim formulated by Lessenich: it becomes rather unclear against whom or what (or even more importantly: for whom or what) and in whose name resistance should be organised.

By following this line of 'contradiction', Lessenich, as mentioned above, ultimately does little more than repeat Offe's and Habermas' critique of late capitalism: since capitalism necessarily produces external effects that jeopardise its own conditions and requirements of existence and functionality, it inevitably depends on external controlling institutions and interventions, and the entity that performs these interventions in all capitalist social formations up to the modern day has been and is the state. What is then essential, as Offe sees it, is the development of 'systemic elements that are alien to the structure but functionally necessary for the maintenance of the system.'[23] Accordingly, in order to exert the required degree of management, the state must systematically divert resources from the economic system, which it can then deploy to restrict that very system in its operational logic. 'In order to stabilise the system, the state resorts to measures that are essentially incompatible with that system', and 'that this arrangement cannot function smoothly over a longer period of time' Lessenich considers to be 'rather obvious'. Is it really? Surely, the capitalist state's structural and functional problems are intensified by the fact that it requires not only relevant economic resources but also *democratic legitimacy*; as a result, it comes under

---

23   Offe, *Strukturprobleme*, p. 75, (quoted in Lessenich, p. 113 in this volume).

permanent fire from two sides – from the interests of capital valorisation on the one hand, and the democratic interests of social participation and redistribution on the other. Lessenich does indeed consider this feature, deemed crucial by Habermas, to be a central problem; it is thus all the more surprising that he only returns to this issue late in his text, giving the impression of an 'additional argument'. We seem to have identified two fundamental contradictions: the state is forced to act, *in* the interest of capital and with *capitalist*-produced means, *against* the interests of capital; meanwhile, it relies on legitimation by those very groups *disadvantaged* by the interests of capital in order to do so. Lessenich acknowledges this circumstance, labelling it a 'double-bind' situation.[24] Over the course of the twentieth century the state managed to (temporarily) resolve this difficult twofold 'balance problem' by creating and expanding growth-oriented welfare state regimes. By the 1970s, this model was being called into question and was threatened by over-extension. It seemed obvious that further expansion of welfare functions would generate system-threatening instabilities, but it appeared virtually inconceivable that the state would be able to perform its balancing act *without them*. Thus the state's options seemed, as both Offe and Lessenich note, 'categorically exhausted' – indeed, the state was at risk of being 'torn apart'.

However, Lessenich (in this volume, and in his recent book)[25] brilliantly illustrates the way in which the late capitalist social formation escaped from this functional crisis: through the re-invention of the social, through the establishment of a labour regime which not only places the state's social responsibilities in the hands of its subjects, but also its responsibility to control and direct. Contrary to any talk of 'categorical exhaustion', in this aspect Lessenich observes a (ingenious and highly innovative) categorical extension of the state's repertoire of action – one which provides relief for the state on two sides: subjects now blame themselves for social failure, they assume 'self-responsibility', which means the state requires less tax revenues than it did before. (Though it may be accurate to say that the new form of control has in the meantime proven to be deeply inefficient, as evidenced by the current financial and economic crisis, this circumstance has no direct impact on an analysis of the current social formation's functional logic. The fact that, politically speaking, the crisis thus far has not threatened the system – it is the FDP [Free Democrats] and not Die LINKE [Left Party] that is winning votes in the crisis – only seems to be more proof of the successful re-constitution of the social.)[26]

---

24   Lessenich, p. 117 in this volume.
25   Cf. S. Lessenich, *Die Neuerfindung des Sozialen*, Bielefeld 2008.
26   [Trans. Note] at the time of this book's original publication (2009), this

Rising public expectations regarding democratic claims to participation and co-determination[27] in the 1970s, as presumed by Lessenich, surely signalled an intensification of the problem of legitimation – in the year 2009, however, following the *re-invention of the social*, this is hardly noticeable: the activation regime activates citizens economically and 'entrepreneurially', but not politically; one could almost think that Lessenich has gotten the centuries mixed up in this regard. That might be due to the fact that – in contrast to what Lessenich believes – the social is not (or only to a minor extent) incorporated as something *intentional*, but instead as a 'negative', as a liability; not as positive motivational force (or 'driving energy' [*Triebenergie*]), but merely as a *feeling of guilt*. His contention that the subjectification of the social must always be 'beneficial to the common good' or 'in pursuit of a 'higher (social) cause' strikes me as analytically false: no one would seriously suggest that Bill Gates or Silvio Berlusconi base their actions on what is beneficial to society, and yet they fit the criteria of 'active citizens' perfectly. In my view, all this re-invention of the social implies is that 1) the active and vigorous pursuit of one's own interests (as long as one adheres to the rules) creates – wholly in the sense of Mandeville or Smith – a positive effect for the common good, and in particular 2) that lethargy, inflexibility and the inability to care for oneself are downright 'anti-social' (*asozial*) behaviours.

Irrespective of this (or rather, because of it), the following is true: it is precisely because Lessenich's reconstruction of the state's logic of activation, which permeates all strata and social spheres, and the creation of the 'subjectification of the social' in which the state participates, is so convincing, that his *diagnosis of contradiction* fails. What is impressive about his depiction is how the three axes of knowledge (after all, science has long 'proven' that physical exercise keeps us fit, that mental mobility and flexibility make us happy and satisfy us, that self-efficacy can prevent cancer), power (from Hartz IV via anti-smoking laws through to the award criteria of the *DFG* [German Research Foundation]), and ethics (who does not feel a pang of guilt when they catch a cold – not enough exercise! – or when the topic of one's insufficient retirement planning is raised!) are interwoven to such an extent that activity appears as (ethically) good, (morally) correct and (anthropologically) true. This is exactly why his attempts to

---

was indeed the case. By 2014, however, the Free Democrats had failed to be re-elected to the federal parliament and lost a series of regional elections. At the time of this writing, many journalists and political analysts are speculating about the definitive end of the FDP as a national political force. Vote returns for Die LINKE continue to fluctuate, but the party remains a force in parliament, receiving just under 8 per cent in the 2013 elections.

27 Lessenich, p. 122ff in this volume.

prove the continuous existence of irresolvable paradoxes and contradictions remain fruitless: it may be accurate to claim that the state seeks to control and prevent certain movements (for example, those of immigrants or social movements of disadvantaged groups) as opposed to promoting them, but this does not constitute a fundamental contradiction. To me, this is where that fatal tendency in Lessenich's line of argument of wanting to – or, due to his theoretical disposition: *feeling obligated to* – elevate any difficulty and every balance problem to an indissoluble paradox becomes apparent.

This is all the more true for the second, allegedly categorical, paradox identified by Lessenich: the neo-social 'active self' supposedly represents a 'highly contradictory social character', for it must firstly be established by massive political intervention (Hartz IV, educational programmes, etc.), while, secondly, it is naturalised as the quasi-anthropological 'natural form' of the subject.[28] I cannot find any incompatibility, let alone paradox, in this whatsoever: after all, the standard neo-liberal (or neo-social) similitude states that 'humans' are creative, active, competition-oriented, greedy and innovative by nature, but that long phases of bureaucratic- welfare-statist or even state-socialist protection have spoiled and alienated them, that they have even 'degenerated', and that this is why they now need to be, by way of state-paternalistic intervention, 'normalised' and 'naturalised' (and thus 'liberated' back to their true natures) once again. Yet what seems valid and significant to me is the fact that this always produces guilt-ridden subjects, since they can never possibly be *active enough*: I consider this a fundamental starting point for a normative critique of this social formation, but not as a functional contradiction. The same applies to that 'tragic social character of the "active loser"':[29] indeed, that even the activated society produces or reproduces inequality, and that the losers in this process (the 'precariat', in the words of Dörre) are unjustly excluded from the distribution of wealth, seems to me equally certain and deplorable – nevertheless, it does not constitute a discernible functional crisis. Capitalism has thrived off the production of inequality and exclusion for centuries.

The question remains: what exactly constitutes the irresolvable paradox that Lessenich repeatedly postulates throughout his argument? 'Activation' is the contemporary expression of the unresolved – and systemically indissoluble, as it must perpetually be contained and processed anew – fundamental contradiction of the democratic-capitalist social formation between requirements of economic productivity and demands for social participation',[30] as Lessenich concludes his chapter. However, it is Lessenich himself who

---

28 Lessenich, p. 132 in this volume
29 Lessenich, p. 134 in this volume.
30 Lessenich, pp. 134–5 in this volume.

shows that aspirations to economic productivity and social participation are brought together in the activation formula in a way that allows them to seem not only consistently compatible but even synonymous, while simultaneously relieving the state; in doing so, he has, quite elegantly, disproved his own central thesis of irresolvable paradoxes. This is exactly why he explicitly and logically shifts the focus back to the second, genealogical perspective of critique at this point: in the final passages of his contribution, it is not the functional contradiction that features as the aspect of capitalism deserving of criticism, but the existence of an apparently significant, yet undisclosed *shift in meaning*: the idea of social participation contained in the activation formula, as Lessenich suggests, is not the 'right one' – following Brieler, he considers this a loss when measured against the *expectations of the past* and in some ways even a *betrayal of the future* – since it does not realise the 'possible'. Lessenich juxtaposes this with the political hope that subjects will engage in *resistance* against the late modern, active society-based type of subject and knowledge production.[31] Though I do agree with this, there is one problem: *resistance* does not necessarily mean (functional) *contradiction*, as the former requires normative motivation; this brings Lessenich into the Foucauldian dilemma: why should one type of self-governance, or rather one type of knowledge/power/ethics-formation, be better or worse than any other? Because Lessenich systematically refuses to state normative criteria of any kind – after all, what exactly is the promise of the past that was 'betrayed'? The promise of autonomy, perhaps? What precisely are those potentials that could be realised? And why should the promises of the past, as well as the very potentials of the future Lessenich envisions, be worth fighting for politically? – he is forced to retreat from his political and normative-critical claim to such a degree that hardly anything remains of it at the end of his contribution. It is empirically open-ended whether the subjects will 'play along' in the long term, he writes; sociological critique consists of *distrusting the art of political governance over people* (though, honestly, this attitude can be found in any corner pub or FDP convention) and to have faith in the people's obstinacy (which in itself does not constitute any sociological, political, critical or other contribution whatsoever). For Lessenich, then, this already marks the limitations of scientific critique. One has to read this passage several times before believing the words on the page – is this really the same author who at the beginning of his contribution so boastfully announced a critique of 'the whole, the principle, the absolute'[32]?

In my view, the fact that one *can think about something* – including about oneself – *in a different way* does not imply a critique of existing conditions

---

31   Lessenich, p. 137 in this volume.
32   Lessenich, p. 99 in this volume.

as such, even though it is, a (non-trivial, as Adorno has taught us) precondition of critique to not mistake the existing for the naturally given; and it is only subversive to the extent that this *different way* proves to be an appealing alternative. In other words: precisely because capitalism (obviously) does not intend to perish of its own contradictions, we will not be rid of the 'old rascal' automatically – but in order to engage in struggle against it we require normative criteria, or at least motivational political guiding images.

Understandably, I do not wish to end this chapter without pointing out the proximity and complementarity of the diagnoses of acceleration and activation. As far as its subjects are concerned, capitalism has thrived off of exposing individuals to notorious anxiety since its early stages: what Max Weber identified as the 'Protestant Ethic' (of which a key element is 'restless striving and activity') was nothing but a gigantic programme of activation which led to an acceleration of the speed of life – defined as a systematic and methodical increase in the number of actions performed per time unit – that was equally comprehensive. Late modernity's activation regime, as depicted by Lessenich, simply represents a further step in this process: it increases subjects' 'immanent asceticism' and the desire for movement far beyond the economic sphere observed by Weber, and relentlessly inscribes this asceticism into each and every impulse of the 'late modern habitus'. All this remains unaffected by the fact that the setting-into-movement and activation, as Lessenich rightly observes, exhibit simultaneous complementary tendencies of immobilisation or even solidification at all times; for example, while everything seems to fall into movement and become more flexible in the 'substantial' social areas, the capitalist structural and functional logics (and, surprisingly, even the reproduction of social strata, which in terms of individualisation and theories of justice is truly outrageous) appear all the more solidified and immovable. The flipside of these high rates of acceleration seems to be solidification, even historical stagnation – the 'frenetic standstill', or in Lessenich's earlier diction: the *dynamic immobilism*.[33] Yet what I have most trouble discerning is whether there is an *interplay* or a *game of escalation* occurring between the tendencies of movement and immobilisation, respectively – and whether Lessenich considers these forces of movement and immobilisation to be symmetric or asymmetric. According to my understanding, the tendencies of dynamisation systematically outweigh the forces of inertia in capitalist modernity; and this sets in motion a game of escalation which continuously leads to higher velocity throughout society (and affects any type of social or economic transaction),

---

33   Cf. S. Lessenich, *Dynamischer Immobilismus*, Frankfurt a.M., New York 2003. This is precisely one of the main theses of my 'acceleration book': cf. Rosa, *Social Acceleration*, p. 277 ff.

yet, complementary to this, ever-stronger tendencies toward solidification as well. If we are able to agree on this formula, then it begins to become clear how the three diagnoses presented here may be combined: acceleration, *Landnahme* and activation are, taken together, the manifestation of the principles of process, substance and political-ethical control of one larger process: the endless movement of capital.

CHAPTER 6

Artistic or Social Critique? On the Problematisation of a False Alternative

STEPHAN LESSENICH

For the formation of a comprehensive socially critical movement as witnessed in 1968, it is imperative that a critical discourse emerge capable of combining the myriad varieties of critique in a hegemonic manner.
– A. Demirović, 'Leidenschaft und Wahrheit. Für einen neuen Modus der Kritik'

Social critique is a risky kind of sociology. Indeed, the critique of society put forth by established professors in the academic 'security zone' no longer represents a direct material, let alone existential, threat to its authors (at least not in this country). However, a sociological critique of society runs the more general intellectual risk of failing to accomplish the objective of its critique – that is to say, an analysis of the social status quo encouraging change for the 'better' – by either systematically falling short of or surpassing the level of analytical distance from the status quo that such a critique requires. 'Critique can either maintain a distance from its object of critique to such an extent that it loses its reliability, or it can be too close to the object.'[1] This problem of proximity versus distance emerges for precisely the type of sociological social critique which seeks to or – more accurately – is convinced of *having* to consist primarily of a critique of capitalism; it is thus no coincidence that this problem appears in the introductory chapters of both Klaus Dörre and Hartmut Rosa. In the following, I will attempt to show that a critique of capitalism that explicitly rejects a materialist grounding of its object of critique and commits itself to the perspective of the reconstruction of, as it were, a 'pre-social' identity of the modern subject (Rosa), loses social traction and must necessarily remain socially ineffective; whereas a

---

1   A. Demirović, 'Leidenschaft und Wahrheit: Für einen neuen Modus der Kritik', in: A. Demirović (ed.), *Kritik und Materialität*, Münster 2008, pp. 9–40, here: p. 15.

critique of capitalism which, in its scientific reconstruction of the material movements of the system in capitalist economies, does not advance to an analysis of modern subjectivity (Dörre), must likewise encounter problems in its diagnosis of the limits of systemic reproduction, as well as in its answer to the question about the (continuous) political modification of these limits. In combining this twofold critique I will conclude by claiming (in this volume, how could I not?) that my own analysis and critique of contemporary society as the 'active society' in its position to stated dangers in fact avoids both – an unreliable distance or an overly committal proximity. I will then attempt to explain the reasoning behind this strong statement by responding to my two critics, who I am about to criticise myself.

1. The temporary worker confronted with social critique – baffled

According to Boltanski and Chiapello, two historical traditions of the critique of capitalism can be distinguished from one another: while 'social critique' addresses capitalism as the source of phenomena such as poverty, inequality and social disintegration, 'artistic' critique by contrast places processes of loss of individual autonomy, authenticity and creativity at the centre of its engagement with the capitalist social formation.[2] 'Alienation' here and 'exploitation' there: these were, as expressed in these succinct slogans, the anti-capitalist impulses contained in the movements of cultural and class struggle throughout the nineteenth and twentieth centuries. If we accept the lucid analysis of those two aforementioned French sociologists, then the secret of capitalism's success in socialisation consisted of, and still consists of, its capacity to incorporate and institutionalise this twofold critical impulse; that is to say, its systemic capability to accomplish a 'subsumption of subversion'.[3] With the introduction and expansion of the welfare-state agenda on the one hand, and the shift in labour policy towards flexible and co-determined forms of the organisation of production on the other, came another historic shift: it became possible to harness the anti-systemic capacities of both artistic and social critique; that is to say, to disarm and depreciate them, through systemic capitalist co-optation. If we accept this (in my view) rather convincing diagnosis, then any adaptive continuation of either of these two lines of critique (along with any attempt at a

---

2   Cf. L. Boltanski, È. Chiapello, G. C. Elliott, *The New Spirit of Capitalism*, London, New York 2007, p. 38ff.

3   Cf. T. Künkler, 'Produktivkraft Kritik. Die Subsumtion der Subversion im neuen Kapitalismus', in R. Eickelpasch, C. Rademacher, P. Ramos Lobato (eds), *Metamorphosen des Kapitalismus – und seiner Kritik*, Wiesbaden 2008, pp. 29–47.

combination of both strains), regardless of which one, runs the risk (apropos of risky kinds of sociology!) of providing additional material for the perpetuation of capitalism's success story; a risk which thus must be taken into consideration in the course of the critique being practised in this volume. Within this dualism of social and artistic critique, Klaus Dörre's contribution leans decisively toward the former. His reconstruction of capitalist development, as a sequence of specific forms of *Landnahme* of previously not yet economically valorised spaces and resources, which he bases on Luxemburg, Arendt, Lutz and Harvey, culminates in an analysis and critique of contemporary finance capitalism and the social phenomenology of increasing precarity it generates with respect to the conditions of work and life for ever-wider strata of the population. The inquiring temporary worker, whose lamentations about his systematic disadvantages when compared to his colleagues mark the leitmotif of the text – earning only 'two-thirds of their wage, [having] five fewer vacation days, no bonuses, only half of the overtime pay, no extra money for meals, no retirement plan, no company pension, no raises, no parking spot'[4] – is representative of the sociologist's concern for and bias towards the 'weakest groups in society':[5] according to Dörre, social critique must start from 'the "exterior" generated by the finance-capitalist *Landnahme*'.[6] As instructive as the *Landnahme* thesis is – taken either individually or as an interpretational frame for both the 'acceleration' and 'activation' theses argued in this book – and as heartwarming as the scientist's apparent concern for the grievances of the helpless temporary worker may be, the answers he provides also raise many questions. In the following I would like to formulate and discuss five of them.

The first question (or rather set of questions) arises from the markedly economistic tinge of Dörre's study of the finance-capitalist social formation's genesis and mode of operation. Though the author explicitly favours a 'non-economistic, multi-causal interpretation of the crisis'[7] with view to the crisis of transformation of Fordism, his analysis is actually only multifactorial in a very limited sense: the economic is largely explained by itself, without any systematic reference to the political or, even more importantly, the cultural (i.e., to the state and its subjects); the economic formation thus appears to reproduce itself almost autopoietically on a correspondingly higher, or rather (in the sense of the *Landnahme* thesis), expanded scale. 'Capitalism' in its respective historical form appears as an actor 'capable

---

4 Dörre, p. 11 in this volume.
5 Dörre, p. 64 in this volume.
6 Dörre, p. 64 in this volume.
7 [Trans. Note] this passage did not actually appear in the final edition of the book, but has been retained for the sake of preserving the author's original remarks.

of shedding its skin at certain conjunctures of its development'[8] and that, moreover, executes radical changes in the relations of property, production and regulation on an international scale, 'with the aim of preserving [itself]'.[9] That such an explanation, unless it represents a stylistic device of quasi-personifying speech, cannot satisfy sociologists is rather obvious. Ultimately, the question remains as to who is the actual actor when 'capitalism transforms itself': what brings about the societal hegemony of financial markets and their functional logic, how does it establish itself? Has 'politics' played a merely reactive (as opposed to constitutive) role after all, as it may presently appear in light of the oft-invoked 'last resort' of multi-billion dollar state-sponsored rescue packages? How were citizens 'captured' by this new formation; how did finance capitalism bring subjects 'to its side'? Some valuable clues about how to answer this question come, for example, from Christoph Deutschmann's reading of financial markets as an expression of a 'collective *Buddenbrooks* effect':[10] his economic-sociological interpretation of the crisis currently unfolding emphasises the fact that broad sections of the population wanted to participate in the huge finance boom without being honest with themselves about the problem of the collective effects incurred by a decoupling of individual expectations of profitability from value creation processes in the real economy. This points to phenomena of both social knowledge and political knowledge production, which remain underexposed if not completely obscured in Dörre's analysis: the political promotion of the 'people's share' (*Volksaktie*) and public talk of a 'nation of shareholders'; the social proliferation of the belief in quick profits, in limitless earnings, in almost magical multiplication of money, in 'working money'; the social generalisation of the shareholder's credo of a right to rising profits, and, more generally, the society-wide implementation of the illusion of everlasting, boundless growth. All these represent dimensions and aspects of finance capitalism's cultural base, without examination of which both the success and the crisis of this new social formation will likely remain uncomprehended.

This leads directly to a second, deeper question: why does Dörre not push the analysis of the capitalist *Landnahme* further, to the point – in my view decisive for a social diagnosis – at which its dynamic begins to

---

8   Dörre, p. 28 in this volume.

9   Dörre, p. 28 in this volume.

10   Cf. C. Deutschmann, 'Der kollektive Buddenbrooks-Effekt'. Die Finanzmärkte und die Mittelschichten', *MPIfG Working Paper* 5, Cologne 2008.

[Trans. Note] *Buddenbrooks* is a novel by Thomas Mann which was published in 1901; it deals with the gradual decline of a wealthy German merchant family over several generations.

encroach upon its subjects, incorporates their subjectivity, and is thereby able to reproduce itself precisely through this access to subjects? To take this analytical step would entail taking into account the fundamental social-theoretic insights of what is referred to as 'governmentality studies':[11] in the present social formation, subjectivity 'is no longer the last refuge or node of resistance, but has long been incorporated (by the capitalist system as a whole) into the continuously expanding imperatives of optimisation'.[12] Hence, a contemporary social critique would also have to take into consideration and integrate this dimension of capitalist *Landnahme*, and thus the 'artistic impetus' of the critique of alienation, into its analytical framework – at least to the extent that it not only lives off of and for the 'everyday lamentations' of temporary workers and other underprivileged groups, but in fact 'requires social subjects to whom it refers' in its orientation toward changing the existing status quo. Governmentality theory's thesis of incorporation, however, obviously poses a serious challenge to an analysis à la Dörre, i.e., an analysis that postulates the constant production of an 'exterior' in which the 'victims' of a respective mode of capitalist socialisation are then placed: it raises questions regarding in what sense, in reference to what, and in relation to whom the social space of phenomena such as precarity really represent such an 'exterior' of *Landnahme*, from which the social critic would then hope to see an attack of some kind on (or a collective movement away from) capitalism's 'interior'.

That Dörre the social critic is driven by such hopes is evidenced in the last paragraph of his contribution, in which he deals with the option of local experiments with solidary alternatives to the capitalist mode of production – and thereby with the revitalisation of those 'principles of rationality which the internal imperialism of the finance-capitalist system seeks to advance'.[13] Beyond and before this concluding statement of perspective, however, the reader must ask, thirdly, what exactly the object and thrust of Dörre's social critique is. What exactly does the 'social question' of, or rather in, finance capitalism consist of? What sparks the temporary worker's criticisms, how are his grievances reformulated in an empirico-analytical manner, and what recommendations for action emerge for the plaintive subject? All of this remains, upon closer inspection, rather unclear. After all, the problem diagnosis put forth by the inquiring worker does not directly imply an antagonistic position vis-à-vis his exploiting counterpart, but instead

11 Cf. G. Burchell, C. Gordon, P. Miller (eds), *The Foucault Effect*, London 1991; U. Bröckling, S. Krasmann, T. Lemke (eds), *Gouvernementalität der Gegenwart*, Frankfurt a.M. 2000.

12 Künkler, 'Produktivkraft Kritik', p. 33.

13 Dörre, p. 66 in this volume.

consists mostly of feeling like a 'second class citizen' – and thus in subjective opposition to members of the 'first class' of the privileged exploited (i.e., the permanently employed). Dörre the sociologist reacts to these grievances – after the plaintive inquiring worker exhibits 'impatience' with the sociologist's analyses – with an 'attentistic' appeal to sit tight and hang on until the system eventually reduces itself to absurdity: 'Finance capitalism will not last forever!'[14] Yet shortly thereafter the author, so it seems, calls for a new reformism, an ecological 'New Deal', or rather *Kondratiev*, which on the one hand seems rather 'voluntaristic' due to its allegedly necessary bias towards those 'out there' (in the exterior), and which, on the other hand, seems not to present any more than, or differ significantly from, a global social democratic agenda for the twenty-first century (perhaps we should be a bit more careful, and note: at least as far as we can tell). This is in turn followed once more by Dörre's hinting at a 'yet-to-be-realised project of an egalitarian democracy encompassing the economic system',[15] and thus at the related system alternative of a 'solidarity economy'.[16] If at this (and Dörre's) point we try to put ourselves in the shoes of the inquiring temporary worker one last time (as the author does shortly before in a rather emphatic way), then I believe we will find him even more perplexed than before – thanks in no small part to the socially critical emotional roller coaster provided to him here.

The vagueness of the critique and, related to it, the ambivalence of the vision of social change it develops may well be owed to an analytical artifice of Dörre's, which in turn takes us to a fourth set of questions. In the first paragraph of his contribution dealing with terminology, he explains to the inquirer 'that the market economy and capitalism are not identical',[17] defining 'capitalism' in economic-sociological terms, as an arrangement of market exchange plus non-market-conforming institutions which neutralise the self-negating tendencies of the market system – a capitalist logic of constitution which in the procedural logic of *Landnahme* appears as an 'interplay between market liberalisation and market delimitation'.[18] What remains perfectly logical and consistent in terms of the contribution's main thesis, however, in its argumentative logic has the effect of making the systemic dynamic of the 'internal-external dialectic',[19] as it were, obscure the social dynamic of

---

14   [Trans. Note] This passage also did not appear in the final edition of the book.

15   Dörre, p. 66 in this volume.

16   Dörre, p. 66 in this volume.

17   Dörre, p. 23 in this volume.

18   Dörre, p. 32 in this volume.

19   Dörre, p. 38 in this volume.

the capitalist mode of socialisation – thus blurring the once-clear contours of a potential social critique of capitalism. The question, of the social consequences of capitalism, that is essentially posed by mentioning 'capitalist realities' such as structural power asymmetry, the antagonism of interests in terms of class politics, and the relations of exploitation, disappears in the course of the analysis behind detailed answers to the guiding question: 'How exactly does capitalism develop?'[20] As it were, accomplishing the author's obviously socially critical intention would require a more precise social structural analysis of finance capitalism, which could deal with, inter alia, questions concerning the social significance of 'shareholder-esque' modes of behaviour by the middle classes, or precarity-induced fault lines within the overall workforce. Keeping in mind such a seemingly contradictory neglect of the *social* aspects of capitalist socialisation – and with view to a precise and well-founded social critique – Dörre, the critic of capitalism, is 'too close' to the specific logic of contemporary capitalism as an economic system.

Finally, a fifth question that may 'put the saddle on the wrong horse' within our circle of three sociologists critical of capitalism shall nevertheless, for strategic reasons in the interest of a necessary discussion about the reach and efficacy of scientific critique, be posed at this point. Though not as strongly as in Hartmut Rosa's contribution (but still noticeably), Klaus Dörre's text is marked by a tendency to mourn the 'good old' capitalism of Fordist-organised 'second modernity',[21] or at least – as generally seems to be the danger in all critical analyses of the present – to normatively elevate it in retrospect, which is again another expression of Dörre's excessive proximity to the object of critique. Though the explicit formulation actually reads that the transition to finance capitalism threatens to 'squander' the functional strengths of 'Rhenish capitalism';[22] one nevertheless senses an authentic appreciation of 'social capitalism'[23] (of the German variety) behind this – a position which, beyond all adjectives, runs counter to a radical critique of capitalism and which accounts for the contribution's relative restraint in its discussion of not only possible, but indeed conceivable system alternatives. That said, just to be sure: the matter at hand is by no means a cheap, verbally radical 'professor's socialism' advanced by a new generation of 'scientists with such tendencies' in Jena.[24] However, it should, or must – in the

---

20   Dörre, p. 23 in this volume.
21   Cf. P. Wagner, *A Sociology of Modernity*, London, New York 1994.
22   Dörre, p. 3 in this volume.
23   Dörre, p. 61 in this volume.
24   Cf. M. Steinbach, Ökonomisten, Philanthropen, Humanitäre, Berlin 2008;
J. Opitz, 'Tendenzwissenschaft' an der Universität Jena: Die Jenaer Nationalökonomie

context of this volume – be the task to 'put one's cards on the table' in terms of personal-political preferences; this must consist of more than the refusal to 'exclude the possibility of a transformation of the system from the spectrum of potential social development paths'.[25] It should and would have to be about saying, openly and clearly, that capitalism, which today dominates us in its finance-driven form, has to be done away with – because it destroys people, society, and not least nature – if only for the reason that its workings are diametrically opposed (regardless of our respective personal versions) to our concepts of a 'good life'. We will definitely have to return to this question later.

2. THE SOLITUDE OF ARTISTIC CRITIQUE

It so happens to be the case – quite beneficially for an intense and productive sociological controversy between the three authors of this volume – that Hartmut Rosa, in contrast to Klaus Dörre, is not particularly fond of any kind social critique of capitalism, but instead is fully committed – in explicit dissociation from the former – to the mode of artistic critique of contemporary society. In an age that he considers particularly determined by changes in its time structures, and in a capitalist social formation likewise determined by the quasi-totalitarian dominance of a regime of acceleration of individual and collective work and life arrangements, he views key achievements of the project of modernity as not only endangered, but in many cases already destroyed. Here we once again encounter the concepts of a 'good life'[26] mentioned previously, those societal conceptions of 'a successful life'[27] which Rosa critically poses against the de-civilising effects of the dynamic of social acceleration that, in a way, chip away at the normative legacy of the Enlightenment. Like Dörre's *Landnahme* thesis, the thesis of acceleration, which quite rightly enjoys broad public resonance at the moment,[28] is of remarkably high epistemological value as a socially critical diagnosis of the times – and not least as a social-theoretical supplement to my own thesis of activation as well. Having said that, however (and how could it be any other way?), this thesis in particular thrusts the sociological reader

---

zwischen ‚Kathedersozialismus' und bedarfsorientierter angewandter Wissenschaft', in: M. Steinbach, S. Gerber (eds), *'Klassische Universität' und 'akademische Provinz'*, Jena 2005, pp. 357–78.

25   Dörre, p. 65 in this volume.
26   Rosa, p. 67 in this volume.
27   Rosa, p. 67 in this volume.
28   H. Rosa, *Social Acceleration: A New Theory of Modernity*, 2013.

into a world of doubt, which I intend to engage with in the following. As in the preceding chapter, I will complete this treatment by way of posing and explicating five questions (or rather, sets of questions). However, since Rosa outspokenly purports to be a critic of social critique, I have another, sixth question which I will also pose to Rosa – a personal question, so to speak. Fortunately, the construction of this volume as a trialogue between three amicable colleagues allows me to not only pose said question, but also (and especially) to expect a productive response from the author in question.

Rosa's opening question about the 'good life', or rather his opening claim that 'the analysis of the social conditions under which a successful life is possible' must be considered as 'the ultimate object of sociology, though rarely articulated (at least not consciously)', already provides an occasion to ask an initial, fundamental counter-question. For it is one thing to consider the establishment of such a specific object and purpose of sociology indispensable and to argue for it – although the *topos* of the 'good life' already indicates the rootedness of Rosa's thoughts in communitarian social critique. But it is another thing entirely – and the author clearly displays a strong tendency to do so – to not only accuse colleagues who do not share one's recognition of 'this motivational origin and legitimising anchor of sociology' of being mistaken, but in fact to insinuate false consciousness as the cause of their actions: for their scientific endeavours – though Rosa claims that they 'deliberately attempt to deny this' – are also 'ultimately motivated and legitimised by nothing else than this very question [about the 'good life', S.L.]'. So is the empirico-analytical sociologist, who, as it turns out, may seek to go beyond simply playing with numbers (as the notorious figure of the 'bean counter' suggests); and who may actually be interested in explaining the social world in comprehensible terms, nothing more than a deluded denier of the 'real' purpose of sociology (possibly even acting against his or her better judgement)? Despite sharing the conviction that sociology is (or should at least strive to be) more than just the analysis of that which exists and that which has become, that it lives more so and particularly from its extra-analytical surplus, I would not be inclined to agree on the (seemingly) slightly revanchist gesture of excommunicating all those whose self-understanding of sociological motivation is *not* derived directly 'out of the diffuse but nevertheless probably universal basic human perception that "something is wrong here"'[29] from the 'scientific community'. *Should* sociology always be understood as part of a socially critical praxis? Absolutely! And should we personally contribute to disseminating and expanding such an understanding of sociology – especially vis-à-vis the young generation of

---

29 Rosa, p. 68 in this volume.

students and scientists? By all means! Parading around a kind of sociological imperialism with somehow socially critical intentions, however, is not conducive – is in fact counter-productive – to these ends.

Having established this point, the centrality of the question of the 'good life' in Rosa's approach raises another follow-up question: after all, Rosa selects as the point of reference for his critique of social relations 'the guiding normative concepts, or rather the conceptions of a successful way of life which individuals adhere to either explicitly or – far more often and to a much higher degree – implicitly'. At the beginning of his analysis, we thus encounter the (quite charming) call for an empirical, or rather practical, social theory that elevates people's everyday conceptions of a 'happy' life to the criterion of a critique of the status quo. Unfortunately, Rosa's contribution abandons this aspiration almost immediately, for over the course of the chapter the central value references of individual and collective thought and action under capitalism are precisely *not* extracted from the subjective legitimate orders of the subaltern(s) (as expressed in the terminology of social critique), but instead derived theoretically from the writings of 'leading social philosophers'. If one is then to follow Rosa's social-philosophical value testing, the 'defining cultural ideal' in modern capitalism is the quest for 'autonomy', supplemented by the claim to 'authenticity'. Through this praxis (itself lacking any practical relevance) of determining what is 'good', the author betrays his own aspirations, and in a way comes under that 'suspicion of ideology and reification',[30] which he himself (correctly) attributes to a sociology that 'considers itself to possess knowledge of the 'true nature' or the 'true needs' of humanity, as opposed to the active subject.'[31] The fact that he does *not* derive the value references of his social critique from the mouths of those affected, but instead conjures them out of the (not particularly novel) hat of social theory, may be interpreted as the first act of distancing himself from his object – an act which, as we will see, will be followed by more to come.

A third aspect of Rosa's analysis seems particularly dubious to the sociological reader: namely, his proposition – as bold as it is foundational – that 'autonomy', as the highest value reference of human life and ambition, represents not only the 'fundamental promise of modernity'[32] but also the 'aspect of promise within capitalism'.[33] Rosa's interpretation and critique in this regard becomes all the more difficult, as the author does not clearly terminologically–conceptually distinguish between 'modernity' and 'capital-

---

30   Rosa, p. 70 in this volume.
31   Rosa, p. 70 in this volume.
32   Rosa, p. 72 in this volume.
33   Rosa, p. 73 in this volume.

ism', and increasingly conflates the two in the subsequent trajectory of his argument. While autonomy initially trades under the name of a 'cultural and political project' – or sub-project – of modernity, and manages to hold out both analytically and practically 'in the face of the processes of (capitalist) modernisation that have taken on a life of their own' – that is to say, in the face of that economic sub-project of modernity called 'capitalism' – in a subsequent step it ascends to the level of the 'leading cultural idea of capitalism' *itself*. It seems as if the economic subsystem of society has set out on its own modernist offensive, based on its very own 'promise of being able to lead a self-determined life according to one's own standards'. It is, however, essential that we formulate and argue very accurately when discussing this matter. I believe that Boltanski and Chiapello allow us to safely conclude that capitalism's promise of autonomy is not and has not been by any means intrinsic to the system: 'Unable to discover a moral basis in the logic of the insatiable accumulation process … capitalism must borrow the legitimating principles it lacks from orders of justification external to it'.[34] If one accepts this proposition, then the modern progress-driven hope, not only for material prosperity but also for 'genuine cultural autonomy'[35] which, according to Rosa, 'has always been implicitly and explicitly tied to capitalism'[36] arises not from the economic system itself, but is induced from outside – from other social subsystems, or rather from social bearers of ethical, moral, social-philosophical, cultural, political, etc. aspirations and demands. If these cultural hopes for progress as found in society are then historically as well as presently negated (as Rosa diagnoses), it is not to be understood as the 'perversion of the leading cultural idea of capitalism',[37] but as the *démenti* of a modern cultural ideal by the capitalist economy's laws of movement. How else could one reasonably – and with a critical objective, as Rosa implicitly does himself – speak of, for example, an 'economisation of the social' if the 'economic' within capitalist society has always entailed the promise of autonomy and authenticity and continues to do so? One can undoubtedly and with ample justification engage in a cultural criticism of capitalism – but if that is the case, one should then refrain from measuring capitalism by its own standards; one does not beat it at its own argumentative game, but instead by increasing one's distance to these very standards – including, say, that of efficiency (in classical capitalism), or that of flexibility (in contemporary capitalism) – instead applying external standards to it, imposing one's own game on it, so to speak.

---

34   L. Boltanski, È. Chiapello, G. C. Elliott, *The New Spirit of Capitalism*, London, New York: Verso, 2007, p.487.

35   Rosa, p. 75 in this volume.

36   Rosa, p. 75 in this volume.

37   Rosa, p. 75 in this volume.

Thus I am more than a little critical when near the end of his contribution Rosa declares that not only the aspiration to autonomy but even claims to collective self-determination, to a 'configuration of the way of life as a whole to become a democratic political project along self-defined normative standards', are 'fundamental promise[s] of capitalism'[38] – this could not be further from the truth. In reality, a democracy understood in this way can and must always be contested and struggled for – in *conflict* with capitalism. One could also put it this way: *that is why we are here.*

Before I address a similarly crucial point of critique, I would like to segue into it by – fourthly – inquiring as to why, in Hartmut Rosa's juxtaposition of three phases of the modern history of acceleration, the 'classical modernity' of 'organised capitalism' appears as the golden age of albeit not unlimited but nevertheless extensively enforced, institutionally protected, individual autonomy – far more so than in Klaus Dörre's chapter. 'During working hours subjects were 'heteronomous', yet it was through work that they acquired the resources to compose their 'life sphere' autonomously':[39] one would assume that until not too long ago the realm of freedom began at the factory gates; the Fordist subject lived in two distinct worlds – being a wage earner Monday to Friday from nine to five, and leading the life of a self-directed hedonist the rest of the time. By contrast, under the present regime of intensified acceleration, as the author notes at several points throughout the text and with an emphasis appropriate to the historical break he postulates, 'forms of subjectivity lose their claim to participation and development and thus to autonomy as acquired in classical modernity'.[40] Here, the narrative of a cyclically accelerating modernity appears as a history of gradual decay: accordingly, under Adenauer or at least under Brandt (as one is tempted to polemicise), things were better – or in any case, as is suggested in retrospect, at least not so bad in terms of autonomy. This, incidentally, makes it clear why, in Rosa's eyes, a utopia of social change must not necessarily be quite as radical as the recipient of his critique of acceleration may at first assume.

This brings us to my fifth query directed toward Rosa's diagnosis, to which I would ascribe paramount importance, all the more so in the context of a critical juxtaposition of artistic and social critique – for the acceleration thesis consistently and aggressively abstracts, in the sense of distancing itself from the social 'reality' it criticises, from basically all socio-structural differentiations within capitalist society. From the perspective of a socio-structural analysis, then, one could say that Rosa reveals himself to be a

---

38   Rosa, p. 89 in this volume.
39   Rosa, p. 92 in this volume.
40   Rosa, p. 84 in this volume.

genuine anti-sociologist. Rosa counterposes his appreciation of the 'good life' against the option of '(distributive) justice ... as the guiding standard of social critique'[41] right at the outset of his analysis. In the subsequent passage, as he raises (seemingly in accordance with Dörre) 'the affected subjects' experience of suffering ... when and if they systematically result from social relations'[42] to the status of a criterion of sociological diagnosis, one begins to wonder if he does perhaps have a soft spot for social critique after all. However, his diagnosis of social suffering in the present goes on to state that (resembling previous diagnoses of 'risk societies') in an age of acceleration there are no longer any socially relevant, classical vertical lines of differentiation or distinction: we are all victims of acceleration. Looking retrospectively at the golden age of Fordism, Rosa sees 'a decent standard of living, but also status, recognition, security and, in particular: spaces of autonomy' as economically institutionally secured through occupational positions at the upper as well as at the lower 'end of the social spectrum'.[43] (It would have been interesting to read more extensively about, for example, the 'permanently employed cleaner's[44] spaces of autonomy in these so-called 'good old days'.) The assumption of a quasi-democratic because universal impact (*Allbetroffenheit*) of acceleration, however, is all the more valid for the current, post-Fordist workings of acceleration: here, questions of social inequality supposedly play no part, and there is no mention of resource-, opportunity- or power gradients. The assertion of a 'situational identity',[45] for example, as the 'self-relation corresponding to the *temporalised* time of late modernity', is not furnished with any kind of social structural-analytical index: 'one is married to X *at the moment*, one is *currently* working as a graphic designer, one voted Green *during the last election*, etc.'[46] – indeed, the question of whether the aforementioned phenomena (a liquefaction of the social throughout all strata and milieus, across all social groups and positions of social status) are accurately portrayed seems to be either already clear or irrelevant; whatever the case, the question is not even posed. 'Acceleration devours its children, the big ones and the little ones too.' This line must read like a contemporary reproduction of that eternal (and now truly) capitalist promise according to which 'we' are all in the same boat.[47]

---

41   Rosa, p. 70 in this volume.
42   Rosa, p. 71 in this volume.
43   Rosa, p. 86 in this volume.
44   Rosa, p. 86 in this volume.
45   Rosa, p. 85 in this volume.
46   Rosa, p. 85 in this volume (emphasis in the original, S.L.).
47   Cf. G. Vobruba (ed.), *'Wir sitzen alle in einem Boot'*, Frankfurt a.M., New York 1983.

Incidentally, this obfuscation of structures of social inequality corresponds to the overall neglect of the state in Rosa's analysis: the state, along with its 'political modes of governance',[48] appears at best as a dependent variable of the 'revolutionising of capitalist production regimes'[49] and particularly of the regime of social acceleration, in the face of which it finds itself 'completely powerless'.[50] But whether or not the state – much like 'the market', now as much as ever – is a major and independent structuring instance of social inequality is not particularly important if we assume that the social structure of the activated society is homogeneous, levelled and de-structured.

Last but not least, there still is that 'personal' question for Hartmut Rosa that I announced previously – namely, that of the locational dependency of his critique of capitalism. For if Rosa does at times diagnostically assert social differentiation, then this indicates not least the author's own socio-cultural status. For example, when he refers to the thesis of the acceleration-induced loss of autonomy to 'material and technical structures integral to our daily lives',[51] he adopts the position of the 'cultural elites'[52] – as if these technical activities pertained, as his example states, to '[listening] to the music that means something to us'.[53] For Rosa, the hunt for 'capacity increases' by means of mastering everyday inconveniences through the purchase of technical devices has increasingly turned into an 'underclass phenomenon'; he believes that the cultural elites are already in the process of realising the futility and contradictoriness of this undertaking. These deliberations are reinforced by the – once again seemingly social-structurally agnostic, yet de facto socio-structurally grounded – claim that late modern society is characterised by a 'far-reaching *ethical autonomy*',[54] or rather an ethical code with 'only minimal restrictions':[55] 'there are hardly any ethical-collective compulsions to do or believe or like anything specific – or *not* to do so'.[56] This claim, which, if anything, reflects the post-conventional lifeworld of a middle-class intellectual operating within a social context of only minimal ethical restrictions, may serve as a representative example of the problem of social critique's distance from its object as mentioned at the beginning of this chapter: an artistic critique of the capitalist social formation which

---

48   Rosa, p. 78 in this volume.
49   Rosa, p. 78 in this volume.
50   Rosa, p. 90 in this volume.
51   Rosa, p. 87 in this volume.
52   Rosa, p. 88 in this volume.
53   Rosa, p. 87 in this volume.
54   Rosa, p. 90 in this volume.
55   Rosa, p. 90 in this volume.
56   Rosa, p. 90 in this volume.

has shifted far – perhaps too far – away from the latter's foundations. I hope I am not being unfair to the author and his critical impetus by saying that to me his thesis of acceleration in its present form seems like a social critique by cultural elites for cultural elites, as an artistic diagnosis of the times for readers of *Die Zeit*. Should this be the case, that would by all means be legitimate – but the question must be raised as to who exactly is the subject of radical change, of a social overcoming of the acceleration regime: can we really expect the cultural elites, the materially well-off (to make use of a classical category of social structural analysis) in this social formation, to collectively and intentionally stage its overthrow? Rosa seems to be thinking in this direction when at the end of his contribution he points out that the accelerated society represents 'a limitless game of escalation that eventually throws even the profiteers and winners into misery'.[57] But are they really capable of leading a social upheaval in the common interest of all, a negation of what they conceive of as the 'good life' (as Rosa seems to believe)? One may understandably have reservations about this. Or perhaps the revolution will be called off by artistic critique itself after all: for Hartmut Rosa in the end carefully suggests that a sociology of social critique should become 'a constitutive corrective instance, especially with respect to those social developments that take on a life of their own'.[58] This, in turn, indeed sounds – very much like what Klaus Dörre is saying – like a re-incorporation of social critique into a reformist political praxis in the spirit of classical-modern, democratic capitalism. To cut a long story short: is 'affirmative protest'[59] really all that critical sociology is destined to amount to?

3. WHAT IS TO BE DONE? TOWARDS A RADICAL SYNTHESIS OF ARTISTIC AND SOCIAL CRITIQUE

As I remarked in the introduction, sociological social critique must reflect and productively resolve its constitutive problem of distance versus proximity: it must address the danger of adopting a position of either too great a proximity or too great a distance toward the object of critical scrutiny – i.e., the capitalist social formation of one's own, of 'our' time. While Klaus Dörre in some ways operates 'too close' to capitalist *Landnahme*'s systemic laws of movement, which then, despite his attention to the critical issues of the losers

---

57   Rosa, p. 97 in this volume.
58   Rosa, p. 96 in this volume.
59   Cf. S. Kluge, 'Affirmativer Protest – Ambivalenzen und Affinitäten der kommunitaristischen Kapitalismuskritik', in Eickelpasch, Rademacher, Lobato (ed.), *Metamorphosen*, pp. 59–79.

of the finance-capitalist transformation, limits his grasp of the specificity of the current mode of socialisation of capitalist subjects, Hartmut Rosa's analysis, by contrast, assumes it can establish the social self-definition of bourgeois modernity, the eternally unrealised dreams of the Enlightenment for autonomy and authenticity, as value reference even for contemporary capitalism, thus ultimately setting himself 'too far removed' from the experiences (explicitly not irrelevant to him) of suffering as experienced by the average member of society. If one reads Dörre as social critic and Rosa as artistic critic of the dominant social formation, then the task at hand is now – to paraphrase Dörre's paraphrase of the 'Theses on Feuerbach' – to unify both roles, or rather both perspectives of critique, in a single person – that of exploitation as well as that of alienation – in an analytical-diagnostic position, in order to thereby bring 'the cultural significance of social critique as well as the social dimension of artistic critique'[60] to bear.

What I wish to argue here, and what I will further elaborate on in my riposte to both Klaus Dörre's and Hartmut Rosa's criticisms of my own introductory text, is that the critical analysis of the late capitalist 'active society' as I have presented it is capable of performing precisely such a synthesis. The sociological imperative of a productive engagement with the proximity-distance problematic indicates that social critique 'must be intrinsically versatile and flexible'[61] – just like the society it declares the object of its critique. The critique of activation I have put forward accommodates the artistic motif of the capitalist perversion of 'freedom' into an institutional demand of (pro-)active social responsibility, thereby validating this motif, so to speak, on the basis of the question of a social critique of the opportunity structures – which are unequally but systematically distributed throughout capitalist society – 'of being able to materially afford and to live up to, in everyday practical terms, the claim to a self-reliant [and socially responsible, S.L.] way of life raised, in the meantime, to the status of a universal norm'.[62]

The 'only' thing this synthesis then still lacks is an operative plea for the overthrow of the capitalist social formation, for a radical restructuring of capitalism's current form of the active society, derived from the synthesis itself. As emphasised at the beginning, social critique is a risky type of sociology – but if one is willing to take that risk anyway, then why not go all the way? 'Critique is not just about lamenting, demanding, or about stating

---

60   Demirović, 'Leidenschaft und Wahrheit', p. 19.
61   Ibid. p. 15.
62   F. Schultheis, 'What's left? Von der Desorientierung zur selbstreflexiven Standortbestimmung linker Gesellschaftskritik', in Eickelpasch, Rademacher, Lobato (eds), *Metamorphosen*, pp. 21–8, here: p. 27.

which aspects of the existing order should function better, but about recognising why the total context of social reproduction remains perpetually crisis-prone and what social forces have an interest therein, in order to then finally move beyond'.[63] To finally move beyond: if sociology aspires to be more than just a servant of intellectual distinction, then sociological social critique cannot fall behind this self-proclaimed objective.

---

63   Demirović, 'Leidenschaft und Wahrheit', p. 32.

Section III

RIPOSTES

CHAPTER 7

Landnahme, Social Conflict, Alternatives – (More than) a Riposte

KLAUS DÖRRE

François-Henri Pinault ... experienced more than the usual traffic jam when he tried to take a taxi through Paris ... The 'serial entrepreneur' became the most prominent victim of what has been a series of unlawful detentions by French workers. In Grenoble, protesting workers prevented four managers from leaving the factory premises for twenty-four hours after an announcement that 733 jobs were to be eliminated. Held captive inside their own offices, the managers of M3 and Sony also had to suffer the consequences of anger triggered by job cuts.

– G. v. Randow, 'Arrest für den Boss', in *Die Zeit*, 8 April 2009

Fearing the dramatic consequences imposed by global crisis, some address-ees of social critique are moving into action. French workers, faced with the relative inefficacy of their trade unions for some time now, are reviving the tradition of 'bossnapping'. In doing so, they engage in both the con-struction and practice of social antagonism(s): 'France thinks in terms of class. Us down here versus you up there. And now that many of president Nicolas Sarkozy's low- and middle-income voters have turned away from him in disillusionment, the 'You' has come to include the political class'.[1] For sociology, this is the point where things start to get interesting. The fact that people think in terms of class is not something that we can take for granted, even in France. For in no other country has the decline of a militant working class culture had such severe consequences as in the case of Germany's southwestern neighbour.[2] Nevertheless, and in contrast to the situation in Germany, scientific social critique was never fully silenced in France. In France we find intellectual reference systems which can be

---

1   G. v. Randow, 'Arrest für den Boss', in *Die Zeit*, 8 April 2009, p. 9.
2   Cf. S. Béaud, M. Pialoux, *Die verlorene Zukunft der Arbeiter*, Konstanz 2004.

updated and re-vitalised should the need arise. This is not so in Germany. To sociological normal critique, nothing could be more boring and tedious than the modern-day descendants of the Marxian proletariat who 'tired and half-heartedly' participate in obligatory demonstrations, waving their 'little bannerette of co-determination' and wearing their 'silk scarves'.[3]

Often the outcome of an 'unrequited love' (for the working class), these sorts of conceptual bias obstruct an understanding of changes in everyday consciousness that are happening even in Germany. Public acceptance of capitalism is declining, particularly among those who are capable of doing serious damage to the system – workers and employees who used to belong to the secure groups in society. So far, this de-legitimisation finds expression in letters to the editor and e-mails instead of public protest. Nevertheless, it is definitely happening. The only question is whether sociology, including critical sociology, realises this. The following riposte revolves around this problem. I shall begin by asking for general absolution. Many of the comments regarding omissions and selectivity in my line of argument are absolutely accurate. These gaps are owed in part to the draft character of the argument itself. Other aspects, such as Rosa's point concerning state social-ism and systems rivalry, would indeed require a lengthier response.[4] Since this is not feasible in the context of this chapter, I will confine myself to a few points.

1. LANDNAHMEN AND THE CRISIS OF TRANSFORMATION

Both of my co-authors describe my approach as economistic. And, admit-tedly, the argument definitely contains some degree of bias in this direction. However, in this case the politico-economic focus was chosen quite deliber-ately. The justificatory regime of contemporary capitalism itself is profoundly economic. The only way to attack capitalism at the very core of its substance is through analysis on the plane of economy and labour. Currently, sociology exhibits multiple blank spots in this regard. Excessive critiques of economi-sation often seem helpless, for they possess very few factual arguments with which to counter market fundamentalism – and market fundamentalism, like it or not, tends toward the economistic. Given that, my central theses

---

3   D. Rucht, 'Ruhe ohne Sturm', in *Die Tageszeitung*, 14 April 2009, at http://www.taz.de/1/debatte/ kommentar/artikel/1/ruhe-ohne-sturm/ on 20.05.2009.

4   In contrast to, for instance, Eric Hobsbawm, I consider the participation of wage earners in productivity increases that could be based on prosperity and effi-ciency to be far more important than the competition posed by state socialism, the rejection of which was widespread in the West.

contained in this book are treated far too generously. Indeed, one could have justifiably asked whether developments leading to the total meltdown of the financial system can be adequately analysed using the concepts of financial market capitalism and *Landnahme*. Economists such as Robert Brenner reject this notion. Brenner considers the term 'finance-driven accumulation' to be a contradiction in itself, because it implies that fictitious capital can become the real economy's structuring force.[5] Some view financial market capitalism not as a formational term of its own accord, but more as of a product of Fordism's decay, while others dispute that the dominance of finance capital is an adequate criterion of periodisation in the first place.[6]

Irrespective of the general difficulty in establishing accurate and appropriate phases of capitalist development at all, both the *Landnahme* theorem and the resulting crisis diagnosis are without a doubt highly controversial. This ought to be noted down; otherwise the very real need for discussion threatens to be all too easily lost behind some blanket accusation of economism. There is, however, one crucial aspect in which the preceding criticisms must be firmly contradicted. In its theoretical substance, the *Landnahme* theorem represents the exact opposite of an economistic approach, for it generalises what Marx had still believed to be valid only for capitalism's initial phase of primitive accumulation: in order to function, capitalism periodically requires a political force that disrupts economic 'regularities'.

This also touches upon an important criterion of any periodisation: namely, that one can only reasonably speak of financial market capitalism as a specific capitalist formation if the latter involves more than just an economic principle. What marks the qualitative novelty of capitalist socialisation in each phase, according to the conceptualisation presented here, are particular, more or less political, *transfer mechanisms* that facilitate a transmission of the finance-capitalist logic of competition to spheres of society that were until then structured in a completely different manner. Yet my critics assert that the *Landnahme* theorem is in its essence 'sociologically unsatisfactory', imprecise (Lessenich) and better suited to the analysis of finance capitalism than Fordist capitalism (Rosa). And indeed: the concept as it stands is more of a research programme than a mature and fully developed theory. However, some clarifications are nevertheless possible. First of all, Hartmut

---

5   Cf. R. Brenner, 'A Way Out of the Global Crisis?', Interview with Robert Brenner by Jeong Seong-Jin, 4 February 2009, at http://english.hani.co.kr/arti/english_edition/e_international/336766.html.

6   Cf. J. Bischoff, R. Detje, 'Eine neue gesellschaftliche Betriebsweise?', in K. Dörre, B. Röttger (eds), *Das neue Marktregime*, Hamburg 2003, pp. 55–71; W. F. Haug, 'Krise des Kapitalismus – Krise seiner Naturverhältnisse', in *Das Argument* 279(6), 2008, pp. 785–94.

Rosa's proposal to conceive of *Landnahme* and 'land surrender' as one unified process is perfectly consistent with the theorem's objective. The same is true with respect to Fordist capitalism. The 'liberation' of labour power from the traditional sector (*Landnahme* as commodification) became possible as welfare-state institutions adopted the function of primary or secondary social networks (de-commodification and 'land surrender').

A second suggestion of Rosa's also seems sensible to me. Essentially, there can be no *Landnahme* based exclusively on de- or re-commodification. The historical modus operandi of capitalist *Landnahmen* each entails a wide range of strategies. In part, the deployment of these strategies occurs randomly, and is thus contingent. However, every modus operandi encompasses a dominant strategy that can only be altered through extensive transfer crises. The (German) Great Depression of 1929–1932 was accompanied by such a shift. The tenets of *laissez-faire* capitalism were abandoned across an extremely polarised spectrum of social development possibilities, spanning the fascist dictatorships of continental Europe, the US-American New Deal, and Sweden's Industrial Democracy. The counter-movement began to pick up speed around the crisis of 1973–1975. Ultimately, historical evaluation of the global crisis of 2008–2009 will be decided by the question of whether the forms of state crisis management will in fact signify a change in the modus operandi of capitalist *Landnahmen*; that is, of whether a phase of market opening will indeed followed by a phase of market closure.

Hartmut Rosa now complains that my approach contains no logic of escalation, which – analogous to the principle of acceleration – should imply a perpetually intensifying crisis of capitalist socialisation (*Vergesellschaftung*). Here, Rosa hits the nail on the head. Still – I will not make any theoretical concessions on this question. In contrast to market orthodoxy, I consider capitalism to be intrinsically crisis-prone. That said, this type of society will certainly not perish on account of its economic crises – which continually return on an expanded scale – or its drive to acceleration. Crises lead to changes only if and to the extent that they are political. Should movements and alternative models of society that could potentially transcend the system fail to materialise, then changes in the mode of socialisation occur within the capitalist form.

However, one should add that the integration of subaltern classes and groups in such cases nevertheless remains fragile. Finance-capitalist rationality cannot be singularly imposed from above without encountering problems. Starting at the level of the international system of states, this rationality collides with various competing policies. Indeed, there are only a few states in which the finance-capitalist model has actually been generalised in all of its core facets. Frictions, tensions and contradictions with the potential to develop into 'trouble spots' occur all the time, both inside and outside of states. In this sense, the differentiation between periods of crisis and those of stability is 'always relative'.[7] The adoption of the finance-dominated accumulation regime also forestalled the 'epicentre of future crises'.[8] Despite this, some of the tensions and contradictions generated by finance capitalism will still be effective (perhaps even more so) after the acute crisis of this social formation has been resolved.

2. SOCIAL CONFLICT AND ECOLOGICAL CRISIS

This is particularly relevant with respect to the return of the social question to the public political arena, to the tensions and conflicts I have subsumed under the label of *discriminatory precarity*. This term contains a social-structural assertion that Stephan Lessenich does not take into account. It signals a reconstruction of 'networks of class power', i.e., successful redistribution to the benefit of privileged asset owners and income recipients, as has been occurring in all developed capitalisms since the 1970s. Yet the term also illustrates that precarisation within the wealthy Western societies does not imply the return to past manifestations of the social question.

Hartmut Rosa is particularly oblivious to the explosiveness of the new social cleavages, because he adheres to an interpretational framework according to the logic of which the 'problems of "overweight"'[9] ultimately mitigate the explosive power of struggles over distribution. The anti- or post-productivist turn of sections of German sociology has apparently impeded the ability to grasp the fact that the termination of the Fordist class compromise imposed 'from above' has damaged the mode of intermediary conflict regulation over the longterm. If diagnoses of the times, such as the 'colonisation of lifeworlds'[10] were still based on the welfare-state pacification of class conflict, then the finance-capitalist *Landnahme* now disables this very regulatory capacity. The result is neither a 'disorganised capitalism' nor the return of industrial class conflict in its known historical form.

---

7   J. Hirsch, 'Weshalb Periodisierung?', in M. Candeias, F. Deppe (ed.), *Ein neuer Kapitalismus?*, Hamburg 2001, pp. 41–7, here: p. 45.

8   F. Chesnais, 'Das finanzdominierte Akkumulationsregime: theoretische Begründung und Reichweite', in C. Zeller (ed.), *Die globale Enteignungsökonomie*, Münster 2004, pp. 217–54, here: pp. 219 and 242.

9   U. Beck, *Risk society: Towards a New Modernity*. Reprint. (Theory, Culture and Society), 2009 [1992], p.20.

10   Cf. J. Habermas, *The Theory of Communicative Action vol. 2. The Critique of Functionalist Reason*, Oxford 1989, p. 196.

Social conflict has become fragmented. The breakdown of organised labour relations in some sectors and countries is accompanied by new workers' movements in other states and regions. What remains crucial, however, is that collective interests are often no longer articulated within standardised conflicts. In quarters and regions that have fallen far behind in terms of their relative economic competitiveness, 'bargaining by riots' has long become commonplace; these 'riots', despite the undeniable relevance of ethnicity- or gender-specific constructs, are widely motivated by spontaneous or organised class action. The (sub)urban riots in France and Britain represented class-specific bread-and-butter conflicts to a large degree.[11] Just like the renewed militancy of well-educated Greek youths or French workers, this illustrates that outdated forms of intermediary conflict regulation no longer function for large social groups, even within the capitalist centre. The more that institutionalised forms of workers' power come under pressure, the more pronounced is the readiness of under-represented groups to express anger, disappointment and frustration in non-standardised conflicts.

The image of a struggle for the 'poisoned pie',[12] the consumption of which then further propels the spiral of destruction, hardly captures the reality of this development. The wage share that has stagnated since the 1990s and the declining actual wages among the bottom quarter of wage earners (in Germany a reduction of almost 14 per cent between 1995 and 2006) will contribute as little to deceleration as will the explosion of profits in the private economy (an increase by 25 per cent in the eleven quarters of the short-lived economic boom alone).[13] Instead, the opposite is occurring: profits that are not re-invested simply fuel 'Casino Capitalism' even further. Before the outbreak of the financial crisis, excess capital flowed into food speculation to a truly grotesque extent. This resulted in the price of wheat and other crops increasing, thereby intensifying the hunger crisis in the world's slums. Poverty and precarisation, for their part, destroy an awareness of the future and thus also obstruct the adoption of anti-consumerist lifestyles. Bargain hunting, of which Rosa accuses the 'underclasses' (and which of course is pursued by other groups as well), is by no means an expression of luxury. It is motivated by relative poverty as compensation for social insecurity and as an expression of cultural discrimination. It is unthinkable to speak of false

11   Cf. L. Wacquant, 'Die Wiederkehr des Verdrängten – Unruhen, Rasse' und soziale Spaltung in drei fortgeschrittenen Gesellschaften', in R. Castel, K. Dörre, (eds), *Prekarität, Abstieg, Ausgrenzung*, Frankfurt a.M., New York 2009, pp. 85–112.

12   Cf. U. Beck, *Gegengifte*, Frankfurt a.M. 1988, pp. 209–55.

13   C. Logeay, R. Zwiener, 'Deutliche Realeinkommensverluste für Arbeitnehmer: Die neue Dimension eines Aufschwungs', in *WSI-Mitteilungen*61 (8), 2008, pp. 415–21, here: p. 420.

wants and corresponding forms of consumption without addressing the question of re-distribution in favour of weaker interests. After all, anything else, especially given the widespread immiseration in developing countries, would amount to an ecological counter-revolution.[14]

3. HEGEMONY AND SUBJECTIVITY

Another point of criticism formulated by both Hartmut Rosa and Stephan Lessenich is in fact valid. My construction does indeed lack any deliberations concerning hegemony or subject theory. Therefore, it may seem in parts of my contribution as if finance-capitalist structures emerge outside of praxis and subjectivity. This is – of course – not the case. If one goes back to the genesis of shareholder value forms of management, it quickly becomes evident that this transfer mechanism consists of contingent actor strategies and micro-policies, as well as countervailing practices. The implementation of this form of governance can be constructed, in reference to Foucault, as 'subjectless' hegemony. Based on Antonio Gramsci, it is then possible to map out, moreover, the embattled, adversarial moment of hegemony formation. In doing so, however, the limitations of a governmentality- or discourse-theoretical reconstruction of subjectivity must be taken into careful consideration. The reconstruction of modes of governance, in the style of Foucault, does not transcend the level of guiding images and concepts, the relevance of which for (any type of) action is presupposed but not proven. Between the guiding images of shareholder value management on the one hand, and the *dispositif* (that is to say, the level of management practices) on the other, lie numerous social fields with their own respective rules, rationalities and logics of action. Even after reaching this level, one still knows very little about the subjectivity, the explicit consciousness, or the forms of habitus.[15]

These layers of everyday consciousness can only be reconstructed with the aid of sophisticated empirical research. More recent studies have raised

---

14   At this point even Ulrich Beck speaks of a 'fatal magnetism between poverty, social vulnerability, corruption and the accumulation of dangers'. (U. Beck, 'Jenseits von Klasse und Nation: Individualisierung und Transnationalisierung sozialer Ungleichheiten', in *Soziale Welt*, 59 [4], 2008, pp. 301–25, here: p. 313).

15   On the mutual, dynamic convergence and divergence of collective guiding images and practices as well as of subjective self-conceptions and habitus formation cf. H. Rosa, S. Schmidt, 'Which Challenge, Whose Response? Ein Vier-Felder-Modell der Challenge-Response-Analyse sozialen Wandels', in D. de Nève, M. Reiser, K.-U. Schnapp (eds), *Herausforderung – Akteur – Reaktion*, Baden-Baden 2007, pp. 53–72.

doubts about whether such terms as *subjectification, labour force entre-preneur*, or *the entrepreneurial self* really allow for an adequate depiction of characteristic forms of consciousness. Accordingly, it is very unclear whether a planned economy in the service of profit maximisation has ever been a hegemonic project actually resting on broad consensus. Recent research, including that of my own team, suggests a different conclusion. The market-centred mode of control forces workers and employees to per-manently devote themselves to the limitation of market risks. Though this occurs more or less successfully, it need not necessarily be related to an approval of the corresponding control practices. Strict profit management is often criticised quite harshly, even rejected; people simply see no chance of escaping it. Subjects therefore remain within action corridors, the limits of which seem like an impenetrable wall. This does not mean, however, that their behaviour indicates a form of consent. When surveyed workers and employees conceive of their own company as the 'good', which is to be pro-tected against the 'bad' (because crisis-prone, unjust, and unsustainable for future generations) society, then their own qualifications and performance levels serve as points of reference. Management and its business concepts and promises of freedom, by contrast, embody the disregard for perfor-mance and the production of insecurity.[16]

This *non-correspondence* of guiding images, institutional practices and subjectivity is what really requires an explanation. The impacts of transfer mechanisms such as strict profit management of companies have unfolded over a long period of time *despite* the fact that, or perhaps precisely *because*, corresponding regimes have generated a vast number of obstinate forms of processing for the respective action requirements. Hartz IV, for example, takes effect among the long-term unemployed not because of but *despite* strict rules of conditionality, which either have no effect whatsoever on (the pro-active efforts of) a large proportion of those affected, or are simply per-ceived as additional bullying on the part of the state.[17] To phrase it more generally: the neo-liberal mode of governance's promise of freedom, like the ideologies of activation and acceleration, has long since begun to collide with bulky subjectivities. If finance capitalism does indeed rely on consent,

16   Cf. M. Behr, K. Dörre, 'Arbeitsbewusstsein, Interessenorientierung und Gesellschaftsbild von Beschäftigten in Ostdeutschland – Ergebnisse einer Belegs-chaftsbefragung in einem Unternehmen der Optischen Industrie in Thüringen', Jena 2008 (MS); D. Eversberg, 'Lebenssituation und -perspektiven jüngerer Arbeitne-hmerinnen und Arbeitnehmer – eine Literaturstudie', Jena 2008 (MS). Cf. also T. Kämpf, *Die neue Unsicherheit*, Frankfurt a.M., New York 2008.

17   Cf. P. Bescherer, S. Röbenack, K. Schierhorn, 'Eigensinnige, Kunden' – Wie Hartz IV wirkt … und wie nicht', in Castel, Dörre (ed.), *Prekarität*, pp. 145–56.

then it is a passive consent. The questions of how dominance accommodates obstinate practices, at what point obstinacy becomes everyday life resistance, and under which conditions such everyday resistance turns into collective, organised political agency can only be answered by means of thoroughly empirical subject research.

4. THE MODEL OF CRITIQUE

The question of the critical sting of such research types also addresses the model of critique my co-authors find lacking in my approach. In his book *Zweifel und Einmischung* (Doubt and Intervention), Michael Walzer distinguishes between two groups of social critics: those who adopt the standpoint of transcendence and consider themselves, as it were, outside of or beyond society; and those who remain 'inside the cave' and feel obligations to a moral community which determine their standards of critique. Walzer favours the second group – intellectuals who are at all times aware of the moral foundations of their social critique and the social ties which motivate their partisanship in social conflicts. Though Walzer's reasoning, based on a contraposition of two prototypical representatives of each group (Gramsci versus Silone), is not convincing in each and every aspect, I do agree on one important point.

The normative content of every social critique originates, ultimately, in a specific moral community. At this point a few lines addressing my own biographical context are in order: for me, this moral community is the world of workers, employees and ordinary civil servants, whose lifestyles are 'too readily imputed to the conservatism of proletarians (or that of their "apparatuses")' and described 'as signs of embourgeoisement'.[18] I stopped belonging to that world long ago. As an adolescent, I considered the concepts of a successful life entrenched in that world to be pure snobbishness. Today, confronted with its presumably irreversible decline, I treat this lived 'scarcity in the midst of prosperity' with far more respect than before. Much of what at the time seemed stuffy to me from an analytical point of view (the concentration of all resources on building one's own house, for example) represents nothing more than a quite elaborate form of personal security, derived from extensive life experience, against major social risks – old age, illness, poverty, social disregard, disability; risks which have never fully disappeared from the lives of wage earners and their families. Having respect for this has nothing to do with conservatism. It is rather a scientific scepticism toward

---

18   P. Bourdieu, *Algeria 1960*, Cambridge 1972, pp. 62–3.

any kind of scheme that elevates highly flexible artists' job markets to the future reality of society, only to simultaneously label all those who insist on security and collective protection as hopeless traditionalists. Workers and employees, who even in the era of finance-dominated capitalism still constitute the majority of the working population, suffer a fate similar to that of Bourdieu's Algerian sub-proletarians. They are constantly assessed against a supposedly ineluctable ideal of modernisation which, considering their life circumstances, they cannot and do not wish to fulfil in the first place.

Even reconstructions of neo-liberal 'governments of freedom' composed with critical intent are not beyond committing such analytical fallacies. They commonly lack a necessary feel for the subject area of social critique. In a social constellation in which precarisation and unemployment lead to the perception that it is a privilege to be the 'object of rational exploitation',[19] the silencing of social critique is disastrous. Nancy Fraser was one of the few who urged us 'to demystify "post-socialist" ideologies concerning the shift from redistribution to recognition'.[20] This does not imply a preference for social critique over diagnoses of alienation and policies of recognition. Both variants of critique move (not exclusively, but also) on the terrain of the capitalist mode of production and heteronomy. If these variants seek to qualitatively distinguish themselves from conservative, backward-looking critiques, or from those merely interested in the preservation of the status quo, they must not leave the normative frame of reference stipulated by the principle of equality. Despite all difficulties of definition, it is with regard to *egalité* that leftist and rightist critiques of capitalism differ.[21]

It is for this reason that I do not call for simply abandoning the conceptual framework of equality. The waning of social protections is a problem of deprivation and thus a genuine object of social critique. However, what a socially critical perspective does not accomplish is the conceptual accommodation of the perceived gain in freedom through flexibilisation – as is characteristic, for example, of single self-employed and creative workers. From the perspective of those working on monthly contracts in the film business, or the hopeful small business owner running his or her own techno label, or the journalist who works as a subcontracted freelancer for TV and radio broadcasts, the equation of the erosion of welfare-state-protected 'normal employment' with social decay, as seems to be suggested by Robert Castel, inevitably appears as nostalgia for an overwhelmingly male and, meanwhile, dying form of industrial wage labour. A critique that

---

19   Ibid.
20   N. Fraser, *Justice Interruptus: Critical Reflections on the 'Postsocialist' Condition*, New York 1997, p. 4.
21   Cf. N. Bobbio, *Rechts und Links*, Berlin 1994.

seeks to have an impact can only avoid this dilemma of a fragmentation of the modes of critique if it insists on developing an appealing synthesis of social and artistic critique. This is where the inquiring temporary worker comes into play. Surely, he also serves as a stylistic device, yet is not quite an 'artifice' as Lessenich implies. My introductory statement comes from a real person. Throughout my deliberations, the temporary worker epitomises several meanings. Firstly, he represents the necessity of re-defining equality with due regard to the subalterns in times of precarisation. 'Equal pay, equal treatment' is an age-old socialist demand no longer to be realised only 'within the class', but, in a situation of increasing precarisation, perhaps even in terms of an approximation *between* classes (or class currents). *Secondly*, the temporary worker illustrates an everyday practical permutation of social and artistic critique. The matter at hand is not only distributional justice. Just to underline the demand for equality, the temporary worker – despite being male, white and well-educated – must insist on the recognition of his special status, namely that of difference. For this reason, the e-mail, *thirdly*, contains an implicit critique of trade unions and political parties which practically deny such recognition of difference, thereby impeding policies of de-precarisation. And finally, *fourthly* – this is the crucial point – doubts concerning the legitimacy of existing capitalism arise precisely from those daily experiences of discrimination which Hartmut Rosa deems irrelevant. A notion of the good life that relies to a large extent on norms of equality and needs for recognition collides with the fundamental experience of being treated as a 'second class human'. This generates doubts about the system.

These are the experiences a sociological critique of capitalism can, in fact must, begin from. Equipped with an analytical sensorium for these kinds of everyday complaints about social injustices, it then goes beyond this basic form of social critique and transgresses the consensus offered by the community of 'common values'. Its criteria are not produced exclusively within the moral community, but throughout society as a whole. Every form of capitalism corresponds to a justificatory regime which standardises demands and expectations, the worthiness of which can then be evaluated. A critic of capitalism demanding and promoting such evaluation by no means removes him or herself from society. He or she may be distanced, but does not stand outside of the object of critique.

5. ALTERNATIVES

It is from this perspective that I formulated my critique of financial market capitalism. It is aimed at the corresponding justificatory regime and the structures which legitimise it. The fundamental promise of the market-based *cité* was that (re-)commodification would lead to increased economic efficiency and growing prosperity. The intensification of social inequalities has surely been accomplished; however, the promised positive results of increases in efficiency and prosperity have thus far failed to materialise. After a few decades of deregulation and privatisation, the economy of the developed countries (though they are by no means the only ones affected) is in worse condition than ever before. Numerous efforts at adjustment to the supposed imperatives of globalisation now appear in a different light altogether. The price paid to shore up the economy in the name of global *Standort*-competition is no longer legitimised by anything. In fact inequalities, dislocations and crises have grown to an extent that they are beginning to be dysfunctional for the system itself.

The task of a sociological critique of capitalism is to reveal the reasons for this gigantic system failure. Militant actions like 'bossnapping' are viewed by this critique as initial attempts, albeit limited in effectiveness, at rendering identifiable the 'faceless collective capitalist'[22] who gradually draws individual capitalists into subjugation. In doing so, however, the critique does not adopt the victim's perspective. Its actual objective lies in the attempt to confront both those lamenting and those already in revolt with the message that behind those rational sub-systems lies a system which in its totality amounts to a complete absurdity. The moral critique is suspended and replaced with a critique that starts from the contradictions and crises of capitalist socialisation itself.

The question, then, is: what might such a critique aim for? Which alternative project might it pursue, in our post-socialist times? Does it attack only one particular variant of capitalism, or capitalism itself (Rosa)? Does it fight for a new social democratic project, or for the 'overthrow' of capitalism (Lessenich)? At this point I could take the easy way out by reminding my esteemed critics that they demand from me a stronger commitment than they themselves are prepared to make. Another line of argument could be that which Marx deployed against his anarchist critics: capitalism, just as the capitalist state, cannot be 'abolished'. More likely is that it will, quite

---

22 M. Castells, *Der Aufstieg der Netzwerkgesellschaft*, Opladen 2001, p. 532; W. Streeck, 'German Capitalism: Does It Exist? Can It Survive?', in: C. Crouch, W. Streeck (eds), *Political Economy of Modern Capitalism*, London 1997, pp. 33–54, here pp. 51–3.

similar to the phase of primitive accumulation, gradually wither away as its functional mechanisms are suppressed and replaced by new principles of rationality. However, as I am happy to concede, the inquiring temporary worker deserves a more precise answer. The first part of this answer, my dear colleagues, will probably be far worse than you expected. For I call not only for a double strategy, but for a multiple strategy – not least because of my deep distrust of hermetically sealed scenarios. For example: a good decade ago, shrewd analysts predicted that the 'deregulatory bias of globalisation' would lead to the 'perverse outcome' that the 'less well-performing Anglo-American model of capitalism' would '[outcompete] the better performing "Rhenish model"'.[23] Because the cage of globalisation was portrayed as being even more restrictive than it really is, the only remaining lifeline was a supply-side corporatism, which found political expression in the *Bündnis für Arbeit* (Alliance for Jobs). But even without this (ultimately) failed alliance, 'German capitalism' has approached the Anglo-Saxon model through expansion of the low-wage sector. And yet it is this latter variant of capitalism in particular, which incidentally served as the blueprint for political adjustment in the first place, that is now coming under fire in the financial crisis.

Bearing this in mind, a serious critique of capitalism must broaden its perspective to include scopes of action within the system. Much of what is necessary and possible under the conditions of crisis will surely stabilise capitalism. And, taking into consideration the danger of a new authoritarianism, this is by all means imperative. Whether speaking of the introduction of stricter rules for financial market actors, effective measures against the global food crisis, reducing the most severe manifestations of poverty, protection against precarisation via legal minimum wages, or the levelling of the wage gap between men and women (which in this country still reaches 20 per cent in some places) – none of this would necessarily bring capitalism to its knees. In this sense, there is no fundamental reason that 'we could not overcome the three greatest consequences of class differences: unequal access to education, to health services, and to a guaranteed decent income throughout life'.[24] Quite frankly, implementing all of this outside of commodification would not even amount to a social-democratic project. If one imagines this theoretically feasible project on a global scale, however, it seems downright utopian.

This statement is even more valid with regard to a new social-democratic

---

23 I. Wallerstein, *Utopistics, or: Historical Choices of the Twenty-First Century*, New York 1998, pp. 78–9.

24 Ibid.

platform, an eco-social New Deal. Even in its technocratic version of an eco-logical industrial policy, it contains numerous unknowns: For example, no one knows whether or to what extent a major shift toward renewable energy production would create new employment opportunities. What is obvious, on the other hand, is that the dynamic of innovation in energy production and application must be accelerated if we are to even come anywhere near meeting climate goals such as the necessary reduction of CO_2 emissions. The respective social orientation that lies behind such necessary innovations in turn holds great conflict potential. After all, the large-scale technologi-cal solutions favoured by the energy corporations and their lobbies, and decentralised solar energy as proposed by people like Hermann Scheer,[25] are worlds apart. A critical sociology must intervene in these controversies instead of attacking some vague elite deals beforehand (which may or may not materialise, and even if they do, it is unclear what they will look like).

Ultimately – and this is my most important argument – even a mere social-democratic project would only stand a chance of realisation if an antagonistic force emerges that is actually capable of challenging post-democratic elites. I hold three substantial minimum requirements for the coordinate system of such a force to be more or less obligatory. Firstly, a counter-hegemonic concept must exhaust the socialisation potential of modern productive forces. That means assuming a state of development 'where nobody has one exclusive sphere of activity but each can become accomplished in any branch he wishes; society regulates the general produc-tion, making it possible for me to do one thing today and another tomorrow … without ever becoming a hunter, fisherman, herdsman or critic'.[26] I con-sider such a conception to be possible already, at least in the developed countries. It would have to be a flexible phase model allowing for changes of occupation throughout one's lifespan, as opposed to some naive postulation of the general abandonment of the division of labour altogether. An insti-tutionalised status of activity allowing for the option of being hired for any paid activity after having worked in a certain gainful activity for a period of time would render accessible a mode of flexibility that would surely entail an increase in the quality of life for the largest possible share of the population.

A higher quality of life, however, can only be delivered by such a concept if it, secondly, is tied to an egalitarian distribution of assets and incomes, as well as employment opportunities, education and participation. Without

---

25   Cf. H. Scheer, 'Energie – neu denken!', in *Widerspruch, Beiträge zu sozialis-tischer Politik* 54, 2008, pp. 53–62; U. Brand, 'Umwelt' in der neoliberal-imperialen Politik. Sozial-ökologische Perspektiven demokratischer Gesellschaftspolitik', in: ibid. pp. 139–47.

26   Marx, Engels, 'The German Ideology', *Collected Works*, vol. 5, p. 47.

such redistribution and a restriction of 'negative freedoms' (Polanyi), exercised at the cost of large social majorities, the expansion of individual options in life remains for many a mere fiction. In a society in which any demand for redistribution immediately provokes accusations of social envy, the task at hand is a very arduous one. But again, redistribution is not only about money and assets – it is also about working and (especially) nonworking hours. Shorter full-time working hours (which would translate, on average, into longer working hours for women and shorter working hours for men) remain an indispensable goal – particularly in terms of gender justice – for the future.[27]

If the question of sensible patterns of production and consumption is to be not only asked, but also given a proper answer, then it immediately raises the related question of alternative, more rational forms of economic life. In other words, it is not only a problem of individual life planning, but also of the social planning of production. This is precisely what the term *economic democracy* (*Wirtschaftsdemokratie*) encapsulates, with which I intend to sketch out a perspective for the inquiring temporary worker. At this point, the task cannot be to present a feasible democratic economic model. My proposed periodisation of capitalist development shows that it would be foolish to simply inherit and adopt previous social-democratic (Fritz Naphtali) or left-socialist (Viktor Agartz) conceptualisations. In my view, however, it is the crisis of finance capitalism itself that raises the question of new forms of economic democracy. It has become commonplace across the diverse spectrum of 'management philosophies' today to acknowledge that processes of rationalisation and innovation depend on the informal knowledge of employees. That which is demanded, albeit rarely consistently practised, on a company level can hardly be all that far-fetched for society as a whole in terms of the *what* and *wherefore* of production and consumption. This is all the more valid since, for example, crisis management in the banking and automotive sector has depended on planning mechanisms being established (beyond any democratic public, of course) by those very same 'expertocracies' whose (excessive) influence led to the worldwide financial market disaster in the first place.

Approaches to economic democracy must be established on at least four levels: direct participation by employees at the workplace and within the company; collective self-direction within the context of large companies, thereby rendering explicit that such economic organisations essentially represent public (and thus social) institutions; regional and national economic

---

27   The close connection between a well-financed public sector and high rates of employment of women indicates how this could be realised. Cf. G. Bosch, S. Lehndorff, J. Rubery, *European Employment Models in Flux*, Houndmills, Basingstoke 2009.

and structural councils; and democratisation of important international institutions. The latter would initially entail an Europeanisation of co-determination, but also a self-critical appraisal of corruption within the ranks of worker's interest representation and, moreover, the inclusion of representatives of reproductive interests (environmental and consumer protection organisations) in important company decisions. The extension of democratic participation to the strategic investment decisions of large companies could well be integrated into such a programme. Democratic legitimation and participation by wage earners could also help distinguish public state intervention from the authoritarian protectionism being suggested to the population as a system-preserving, problem-solving strategy today. Economic democracy would by no means be the counterpart to a 'zero option', but instead, and here I am in agreement with Burkart Lutz, the regulatory system of a new constellation of prosperity which gives large numbers of people the ability 'to live their lives the way they want to'.[28]

Epilogue

Is this vision really attractive enough to at least spark a debate about necessary changes? And if so, what force would be available to realise such changes? My – admittedly, not particularly satisfying – answer to this is: the sources of workers' power have not yet run completely dry and could perhaps be harnessed more intensely once again. Ultimately though, the goal must be to weave together in new ways the power of wage earners with political publics, consumer and discursive power, the influence of protest movements, non-profit organisations, cooperatives, and other civil society organisations into a single fabric. We are talking about a form of power which capitalises on new information and communication technologies, creates publics and – perhaps in the Habermasian sense – has faith in the informal force of the better argument to widen and generalise the finance-capitalist regime's problems of legitimation. For the time being, I will refer to this combination, of oppositional discursive power, the power of wage earners, and cooperation with other civil society actors, as *associated power*. Should such a patchwork left, or 'mosaic left'[29] of the 21st century emerge, it will require both the astute 'abolisher of capitalism', Lessenich, and its no less

28   B. Lutz, 'Sozialismus, warum denn nicht?', in *Mitbestimmung* 55 (1/2), 2009, pp. 48–51, here: p. 51.
29   Cf. H.-J. Urban, 'Die Mosaik-Linke. Vom Aufbruch der Gewerkschaften zur Erneuerung der Bewegung', in: *Blätter für deutsche und internationale Politik* 54 (5), 2009, pp. 71–8.

prudent 'beguiler', Rosa. Since the effort toward a reanimation of social critique seeks more than anything to empower marginalised groups, it relies on support from social sectors that are utterly unfamiliar with socially critical arguments. For the continuation of the discussion, however, we can make use of a rising level of public interest. As sociologists, we have at our disposal a forum that in fact invites the addressees of critique to direct exchange. Accordingly, our e-mail discussion partner gets the last word:

> Well, you seem to be very optimistic that the local subalterns will learn one day.
> ... I'm afraid that they'd sooner beat their children to death, while unions like
> IG Metall go on dutifully producing placards. I don't even want to go into the
> ecological consequences of an industrial policy and way of life that is not generalisable on a global scale.
>
> (A friend who works in political education)

One could see things this way, and despair.

> Let me give you an example of how things are done in the German metal industry
> these days. Let's get to the point ...: there is a war going on within German businesses ... At first glance, employees seem satisfied, as one always tries to keep
> one's composure. But don't ask them about their degree of satisfaction with their
> job or income, otherwise you will quickly see how seized by bitterness and anger
> they really are. Really, it makes you want to puke. Many colleagues are burnt out
> and exhausted, and on top of that, we now have to worry about whether our jobs
> are safe again. Well, great! Things really have to change ... for the simple reason
> that it can only get better if we work together.
>
> (An engineer, metal works company, 450 employees)

I hope so too!

CHAPTER 8

Antagonists and Critical Integrationists, or: What Do We Do with the Spoiled Pie?

HARTMUT ROSA

Sometimes it is the simplest of images that prove most useful in identifying the core aspects of complex problems. The debates in this book, which I find very illuminating indeed, are permeated by two moments of tension that surface repeatedly throughout the text and which are more closely related to one another than may initially appear. On the one hand, we have continually counterposed the perspectives of artistic and social critique of capitalism (or those of a moral and an ethical critique); on the other hand, it is apparent in the introductory texts and above all in the criticisms (especially in my own) that there exists a profound disagreement between our respective diagnoses of the times and formation analyses with regard to that question about the 'boat' – and who exactly is sitting in it, and where. Are 'we', as subjects of late modern societies, all in the same boat – or is that a misleading metaphor concealing the true constellation of social interests? Are we perhaps sitting in two different boats, perhaps even two different gunboats, altogether – and headed on a collision course? Behind this metaphorical question we find two long-standing traditions of the critique of capitalism, which for our purposes I would like to refer to here as the 'antagonistic' and the 'integrationist' positions. I will attempt to explicate this view by using another image – that of a pie to be baked and then shared. Societies collectively produce a 'pie' of goods and services (the 'social product'), yet also of opportunities, privileges and (secure and insecure, desirable and undesirable) positions, all of which must then be shared and distributed. Antagonistic critiques of capitalism mainly focus on the unjust distribution of this pie: some receive larger pieces than others, some hardly receive anything at all, some pieces contain juicy cherries while other pieces may only have bitter crumbs. One variant is the critique of the pie's *production*: not everyone has to work equally hard, some have to produce under miserable conditions while others are excluded from the production process altogether. This is the source of the very real conflicts of interests and distribution battles of which both my colleagues Lessenich and, even more insistently, Dörre, remind us. This is where social critique that focuses on inequality, injustice, and exclusion, as well as class-, strata-, or gender-specific inequalities originates. Incidentally, Stephan Lessenich seems to be of the opinion that only a sociology which actually bases itself on an analysis of these inequalities is real sociology, as he accuses me of an 'anti-sociological' approach that largely ignores or disregards these issues of distribution. Klaus Dörre also voices this allegation quite explicitly. However, there is a second form of this pie-critique, namely the 'integrationist' form: it does not deal with how the pie is produced per se, but (instead) with its texture. To put it more succinctly: its objection (which often appears in the guise of 'artistic critique') is that the pie as a whole is, for lack of a better word, spoiled. In its mild variant this could mean that the pie does not taste good (i.e., it is based on a false understanding of prosperity or well-being), while in its more radical version it states that the pie is mouldy or poisoned (and thus necessarily makes all those who consume it unhappy). I call this critique 'integrationist' because it is inclined to forgo internal differences within the community of pie-eaters: the pie is rotten for all of 'us', independent of our respective position in the social hierarchy; it is a problem affecting all, or in fact affecting those who receive the largest slices (the 'winners') even more.[1]

If we apply this metaphor to the diagnoses of reality put forth in this book, then the significance of the argument quickly becomes clear: *Landnahme*, acceleration and activation are, in my view, far more effective, radical and conclusive when examining the elites than when seeking to understand the phenomena of precarity and exclusion. Economic, cultural and political elites devote themselves to the 'engine of acceleration and activation' far more easily and with much less resistance; they are much more likely than members of de-privileged strata to accept or even embrace that their way of life, their creativity and their subjectivity are to be subjected to a radical *Landnahme*. The latter are quite frequently (and involuntarily) 'decelerated by force' and pacified. This is exactly what Klaus Dörre accuses

---

1 That the (re-)production of the pie can of course be threatened by operation-logical contradictions in the production process is beyond dispute. This is the domain of functionalist critique. I explicitly agree with Klaus Dörre – not only that the capitalist acceleration regime includes by functional necessity a 'downside', that is to say, that it can only be maintained under certain legal, political, infrastructural and even biographical conditions of stability, but also in the diagnosis that late modern 'turbo-capitalism' has unchained and radicalised the forces of acceleration to such an extent that the conditions of stability run the risk of being eroded. This is precisely what the third and thirteenth chapters of my book on acceleration address.

Stephan Lessenich of when he points out that the precariously employed in particular have not internalised the logic of activation nearly as thoroughly as it may seem to cultural elites. This is *not* to say, of course, that the disadvantaged do not suffer under such conditions (or not *more so*): if they do not eat from the pie, or only very little of the pie, they may not ingest as much poison – but poison or no poison, if they do not eat they will eventually starve. At this point, however, I would like to defend my general diagnosis of acceleration against the accusation issued explicitly by Stephan Lessenich in this volume, but which has also been and is being formulated by many other critics elsewhere; namely, that it only describes the lifeworlds of elites, that it is a 'social critique by cultural elites for cultural elites … an artistic diagnosis of the times for readers of *Die Zeit*'. There is virtually no social field in which we do *not* observe the phenomena of acceleration I have identified: I have received incessant, at this point countless reactions from educational institutions, churches, theatres and museums, from representatives of the media and politics, but also from hospitals, care facilities, business associations, recreational facilities, and even from the *Bundeswehr* (German armed forces) identifying the acceleration phenomenon as a central problem for their respective field or institution. Whoever thinks that less privileged strata are not affected by the compulsions of acceleration should perhaps spend a day with hospital staff, mobile care service personnel, supermarket cashiers, construction workers (who almost always have to work under tightly calculated deadlines, the non-attainment of which incurs contract penalties) or long-distance lorry drivers: indeed, I am rather suspicious of the empirical 'proximity' of sociological researchers who claim in all seriousness that acceleration is only a problem of the elites. That the compulsions of acceleration are perceived as more of an *external compulsion* than voluntary self-constraint by the lesser-favoured strata is a logical consequence of the different degrees of 'internalisation' (or 'poisoning') that I postulate.

However, time and again, my argument seems to drive the 'antagonists' to suspect that what I am asserting is that the elites are 'suffering even worse' than the underprivileged; that my critique really only echoes the conservative self-pity of the cultural elite, which is allegedly even worse than the 'one-boat rhetoric'. Yet whether it is worse to starve or to be poisoned essentially depends on the respective ratio of poison to hunger. This pivotal question of relation is almost inevitably distorted by the perspectives of both approaches. This is the reason for the necessary complementarity of the two.

Keeping in mind the aforementioned image of the rotten and unfairly sliced pie, it becomes apparent that this (necessary) complementarity of critique(s) is not that simple, since 'antagonists' and 'integrationists' will almost inevitably clash with one another (as demonstrated, at least by tendency, by the three of us here): even if both may be equally correct – i.e., the pie is both unfairly distributed *and* poorly made – it becomes rather evident why the two arguments tend to undermine one another in real social conflict.

The assertion that the pie *does not taste good anyway* helps to easily 'get rid of' or deflect justified demands for redistribution: the integrationist arguments of 'democratic *Allbetroffenheit*' (Beck/Dörre) quickly assume an ideological function, which is of course precisely what Klaus Dörre (rightly) suspects is looming behind the 'one-boat rhetoric' of a Josef Ackermann. Responding to the exclamation 'I am hungry!' by saying 'the bread has gone bad' is highly unsatisfactory, and to say 'the bread does not taste good' sounds downright cynical. In contrast, replying 'but sometimes some people get a bigger piece than others' misses the point dramatically if the real problem is that the pie has already spoiled. Even worse: the demand for a bigger piece, the suggestion of a blatant injustice in distribution, will inevitably increase the overall appetite for pie and the desire for a bigger piece of it in the first place – and also stoke the fears of the 'haves' that they will be forced to share a larger portion of their pie with the 'have-nots'. It therefore seems as if the other form of critique really only contributes to the ideological stabilisation of the criticised condition itself: from the perspective of the 'antagonists', styling us all 'victims of the system' in the spirit of a politics of 'sour grapes' or 'money alone does not bring happiness' greatly aids in concealing opposing interests, in hiding injustices, and in fending off legitimate demands. By not conceiving of capitalism as an instrument of oppression and exploitation in the hands of the propertied, but instead allowing it to appear as a kind of universal virus, the critical integrationists risk crippling social potential(s) for resistance. I presume it is not least this concern – namely, that a critique of capitalism like the one I formulate may ultimately contribute to maintaining the status quo – that constitutes the reason why I am repeatedly accused (including in my colleagues' contributions) of conservatism, without it ever being made clear what exactly constitutes this alleged conservatism. Conversely, to the 'critical integrationists', the antagonists' demands for a greater share of the pie seem like a central propellant for the 'engine of acceleration and activation'; indeed, they provide the fuel that the relentless rat race the capitalist game of escalation has become requires. The trade unions *do* demand a larger piece of the pie, but growing the overall pie is more or less the only way to realise larger pieces for wage earners *within the system*. To name another example, the struggle for shorter working hours (which was necessary for a long time) ultimately came at the cost of massive compulsions of acceleration, as Marx had already observed: labour did not and does not reduce in quantity, it simply occurs at a higher pace. Similarly, the consideration of gender inequality, wherever it finds a hearing, frequently leads to women being 'fully included' in the capitalist engine. Complaints about the development gap between North and South triggers responses from the antagonistic critics that almost always amount to the 'full inclusion' of excluded or marginalised groups. By identifying the presence of winners and losers in the game of escalation, the pie remains appealing to both.

In other words: *Landnahme*, acceleration and activation are the very modes of reaction with which the capitalist system has always responded to antagonistic critique; indeed, such critique plays a significant role in producing such reactions in the first place. Antagonistic critique therefore rarely moves beyond the realm of competition and social comparison on which capitalism thrives; it is in fact an element of this competition.

But if this is really the case, then which variant of critique should one favour? The crucial factor here is obviously the analysis of social relations: if one is hungry, bread that tastes bad is surely better than no bread at all; and for someone who is starving, even mouldy bread is better than nothing. Inversely, for well-fed subjects it is at best questionable to continually desire more of an unhealthy food, but it is considered brave or daring to consume mouldy goods. In my view, in such a situation a sophisticated sociological critique of capitalism can no longer refrain from a reflection and analysis of aspirations and wants or, more precisely: a renewed attention to the discussion around the foundations, conditions and possibilities of a successful life. This is the only way to discern the relative weight of hunger and poison, respectively. Yet, surprisingly, it is precisely this deliberation that antagonistic social critics avoid like the plague. This can be observed in my colleagues' texts, in which both respond to the question of the good life, or rather to any sort of value-related questions, with an almost reflex-like proscription. Accordingly, Stephan Lessenich polemicises against my 'value testing', while Klaus Dörre seems to fear that my call may essentially (and contrary to my intentions) amount to the 'sociological headmaster, as accomplice and pontiff of an authoritarian … value-imposing elite (*Wertelite*)' wanting to prescribe a compulsory normative framework of a good life.

I propose nothing of the sort. *Au contraire*: the conceptions of a successful life which may be suitable to provide a criterion or framework for critique are pursued by subjects themselves; they already form the basis of their outlook vis-à-vis the world and their action orientations. My claim, for example, that autonomy and authenticity represent guiding images that indeed have a significant impact on subjects' everyday actions with respect to life choices and notions of happiness throughout modern western societies is based on an evaluation of roughly 200 narrative biographical interviews with members of all social strata,[2] not on some philosophical or ethical 'value test'. There is, however, one point on which I agree with Lessenich: sociologists must first *listen* and *observe* in order to find out what concepts of happiness subjects pursue and why realisation of their pursuit often fails. And when we listen more closely, it is impossible to not notice how strongly the moral aspiration to 'decide things by oneself' persists, even in areas where there is effectively nothing left to decide on: we frequently observe that subjects tend to attribute occurrences to themselves ('so then I left the place') when, in reality, the experience was entirely involuntary (such as being fired). In a similar way, actions and decisions are explained time and again by the subject's desire to 'stay true to themselves', that they could not 'bend or break' any longer, or that they got the feeling that something *was* or *was not* 'the right thing for them'. I have never doubted that these value orientations are themselves socially and culturally determined. Demands for autonomy and the aspiration to authenticity to me do not represent some kind of anthropological constant, but rather the outcome of a long occidental history formation. This cultural formation is also, though not exclusively, informed by capitalism: the capitalist economic system and its institutions in turn require – particularly during their early stages of development – a cultural foundation. They became plausible and justifiable against the backdrop of a modern cultural horizon I have tried to characterise by utilising the term 'project of modernity'. Autonomy and authenticity – that is to say, the prospect of a self-determined way of life corresponding to subjects' proclivities, aptitudes and needs – represent the major ideological pillars of this interpretation of the world and its corresponding value system. Against such an ideological backdrop, the establishment of a global capitalist system seemed not only plausible, but even promising, as its alleged efficiency promised to develop the economic resources and political-social freedoms necessary for the realisation of the 'project of modernity'. Surely, one could justifiably raise the objection, in Lessenich's terms, that this autonomous life design left much to be desired for most wage earners, even in the Fordist phase of capitalism: hence, the passage in the text Lessenich criticises does not speak of an *accomplished* autonomy of subjects in 'classical modernity' at all, but rather of their aspirations to such an autonomy. In the 'classical' or 'Fordist phase' of capitalism, the promise that one would, through continual wage increases and reductions in working hours, achieve ever greater spaces of autonomy in the form of a 'pacified existence' (Marcuse) insulated from

---

2   The data was collected in the context of a sub-project ('Soziomoralische Landkarten engagierter und distanzierter Bürger in Ost- und Westdeutschland') of the *Sonderforschungsbereich* (special research area) 580 Jena/Halle conducted by Hans-Joachim Giegel, Michael Corsten and myself.

everyday economic pressure was still effective and sustainable – under the flexible accumulation regime, however, this promise can hardly be felt. In anticipation of a further intensification of competition, the promise has not only become progressively vague and obscured, but has been reversed: what is expected is instead further erosion of such autonomous spaces, as we will 'not be able to afford them for much longer'.

This is what I mean when I speak (admittedly, perhaps a bit too carelessly) of the promise of capitalism: of course an economic system as such does not make promises, it does not even care about normative or ethical standards – how could it? But its institutions require (as all social institutions do) cultural legitimation and justification, and this can only be achieved by promising the realisation of culturally meaningful goods. Thus, from Adam Smith to Ludwig Erhard and even through to the transitional period of 1989, the legitimation of capitalism has always been accomplished (I am repeating myself here) with the argument that this organisational form's economic efficiency will generate so much prosperity that people, relieved from the economic struggle for survival, will be able to, again in that sense of a 'pacified existence', freely develop and pursue their individual conceptualisations of a successful life. This is the normative relation between the 'project of modernity' and the capitalist economic system; herein lies the unspoken 'promise of capitalism' in the sense of an objective genitive – that is to say, what capitalism was supposed to do. I agree with Stephan Lessenich that capitalism does not promise anything[3] – still, its subjects have always and still to this very day expect capitalism to provide them with chances and opportunities for autonomy (and authenticity) which, however, are more and more obviously being eroded by the intensification of the compulsions of acceleration and activation, i.e., through the concentration of all energies on economic competition. Accordingly, then, my point of departure does not consist of some set of 'pre-social identities' or extra-social subjects, as not only Stephan Lessenich insinuates in his (friendly) criticism but which Armin Nassehi has elsewhere alleged in a decidedly more vicious tone,[4] but instead the individuals who move within the horizon of modernity's

---

3   I am guilty of a careless and misleading (over-)simplification elsewhere as well; namely, in my depiction of time as a factor of production, which Klaus Dörre immediately registers as a categorical error on my part: of course, I did not in the least intend to propose that time becomes a production factor essentially of its own accord, thus potentially eventually replacing labour, but rather that labour continually enters a product via socially necessary paid labour time, thus influencing its value and making time and labour so inextricably linked to one another that time can no longer be separated from the production factor of labour.

4   Cf. die Einleitung von A. Nassehi, 'Gegenwarten', in A. Nassehi, *Die Zeit der Gesellschaft*, Wiesbaden 2008, pp. 11–34.

'cultural meanings' – in the context of the new 'moral map' of modernity, the culturally contingent construction of which was reconstructed (or at least attempted) by, say, Charles Taylor (and from a different perspective, Michel Foucault).[5]

Incidentally, because we as sociologists cannot help but orient our terminological and observational apparatus toward those cultural meanings without which (as we know since at least Max Weber) we would be limited to a 'chaos of existential judgements', sociology's objects of study have likewise also always been linked to these cultural meanings by a profound underlying 'value relation'.[6] The question of what aspects of reality we deem relevant and worthy of study (and why they seem worthy of study to us) is determined by a horizon of cultural meanings that is always normatively tinted, for it is linked to a conception of what life is all about, i.e., what actually constitutes a good life. Because we all as cultural beings are forced to respond either positively or negatively to the phenomena of the world in a meaningful manner, and because these responses determine our terminological apparatus and observational standpoint, we can, even as sociologists, never fully evade the question of the good life. This is why, when Stephan Lessenich refutes my thesis (which, by the way, was intended descriptively and not normatively) that the source of sociological inquiry is always tied to the question of the good life, calling instead for a mere analysis of 'that which exists and that which has become', we must answer clearly that such an analysis is, according not only to Marx but also to Weber (who is, after all, the father of the so-called 'postulate of value-freedom'), not even possible. That Lessenich would rather expose himself to accusations of positivism than permit this question to be a constitutive feature of sociological inquiry is proof once more of the New Left's fear of value-related questions. And yet it may be this very fear that prevents the theories of the Left from entering into a more productive relationship with current social movements. It was not least the willingness of the young Marx but also of, say, Erich Fromm or Herbert Marcuse (and to some extent even Adorno) to address the conceptions of a good life, of happiness, as well as their non-attainment due to the influence of false consciousness and processes of alienation, that not only helped these authors to distinguish themselves but also helped them to

---

5   Cf. C. Taylor, *Sources of the Self: The Making of the Modern Identity*, New York 1989; H. Rosa, *Identität und kulturelle Praxis*, Frankfurt a.M., New York 1998.

6   M. Weber, "'Objectivity' in Social Science and Social Policy'. In *Max Weber* (ed.), *Readings in the Philosophy of Social Science*, Cambridge, MA 1994, pp. 535–45. For a more elaborate treatment cf. H. Rosa, 'Paradigma und Wertbeziehung. Zu Sinn und Grenzen des Paradigmenkonzeptes in den Sozialwissenschaften', in *LOGOS: Zeitschrift für systematische Philosophie*, N. F. 2,1995, pp. 59–94.

achieve genuine *political effectiveness*. People develop an interest in sociological theories and critiques to the extent that they seem relevant to their
own lived experiences.

What is conversely true, however, is this: only those who inquire about
culturally effective conceptions of a successful life can begin to identify
those aspects of social relations that prevent the former's realisation: either
a poisoned pie, or a lack of any pie whatsoever. But since the younger,
'antagonistic' left unthinkingly adopts the liberals' claim (which was deeply
ideological from the outset) that questions concerning the good life and
happiness are private matters only relevant to conservatives, it unnecessar-
ily places itself in the awkward position where it can either demand bigger
pieces of the pie (in normative terms) or confine itself to a functionalist
critique, i.e., a critique of how the pie was baked. It is my view, however,
that this self-confinement contributes extensively to the preservation of the
capitalist rat race and its game of escalation: *whatever you do, don't ask questions about why growth and acceleration, activation and productivism and*
(thus ultimately) *economistic Landnahme are supposedly good for us in the
first place*; but that also means: *do not mention the fact that the pie has long
since spoiled*. What is needed not only for sociology, but for society as a
whole, is democratic deliberation, a collective discussion about an appropriate definition of prosperity and quality of life. What we require for this
discussion is, firstly, practical, i.e., real economic *room for manoeuvre*: as
long as we are forced, individually and collectively, to more and more des-
perately maintain our *Standort*-related (business-locational) advantage and
competitiveness, as long as we are trapped in an ever-quickening rat race, it
will remain difficult to focus on the question of the good life at all. A 'pacifying' basic income could perhaps be a good starting point for doing so. In
addition to this economic 'room', we also require *theoretical space*: sociology
cannot just mean deciding the question of the good life 'sociologically' and
in an elitist manner, i.e., by simply prescribing an ethical framework; it must
also mean *asking* (and in particular from the subject's perspective) *the right
questions*. An experienced analytical eye can in fact formulate these questions – if it rids itself of the fear of addressing value-related questions and of
rethinking the concepts of false needs and alienation under contemporary
social conditions.

Such a perspective would, among other things, reveal the quite remarkable fact that modern western society confuses 'purchasing' with 'consuming'
(and, as the financial crisis has made clear recently, 'making profit' with
'producing', but that is another story) to an increasing degree. To this end,
sociology could take Marx as a direct point of departure: when have we
really consumed a commodity or a good: when we have bought it – or when

we have used it or used it up? Surely, a book is not consumed (apart from the limited and derivative possibilities of ostentatious consumption) until we have actually *read* it. However, empirical findings indicate that Germans as well as Americans, for example, continue to *buy* more but *read* fewer books every year. The same is true for audio recordings: technically, we have not consumed a CD after we have heard it once, but only after we have heard it 'exhaustively' (as difficult as this may be to define). Likewise, a piano or keyboard is not 'consumed' at purchase, but by use. The buyer, it seems to me, is still motivated to purchase by the prospect of the cultural good's 'adaptation' (*Anverwandlung*), yet frequently this adaptation no longer occurs: food goes stale before it is eaten, shoes and clothes are donated to the Red Cross without ever having been worn, newspapers and magazines are hardly even looked at before being scrapped. The discrepancy between the rate of purchasing and actually consuming may be even greater in other areas: astronomical societies report rising sales figures for telescopes, yet none of them are reporting rising numbers of sightings or observations. The most conspicuous example of this is probably found in children's bedrooms: considering the German population ratio of ten adults to every two children, those anonymous, unused, hardly even unwrapped toys pile up quickly. More is purchased, but (if for no other reason than a lack of children) less is played with. While the struggle over shop opening hours on Sundays is usually discussed in terms of whether the seventh day of the week should be 'opened up to consumption', this is actually highly misleading: open shops not only imply (as the antagonistic critics emphasise) excessive and unreasonable working hours for employees, but also an additional extension of 'buying time' at the cost of 'consumption time': after all, (s)he who is out shopping cannot consume. If shops were closed on Sundays we would have the time to read those books, play that keyboard, try out that new software, and listen to those CDs. This difference between the act of purchasing and the time required for consumption is just as interesting with regard to an adequate analysis of capitalism as it is illuminating for an up-to-date diagnosis of the times: the act of purchasing can be accelerated virtually infinitely – essentially, it requires no time resources – while the act of consuming, by contrast, continues to be time-consuming. The more complex and high-powered a purchased product turns out to be, the longer it usually takes to be able to operate it adeptly. The difference between physical and moral strain, to paraphrase Marx, continues to grow, not only in terms of instruments of production, but of consumer products. A careful analysis of psychological mechanisms of action may well conclude that the act of buying has almost begun to serve as compensation for unfulfilled consumption (for example, taking pictures while on vacation may compensate for actually 'consuming' the landscape): we buy *new* books *because* we have not read the old ones properly – and because we do have the time to purchase new books, whereas we do not have the time necessary to read the old ones. *Landgenommene* (conquered or appropriated), accelerated, activated subjects caught in the rat race prove their hedonism through *buying*, not through *consuming*, as they simply do not have time for the latter. Acts of purchasing must suffice to convince them that their activity is worthwhile, that they can 'afford stuff', that their lives are pretty good after all. From this perspective, it strikes me as only logical that during the most recent boom cycles, elites in particular bought assets which not only required no 'real consumption', but which no longer even relied on *real production*. Though such a virtualisation of production and consumption may be included in the logic of acceleration – real production and actual consumption are only accelerable to a limited degree, whereas financial transactions are infinitely accelerable – it sooner or later pulls the rug out from under the real economy's feet through (material and temporal) decoupling from financial markets.

In this we see the enormous integrative 'achievement' of capitalism as originally identified by Weber repeating itself once more. Weber saw that a formation was emerging that motivated subjects (initially in the guise of the Protestant entrepreneur) to amass wealth through hard, ascetic and systematic labour without consuming it: he considered capital accumulation through re-investment of profits to be so improbable and, as it were, utterly 'unnatural', that he thought only a religious force – the Protestant work ethic – could be capable of implementing it. However, this was no longer sufficient in developed capitalism: the commodities produced have to be sold one way or another; rising productive capacity must be matched by an equally large capacity for consumption. This is where capitalism actually performs an even greater miracle without religion: it 'educates and selects' subjects who not only *produce* without consuming, but who also *purchase* without consuming! In this, hedonism and the Protestant ethic coalesce into a conceptual relationship as impossible and unlikely as it is stable.[7] If the left had the courage to address the question of false needs and compulsory compensatory actions once again, what could possibly be a more appropriate starting point than this? Once again: sociology cannot be a matter of authoritatively distinguishing false from correct needs, but asking the right

---

7   Here is where the explanation for the 'cultural contradictions' in developed capitalism identified by Daniel Bell seems to lie: Bell appears to have considered a hedonistic consumptive orientation to be incompatible with a Protestant-ascetic work ethic, even though both are functionally necessary for advanced capitalism. Concluding from my analysis, what the late capitalist ethos truly represents is a form of the Protestant work ethic heightened beyond belief.

questions may help determine the distinction of the two from the perspective of subjects.

Are we, then, all in the same boat? My colleagues will certainly object that the unread books and still-wrapped telescope are surely of no concern to those who have just lost their jobs or who can no longer pay their rents after being forced to subsist on the meagre benefits of Hartz IV. This is, of course, obvious. Nevertheless, both groups – the forcibly decelerated and thus 'inoperative' along with those still stuck in the rat race – stand in the shadow of a massive 'engine of acceleration and activation', the functional mode and effects of which they *could not possibly want*. The precarised and excluded are already aware of this. The privileged still have to come to terms with this reality, but they will not learn if they keep being referred to as 'winners'. Admittedly, we are all affected by the capitalist system's formational logic *in different ways*. Yet beyond the antagonisms of class conflict, this formational logic shapes *all* its subjects – an insight also shared by Marx. The social 'being' that determines consciousness is in turn not only determined by positional differences – even the capitalist is not free; he (or she) acts as a 'character mask', but is also, according to Marx, 'driven' by the endless movement of capital, the instrument of which he or she also acts as. After all, with view to a potential ecological cataclysm or nuclear holocaust, we certainly are all in the same boat: in such an event, the fact that some of us have life jackets and safety buoys will not do much good.

CHAPTER 9

The System in/on the Subject, or: When Three People Quarrel, (Critical) Sociology Rejoices

STEPHAN LESSENICH

> Commitment in politics only arises where there is collective action, and not in instances where someone thinks of something by him or herself – regardless of how compelling that thought may be.
>
> – D. Dath, *Maschinenwinter*

It is certainly a rarely experienced (and rarely experienceable) joy for a scientist when one's own texts are not only read, but even critically appreciated and commented on with the intent of achieving genuine clarification and understanding. I do not wish to take this (hopefully not unique) opportunity to deal with my two colleagues' – in most aspects absolutely legitimate – reprimands in their entirety nor in every particular detail. Rather, I will limit myself to a discussion of several selected points of criticism, which in my view seem to touch upon the key objective and main concern of my analysis and which for this very reason are best suited to serve as points of convergence for a productive combination of the three approaches collected in this volume. As Klaus Dörre also points out in his contribution, a logic of *critical critique* must abstain from becoming 'affirmative in relation to itself'.[1] The present volume's dialogical (or rather, trialogical) construction facilitates not only an individual and collective epistemological advance for the authors involved, but also systematically promotes precisely such a critical self-reflection of critique. It thus proves to be a form of scientific debate which – consider this a friendly proposal – should become a (more) common academic practice.

It is no coincidence that both Klaus Dörre and Hartmut Rosa's critiques revolve, each in its own way, around (in the terminology of my own

---

1 A. Demirović, 'Leidenschaft und Wahrheit. Für einen neuen Modus der Kritik', in A. Demirović (ed.), *Kritik und Materialität*, Münster 2008, pp. 9–40, here: p. 26.

contribution) the 'late capitalist' link between the logic of the system and subjectivity. For that is exactly what my contribution places at its heart: the analysis and critique of the political formation of compatible, 'fitting' subjects in contemporary capitalism. In this sense, Klaus Dörre is only partly correct when he asserts that the activation thesis deals only with social 'surface level phenomena'.[2] This may be true, at least to the extent that the question I deal with – i.e., how flexible capitalism, which has attained 'economic dominance' (as well as other forms of dominance) over the last two or three decades 'educates and selects the ... subjects which it needs'[3] – is an expression of a Weberian shift in the Marxist perspective: the search for the factors of social stabilisation, 'for the specific rationality of the evident irrationality of capitalism'[4] then directs attention not to 'the economic circuit of valorisation, but to sociological and social-psychological processes of socialisation. The contradictions are thus not to be found within capitalist relations, but in subject relations'.[5]

At the same time, however, this subject relation (in its respective historical form) remains deeply tied to the capitalist valorisation process and the dynamic thereof. As far as the ongoing process of an 'activating' reconstruction of the welfare state and the heteronomously and autonomously effected socio-political mobilisation of its citizens is concerned, this development is normatively and functionally linked to the emergence of flexible capitalism,[6] which requires specific dispositions and motivations on the part of (economic) subjects for its establishment and reproduction, and which seeks – politically aided and expressed in Weberian terms – to instil a 'manner of life ... adapted to the peculiarities of capitalism'[7] in people.

It is true, as Dörre critically notes, that I in fact 'presuppose' capitalism in my analytics of sociological activation – yet I do this most certainly in the spirit of Dörre's own work: after all, the activation regime confronting people in this country has been proven throughout our analysis to be a political arrangement of subject formation *by* capitalism *for* capitalism. The 'engine of activation' and the movement it seeks to effect have the systemic goal of M'. To presuppose this may simply mean that one does not wish to make flexible capitalism's regime of labour, production and accumulation

---

2   Dörre, p. 162 in this volume.
3   M. Weber, *The Protestant Ethic and the Spirit of Capitalism*, 23rd print. London, New York 2001, p.20.
4   H. Bude, *Wie weiter mit Karl Marx?*, Hamburg 2008, p. 23.
5   Ibid.
6   For a more elaborate treatment cf. S. Lessenich, *Die Neuerfindung des Sozialen*, Bielefeld 2008.
7   Weber, *The Protestant Ethic*, p. 20.

the object of one's own study (alternatively, speaking as a sociologist, one could simply appeal to the graces of a sociological division of labour). This does not imply that I am masking, or trying to mask, the question of who is activating whom and why. Yes: 'activation' in flexible capitalism is an amalgam of practices of domination, constellations of interests, gradients of power, structures of inequality, processes of exploitation – a socio-political surface-level phenomenon, if you will – which has nevertheless developed and continues to develop in elective affinity to the deep politico-economic structure of the present social formation. That I am able to emphasise this point – while at the same time explicitly stating that I do not *by any means* consider the welfare state to be a 'more or less neutral instance', that I do not, *even remotely*, deny the role of the 'visible hand' of political coercion and that I am *far from* diagnosing the 'rule of freedom' as a broad social condition – is in my opinion the first tangible result of clarification (owed especially to Klaus Dörre's trenchant criticism), which also marks our potential trajectory of conciliation: the contradiction theoretician Lessenich is not only active at the systemic level of competing control requirements directed at the democratic-capitalist state, but also at the level of social antagonisms which also find expression in the political activation arrangement of the 'investive welfare state'.

Above all (and here too we find potential for mutual approximation hidden beneath the surface of analytical pretence), Lessenich the neo-Marxist theoretician of contradiction need not be defended against his *alter ego*, Lessenich the late Foucauldian theoretician of governmentality (or vice versa) – an impulse which both of my amicable colleagues appear to share. Nevertheless, both display an understanding of Foucault in their analysis and criticism of my approach – which is not the Foucault of *Governmentality Studies*, or at the very least has little in common with my understanding of it. After all, an analysis of society based on the theoretical terms of Foucault's studies of governmentality alone *does not* – or rather: *need not* – by any means claim that late modern institutions are 'seemingly coherent spaces and figures' (Rosa) or represent social constructions of an 'almost perfect-seeming disciplinary mechanism' (Dörre). What *is* analytically presumed, a priori, is the aspiration to control and leadership (and, as we have seen, the constitutively capitalist character) of institutions, in this case the socio-political regimes of late modernity; what *is not*, however, is the effective power of the latter's control and leadership, as this – as I repeatedly emphasise in my introductory text – can only be accurately evaluated *ex post facto*. The systemic contradictions which in my view ineluctably engulf late-capitalist state activity are precisely *not* always quasi-pacified through certain modes of subjectification – at least if this pertains, as Klaus Dörre suggests, to the neutralisation or de-substantialisation of these contradictions. My reading of Offe and Foucault is rather that both authors – on different levels ('system' versus 'subject'), yet in a complementary sense – refer to the circumstance that the moments and motives of contradiction within capitalism can only be fenced in and absorbed provisionally and temporarily, but ultimately cannot be resolved sustainably, let alone permanently. Even the presently occurring – to be sure: *attempted* – activation-state-induced transfer of social management requirements and claims to political leadership onto subjects does not represent a de-problematising suspension, but rather a problem-displacing reallocation of systemic contradictions. In this sense, it is precisely *not* the case that – contrary to what Hartmut Rosa believes – my genealogical revelation of 'the activation regime's efficiency and efficacy' renders my simultaneously developed model of contradiction 'implausible'.[8] In my view, the systemic contradictions – for instance, of mobility versus control, but also of ownership versus non-ownership of socially relevant resources, of domination versus subjugation, freedom versus coercion – instead remain intact, even within the process of their politically orches-trated, intended subjectification. If and how, when and where they (in altered form, of course) erupt can never be determined *ex ante*, but instead can only be ascertained (this is the sociologist speaking) *empirically*. The fact that the mainstream of governmentality theory is apparently and even explicitly not interested in such a research strategy deserves criticism indeed (as Klaus Dörre does in fact provide).[9] The study of the empirically ascer-tainable aspects of late capitalist governmentality, however, is among the tasks that 'Jena Sociology' has committed itself to – as we are convinced that a critical sociology must always represent both a theoretical diagnosis of the times and an empirically grounded social analysis in equal proportion.

Such a research agenda, moreover, aspires to combine the genealogy of present-day capitalism with a normative-critical impulse – despite the fact that Hartmut Rosa believes this to be impossible for those following the Foucauldian tradition; or rather, regardless of whether or not it is possi-ble, he at least thinks that my approach does not accomplish such; indeed, it remains entirely unclear to him 'against whom or what (or even more importantly: for whom or what), and in whose name resistance should be organised'. Rosa's complaint is directly related to the crucial question he raises, which haunts all critiques of capitalism: the question of what exactly the problem with capitalism is: 'What is wrong with (contemporary) capital-ism?' As analytically self-evident and politically meaningful as this question

8   Rosa, p. 174 in this volume.
9   Cf. z.B. U. Schimank, '"Wissen ist Macht" – Das "Glossar der Gegenwart"', in *Soziologische Revue* 28(4), 2005, pp. 301–8.

may be, it strikes me as incorrectly phrased while appearing overly defensive at the same time. It should be, in reference to Philippe van Parijs, turned back on its feet and thereby radicalised, after which it would have to read: 'What (if anything) can justify (contemporary) capitalism?'.[10] Reversed in this way, the question addresses capitalism's systemic need for legitimation, the structural legitimatory problems of a form of socialisation *incapable* of justifying itself of its own accord, but instead requires permanent, and if need be 'external' legitimatory resources in order to ensure the social acceptance and acceptability of the order it creates. In fact, Claus Offe's theory of late capitalism, to which I make analytical reference, does not take this fundamental aspect into account when it categorises democratic institutions and procedures as mere organisational means of state activity – and localises the late capitalist requirement of legitimation exclusively in the political system. After all, the production of 'affirmative subjectivities'[11] in modern capitalism requires more than just the formally democratic organisation of adulatory mass loyalty, as envisaged by Offe. In welfare-state-regulated capitalism, too, state actors are not the only ones accountable for their regulatory action; 'the economy' is equally compelled – even though it usually attempts to project some sort of legitimatory kinship with the state – to explain why, despite chronic unemployment and multi-million Euro salaries, resource depletion and world hunger, life under capitalism is just fine. One could perhaps interpret this order of justification – and again, it does not seem all that far-fetched to infer a path of analytical (re-)conciliation with my critical colleague here – as a response to the question of the 'good life' (or at least a better life than anywhere else). However, what I consider essential and of primary interest is how (to wit: based on which instrumentarium and on which mechanisms) this response is generated under present-day capitalism.

One may justifiably understand the agenda of activation, in Rosa's sense, as the welfare-state 'promise' of the present, but one cannot safely assume that the idea of activation, which he considers 'ingenious and highly innovative', will automatically be realised throughout society – at best, this will be true of only a small part of society, at a great cost to the vast majority. This actually suggests a normative line of critique, as rises from the 'subtext' – in which Rosa believes the normative claim of my analysis to be buried – to the surface, and manifests itself as a mode of critique that adopts and is capable of combining elements of both social and artistic critique. In the project-based order of flexible capitalism as already described (albeit necessarily

---

10   P. van Parijs, *Real Freedom for All*, Oxford 1995.
11   Bude, *Wie weiter mit Karl Marx?*, p. 23.

somewhat roughly) with reference to Boltanski and Chiapello[12] in my intro-ductory text, activity becomes the most important social-political reference criterion and standard of evaluation of any action: whoever 'distinguishes him or herself through unlimited flexibility, mobility and adaptability'[13] – and contributes to the common good in doing so – can become 'hugely successful' in the truest sense of the term. But what, then, is wrong with this order, or rather, how could it possibly be justified? Though I do not wish to repeat myself at this point, it does seem rather appropriate, in light of the reactions of my two critics who lament the 'vagueness' (Rosa) or even 'toothlessness' (Dörre) of my critique, to return to the essence of my point once more.

The politico-social hegemony of the norm of activation has an equally alienating and exploitative character. As far as the alienation aspect is con-cerned, the agenda of activation refrains from prescribing subjective value systems for its addressees in order to thus mobilise them in the full sense of the value norms of a wage earners' society. 'Whatever creates jobs is socially just': activation signifies nothing more than integration into 'employ-ment'. 'Inclusion', that is to say, the activating welfare state's social-scientific formula of legitimation, seeks only one thing: participation in the labour market. Regardless of who falls prey to activation policy, whether pre-school aged children or university students, the unemployed or old-age pensioners, the employment system consistently marks the long-term target of politi-cal intervention, while the norms of life conduct and productivity serve as a conceptual yardstick for social expectations. It is simply irrelevant to the late-capitalist activation regime what form and substance people themselves may associate with and desire in an 'active' life. Whoever manages to realise these ideas for themselves under existing conditions has either already suc-cumbed to the social norm of activation, or is one of those 'high potentials' revered by flexible capitalism's active society the world over.

The fact that the late-capitalist regime of activation, when viewed from this perspective, also represents a veritable regime of exploitation is under-exposed not only in my own analysis, but is inadequately addressed in the current social political debate more generally. It is Luc Boltanski and Ève Chiapello who seek to rehabilitate the concept of exploitation, in terms of a diagnosis of the times, with their analysis of the interconnected world

---

12   Cf. L. Boltanski, È. Chiapello, G. C. Elliott, *The New Spirit of Capitalism*, London, New York 2007.

13   T. Künkler, 'Produktivkraft Kritik. Die Subsumtion der Subversion im neuen Kapitalismus', in R. Eickelpasch, C. Rademacher, P. Ramos Lobato (eds), *Metamorphosen des Kapitalismus – und seiner Kritik*, Wiesbaden 2008, pp. 29–47, here: p. 34.

of 'connexionist capitalism'[14] – in contrast to the sociologically stabilised domination of the rhetoric of 'exclusion' and 'marginalisation'.[15] The authors emphasise, and rightly so, that the mobility profits of the 'top performers' of the active society are inversely linked to the mobility deficits and impediments for those underprivileged in the active society. Flexible capitalism produces and reproduces a socio-structural 'mobility differential', an exploitative structure of the active society, in which 'the immobility of one group is the precondition for the mobility of the other, while the contribution of the immobile to the capital valorisation process is not adequately remunerated'.[16] Thus, on one side there are those who fail to meet the prevailing requirements of activation, who are overwhelmed by them – or even (social-)politically prevented from activity and controlled in their mobility. On the other side are those whose lifeworld and way of life has always corresponded to the prescriptions of the activation regime, or who manage to utilise the new opportunity structures of a policy based on 'active citizens' in order to attain relatively privileged life opportunities. The emerging active society is an arrangement of unequally distributed opportunity structures for a way of life adapted to and adequate for the political norm of activity. This society not only includes – to use a social fault-line more recently popularised as a result of the crisis – the bonus-laden top manager living at the cost of the 'honest taxpayer'; in fact it is the active, mobile, flexible and 'productive' who live at the cost of citizens who allegedly (or actually) do not match this social profile (although the opposite is commonly portrayed in public discourse). Additionally, this discrepancy is by no means a mere 'surface level phenomenon', but presents itself as a social antagonism closely associated with the social relations of production and reproduction in flexible capitalism.

Perhaps we can move a step closer to clarifying two additional questions raised in my critic Hartmut Rosa's conclusion at this point. To begin with, the preceding deliberations might have made it a bit clearer that mobility and control enjoy a rather asymmetrical relationship to one another – at least to the extent that mobilisation represents the dominant strategy of political action in the active society, and measures of control affect and are directed towards those considered 'difficult to train' for the active society or whose activity profiles are too far removed from the applicable norm of activity. In this context, the question of whether there is an 'interplay' or a

---

14   Cf. Boltanski et al., *The New Spirit of Capitalism*, 2007.

15   Cf. e.g., H. Bude, *Die Ausgeschlossenen*, München 2008.

16   Künkler, 'Produktivkraft Kritik', p. 40; cf. S. Lessenich, 'Beweglich – Unbeweglich', in S. Lessenich, F. Nullmeier (eds), *Deutschland – eine gespaltene Gesellschaft*, Frankfurt a.M., New York 2006, pp. 336–52.

'game of escalation' between the active society's tendencies of mobilisation and immobilisation seems unanswerable in the form of an alternative (at least in my interpretation of the latter); in my view mobility and control do not balance each other out in their counter play, but instead initiate a dynamic of mutual escalation. This is due, among other reasons, to the fact that the agenda of activation, and especially the operative politics of activation, are far from being so perfect and sealed off as to leave no room for unintended effects and undesired practices. In a situation in which more individual movement motivated by social objectives is both expected and demanded the society over, it surely cannot be ruled out that the (politically 'programmed') social intent of individual movement is missed – or (or: and) individual movement will begin to grow into collective movement. In other words: though it cannot be predicted, neither can it be prevented that movement fails to move in the desired direction and thus instead becomes *political* on its own terms. What my colleague Rosa somewhat incredulously depicts as a romantic delusion from another century (but which one exactly?) to me seems anything but delusional: the good old possibilities for political activity still exist – along with many new ones.

This brings us to the positive and hopeful aspects, namely the potential(s) for 'resistance of subjects against the instrumental and unreasonable demands of the capitalist way of life'[17] even in their everyday confrontations with today's flexible capitalism – and to the contingencies of their resistance against the exploitative properties of the activation regime. Concerning this matter I feel obliged to reassure Klaus Dörre that the 'bulky aspect of habitus' – or what I would call: people's obstinacy rooted in individual experience of the social world – is by no means 'systematically neglected' in my analysis, or rather, in the conception of the subject underlying it. On the contrary: the potential for resistance buried within subjects' obstinacy (and prone to flare up from time to time) is precisely the point of an approach which, in its analysis of systemic contradictions – as my critic Dörre correctly asserts – reveals paradoxical dynamics that nevertheless manifest as moments of at least potential contradiction at the level of praxis. If Hartmut Rosa takes the view that it is uncritical or even apolitical, and in any case far removed from the standards of fundamental critique, for a social scientist to take people's obstinacy and their divergent everyday praxis as a point of departure, then I admit that I do not share this assessment – just as I would vehemently challenge the assertion that a sociological scepticism vis-à-vis 'the art of political governance over people' in the active society (or

---

17   A. Honneth, 'Eine Physiognomie der kapitalistischen Lebensform: Skizze der Gesellschaftstheorie Adornos', in A. Honneth (ed.), *Dialektik der Freiheit*, Frankfurt a.M. 2005, pp. 165–87, here: p. 186.

any other one) is a social-political postulate that could just as easily come from the lips of a liberal like Guido Westerwelle.[18] To summarise my view: the 'beyond' capitalism will not come – that is, if it ever comes – from the 'exterior', but rather from below; and it will come, in terms of Weber's classical typology of actors, not from the thinking academic, but from the willing individual.

That does not mean that the thinking academic may not (at least from the sidelines) state what he or she would want, from his or her perspective as a willing individual. Philippe van Parijs' equally simple and compelling answer to his aforementioned question about the possible justification of capitalism, for example, is that only the freedom guaranteed by an unconditional basic income granted to every single member of society could render the modern capitalist complex of socialisation acceptable. My personal formula for political legitimation would (currently) be that of a 'basic income *plus*', that is to say, a comprehensive and complex social reform which, through realisation of the right to work, to education, to participation, to autonomy and to leisure would facilitate a lasting and sustainable shift beyond the industrial 'quota system' of welfare-state promises of benefits.[19] Both answers, that of van Parijs and my own, would tend to exhibit – if they ever came to fruition – implications that transcend the current capitalist social formation and its political and economic organisation. Whether they are ever to be realised, either in this manner or a similar one, will not be decided at the intellectual's desk – at least not if he or she is there by him or herself and considers this alone to be his or her destiny.

Let me conclude my contribution to this book by returning to Klaus Dörre's criticism of the ideology and rhetoric of the 'one' or 'same boat'[20] that has enjoyed such a revival during the crisis, in order to subject it to a further, more productive turn. I too consider it essential to defend oneself against and repudiate the pseudo-collectivist and pseudo-democratic gesture toward *Allbetroffenheit*: similarly, in the same way that 'we all' are not profiteers of the active society, 'we all' are not victims of activation – or, for that matter, of *Landnahme* or acceleration. Nevertheless, there are some common boats – it is just that they are much smaller, and they are navigating very choppy waters indeed. In that sense, the three authors of this book are definitely 'sitting in the same boat'. I dare claim that we all

---

18   [Trans. Note] Guido Westerwelle served as leader of the vehemently neoliberal Free Democratic Party and German Foreign Minister from 2009 to 2013.

19   Cf. S. Lessenich, *Das Grundeinkommen in der gesellschaftspolitischen Debatte*, Bonn 2009, esp. p. 12ff.

20   On this cf. (in remarkable anticipation) G. Vobruba (ed.), *Wir sitzen alle in einem Boot*, Frankfurt a.M., New York 1983.

share – sometimes silently, at other times more vocally – the insight found at the beginning of this riposte: commitment (and here: the obligation of critique) does not emerge – not only in the political but also in the scientific sense (and even in the space between the two) – when one person thinks of something by themselves, however accurate that thought may be. That which makes critique connective and committal, what ensures its durability and effectiveness, cannot have an impact through reasoning alone, but only through common action.

The critical debate between Klaus Dörre, Hartmut Rosa and myself was not about tallying up some kind of analytical-intellectual 'points' to determine a victor. Our motivation was not to enact yet another round of squabbles between irrelevant left wing sects, but rather to map out the most accurate, and indeed penetrative, characterisation of the social adversary possible. As a result of the rounds of argument, positions, criticisms and ripostes documented here, we are somewhat wiser than before (which in itself is by no means insignificant!), despite the many unanswered questions that remain. We hope that critical sociology may rejoice at our quarrel. Of course, whether capitalism ought to tremble in the face of our exchange is another story – a story that, as far as I know and whether we accept it or not, has not yet been written, either in general terms, or by us. In such circumstances, one should be permitted to raise (and perhaps *should* raise) the bar for radicalism much higher where desired social change is concerned – not to try to jump over it by oneself as an act of intellectual heroism, but to provide a benchmark for confident and collective movement in the everyday praxis of working and living people. After all, one thing is certain: radical change and the subversion of the existing order occurs wherever subjects – who are far from being fully programmed or even programmable in the flexible-capitalist sense – begin to move. The system is not simply *in* the subject – and the subjective operates systematically, even and especially in flexible capitalism.

Landnahme – Acceleration – Activation: A Preliminary Appraisal in the Process of Social Transformation

> I think that the ethico-political choice we have to make every day is to determine which is the main danger.
>
> – M. Foucault, *On the Genealogy of Ethics*

At the end of this volume it may appear to the hasty reader as if there are more – and more substantial – issues that divide us than unite us. From our perspective, that impression probably represents more an unintended effect of the dramaturgical-trialogical sequence of our contributions than an accurate reflection of our analytical and normative standpoint in the contemporary discursive space of late modern society. Admittedly, the preceding debate has revealed beyond doubt that the three of us disagree on a number of points when it comes to the exact rationale and derivation of normative criteria, the appropriate differentiation of levels of critique, the designation of potential protagonists of a desired change, and the exact depiction of the functional crises we identified. That said, if one approaches these differences from the necessary distance, or rather from an external perspective; that is to say, not from the perspective of an internal theoretical dispute as is so cherished by the political left in particular, but instead from that of the contemporary landscape of socio-political discussion (in the context of the crisis), then it quickly becomes clear that the positions presented here are in fact quite similar in several aspects. Not only can they easily and frequently be combined in terms of their political-normative objectives, but they can also complement each other in a sociological 'division of labour', as it were.

The common point of departure for our endeavour was and is the conviction that the basal logic of the (in itself interminable) movement of capital determines the capitalist social formation in all of its phases (including the current financial market crisis) and prescribes not only the latter's economic development but also makes itself felt in its political and cultural possibilities of shaping and formation. In terms of the *factual dimension*, this movement can be depicted, as Klaus Dörre's analysis has shown, as a continuous process of internal and external *Landnahme*: capitalism turns out to be, as it were, a 'greedy engine of incorporation and discharge'; its systemic functional mode is forced to constantly develop new markets, which it sooner or later leaves behind as depreciated 'scorched earth', only to be potentially re-developed at another point in time by a different capitalist formation. As Hartmut Rosa attempts to show with view to the *temporal dimension*, this process of *Landnahme* is inextricably accompanied – across all formational phases – by a constant tendency towards social 'acceleration', which can be understood as the compulsion to increase the speed of circulation, determining not only the logic of economic change, but also that of cultural and political changes. Moreover, it is no coincidence that *Landnahme* (in reality as well as metaphorically) and acceleration appear as spatial and temporal tendencies of change, respectively: the movement of capital leads to a continuous, directed, gradual change of the spatio-temporal regime. Formational shifts can thus also always be conceived as revolutions of the social conceptualisation and cultivation of space and time, although these revolutions are accompanied by critical aggravation and possibly adhere to a more general logic of escalation (as, for instance, David Harvey tries to encapsulate with his term 'time-space-compression'[1]).

The prolonged dynamisation of social, material and intellectual relations in turn necessitates forms of subjects and subjectification willing to 'meet capitalism halfway', so to speak – subjects and subjectification that accept, or render acceptable, the resultant compulsory escalation. In the *social dimension*, the late capitalist regime of 'activation' as described by Lessenich thus appears as the logical outcome of that fundamental mobilisation tendency of modernity which ceaselessly, albeit never entirely, transforms the paralysing external coercion of repressive social formations into restless self-constraint through (if need be violent) political management – thereby transferring the irresolvable contradictions of the social formation determined by the movement of capital onto subjects themselves.

Landnahme, acceleration and activation can thus be described as factual, temporal and social dimensions of a single economic, cultural and political process, the basis of which is the logic of the movement of capital. The combined and complementary impact of the three principles of development is particularly pronounced in late modern society – it is found just as much in the logic of Hartz IV reforms as in the operational modes of financial

---

1   Cf. D. Harvey, *The Condition of Postmodernity*, Oxford 1990.

market capitalism; it manifests itself in the field of consumption no less than in the reorganisation of universities.

Similarly, it surfaces in all the processes that have been known since the 1990s as the subjectification of work[2] (and of the social[3]): because subjects' lifeworlds, as well as their emotions and aspirations, are incorporated into the production process – as even their desires and appetites become factors of production – they are *landgenommen* (conquered) by the process of capital valorisation in an unprecedented manner. This *Landnahme* simultaneously leads to a massive acceleration of the speed of life; it is accompanied by a sense of life taking place on 'slippery slopes' where one can no longer rest because of the ever-present danger of losing one's grasp of the world; that the world may 'run off'. The compulsion to *run faster and faster* in order to maintain the position one has fought so hard for in the competitive system, however, has in itself the effect of a structurally induced activation imperative: the 'entrepreneurial subject', the 'Me, Inc.' (*Ich AG*), etc. is the result of incorporated and subjectivised activation programmes – and wherever this process of activation does not occur 'autopoietically', it is (or at least is attempted to be) induced via external political compulsion. At this point, then, a constitutive limitation becomes apparent in all three process principles: all three authors of this volume postulate structurally inescapable 'phenomena of transition', which denote the radicalisation and flipsides of *Landnahme*, acceleration and activation simultaneously. Especially in places where it has been most successful, *Landnahme* leaves behind 'devastated' terrain; the acceleration logically, but also empirically, reaches a point where it turns into a 'frenetic standstill', in which movement and stagnation can no longer be distinguished from one another, and the concept of dynamic no longer applies.[4] Quite similarly, the attempt at ever-increasing activation ultimately leads to a condition of 'dynamic immobilisation'[5] – or apathy.

These very phenomena of transition can be observed, impressively and fascinatingly if rather unsettlingly, in the form of depression, burnout or (to use a less medically precise concept) the 'exhausted self'.[6] These phenomena indicate a threshold beyond which subjectivities are no longer exploitable

---

2   Cf. G. G. Voß, H. J. Pongratz, 'Der Arbeitskraftunternehmer. Eine neue Grundform der "Ware Arbeitskraft"?', in *Kölner Zeitschrift für Soziologie und Sozialpsychologie*50(1), 1998, pp. 131–51; D. Sauer, *Arbeit im Übergang*, Hamburg 2005; U. Bröckling, *Das unternehmerische Selbst*, Frankfurt a.M. 2007, as well as M. Hardt, A. Negri, *Empire*, Cambridge, MA., London 2001.

3   Cf. S. Lessenich, *Die Neuerfindung des Sozialen*, Bielefeld 2008.

4   For a more elaborate treatment of this cf. H. Rosa, *Social Acceleration: A New Theory of Modernity*, Columbia University Press, 2013, chapter 12.

5   Cf. S. Lessenich, *Dynamischer Immobilismus*, Frankfurt a.M., New York.

6   Cf. A. Ehrenberg, *Das erschöpfte Selbst*, Frankfurt a.M., New York 2004.

and creativity withers away; they transform the affected subject's experience of hectic, trying, accelerated times into a condition of 'temporal suffocation' in which time seems to have come to a halt and morphed into a 'viscous matter'.[7] Burnout sufferers and the seriously depressed can no longer be activated, hence they are forcibly decelerated and 'devastated'; that is to say, they are no longer fit to participate in the process of capital valorisation, at least not on its productive side.[8]

As this example illustrates, the three formational studies presented here are not only by all means analytically complementary, but the three normative perspectives based upon them can be fruitfully combined thanks to their 'division of labour'-like nature: at the end of the day, and as became particularly evident in the last round of our discussion, all three authors depart from and are guided by the suffering experienced by real subjects in their critique – even though these experiences of suffering may be defined quite differently in each approach. While Klaus Dörre concentrates, from the perspective of social critique, on the systemically required inequality, on the injustice and tendencies toward precarisation that accompany the process of *Landnahme* in general (and those associated with the finance-driven regime in particular), Hartmut Rosa's 'artistic critique' is based on the attempt to prove that capitalism's unstoppable tendencies toward acceleration gradually absorb all individual and collective energies, in effect rendering the good life unattainable for both the winners and losers of the system. By pointing out that the activation regime not only – as its inevitable downside – generates immobilisation and blockages, only to then systematically disadvantage those being immobilised and blocked, but also engenders 'imposed' forms of subjects and subjectification due to its politico-economically induced heteronomy, Stephan Lessenich shows the way in which both forms of critique can be brought together productively – and how urgently they require such mutual complementation.[9]

---

7   References and elaborate discussion in H. Rosa, 'Beschleunigung und Depression. Überlegungen zum Zeitverhältnis der Moderne', in B. Hildenbrand, U. Borst, *Zeit und Therapie*, Stuttgart 2009.

8   On this cf. the highly instructive contribution by S. Graefe, 'Subjektivität an den Grenzen der Verwertbarkeit: Anmerkungen zum Zusammenhang von Erschöpfung und flexiblem Kapitalismus', Jena 2009 (MS), to the collective volume compiled as an accompanying project to this book, *Grenzen des Kapitalismus*.

9   In our view, one quite promising possibility of combining social and artistic critique so that both antagonistic and integrationist forms can be accommodated, and one which has not been elaborated on in this book, is the category of 'recognition' proposed by Axel Honneth and currently being debated (cf. A. Honneth, *Kampf um Anerkennung*, Frankfurt a.M. 1994). The 'struggle for recognition' flares up at the moment of excess that is always contained in relations of recognition.

The positions critical of capitalism assembled here are furthermore united, beyond any analytical and normative commonalities, by the conviction that the capitalist system continually generates functional problems that pose an existential structural threat to it, as manifested not least in the current crisis constellation, and can be studied formidably in this context. Even though the analytical determination of those functional crises may play out differently in each of our three contributions, they nevertheless converge on the agreement that said crises can be identified, on the one hand, in the de-synchronisation and relative decoupling of financial markets from the real economy; and in the incompatibility of political-democratic management and distribution in temporal and material-logic terms, as well as capitalist resource protection, on the other. This book thus places itself in a long line of works that fear (or hope, depending on one's perspective) that the capitalist social formation will erode its own conditions of existence in the long run – as can be observed in the age of financial market capitalism; for instance, in the ways deregulation and privatisation have created a systematic myopia that subverts the temporal horizons, stability requirements and possibly even the cultural resources for long-term investments and action strategies.

In our view, the formational crisis currently shattering the world economy thus does not represent a mere temporary 'ailment' of an otherwise 'healthy' system, but is rather the contemporary expression of an intrinsic, structurally insurmountable system error:[10] this crisis reveals the pathology of capitalism not in the sense of the objective genitive but as a subjective genitive – or to phrase it more radically: capitalism does not *have* a pathology, it *is* a pathology (albeit historically a highly fruitful one) – at least in its late modern, democratically uncivilised form.

Yet this, in turn, inevitably means that individual institutional reforms, cultural innovations in the sense of a new 'spirit', or even radical attempts at political redirection cannot fundamentally overcome the crisis, even if they are able to mitigate the analysed functional and normative problems temporarily. The 'system question' has not been resolved – indeed, two decades after the fall of the Berlin Wall, it presents itself more radically and forcefully than ever. However, in our understanding, such a fundamental reconstruction of the system requires a concerted combination of simultaneous economic, political and cultural change(s) – and thus ultimately: a radical formational shift.

---

10   'As long as the social character of labour appears as the money existence of the commodity and hence as a thing outside actual production, monetary crises, independent of real crises or as an intensification of them, are unavoidable'. (Marx, Engels, *Collected Works*, vol. 37 [Capital vol. 3], p. 649.)

Admittedly, and this may come as a disappointment to some of our readers, we can neither present an elaborate conception of transformation nor a ready-made construction of that mighty subject of future change. Here we are in a more comfortable or (again depending on one's perspective) awkward situation than many of the citizens of East Germany were in 1989/90. There is no template for social transformation, no model of society, and certainly no prefabricated set of institutions along which theory, critique and praxis could be oriented.

A sustainable social formation fit for the future should in our view be capable of 'pacifying' human existence in its basic needs:[11] humanity has long developed the resources and productive forces to alleviate the daily economic struggle for existence, at least to the extent that a self-determined way of life free of economic imperatives would be possible. In this sense, an unconditional basic income (*Bedingungsloses Grundeinkommen*), as is currently being debated in Germany, may potentially represent *one* element of a future, less objectionable social formation. To introduce this basic income as the sole measure of reform, however, strikes us as a rather questionable strategy, as such a basic security in the context of a wage earner's society could all too easily result in the social marginalisation of broad layers of the population. We see the need for such a measure to be politically flanked by innovative forms of economic democracy (*Wirtschaftsdemokratie*), rendering not only the ownership of the means of production, but also the establishment of production and development goals as objects of democratic-deliberative decision-making processes. It is highly likely that the cultural conceptions of a successful life would also be set in motion over the course of such economic and political innovation(s). Unflinching in the face of subjects' real experiences of suffering, the cultural justification of the logic of capital valorisation is still grounded in the belief that economic growth, increases in the rate of innovation and intensification of social competition already set the direction for an improvement of human destiny per se. Yet this promise is obviously not being realised for the majority of humanity. We therefore consider collective deliberation on the appropriate definition of prosperity and *quality of life,* beyond the idea of economic and social-comparative increase and escalation, to be absolutely crucial. The destiny of humankind should be determined by guiding ideas that have been arrived at by collective deliberation, and must not be left to the authoritarianism and decisive power of 'visible' and 'invisible' hands any longer. It is in this spirit that possible paths to a new social formation should be explored.

The political subject of such a counter-position cannot yet be identified;

---

11   In this usage we build on conceptions and visions contained in earlier critical theory, as represented by, for example, Herbert Marcuse.

those mighty bearers of a dynamic of fundamental social change are nowhere to be seen thus far. What we do see are numerous, but atomised and fragmented, struggles and expressions of resistance against the impositions of a capitalism built on *Landnahme*, acceleration and activation. Perhaps these individual movements – in the retrospective account of a future historian – mark the beginning of an age of a revitalised, socially critical social praxis, the emergence of a 'patchwork Left' that feels united by its critique of capitalism. It could then, and would have to be, the task of sociology – at least as we conceive of it – to maintain its distance from this process no longer, and to instead use all available means to accompany and support it. There are surely enough examples of such a stance (not only of the spirit) – and we need not return to the year 1848 to find them, either. It was a good century later, in 1959, when C. Wright Mills, that great radical American sociologist, passionately appealed to his discipline to return to the mode(s) of thought set forth by the 'classics'.[12] In an age of accelerated change, Mills said, the task of sociology is to venture beyond elaborate empiricism and *grand theory* and to once more ask the 'big questions' of social analysis, especially those of the sociality of seemingly individual problems, about the social mediation of real people's particular life circumstances – for it is the only way that sociology could regain its long lost cultural and political relevance. We believe that it is time once again – 50 years later – to return to the social-analytical and socially critical 'promise' of sociology as envisaged by Mills. The suffering in this society experienced by millions of people, from the precarious temporary worker to the well-off (mostly male) university professor, is both an expression and a reflection of macro-social processes of *Landnahme*, acceleration and activation. To place these processes at the heart of a critical reflection is to stand with those who deserve to live a better life in a better society. That is the side we wish to take with this book.

---

12   Cf. C. Wright Mills, *The Sociological Imagination*, New York 1959.

Social Capitalism and Crisis: From the Internal to the External *Landnahme*

KLAUS DÖRRE

This book – our attempt to conceive of contemporary capitalism as a dynamic system reliant on endless *Landnahmen*, social acceleration and the permanent activation of subjects for its continued existence – was originally published at the height of the global financial crisis, in the autumn of 2009. The crisis was one expression of an inherent 'system error' located within capitalism itself. Our conclusion: namely, that 'capitalism does not *have* a pathology, it *is* a pathology', was an intentional provocation. Five years down the road we can confidently state that the global economic and social crisis is here to stay – and our 'provocation', in turn, can hardly be considered provocative any longer. In the year 2014, debates revolving around capitalism's decline have (re-)entered the mainstream of the social sciences.[1] Even radical free-market economists are speculating about the end of this social system,[2] while those ideologues who still cling to capitalism find themselves waxing lyrically over the very social capitalist model that (prior to the crisis) was supposedly hopelessly outdated. A good example for this is the philosopher Antonio Baloffi, who claimed, in a vengeful criticism of the Italian left: 'Germany is playing a hegemonic role in Europe today ... I mean that in the Gramscian sense. Here people know what good governance is. Germany has the better social model'.[3]

In the following remarks I would like to develop an alternative point of view – a point of view that contrasts with both romantic hopes for a renaissance of the European social market economy, as well as the various

---

1 I. Wallerstein/R. Collins/M. Mann/G. Derlugian/C. Calhoun, *Does Capitalism have a future?* New York 2103.

2 Th. Straubhaar, Das ist das Ende des Kapitalismus, in: *Die Welt*, 10 June 2014.

3 A. Bolaffi, Interview in: Frankfurter Rundschau. 23 February 2014, pp. 26–27; cf. A. Bolaffi, *Deutsches Herz – Das Modell Deutschland und die europäische Krise*. Stuttgart 2014. p. 26 f.

hermetic scenarios of capitalist decay or even collapse. Just like all other varieties of capitalism, the German version of social capitalism (in truth long extinct) is mired in the depths of an economic-ecological 'pincer-grip crisis',[4] which it will not be able to overcome without undergoing significant change. Throughout the interplay of forces between competing political projects that characterises the neo-liberal era, the creative destruction of this particular variant of capitalism was only taken to a certain point – a point at which what remained of the old model was still sufficiently robust to facilitate a relatively successful strategy of crisis management. What has emerged, however, is not a renewed social market economy – let alone a social market economy that could serve as a model for Europe or the rest of the world. What we now see is a society driven by competition, in which empty gestures of concern, vis-à-vis the 'social', function merely to shore up domestic support and popular allegiance, while simultaneously tying these sentiments to a 'half-hegemonic'[5] politics of dominance within the European space as a whole. The internal *Landnahme* is now followed by an external one. The ongoing expansion of this selective-integrative competitive capitalism may proceed for some time, but it offers no long-term, sustainable solution to the aforementioned pincer-grip crisis in which Germany and the world finds itself. Having said that, this statement should not be taken to imply that I believe there to be a kind of automatism in this decline. The secular crisis is an intersection from which several distinct paths of social transformation depart. I will elucidate this stance, beginning with a rough outline of the crisis (1), which allows, in terms of both crisis theory (2) and time diagnostics (3), for a more precise clarification of the *Landnahme* theorem (4), in order to then conclude with some deliberations on the potential forces and trajectories of social transformation (5).

1. WHAT HAPPENED? THE TRAJECTORY OF THE CRISIS

The great contraction of 2008–2009 was not and is not merely a common crisis like any other. Its causes and effects will continue to challenge and confound social scientists for generations to come.[6] In its wake, we have already witnessed one of the most impressive ideological achievements of the last

---

4   S. Sakar, *The Crises of Capitalism. A Different Study of Political Economy*, Berkeley, New York 2012.

5   J. Habermas, '*In favour of a strong Europe*' – *what does this mean?*, in Juncture, Volume 21, Issue 1 Summer 2014, pp. 82–88.

6   G. Dux, *Demokratie als Lebensform. Die Welt nach der Krise des Kapitalismus*, Weilerswist 2013.

half decade – namely, the successful re-interpretation of the global financial crisis as being primarily a 'home-grown' sovereign debt crisis of the European states. Countries like Greece, so the radical free-market mantra goes, were unable to compete on the global economic playing field 'because the cheap credits that accompanied the Euro became too expensive', thus making them the main culprit of the fiscal crisis.[7] This notion that the countries of the southern and southeastern European periphery had been living beyond their means and thereby caused the crisis is grounded upon a case of severe memory loss (so to speak), for it utterly ignores or even denies the influence the global financial market crash has had on the European situation.

Let us first take a look back at what actually happened. The economic meltdown began, almost unnoticed at first, with bankrupt North American homeowners from the lower social strata. This wave of private insolvencies only began to raise eyebrows when it reached members of the middle class(es). Through securitisation, banks had spread the risks of mortgage loans – subject to flexible interest rates – very widely. This supposed democratisation of risk, intended as it was to minimise the potential for catastrophe, ultimately proved to be the Achilles' heel of the global financial system. These bad loans, no longer serviceable by financially insolvent homeowners, resulted in the bankruptcy of Lehman Brothers and triggered a banking crisis, the ramifications of which reached far beyond the United States. The loss of confidence within the financial system brought interbank transactions and lending to an effective standstill. The crisis in banking and the credit crunch quickly grew over into a veritable financial wildfire, which spread to the real economy (or rather: the productive economy excluding the financial sector) after a brief delay.

At this point, an overarching constellation of crisis encountered economic imbalances and structural weaknesses in the nation-states themselves, some of which long pre-dated the onset of the crisis. When the global economy returned to a growth trajectory in 2010, numerous regional and national trouble spots continued to smoulder. Though the crisis may have had distinct consequences for the different varieties of capitalism, it has undeniably had an impact everywhere.[8] While the economies of China and other emerging countries of the Global South recovered rather swiftly, the crisis took a rather different turn in Europe. In the Eurozone the effects of the crash encountered a fragile supra-national structure integrating countries with

---

7   H.-W Sinn, Verspielt nicht eure Zukunft, München 2013, p. 103.

8   S. Lehndorff, *Spaltende Integration. Der Triumph gescheiterter Ideen in Europa – revisited. Zehn Länderstudien*, Hamburg 2014; K. Dörre/K. Jürgens/I. Matuschek (ed.), *Arbeit in Europa. Marktfundamentalismus als Zerreißprobe*, Frankfurt am Main 2014.

sharply divergent economic output into one unified economic block with a common currency. Aided by the European Union, national governments had managed to codify ruling class political objectives at a supra-national level, which were subsequently used as justification for implementing supposedly 'inevitable' market-centred reforms on the national level. The monetary union and the introduction of the Euro had signified the completion of this project. Since the nation-states had been stripped of the ability to temporarily balance competitive disadvantages through devaluation of their respective national currencies, the one instrument left to the weaker economies was 'internal devaluation',[9] that is to say: permanent downward pressure on wages and social standards.

The global financial crisis had already passed its low point when this fragile European constellation's potential for crisis came into bloom. The chain of events began in Greece, where a national economic model that had attempted to compensate for the displacement of labour forces, from the traditional agricultural and artisanal sectors through an expansion of state and public employment, had reached its limits.[10] Corrupt elites, an inefficient tax system and financial manipulation during the initial accession to the Eurozone had already contributed to an imbalance in the national budget even before the crisis began. When the national deficit rose to 15.6 per cent in 2009, investors (who up until that point had treated Greek bonds no differently than German ones) now demanded higher interest rates. Banks responded with desperate attempts to sell off any and all Greek securities. Due to this decline in value and corresponding rise in interest rates, the Greek state was no longer capable of servicing its debts by itself. But Greece was not alone for long. Rating agencies and institutional investors were on the lookout for other potential weak links within the Eurozone – and Ireland, Iceland, Italy, Portugal, Spain, and Cyprus soon proved to be suitable candidates. Only the European Central Bank's promise to buy up government bonds more or less indefinitely was able to halt the banks' speculative spree. Yet the crisis-stricken countries' structural financial problems remained. In their efforts to secure the survival of ailing banks and other financial institutions, some of the European nation-states, despite (or rather because of) high unemployment and corresponding losses in tax revenue, were willing to accept the potential risks of taking on dramatic new levels of sovereign debt. The same financial institutions that had cried out hysterically for state intervention at the height of the crisis now expected the bill

9   W. Streeck, *Buying Time: The Delayed Crisis of Democratic Capitalism*, London, New York, p.150.

10   A. Steinko, A. F., Portugal, Spanien und Griechenland auf der Suche nach einem Ausweg, in: Das Argument, No. 301, 2013, pp. 140–155.

for these costly government rescue packages to be paid in full. The financial markets' professed loss of investor confidence resulted in the economic punishment of those nations benefiting from infusions of financial aid, particularly in southern and eastern Europe. This 'punishment' came in the form of declining credit ratings and increasing interest rates. It is through this process that the Greek crisis became the veritable midwife at the birth of a regime of European consolidation that prioritises debt reduction and fiscal discipline over everything else.[11]

Under the *diktat* of severe austerity, the economic output of the crisis countries has fallen significantly below 2008 levels. We can no longer speak of a mere 'recession' in the countries of southern Europe today, for what we are witnessing is a sustained process of contraction of entire national economies. A closer look at the Greek situation may help to at least develop a rough sketch of the changes currently occurring in Europe, as Greece has become a laboratory in which the impact of austerity is being tested on the 'living object'. Following 2010, the Troika, a supervisory body composed of the IMF, the EU and the ECB, struck several deals with the Greek government. These agreements stipulated rigid austerity measures, a massive reduction of the public sector, comprehensive privatisation(s), and the annulment of extensive social rights with the alleged aim of increasing labour market flexibility. As was also the case in other crisis-affected countries, however, austerity in fact *accelerated* economic decline.[12] From 2008 onwards, the Greek GDP declined continually, reaching a record low point of −6.9 per cent growth in 2011.[13] Consequently, unemployment rose from 7.7 per cent (2008) to 27.1 per cent (2013), while youth unemployment rose from 22.1 per cent to 59.1 per cent in the same period.[14] In 2010 and 2011 alone, the average income dropped by a total of 8 per cent, wage cuts in the public sector have reached 20 per cent – in extreme cases even 50 per cent. The proportion of jobs not subject to social security or insurance contributions has climbed to 36 per cent. Pension cuts vary between 14 per cent and 48 per cent; homelessness, which increasingly affects even the educated middle classes, is currently 45 per cent higher than pre-crisis levels. As if these statistics were not alarming enough, the suicide rate is hitting record highs: following an increase of 25 per cent in 2009–2010, it rose again by 40 per cent in the following year.[15]

11 W. Streeck, *Buying Time*, 2014, p. 118.

12 J. Leschke, S. Theodoropoulou, A. Watt, *Auf dem Weg ins Europa 2020"? Austeritätskurs und neue Wirt-schaftssteuerung auf der EU-Ebene*, in: Lehndorff (Hrsg.), 2014, pp. 243–272, here pp. 245–247.

13 Weltbank, *World Development Indicators 2012*, Washington DC 2012.

14 Eurostat. Tables, *Graphs and Maps Interface* (TGM), 2014.

15 Cf. M. Markantonatou, *Die Entwicklung der Arbeit, die Automatik der*

And yet, despite all of the sacrifices the Greek people have been forced to make, the country's public debt has increased from 120 per cent of the GDP in 2010 to 175 per cent in 2013.

Behind these figures lies something more significant: the transition to a type of society previously unknown in continental Europe. Greece, along with other crisis-ridden states, has become a precarious society of capitalist slump. We are talking about a European society which, following a thirteen-year growth period, is now marked by economic and social regression. Given that roughly three million people have dropped out of the collective social security systems, many of the most basic social provisions can now only be guaranteed through various forms of self-help.[16] Doctors add extra hours to their official workdays to treat patients who cannot afford or are not entitled to regular medical provisions free of charge. Material scarcity is promoting subsistence production, while networks of barter exchange secure basic provisions for the utterly destitute, and informal social networks offer shelter to families who can no longer afford their rent in the form of crowded apartments or campsites. This way, a radicalised *Landnahme* of the social qua de-commodification generates a non-capitalist exterior, which, as paradoxical as it may sound, temporarily contributes to the stabilisation of capitalist relations of dominance. Precarious societies are now emerging in the heart of the Eurozone in which not only gainful employment, but indeed more or less *all* basic social institutions have become unstable.[17] If we were to include social status insecurity and private indebtedness to this list, we could confidently state that a *majority* of people in these societies live under precarious conditions. Here, governance amounts to maximising insecurities while granting the bare minimum of social security required to avoid the threat of social unrest and revolt (or at least keep them under control).[18]

Such societies are also the bitter (and indeed far more drastic) reality in such eastern European countries as Bulgaria and Romania. Although these societies do in fact possess, at least in the formal sense, a more or less

---

Sparpolitik und die Krise in Griechenland, in: K. Dörre, K. Jürgens, I. Matuschek, Arbeit in Europa, 2014, pp. 217–228.

16   Owed to the vulnerable status of migrants, the already large informal sector had been expanding even before the crisis. Cf. M. Karamessini, *Sovereign debt crisis: an opportunity to complete the neoliberal project and dismantle the Greek employment model*, in: S. Lehndorff (ed.), A triumph of failed ideas European models of capitalism in the crisis, Brussels: ETUI 2012, pp. 161–162.

17   K. v. Holdt, *Bodies of Defiance*, in: M. Burawoy, K. v. Holdt (ed.), Conversations with Bourdieu. The Johannesburg Moment. Johannesburg 2012, pp. 67–73.

18   I. Lorey, *Die Regierung der Prekären*, Wien 2012, p. 14. (English-language version with an introduction by Judith Butler forthcoming in February 2015, published by Verso under the title: *State of Insecurity: Government of the Precarious*)

democratic institutional framework, any decisions concerning the shape or direction of their national future has been taken away from the people of these countries. Assuming that the Greek economy continues to grow at 1.5 per cent, it would still take the country decades just to get back to pre-crisis levels of economic output. Despite economic stagnation or even contraction, the capitalist structures of domination have proven relatively stable in the countries of the crisis. Greece is thus far the only country that has witnessed the emergence of an anti-capitalist formation that enjoys mass support, in the form of SYRIZA; in other countries it is mostly the right-wing populist parties that have benefited from widespread political disaffection. This raises a pressing question: how can we account for the peculiar stability of capitalist relations of domination?

2. WHY DOES IT HAPPEN? *LANDNAHMEN* AND CRISES

A partial answer to this question is simple: because economic crises function as 'the irrational rationalisers of an always unstable capitalism'[19] and never affect all social fields of complex societies simultaneously or to the same degree. Crises are virtually indispensable for the stimulation of growth. This is equally true for the phases of economic turbulence that preceded the global recession of 2008–2009. A crisis management which was underwritten – in sharp contrast to the wildly exaggerated free-market ideology of the time – by massive state intervention(s) ensured that time and again the state that had to step in to rescue investment funds and banking institutions from bankruptcy. Systematic state intervention facilitated a dynamic in which profits were privatised while real and potential losses were socialised. This 'irrational rationalisation', however, led to the development of a 'systemic "moral hazard"'[20] in the case of several important financial market actors. This moral hazard in turn fed into the accumulation of overall crisis potential in the financial sector as a whole. The entire 'service class of financial market capitalism'[21] operated under the impression that they could act at almost no personal risk whatsoever, which (of course) encouraged their inclination toward practices of high-risk speculation even further. From the perspective of investment bankers and their top employees, equipped

---

19   D. Harvey, *The Enigma of Capital and the Crises of Capitalism*, Profile: London 2011, p. 71.

20   Ibid., p. 10.

21   P. Windolf, *Eigentümer ohne Risiko. Die Dienstklasse des Finanzmarkt-Kapitalismus (Owners without Risk. The New Service Class of Financial Market Capitalism)*, in: Zeitschrift für Soziologie (6), pp. 516–536.

with unique insider knowledge (and thus essentially uncontrollable) as they were, it was absolutely rational, when confronted with the prospect of high returns, to take just about any risk imaginable. After all, they knew that it would be others who had to cover incurred losses in the case of failure, and not themselves or their institutions. State-funded rescue packages allowed banks to continue operating without interruption, which in turn prevented market adjustment(s) and seemed to render institutional innovation unnecessary, thereby blocking the crisis mechanism's function of economic cleansing and rectification. The potential for economic crisis was allowed to expand and deepen until finally the flapping of a butterfly's wings was enough to trigger an explosion within the non-linear financial system[22] that would shake the whole world.

Nevertheless, if we wish to fully comprehend the ongoing crisis, we must free ourselves from our fixation on the financial sector and take a closer look at the events and processes leading up to the global crash as well. Numerous commentators draw on the work of Karl Polanyi in order to do so.[23] Yet, aside from the usual difficulties that historical analogies always involve,[24] any reference to Polanyi leaves one central question unanswered: what exactly makes the continuous expansion of the market a non-negotiable capitalist necessity, and how is this expansionist drive related to economic crises overall? An attempt to answer this question (without shelving Polanyi entirely) could take up the line of heterodox Marxist interpretation, which reads capitalist dynamic as prolonged, ongoing *Landnahme*. Irrespective of any otherwise existing heterogeneity between such concepts, they share the assumption that capitalist societies do not and indeed *cannot* reproduce themselves entirely of their own accord. Rather, capitalist development takes place as a complex movement between the internal and the external. It rests upon a dynamic of permanent exchange, which the already-commodified sectors of society cultivate with sectors that are not or not yet fully commodified.[25] This exchange follows the pattern of a continuous cycle of primitive

---

22   K. Mainzer (ad.), *Komplexe Systeme und Nichtlineare Dynamik in Natur und Gesellschaft*, Heidelberg 1999, p. 25.

23   Cf. M. Burawoy, 'Marxism after Polanyi', in: M. Williams, V. Satgar (Hrsg.): *Marxisms in the 21st Century: Crisis, Critique and Struggle*, Johannesburg 2013, pp. 34–52; N. Fraser, *Marketization, Social Protection, Emancipation: Toward a Neo-Polanyian Conception of Capitalist Crisis*, in: C. Calhoun/, G. Derluguian (ed.), *The Roots of the Global Financial Meltdown*, New York 2011, pp. 137–158.

24   J. Kocka, *Geschichte des Kapitalismus*, Munich 2013, p. 18.

25   A capitalist society can be identified at the point where capitalist principles exhibit a certain dominance", that they tend to "proliferate into other spheres beyond the economy" and influence even non-capitalist relations. Cf. J. Kocka, *Geschichte des Kapitalismus*, p. 12.

accumulation,[26] i.e., the separation of the producer from the means of production and the extra-economic disciplining of labour forces so as to adapt them to new methods of production are processes that are never finished, but instead begin again and again at different stages of social development.

The capital surplus absorption problem

So, how are capitalist *Landnahmen* related to economic crises? The capitalist dynamic is mainly a result of the capacity of social actors to turn seemingly absolute boundaries to accumulation into surmountable barriers – a process in which 'production moves in contradictions which are constantly overcome but just as constantly posited'.[27] Crises are conceivable in any and all of the stages of capital flow (production, circulation, consumption). Their roots may lie in insufficient seed capital for capital-intensive innovations, labour force shortages, sectoral disproportionalities, resource scarcity, ecological imbalances, rapid technological changes, workers' resistance, under-consumption, or in the monetary and financial system.[28] Every crisis is unique, and cannot be adequately extrapolated from some abstract logic of capital or from a universal imperative of escalation found within modern societies; if we are to uncover its origins and trajectory, it must be empirically investigated. There is, however, one basic problematic of capitalist accumulation that reveals itself, one way or another, in every crisis. In developing the reproduction schemas contained in the second volume of his main work, Marx attempts – in a remarkably innovative approach for his day – to discuss the conditions of equilibrium in capitalist economies. Like Marx, Rosa Luxemburg also assumes that there is a coercive force continually expanding the reproduction inherent in capitalist economies, resulting from the competition between individual capital units and a permanent increase in labour productivity.[29] Luxemburg, however, laments that Marx's model fails to explain how exactly the extra surplus value of the preceding period of production is realised in the subsequent production cycle.[30]

26   S. Federici, *Revolution at Point Zero: Housework, Reproduction and Feminist Struggle*, San Francisco 2012; M. De Angelis, *Marx and Primitive Accumulation: The Continuous Character of Capital's "Enclosures"*, in: The Commoner 2, www.commoner. org.uk, last accessed: 15 May 2014; M. Backhouse, O. Gerlach, S. Kalmring, A. Nowak (ed.), *Die globale Einhegung: Krise, ursprüngliche Akkumulation und Landnahmen im Kapitalismus*, Münster 2013, pp. 20–39.

27   Marx, as quoted in B. Foster et al, *The Ecological Rift*, New York 2010, p. 285.

28   Cf. Harvey 2011, p. 52.

29   R. Luxemburg, *The Accumulation of Capital*, London 2003, p. 12.

30   Ibid., pp. 432–3.

This notion has been widely rejected by many contemporary Marxists.[31] Yet despite its many 'errors and false conclusions', Luxemburg's argument 'must be regarded as theoretically fruitful'.[32] This is particularly valid when it comes to what David Harvey has since termed the *capital surplus absorption problem*.[33] To put it in simple terms: an economy that grows during a period of production must create markets that are capable of absorbing the extra surplus value during the subsequent period – a task only possible through market-expanding investments. Therefore, the rule of thumb reads: 3 per cent growth requires 3 per cent additional investment.[34] The higher a given society's level of wealth and the greater its economic growth, the more difficult it becomes to acquire and develop new markets. This *capital surplus absorption problem* represents the central macroeconomic driving force of capitalist *Landnahmen*. It explains why the process of capital accumulation requires and demands the ability to 'mobilise world labour power without restriction' so as to 'utilise all productive forces of the globe' – at least to the extent possible within the confines of surplus value production.[35]

Luxemburg rightly views the endless 'setting free' of labour forces to be trained for capitalist modes of production (in turn in a process of transformation itself), the annexation of pre-capitalist forms of production by the money economy, as well as a permanent metabolism between internal capitalist and external non-capitalist markets[36] to be characteristic of any and all accumulation. Writing almost as if she had known what modern theorists meant when speaking of recombination, amalgamation, hybrid conditions, re-interpretations and overlapping as forms of institutional change,[37] she identifies how, in the 'progressive breakdown and disintegration' of non-capitalist forms of production, the 'most peculiar combinations between the modern wage system and primitive authority' emerge.[38]

---

31   One well-founded objection to Luxemburg's deliberations is that her level of abstraction falls short of that found in Marx' reproduction schemas. There is an excellent summary of the debate contained in: M. Turban, *Marxsche Reproduktionsschemata und Wirtschaftstheorie*, Berlin 1980, pp. 132–196.

32   R. Rosdolsky, *The Making of Marx's Capital*, London 1977, p. 505; similar: R. Bellofiore, *General Introduction. Rosa Luxemburg on Capitalist Dynamics, Distribution and Effective Demand Crises*, in: id. (ed.), *Rosa Luxemburg and the Critique of Political Economy*, London, 2009, pp. 1–23.

33   Harvey 2011, p. 26.

34   Ibid., p. 27.

35   Luxemberg, p. 343.

36   Ibid., p. 346.

37   J. Beyer (ed.), *Vom Zukunfts- zum Auslaufmodell? Die deutsche Wirtschaftsordnung im Wandel*. Frankfurt am Main 2003, pp. 7–34, here p. 21.

38   Luxemburg, pp. 342–4.

Credit and innovation as stabilising factors

Yet the foresight with which Luxemburg describes the amalgams of unfree, precarious and only partially commodified labour in its hybrid interconnections to modern capitalist wage labour does not change the fact that her theory of accumulation ignores important stabilisation mechanisms of capitalist accumulation. This includes the functions of credit as well as the significance of process and product innovation in particular. If – in a capitalist economy – there exist no other viable alternative solutions, then money is applied as medium of exchange in order to 'bridge the gap', so to speak, between yesterday's surplus product and today's re-investment(s). Should owners of capital hoard their assets instead of directly re-investing them, then money creation on the part of the banks and deficit spending by the state are the most important means of countering the lack of solvent demand. Moreover, credit stimulates investment, and (in the event of successful implementation) even leads to market expansion.

These two methods of resolving the *capital surplus absorption problematic* are so vital to the maintenance of the capitalist dynamic that special networks or configurations of relations and institutions are relied upon to ensure their smooth operation.[39] *State-finance networks* process problems of finance; they raise capital for elaborate and costly infrastructural projects that are simply too large to be handled by one individual private company alone. This institution-actor network can then go on to develop separate solutions for the *capital surplus absorption problem*. One of the primary methods of dealing with this absorption problem is through the development of innovative new financial products such as derivatives, which serve to spread around and thereby better insure risk, in turn opening up further investment opportunities by ensuring the ongoing improvement and increased circulation of said financial products. The state-corporate nexus deals with any kind of impediment to competition resulting, for example, from economic monopolies, through strict antitrust legislation (as in the USA) or a government agency responsible for regulating economic competition (such as the German *Bundeskartellbehörde*). At the heart of these processes lies the promotion of innovation(s) in the productive economy via cooperation between public research institutions and the research and development departments of private companies. The state-finance nexus and state-corporate nexus ensure that the innovations being funded aid in creating a non-capitalist Other within capitalist societies through creative destruction. Large corporations and the state thus repeatedly find themselves in the position of actively creating an *exterior* within the *interior*

---

39   Harvey 2011, p.48, 92.

of national economies. The production of space through urbanisation is a common way of responding to the forces of market expansion through creative destruction of land and long-term spatial fixation of capital. The list of self-stabilising factors would remain incomplete, however, unless we add a state-labour-reproduction nexus to the two 'central nervous systems' of capitalist accumulation I have described here. I propose that this state-labour-reproduction nexus regulates labour relations in a given society, but is also the institution in which labour capacities are developed, qualified, nurtured and looked after, so as to ensure the proper functioning of social reproduction as a whole. The way in which said networks are institutionalised indicates a particular variety of capitalism,[40] while at the same time also pointing to distinct crisis types.

Types of crisis

It is necessary to distinguish, in a systematic way, cyclical economic crises from a type of crisis that affects the entire ensemble of social regulations and the (re-)productive structures of society as a whole. The same can be said of the various other disruptions to capital flows that every capitalist economy encounters from time to time. Having made that clear, there is nevertheless an intrinsic link between cyclical and secular 'major crises'. Any cyclical disruption of capital flows causes a temporary concentration and centralisation of capital – that is to say, it strengthens the tendency towards a self-negating market economy and thereby weakens the cleansing function that 'minor' crises usually serve.[41] This dynamic can in fact lead to an accumulation and escalation of structural crisis potential(s), which ultimately discharge(s) at a later point, in the form of major crises. Taking the development of the German variety of social capitalism as a test case, such major crises include the Great Depression (or Long Depression, or Great Deflation, 1873–1895), the Depression of 1929 (1929–1932) and the New Depression (1973–1974).[42] The considerable length of crises like the Great Depression are caused by a gap that emerges when established actor-institution networks are no longer able to fulfil their economic regulatory function. They ultimately produce a space of possibility which capitalist actors can harness so as to replace an old, crisis-ridden modus operandi of capitalist *Landnahmen* with a new one.

---

40   Cf. B. Amable, *The Diversity of Modern Capitalism*, Oxford 2003; C. Crouch, *Capitalist Diversity and Change*, Oxford 2005.

41   F. Deppe, *Autoritärer Kapitalismus: Demokratie auf dem Prüfstand*. Hamburg 2013, pp. 38–42.

42   J. Kocka, *Geschichte des Kapitalismus*, p. 83.

There exists a subset of economic literature that depicts the periods between said 'major crises' as long waves of capitalist accumulation. Based upon what we know today, however, we can confidently state that there is no endogenous mechanism or 'law' of economics that could produce or determine any such long wave.[43] Nevertheless, it is still the case that the political and social crossroads that economic crises bring forth necessitate fundamental political decisions and course corrections on the part of institutional actors, which subsequently constitute developmental paths. The world economic crisis of 1929–33 put an end to an era of free market liberalism; at the same time, it generated highly divergent developmental paths, such as the New Deal in the USA, Industrial Democracy in Sweden, and Fascism in Central Europe. Over the course of several epochs, then, capitalist societies in a more general sense move between the Schumpeterian paradigm of creative destruction (dominance of the state-corporate nexus or the state-finance nexus) and Polanyi's embedding of the market into the social (with the labour-reproduction nexus playing the leading role).[44]

Schumpeter and Polanyi describe – from partially contrasting perspectives – an inherent tension which has characterised the capitalist dynamic of accumulation and growth from its onset. Capitalist societies require economic growth and market expansion, in permanence and without interruption. They must also, however, provide for the minimum of social security and stability that makes market-compatible behaviour possible in the first place. Capitalist socialisation (*Vergesellschaftung*) thus represents a process of productive failure, in which the role played by capitalist actors willing to bend or break social rules is just as necessary as that played by social forces capable of imposing a degree of social regulation upon the market. Under capitalist conditions, this tension between creative destruction and social embedding can only be pacified – if at all – for a certain limited period of time. Therefore, and contrary to Polanyi's assumption, the social regulation of market mechanisms is indeed reversible. The structural capital surplus absorption problem necessitates – indeed *forces* – market expansion and fosters the tendency of dominant capitalist actors to call into question, undermine, or even ignore ostensibly binding social rules. In the societies of the twenty-first century, this tension between the pressures of market expansion on the one hand and the required social embedding of capitalist commodity exchange on the other is replacing the opposition

---

43   Cf. Harvey 2011, pp. 98–9.

44   J. Schumpeter, *The Theory of Economic Development: An Inquiry into Profits, Capital, Credit, Interest and the Business Cycle*, New Brunswick and London 1983 [1934]. K. Polanyi, *The Great Transformation: The Political and Economic Origins of Our Time*, 2nd ed., Boston 2001 [1944].

between productive forces and the relations of production as the primary driving force of capitalist development.[45]

3. WHAT IS NEW?

In order to gain a more precise grasp of the defining traits of the current crisis, we must adopt a heuristics that considers the paradox found in the market's contradictory need to expand on the one hand, and the tendency towards the market's social embedding on the other.

Reversing the crisis problematic

During the New Depression of 1973–4, the dominant capitalist actors of the time interpreted the crisis as the result of an overall profit squeeze. Wage earners' power, as it had been institutionalised in the developed welfare states appeared to be the main obstacle to accumulation and market expansion. In response, welfare state institutions became the target of a new round of a mass-scale *Landnahme* of the social. Market actors sought to transform the seemingly absolute barrier to growth posed by the welfare state into a surmountable hurdle. The state-finance nexus assumed the leadership role in this process, attempting to effect changes in the state-labour-reproduction nexus. From the elite's perspective this operation has been hugely successful: both the organised labour movement as well as the institutions designed to restrict market power more generally were weakened to such a degree that the distribution of overall social wealth shifted decidedly in favour of the already-privileged, as was evidenced by how they were best positioned to reap the fruits of the credit-driven boom of the 2000s.

This shift did not come without consequences, however. The erosion of trade union power, the political representation of wage earners and welfare-state institutions also caused a new barrier to further accumulation in the form of structurally deficient solvent demand incurred by wage stagnation and decline. Money that could not be profitably invested in the productive economy was instead diverted to high-risk investments in the financial sector. Furthermore, and particularly with regard to Anglo-Saxon capitalisms, the issuing of mortgage loans to low-income groups was intended to compensate for stagnant wage levels. This linking of the credit system to members of the wage-earning classes led directly to the catastrophe of 2008–09, as the crisis began in the financial sector. The underlying

---

45   In this, I fully agree with M. Burawoy; cf. *Marxism after Polanyi*, 2013.

problem, however, was and remains 'excessive capitalist empowerment vis-à-vis labour'[46] [47] as well as a devaluation of reproductive activities and a general weakening of the social rules which are actually prerequisites for functioning markets. Thus, the fundamental economic problem of the early 1970s has been effectively reversed. Triggered by a profit squeeze, the new *Landnahme* has, by eliminating a specific barrier to capitalist accumulation, created a new one, i.e., structurally insolvent demand, which in turn has evoked the threat of deflation (price slump as a driving force of economic recession) in the Eurozone and which, moreover, holds within it the seed of a new financial crisis.

As should be clear at this point, the capital surplus absorption problem can manifest itself in highly diverse constellations of economic crisis. Disruptions of capital flow influence extra-economic social fields, institutions, and action strategies without determining them as such. Essential social fields of action – Harvey lists technology, family and personal networks, institutional arrangements, work processes, regimes of reproduction, one's spiritual relation to the world as well as society's relationship to nature – develop co-evolutionarily. They influence one another, yet none is able to *control* the others. This is why economic crises can always be alleviated in differentiated societies. However, disruptions of capital flow can also be caused by external shocks.

The commodification of the natural world and the externalisation of the consequences

A vital aspect of an understanding of the ongoing crisis is the evolution of society's relation(s) to the natural world. Michael Burawoy views the commodification of nature as being characteristic of the 'third wave of marketisation'[48] which gradually subordinates land, water, oceans, forests, clean air, and even properties of the human body itself to the principle of competition. The commodification of nature, which really began with the emergence of capitalism itself, produces barriers to accumulation for which the term 'crisis' is not quite an adequate description, even though it is used in this context.[49] Whereas crisis entails a condition that can (at least theoretically) be dealt with and overcome, the creation of global ecological dangers represents a continuous and ongoing process. The

---

46   Harvey 2011, p. 118.
47   Ibid., pp. 122–7.
48   Cf. M. Burawoy, *Marxism after Polanyi*, p. 40.
49   J. B. Foster, B. Clark, R. York, *The Ecological Rift. Capitalism's War on the Earth*. New York 2010, p.399.

beginning of permanent and accelerated interventions into the labour-mediated metabolism[50] of humanity and the earth coincided with primitive accumulation. Industrialisation and the systemic compulsion towards permanent economic growth triggered a kind of expansionism that negates the absolute limits inherent in any metabolism. One pivotal reason for this is the specific form of the capital surplus absorption problem, as formulated in what is referred to as the 'Lauderdale Paradox'. The Lauderdale Paradox posits that private assets in the form of land and natural resources can only be expanded through the elimination or destruction of public assets. This way a lack of x is actively created, where x is something that was once abundantly available as part of the commons (e.g., water, land, and clean air).[51]

This form of primitive accumulation persists and can be observed to this day. An end to these sorts of *Landnahmen* is nowhere in sight, at least not for the foreseeable future. Emissions trading is a striking example of how our very biosphere is being enclosed (through the creation of ownership titles) and assigned a monetary value. So far, the scarcity of natural resources has only been felt indirectly as far as purchasing prices are concerned, and becomes visible as a driver of economic crisis only in a mediated way, as is the case with petrol prices.[52] Reaching 'peak oil' – that is to say, the point of maximum possible output of crude oil – has simply resulted in an increase in high-risk exploration and exploitation (e.g. fracking) of previously unprofitable reserves, also known as so-called 'unconventional oil'. New extraction methods allow for temporarily 'plentiful' oil supplies, and petrol prices drop. As the largest beneficiary, the USA is utilising declining energy prices to finance re-industrialisation. The general rule here is: shortages, which are not expressed in price levels, are not taken into account during the accumulation process unless other regulations necessitate it; these costs are usually externalised and passed on to the wider community (*Gemeinschaft*) as a whole. One fundamental problem of this externalisation mechanism is that it renders the over-stepping of the limits of natural systems invisible over long stretches of time.

---

50   Foster et al. 2010, p. 402. Marx used the term in his analysis of the metabolism of mediation through labour between humans and the natural world. Labour is seen in a broader sense as a life-giving process here.

51   Ibid., p. 432. Private property, profit motive and competition represent specifically capitalist, yet by no means the only causes of economic expansionism. On the ideological and political roots thereof cf. K. Dörre, *Landnahme, das Wachstumsdilemma und die ‚Achsen der Ungleichheit'*. In: Berliner Journal für Soziologie 22(1) 2012, p. 101–128, here pp. 111–113; Ch. Deutschmann, Moderne Ökonomie ohne Wachstumszwang: ein Wunschtraum?, in WSI Mitteilungen 7/2014, pp. 513–520.

52   Harvey 2011, pp. 76–7.

The ongoing commodification of the natural world and the externalisation of ecological risks is resulting in the over-stepping of planetary boundaries. When measured by pre-industrial standards we have already crossed the 'red line' of irreversible damage as far as climate change, biodiversity and the nitrogen cycle is concerned.[53] Acidification of the oceans, lack of ozone, fresh water consumption, land use and atmospheric aerosol loading are all rapidly approaching the limits of planetary tolerance. The main polluters are the growth-driven capitalisms of the North, even though larger emerging economies, such as that of China, are quickly catching up. At present, a quarter of the earth's population – mainly from the Global North – consumes three quarters of its resources and produces three quarters of waste and emissions. If the Global South is ever to have even a *chance* at development, then ecological re-orientation must begin in the historical capitalist centres. The term 'crisis' is appropriate to describe this predicament insofar as phenomena such as climate change are not subordinated to any kind of linear principle of escalation; rather, complex feedback effects ensure that human-influenced natural systems can reach a point at which they are irreversibly destabilised.

This destabilisation, however, does not imply that ecological catastrophes necessarily or automatically bring about a 'final' crisis of capitalism. There are 'endless predictive uncertainties'[54] with regard to the complex interactions between humans and the natural world. Standard values and climate tipping points are dependent upon shared knowledge and definitions; they are also sites of struggle concerning interpretation, political negotiations and social conflicts. What seems safe to assume, though, is that the time frame in which fundamental changes must be implemented in order to allow for a globally sustainable metabolism of the earth cannot be extended indefinitely. The method of overcoming economic crises which has been taken for granted since the Industrial Revolution, namely the generation of economic growth through utilisation of fossil energy sources, has now become a primary driving force of ecological destruction.[55] Essentially, the world has been living beyond its means since the 1970s – and not only in terms of the impact on the climate, but also with view to the actual consumption of finite resources. The ecological footprint, which measures resource consumption in comparison to the planet's overall carrying capacity, represents an important indicator of this. Even before the turn of the millennium, human resource consumption was about 20 per cent above the sustainability

53   Cf. J. Rockström, W. Steffen, K. Noone et al., *A safe operating space for humanity*, in: Nature 461, 2009, pp. 472–475.

54   J. Foster et al., *The Ecological Rift*, 2010, p. 425.

55   Cf. J. Randers, *2052: A Global Forecast for the Next Forty Years*. Chelsea 2012.

limit. During the crisis years of 1980–83, resource consumption had begun to approach the sustainability boundary. It has risen to such an extent since then that we are now approaching the limits of long-term economic growth, at least in the advanced capitalisms.

Given this historically novel accumulation and mutual interleaving of economic, ecological and social dislocations, it seems appropriate to describe the current constellation as an economic-ecological double crisis or 'pincer-grip crisis'. Neither ecological nor economic crises can be traced back to *one* sole cause or origin. The term 'double crisis' depicts mainly a spatial and temporal synchronisation of highly diverse flashpoints and causes. What makes the current crisis constellation a true historical novelty, however, is that the growth dilemma of the advanced capitalisms is being exposed in a qualitatively new way. The tried and true, unquestioned method of overcoming economic crises as described above is currently (and necessarily) leading to an accumulation of ecological dangers. This is the why the capitalisms of the Global North in particular are confronted with a historic decision, essentially between two alternatives: One is to make growth sustainable; the other is to make de-growth stable.[56]

4 HOW DOES IT HAPPEN? THE METAMORPHOSIS OF SOCIAL CAPITALISM

How can we reconcile this crisis diagnosis with German capitalism's ascendency as the leading power in Europe? At first glance, this development, often attributed to the labour market reforms of the Schröder government (the Social Democratic-Green coalition that ruled Germany from 1998 to 2005), seems to elude the analytical explanation of interplay between finance-capitalist expansion and precarisation as put forward in 'the new *Landnahme*'. This requires some clarification. Processes of *Landnahme* occur neither in a linear nor exclusively top-down manner. They are always highly contested processes in which balances of power and justice norms are altered. *Landnahmen* are implemented within as well as through tests[57] which can, in situations of crisis, serve a sort of political-ideological cleansing function. With view to the dimension of power, *Landnahme* means that it is no longer the capitalist market and the profit motive that require legitimation vis-à-vis the representation of living labour; rather, social rules, the welfare state, and democracy itself are forced to 'prove' their market compatibility. In the social-moral dimension, this takes place via changes in the

---

56   T. Jackson, *Prosperity without Growth? Steps to a sustainable economy*. London 2009, p. 128.

57   L. Boltanski, E. Chiapello, *The New Spirit of Capitalism*, London/New York 2005, pp. 520–523.

norms of justice. The equality of status found in social capitalism is gradually being replaced by an equality of opportunities limited to ensuring equal access (i.e., equal opportunities) when it comes to, for example, positions of leadership, educational advancement, or the accumulation of wealth.[58]

Adjustments to the rules of competition, however, cause frictions and dysfunctionalities, but also conscious opposition motivated by the desire to protect against social decline. This is why the creative destruction of social capitalism, quite similar to the 'crumbling' of non-capitalist milieus, has emerged as a re-combination of the old and the new. *Landnahmen*, the protagonists of which regard sectors protected by the welfare state as a commodifiable Other, produce a strange synchronicity of the asynchronous. With the aid of official politics, wage-earners in the relatively protected segments of the labour market are 'set free'. Re-formatted tests at the intersections of core workforces, the precariously employed and the unemployed generate a constant metabolism between those still-relatively-protected interior sectors of the labour market and unprotected, external ones. This has led to amalgamations of wage-earners with and without the status of 'social citizens'. This interpretation will be substantiated in the following six arguments.

Firstly, Germany's relatively successful crisis management rested on the reactivation of an instrumentarium inherited from the social-capitalist tradition. Trade unions and social security systems were still robust enough to launch a 'crisis corporatism'[59] which ensured long-term job security through short-time work and the *Abwrackprämie* for older passenger vehicles. While these were often put into practice only in the face of massive pressure from labour interest groups, in-house deals nevertheless tended to include wage sacrifices, intensification of work and the passing on of job insecurity to the precariously employed. Moreover, this 'crisis corporatism' was not successful everywhere. Job security was achieved particularly for the core workforces in the export-oriented sector(s). It was not, by contrast, as successful in less-organised areas of the service sector with largely female workforces. Thus, this form of crisis management has not been able to correct the asymmetries of power found on the labour market in favour of the 'weak(er) interests'. Rather, the business world quickly realised that precarious forms of employment can be utilised as flexibilisation buffers in times of crisis. These 'buffers' serve to lessen the blows to core workforces and thus minimise social conflict.

---

58 F. Dubet, *Wandlungen des Kapitalismus und Konzeptionen sozialer Gerechtigkeit*, in: Dörre et al. (ed), *Arbeit in Europa*, 2014, pp. 51–70.

59 H.-J. Urban, *Crisis corporatism and trade union revitalisation in Europe*, in: S. Lehndorff (ed.), *A triumph of failed ideas: European models of capitalism in the crisis*, Brussels: ETUI (European Trade Union Institute) 2012, pp. 219–241.

Secondly, aided by 'crisis corporatism', a society of precarious full-time employment has emerged in which a decreasing volume of paid working hours is asymmetrically shared between a record number of economically active people. If the average wage-earner worked 1,473 hours in 1991, this figure had declined to 1,313 by 2013.[60] Though the volume of work has increased since 2005, the number of people in employment has risen even faster. Job creation occurs to a large extent via the integration of female workers in particular into precarious jobs in the service sector. The share of non-standardised forms of employment relations of total employment rose to 38 per cent (in the east, and 39 per cent in the west) in 2013.[61] The low-wage sector, which has come to constitute a significant portion of full-time employment, continually accounts for 22 to 24 per cent of all employment relations.[62] Moreover, while the numbers of those with part-time work (+2.23 million), marginal employment (+770,000) and (single) self-employment (+550,000) increased between 2000 and 2012, the numbers of not only the registered unemployed (-990,000), but also that of the full-time employed (−1.44 million) has declined significantly.[63] As follows from this, the Hartz reforms have by no means created jobs. The 'German job miracle' rests on a reduction of unemployment at the cost of protected full-time employment as well as through the expansion of 'undignified'[64] (because precarious) wage labour.[65]

Thirdly, Germany's economic recovery is owed to a world-economic division of labour, which allows the German export sector to reap the benefits of growing demand in the large emerging economies, and which was quickly restored after the initial outbreak of the crisis. German-made products are

---

60   K. Dörre, *The German Job Miracle. A Model for Europe?* Brussels 2014, p. 42. Figures were obtained from the German Federal Office of Statistics and the IAB.

61   IAB-Betriebspanel. Länderbericht Thüringen. Ergebnisse der 18.Welle, Berlin 2013, p. 24.

62   G. Bosch, *Neuordnung des deutschen Arbeitsmarktes,* in: K. Dörre et al., Arbeit in Europa, 2014, pp. 91–106.

63   Figures obtained from IAB; cf. K. Dörre, *The German Job Miracle,* p. 42; H. Holst, K. Dörre, K., *Revival of the 'German Model'? Destandarization and the New Labour Market Regime,* in: Non-Standard-employment in Europe. Paradigms, Prevalence and Policy Responses. Edited by M. Koch and M. Fritz. Basingstoke 2013, pp. 132–149.

64   R. Castel, *Die Krise der Arbeit. Neue Unsicherheiten und die Zukunft des Individuums.* Hamburg 2011, S. 63. [original French title: *La montée des incertitudes: Travail, protections, statut de l'individu,* Ed. du Seuil, 2009]

65   K. Dörre, Klaus, K. Scherschel, Karin, M. Booth, T. Haubner, K. Marquardsen, K. Schierhorn, *Bewährungsproben für die Unterschicht? Soziale Folgen aktivierender Arbeitsmarktpolitik.* Frankfurt am Main 2013.

in high demand, particularly in China, as they are crucial in these countries' races to catch up to the Global North economically, in addition to being in high demand amongst these countries' rapidly expanding middle classes. This has allowed for increases in industrial value creation despite Germany and its export sector being 'a high-wage economy'.[66] However, the reproductive sphere paid a heavy price for the export sectors' high productivity, even during the era of social capitalism. The powerful export-oriented industries, with their armies of skilled workers in high-tech sectors, is complemented by an expanding sector of low-paid, unstable and often lowly regarded service activities, the labour productivity of which, by any conventional measure, lags far behind that of the industrial sector. In terms of the absolute number of jobs in each respective sector, the balance of forces between the two has shifted noticeably in the past few decades. In the rapidly expanding social economy alone (in which the share of total employment has risen from 4.5 per cent to 6.2 per cent in the last decade), there are about 1.7 million employees in forms of employment subject to social security contributions, and just as many people employed in mechanical and automotive engineering. This shows that, relative to to the highly productive export-oriented sectors, the supposedly less productive yet labour-intensive sector of paid care work (including all those activities aiding in the 'production of labour power') is increasing in importance. From the microeconomic perspective, as well as from that of the export-oriented industries, this appears primarily as a problem of cost, as professional care work is largely funded by the state or via state subsidies.

In an effort to boost the export economy, German state policy has, *fourthly*, structured the exchange between the industrial sector and care work as a metabolism of 'valued' internal and 'devalued' external markets. The provision of care services as a public good has come under pressure due to a lack of state-funded solvent demand. The policy-making response has been to orchestrate state-facilitated markets, commonly referred to as 'quasi-markets', in which private and public providers compete with one another, primarily in terms of wage levels. This policy-making response has resulted in the intensification of work density, the precarisation of employment, increased skill shortages and the retreat of care work into the private household,[67] as well as a full-fledged crisis of social reproduction.[68]

---

66   Deutsche Bank, *Europe's re-industrialisation. The gulf between aspiration and reality*, Frankfurt am Main 2013, p. 7.

67   K. Dörre M. Ehrlich/T. Haubner, *Landnahmen im Feld der Sorgearbeit*, in: B. Aulenbacher, B. Riegraf, H. Theobald (ed.), Sorge: Arbeit, Verhältnisse, Regime. Soziale Welt Sonderband 20, Baden-Baden 2014, pp. 107–124.

68   B. Aulenbacher, *Ökonomie und Sorgearbeit: Herrschaftslogiken, Arbeits-*

This problematic, *fifthly*, coincides with an increase in class-specific inequalities. While the salaries of DAX executives have risen to 54 times that of an average wage-earner's income,[69] real wages have declined by about 4 per cent between 2000 and 2012. According to more recent calculations, the very top one per cent of German households owns 32 per cent of total assets, trailing closely behind the USA where the top one per cent owns 35 per cent of all wealth.[70] Vertical inequalities add more fuel to the fire as far as the capital surplus absorption problem is concerned. The concentration of wealth in the hands of a few means that the appropriated surplus is more difficult to reinvest, as capitalist consumption is of course bounded by physical limits at some point. At the same time, the accumulation of money as a universal form of wealth fosters the accumulation of social power, which can then be used politically to push the implementation and preservation of privileges in tax law. This distributive imbalance reduces the scope for productive state consumption, thus obstructing further public investment. While privately-held surplus capital is concentrated in the financial sector due to a lack of profitable investment opportunities in the so-called real economy, the state – particularly at the local and regional levels – lacks the necessary funds to implement urgently-needed ecological and social infrastructural investment.[71] Social capitalism's creative destruction seems to have shaken the social foundation of investment activity to a degree that this essential stabiliser of the capitalist dynamic's ability to fulfil its systemic function has been substantially impaired.

Sixthly, the result of all this is that the ecological sustainability of German competitive capitalism is in bad shape. Despite the government's decision to phase out nuclear energy and undertake a shift toward renewable energy sources, innovations are largely (if ever) implemented where prospects of market expansion and thus additional short-term profits exist. It appears that investment in green technologies and products remain risky; if they are profitable at all, then they are only so over a long period of time. Profit expectations are either limited, as is the case with renewable energy

---

teilungen und Grenzziehungen im Gegenwartskapitalismus, in: E. Appelt, B. Aulenbacher, A. Wetterer (ed.): Gesellschaft – Feministische Krisendiagnosen, Münster 2013, pp. 105–126.

69   Cf. J. Schwalbach, *Vergütungsstudie 2010. Vorstandsvergütung und Personalkosten. DAX30-Unternehmen 1987–2009*, without obligation, 2011.

70   P. Vermeulen, *How Fat is the Top Tail of the Wealth Distribution?* EZB Working Papers Series, No. 1692, o.O., July 2014; cf. T. Piketty, *Capital in the Twenty-First Century*. Cambridge 2014.

71   Cf.: DIW Berlin, *Fehlende Investitionen kosten Deutschland jedes Jahr 0,6 Prozentpunkte potentiellen Wirtschaftswachstums* ("Lack of Investment is costing Germany 0.6 percent of potential economic growth"), press release 24 June 2014.

production, or require a financial volume that goes well beyond the capacities of even the largest corporations, as can be seen in so-called 'integrated mobility concepts', which seek to re-design urban space and transportation in ecologically sustainable ways. It is for this reason that the German export economy tends to delay major ecological innovations. Thus, rather than legislate binding ecological criteria to determine or at least influence the course of industrial innovation, it is far more likely that politicians will modify existing laws with regard to, say, renewable energy production to fit the needs of industry, or that EU emissions guidelines will be tweaked to fit the profitability forecasts of the domestic automobile industry. This corresponds to the reality that the German export economy's current prosperity rests to a large extent on demand for products and production methods which in many aspects embody the direct opposite of ecological sustainability. In German competitive capitalism, capitalist corporations operate just like Walmart – the company had made significant progress in efficient resource management, and although the increased efficiency did constitute some sort of ecological 'improvement', the money saved was then invested in expansion, the destructive impacts of which far outweighed the ecological improvements gained from initial efficiencies.[72] In the capitalist economy, revenue accrued by way of rationalisation and modernisation with an ecological intent must be re-invested as quickly as possible in order to generate new surplus profit(s). If this development is not reversed, it will lead to increased metabolic conversion, a growth in overall energy demand as well as an increased strain on ecosystems. The assumption 'that capitalism's propensity for efficiency will allow us to stabilise the climate or protect against resource scarcity' is thus, for German capitalism as much as any other variant of democratic capitalism, nothing short of delusional.[73]

5. What has happened, and what can and *should* happen?

To sum up: any talk of the 'German Model' in the present moment refers to a society that has hardly anything in common with the social capitalism of yesteryear. The fact that Germany has navigated through the crisis as well as it has, however, is owed not to the destruction, but indeed to the *preservation* of some lingering remnants of that old model.

Together with the increase in the country's overall geopolitical influence that resulted from German reunification and an economic policy

---

72   J. Foster et al., *The Ecological Rift*, p. 388.

73   T. Jackson, *Prosperity without Growth. Economics for a Finite Planet*, London and New York 2009, p. 86.

consciously oriented towards strengthening the export economy to the detriment of precarised groups, care work, a sustainable human-natural world metabolism and weaker export economies, this ironic historic turn has played a considerable role in Germany's European ascendency. At the same time, the expansive capitalist dynamic's gravitational centre has shifted from an internal to an external *Landnahme*. This development, which has already been described as 'cooperative imperialism',[74] is, upon closer inspection, predicated on the inversion of previous priorities. Whereas colonialism and external expansion in nineteenth- and early twentieth-century imperialism(s) was intended to aid in easing and alleviating internal contradictions within the imperial centre, the exact opposite occurs today. Social welfare and democratic principles are only granted internally if this serves the preservation and even expansion of the country's export capacity and international competitiveness. The minimum wage, a retirement age of 63, and other moderate course corrections, are broadening the social base of support within Germany for a type of politics that amounts to a radicalised *Landnahme* of the social in the EU. Germany's voice is decisive when it comes to the objectives of austerity measures as established by the European Council. These objectives, however, are of course developed in concert with the elites of other European states, who help design, legitimate and ultimately implement said policies. The new form of wage policy-related interventionism as formulated in the European Fiscal Compact – the 'Two-pack' and the 'Six-pack' – amounts to a continual expropriation of social goods and the commons in the crisis states. Minimum wages are being lowered, social rights curtailed, collective bargaining agreements dissolved (or so heavily perforated as to be meaningless), protection against unlawful dismissal undermined, trade unions weakened, state enterprises privatised, public assets sold off, and entire societies driven into impoverishment and precarious living conditions. In short, the German prescription for a *Landnahme* of the social is being administered as a transnational project of European elites, albeit far more brutally, to European countries which exhibit drastically different economic, cultural and political contexts than those found in 'half-hegemonic' Germany. The other EU member states could not copy the German export and industrial model even if they wanted to. On the contrary: the crisis had the most devastating impact on those countries that had advanced most radically in terms of the flexibilisation of labour markets and the de-collectivisation of social security systems.[75] Conversely, it was

---

74   H. J. Bieling, *Cooperative Imperialism? The Global Political Economy of Contemporary Germany*, Tübingen (without obligation) 2014.

75   O. Struck, *Europäische Arbeitsmärkte – Arbeitsmarkt Europa*, in: Dörre et al. (ed.), Arbeit in Europa, pp. 125–164.

the countries that had retained more basic welfare-state security where inequality within the subaltern classes did not increase during the economic crisis.[76] When large countries such as Italy or France are granted budgetary concessions only after they acquiesce to labour-market reforms guided by the German example, it can only mean further stagnation and contraction as far as their national economies are concerned. As a result of this, Europe's economic and social fault lines will widen and deepen. The Troika sets the agenda for crisis management, effectively leaving the populations of the crisis countries without a political alternative. Those unsatisfied with these policies can of course protest against Angela Merkel and the austerity drive she represents, but they cannot vote the German chancellor out of office. A subtle de-democratisation of the EU, the fragility of central European institutions and the difficulties of achieving even small steps toward taming the financial markets (e.g., by means of a financial transaction tax) all bear witness to a major crisis of capitalist accumulation and regulation in which the political and economic elites and the projects they pursue are not only driving said crisis forward, but also being driven forward *by* it.

Is the capitalist world system capable of overcoming its economic-ecological 'pincer-grip' crisis? Of course! That is, at least temporarily and within specific geographical regions. This does not mean, however, that capitalism's continued existence is guaranteed. In order to explore different paths of social transformation it seems reasonable to think of capitalism as a system which resorts to a plurality of modes of exploitation in order to maximise profits. Following Marx, two entirely different modes of exploitation can be distinguished (at a high level of abstraction). *Primary* exploitation, which determines the capitalist formation as such, follows the principle of exchange of equivalents (labour power for an equivalent remuneration). It is embedded, as is common in internal markets, in contractual relationships between free and equal parties. It constitutes exploitation because wage-earners are paid for their labour power instead of their labour product. The appropriation of unpaid additional labour by the owners of the means of production first becomes possible 'beneath the surface' of the formal freedom of contract. This mode of exploitation ideally requires no extra-economic coercion. In principle, it operates without any consideration for colour, race, creed, gender, any dependence upon extra-economic inequality or difference.[77]

It is a different matter altogether with *secondary* (because not specifically

---

76 J. Wickham, *Das irische Beschäftigungsmodell, die Krise und das eigenartige Überleben des Sozialstaats*, in: K. Dörre et al. (ed.), Arbeit in Europa, 2014, pp. 181–196.

77 E. Meiksins Wood, *Democracy against Capitalism: Renewing Historical Materialism*, New York 2008, p. 267.

capitalist) exploitation. Here, exploitation means value by 'violently tak[ing] that which was not produced by one's own labour; ... tak[ing] something without giving something of equal value in return'.[78] In this model exploitation is based primarily on extra-economic coercion. Moreover, it is most certainly an unequal exchange in both essence and form. Secondary exploitation always implies the use of either symbolic-culturally or state-politically legitimated disciplinary mechanisms in order to preserve internal-external differences so as to suppress the price of labour power or the living standard of social groups below a generally accepted guaranteed wage and repro-duction level, e.g., through racist or sexist debasement, or, as it were, so as to make use of reproduction activities as an unpaid resource free of cost to capital.

Thus, exploitation occurs not only within companies and regular wage labour, and it refers not only to paid forms of work. Instead, extensive access to the entire range of different labour capacities triggers battles over shift-ing borders between paid and unpaid labour, which are in turn fought out within the corresponding tests. Essentially, the dynamic competition-driven *Landnahme* rests largely on the creation of opportunities for dominant capi-talist actors within as well as outside of the wage-labour system to utilise flexibilisation and related activities as a cost-free resource. Redundant (often non-formalised) unpaid or badly paid activities appear as 'Land', the exploi-tation of which offers unique gains in flexibility. The key to understanding this problematic is a distinction between labour power and a multiplic-ity of labour capacities as proposed by Negt and Kluge. According to this notion, wage labour, unpaid care work, pro-active, self-directed labour, and activities exclusively in pursuit of individual self-realisation, all rep-resent distinct labour capacities, respectively. These must be linked to one another and coordinated through navigational labour (*Steuerungsarbeit*), which constitutes a labour capacity in its own right. Navigational labour (*Steuerungsarbeit*) in a sense represents the creative centre of human activ-ity. The multiplicity of labour capacities opens up the possibility for both private as well as state appropriation of unpaid life activities. The unem-ployed who participate in civic engagement and who contribute to social cohesion by means of their unpaid or poorly paid activity, are also part of the secondarily exploited.

One common feature of the manifold forms of secondary exploitation is that, due to their expansive access to the entire range of labour capacities,

---

78 M. Mies, Subsistenzproduktion, Hausfrauisierung, Kolonisierung, in: Beiträge zur feministischen Theorie und Praxis 5, Zukunft der Frauenarbeit. Köln 1983, p. 120.

they can produce[79] continuous strain which eventually affects the body, health, the physique, and not least the mind. After all, 'the alleged commodity "labour power" cannot be shoved about, used indiscriminately, or even left unused, without affecting also the human individual who happens to be the bearer of this peculiar commodity.'[80] Access to the full range of labour capacities originates from the same expansive logic that underlies the commodification of the non-human natural world, the authoritative enforcement of the corresponding property rights, as well as the extent of secondary exploitation related to this. Dominant capitalist actors can, to a certain degree, determine the combination and use of multiple mechanisms of exploitation. This is why modes of exploitation and social antagonisms can coexist in varying combinations and to varying degrees. Plural relations of domination and exploitation engender heterogeneous social forces with specific and sometimes competing interests – labour movements, NGOs, cooperatives, ecological and feminist movements, initiatives for and by migrants, political parties, trade unions, charitable enterprises and many other actors – which, in an ideal scenario, could mutually reinforce one another through their respective activities within different fields of action. What is valid for the *Landnahme* of the social, however, is that the multiplicity and complexity of relations of exploitation impedes the formation of collective identities of subaltern groups and has limited the possibilities for establishing any kind of countervailing power or hegemonic bloc. The erosion of wage earners' status of social citizen and the seizure of reproductive activities are based, both structurally and subjectively, on an expansion of secondary exploitation.

Paths and Coordinates of Social Transformation

Whether or not this process is to continue is decided in the tests of new competitive capitalism. In the long term, three different paths seem plausible.

(1) One possibility is the emergence of an order of exploitation which is no longer based on the compulsion to permanent economic growth. Such a transformation becomes probable should economic growth fail to materialise over a longer period of time, re-distribution from top to bottom be blocked and capitalist *Landnahmen* be forced to draw on already existing substance. In such a scenario, that which remains latent throughout the continual

---

79 Negt and Kluge speak of a "balance imperialism" that operates via the "withdrawal of coordinating energies" needed to absorb competition-driven flexibility requirements. O. Negt/A. Kluge, *History and Obstinacy*, Cambridge: MIT Press 2014.

80 Polanyi, *Great Transformation*, p. 76.

primitive accumulation may become dominant. A financial oligarchy deploys its wealth in order to maintain an order of exploitation primarily by means of extra-economic coercion and violence. Projects intended to open up new markets for capital, as are currently being advanced in the form of the proposed Free-Trade agreement between the EU and the USA as well as the EU and Canada, TTIP and CETA, can only be implemented to the detriment of competing economic and geopolitical interests. This tension will manifest itself in rivalries over mineral deposits, scarce resources and spheres of influence, and constitutes a tremendously dangerous development. Such rivalries can reinforce global tendencies toward anti-democratic, and indeed civilisation-threatening, geopolitical escalation, as we have already seen in the guise of a renewed confrontation between East and West (Ukraine), in ethnic nationalism consuming and destroying entire countries (Yugoslavia), in the right-wing populist 'tsunami' in Europe (e.g., Marine Le Pen and the Front National), or, in a totally different form, as organised terrorism motivated by religious fundamentalism (Islamic State). As Hannah Arendt illustrates in her analysis of totalitarianism, a worst case scenario is possible in which surplus capital can merge with the supposedly redundant sectors of society to form a historical bloc. Such a social bloc would give an impetus to an expansive capitalist spirit which gradually detaches itself from socio-economic interests completely, so as to fully commit itself to the accumulation of political power; a force that operates according to the territorial principle and which can only be implemented through the violent drawing and re-drawing of territorial boundaries. In today's capitalist centres, however, it tends to be the relatively secured groups of wage-earners who practice exclusive solidarity,[81] by which they also dissociate themselves from 'below' and from the 'other'. These supposedly 'privileged' sections of the exploited demand zones of protection and demarcations which, should the need arise, may have to be enforced by an authoritarian capitalism. Resembling its imperialist predecessors, such a capitalist state would also base itself on the accumulation of political power. Yet the unlimited accumulation of power permanently 'needs more material to devour in its never-ending process', as it is insatiable, and even 'the last victorious Commonwealth cannot proceed to "annex the planets", it can only proceed to destroy itself'.[82]

---

81   K. Dörre, A. Happ, I. Matuschek (Hrsg.), *Das Gesellschaftsbild der LohnarbeiterInnen. Soziologische Untersuchungen in ost- und westdeutschen Industriebetrieben.* Hamburg 2013, pp. 222–228.

82   H. Arendt, *The Origins of Totalitarianism*, Cleveland & New York 1962, pp. 146–147.

(2) A possible alternative to these apocalyptic visions are neo-Schumpeterian or neo-Keynesian projects of technology- and efficiency-based green capitalist *Landnahmen*. Such projects have already been put forth in the form of the digitalisation of industrial production ('industry 4.0', the Internet of Things),[83] the credo of 'smart growth',[84] or assorted variants of a Global Deal[85] or Green New Deal.[86] There can hardly be any doubt that technological and organisational innovations such as, for example, the transition to renewable energy sources, as well as the improvement of overall energy efficiency and efficacy, are urgently needed if civilisation is to respond to the coming ecological threats adequately. Thus, it would be a mistake to outright reject strategies which rely on 'green' growth, such as the Green New Deal, as some currents within growth-critical movements do. For, as we have learned from European climate policy (as utterly insufficient as it is), even moderate ecological reforms only become a viable political option when a substantial degree of social pressure is present. From the perspective of the emerging economies of the Global South, moreover, they represent 'a stepping stone towards more fundamental options in the longer term'.[87] Any sustainability strategy worthy of the name, however, would be heavily reliant on state intervention, movements of civil society, democratic control of financial markets, public ownership, a revaluation of reproductive labour, a newfound balance between the Global North and South, egalitarianism and reduced overall consumption. The question is: would a society that exhibited all these features still be a capitalist society?

When discussing sustainability, we simply cannot escape the fact that a social system which relies on an inscribed growth imperative will at some point collide with the reproductive capacities of a planet whose resources are finite. The abandonment of the growth illusion may be easier for us once we realise that, as Joseph Schumpeter so brilliantly analysed, creative destruction has long become the creative *preservation* of indefensible and unsustainable social relations. Growth capitalism has become a kind of treadmill (Rosa) that continues to function only because more and more

83   E. Brynjolfson, A. McAffe, *The Second Maschine Age. Work, Progress, and Prosperity in a Time of Brilliant Technologies*, New York 2014.

84   R. Fücks, *Smart Growth: The Green Revolution*, Heinrich-Böll-Stiftung 2013.

85   N. Stern, *The Economics of Climate Change: The Stern Review*. Cambridge 2007.

86   M. Müller, K. Niebert, *Epochenwechsel: Plädoyer für einen grünen New Deal*. Munich 2012.

87   D. Pillay, *Marx and the Eco-Logic of Fossil Capitalism*, in: M. Williams, V. Satgar, (ed.) *Marxisms in the 21st Century: Crisis, Critique and Struggle*, Johannesburg 2014, pp 143–165, see p. 162.

people are forced to expend more and more energy just to avoid falling off of it. Anyone who is serious about sustainability goals has to mount a fundamental challenge to this treadmill itself. This will only be possible if the rest of society (i.e., everything beyond the interests of private profit) exerts its influence over questions of the 'what', 'how', and 'what for' of production and reproduction.

(3) The conscious pursuit of system change requires not only reforms, but also necessitates a break with growth capitalism and a search for viable alternatives in various social fields and action areas. A co-evolutionary anti-capitalist transformation can only emerge from a comprehensive critique of alienation and exploitation that combines radical democratisation and 'substantive equality'[88] into an ecologically sustainable project of emancipation. Sustainable is that which 'stands fast, which bears up, which is long term, resilient. And that means: immune to ecological, economic or social breakdown'. Sustainability is mainly rooted in the 'basic human need for security'[89] – an insight that can hardly be reconciled with a system incapable of distinguishing advance from destruction, or progress from wastefulness.[90]

The only task that remains for sociology, at least for now, may very well be the designation of certain coordinates which could serve as points of orientation for social forces seeking to transform the current system. The *first coordinate* is a conscious social rejection of the imperative of permanent economic growth serving only the self-valorisation of value. However, an ethically-inspired critique of growth which attacks the greedy materialism of the lower classes, because the argument about 'the fair distribution of an assumed yield from human performance' is allegedly really only about 'the appropriation of the spoils that, from an ecological perspective, should have never been created in the first place',[91] is rather misleading. Such variants of critique are likely to drive even those wage-earners who are already critical of the consumerism of capitalist life into the counter-revolutionary camp.[92] A critique of growth that is socially blind and neglects the pressing issue of equality is hardly distinguishable from an intelligent neo-conservatism

---

88   J. B. Foster et al., *The Ecological Rift*, p. 398.

89   U. Grober, *Sustainability. A Cultural History*, Totnes 2012, p. 16.

90   I. Mészáros, *Beyond Capital: Toward a Theory of Transition*, New York 2000, pp. 893¬–94, quoted in: J. B. Foster, The Ecological Rift, p. 410.

91   N. Paech, *Liberation from excess: The road to a post-growth economy*, Munich 2012, p. 35; similar: H. Rosa, *Klassenkampf und Steigerungsspiel: Eine unheilvolle Allianz. Marx' beschleunigungstheoretische Krisendiagnose*, in: R. Jaeggi, D. Loick (ed.), Nach Marx. Philosophie, Kritik, Praxis. Berlin 2013, pp.394–411.

92   Dörre et al. (ed.): Das Gesellschaftsbild der LohnarbeiterInnen, 2013, pp. 215–222.

which utilises ecological crises as justification for declining prosperity and mounting inequality.[93]

To protect against neo-conservative or racist[94] usurpation of our argument, we require a *second coordinate* – namely, a culture of 'substantive equality'. Finance-capitalist *Landnahme* implies that the increasing wealth of a growing yet nevertheless comparatively tiny minority of society carries the poverty, misery and precarity of much larger groups in its wake. Contrary to the widely-asserted claim that the collapse of the financial markets has primarily affected the owners of large fortunes, it has in fact been the poorest of the poor – disproportionately female[95] – who have been hit hardest by the effects of the crisis. In Mexico, Ecuador or Haiti, where entire sections of the population depend on remittances from overseas relatives, the laying off of construction workers or dock workers can lead to widespread malnutrition and even starvation. For this reason alone, an ethically motivated critique of growth cannot dismiss questions of distribution, even if the latter, similarly to projects fighting global poverty, exhibit few if any system-transforming qualities. Equally important is how the production of class-specific inequalities in their interconnections to axes of gender and ethnicity repeatedly function to amplify and intensify ecological crises, which in turn serve as catalysts of social insecurity and inequality. Ecological threats are generally concentrated in the poorest countries. A climate-induced sea level rise will initially pose a problem for countries lacking the financial resources to develop protective measures for their populations. Extreme weather, which is expected to increase in both frequency and intensity, wreaks havoc in the slums of the world's mega-cities. Moreover, the increased strain on natural systems, which is largely a product of Western lifestyles and consumption patterns, is also distributed unequally. As a general rule, it is safe to say that the higher the income, the bigger the ecological footprint.[96]

What is more, benchmarks toward ecological sustainability are far more difficult to meet in countries with more pronounced class-specific inequalities. Inequality fosters positional consumption – driven not least by the fear of losing touch with or decoupling from social norms, or missing

93 Cf. M. Miegel, *Exit. Wohlstand ohne Wachstum*, Berlin 2010.

94 The "Ecopop" initiative in Switzerland, for example, invokes a growth-critical argument in its call for a radical limitation of immigration.

95 For Europe and the USA cf. M. Karamessini, J. Rubbery (ed), *Women and Austerity. The Economic Crisis and the Future for Gender Equality*, London/New York 2013.

96 According to a Canadian study, the top tenth of salaried workers have an ecological footprint that is nine times as high in transportation and four times as high in consumption than that of the bottom tenth. Cf. J. B. Foster et al., *The Ecological Rift*, p. 390.

an opportunity for upward social advancement. The desire to distinguish oneself from others, as well as the activities of the advertising industry as a whole, and unequally distributed decision-making powers as far as investment, products and production methods are concerned, mean that consumers do not really have much choice in how they live their lives. If they did, they would soon realise that a large portion of a society's energy consumption occurs in the productive sector. The lion's share of emissions that affect climate change are produced by private companies; waste is also mostly amassed by industry, not individual consumers. For these reasons, the notion of extensive consumer sovereignty is just as implausible as the assumption that ecological destruction could be countered primarily through conscious consumption.[97]

The coordinate of 'substantive equality' implies the opposite of levelling down; it does, however, entail much more than the concept of an equality of social status as linked to the national welfare state. A culture of 'substantive equality' seeks – and this is the *third coordinate* – a radical democratisation of decision-making in production, meaningful labour and social reproduction. Democratisation represents the only remaining possibility to concentrate and cohere a multiplicity of social identities. What is needed is an 'insurgent democracy'[98] articulating an explicit challenge to capitalist elites. Such a democracy can no longer be understood simply as a political category but must be re-defined as an economic one as well.[99] In a comprehensive sense, it has to prove itself as the social motor or 'driving mechanism' of the economy.[100] Simultaneously, democratisation is linked to a redistribution of resources from the high-productivity to the low-productivity sectors. The latter would imply seeking a break with the capitalist principle of replacing human labour power with machines. Societies that were to conduct a revaluation of care work and care workers within a framework of a comprehensive democratisation strategy, and that were to maintain human labour within digitalised production processes, would become modern postgrowth societies, as they would only grow socially, and thus more slowly and in a different way. Labour productivity would only be increased gradually and not at the expense of living labour and social reproduction. Economic growth would no longer be an end in itself, but merely a consciously applied means that serves the purpose of creating work that satisfies real human need(s). Such a prospect of transformation, which aims at a transition to

---

97   Cf. ibid. pp. 383 ff.

98   M. Abensour, *Democracy against the State. Marx and the Machiavellian Moment*, Cambridge 2011, pp. 47–72.

99   E. Meiksins Wood, Democracy against Capitalism, p. 290.

100   Ibid.

selective, socially and ecologically sustainable growth, ultimately tran-
scends – or at least points to the necessity of transcending – capitalism. Yet
despite all of its crises and ongoing turbulence, capitalism will not disappear on its own accord, it 'will have to be pushed'.[101] Whether or not social
forces and movements emerge which have the stamina and strength to do
said decisive pushing to the capitalist order of exploitation, (probably) following a decades-long period of transition and transformation, remains
to be seen.

---

101   Harvey 2011, p. 260.

Escalation: The Crisis of Dynamic Stabilisation and the Prospect of Resonance

HARTMUT ROSA

1. INTRODUCTION: WHAT HAS HAPPENED SO FAR?

In September 2014, more than 3,000 people from all over the world – scientists and politicians, activists and students, journalists and anarchists – gathered at the campus of the University of Leipzig for the international, week-long Degrowth conference, generating an enormous amount of public interest. The event was a strong indicator of the degree to which awareness of the physical and mental, political and social, environmental and even technical limits to economic growth and the pernicious consequences of the relentless drive towards acceleration, increase and escalation has grown in recent years. Opposition to this drive has been gaining strength globally. Since the publication of the first German edition of our debate in 2009, shortly after the Lehman Brothers collapse and the climax of the global financial crisis, the debate about the irrationality of a growth-dependent form of life and the desirability of a 'post-growth' or 'degrowth' society' has gained significant momentum, producing a wealth of analyses, ideas, suggestions and new forms of social practice. 'Degrowth' (or *Décroissance, Postwachstum, Decrecimiento*) signifies broad social and intellectual currents not just in the affluent European countries, but all over the world, with hubs in Latin America, Australia and parts of East Asia.

The Club of Rome report, commemorating the fortieth anniversary of the original report from 1972, zeroed in on the current predicament with a sharp, clear analysis. This predicament is characterised by two fundamental aspects: firstly, the current form of the world economy is essentially dependent on the logics of growth – without it, its crises cannot be addressed; its operational functions and stability cannot be upheld. Secondly, the prospects for growth grow darker and darker by the day. At least in the so-called developed economies, stable and reliable growth rates appear increasingly difficult to achieve. More and more physical, cultural and political energy and attention are needed and absorbed to keep the engines of growth running (or to get them restarted). At the same time, there are virtually no signs for the empirical realisation of 'green growth' – that is, of a sustainable de-coupling of the utilisation of (natural) resources from economic growth. On the contrary, we are witnessing instead an ongoing increase in the extraction of oil and carbon-based materials, as well as other scarce resources – without any reliable substitutes in sight. This implies that the signs and manifestations of crisis have not vanished after 2008; if anything, they have become even more acute.

Thus, my diagnosis of the current state of growth-dependent societies is this: firstly, it becomes more and more costly (ecologically, politically and psychologically), difficult and stressful to restart the engines of economic growth. Secondly, even where the engines are still functioning, social integration and stability are becoming more and more fragile. As Klaus Dörre's analyses demonstrate in detail,[1] jobless growth, precarisation of large segments of the population, the emergence of a new class of socially excluded people, political dissatisfaction and new forms of social unrest or xenophobia can all be read as symptoms of this form of *growing dynamic de-stabilisation*. Thirdly, even if growth-dependent societies were to successfully manage these two problems, they would not solve, but would actually *worsen* the ecological crisis resulting from extraction and depletion of resources and the production of harmful emissions at a pace too fast to be environmentally sustainable.

Hence, the most pressing and worrying crises of the twenty-first century – the ecological crisis, the financial crisis, the crisis of democracy as well as the psychological 'burnout' crisis – can all be read as crises of dynamic stabilisation, i.e., as inevitable crises emerging from a system that can only reproduce itself and maintain its socio-economic, institutional and structural status quo through growth, escalation, increase and escalation, acceleration and innovation. As long as late modern societies continue to operate in the mode of dynamic stabilisation, these crises will not be overcome; indeed, they will worsen.

In the following, I seek to specify and sharpen this diagnosis (and prognosis) by elucidating my conceptualisation of 'dynamic stabilisation'. I take this to be at the heart of modern, capitalist society: a society is modern, when it can only reproduce and maintain its fabric and structure through economic growth, cultural acceleration, technological innovation and

---

1 See his contributions in this volume, but also Dörre, Klaus and Castel, Robert (eds), *Prekariat, Abstieg, Ausgrenzung: Die soziale Frage am Beginn des 21. Jahrhunderts*, Frankfurt, 2014.

political activation – in short, through the logic of increase and escalation and intensification on all levels of social life. Starting from this, I will try to redefine modern society as a society operating in the mode of dynamic stabilisation – and hence in the mode of ongoing escalation. In the third part of my contribution, I will revisit the dominant crises of the current global age. These can all be consistently re-interpreted as crises of dynamic stabilisation; more specifically, as crises of de-synchronisation. If modern capitalist society can only reproduce itself through progressive dynamisation, it inevitably encounters resistance and obstacles at the 'fringes' of that society, i.e., in those places where dynamisation is difficult or even impossible. Not all spheres of social and natural life can be dynamised to the same degree. Some things simply resist dynamisation: nature, democracy, our bodies and minds are fitting examples. Hence, in its late modern stage, this mode of stabilisation is increasingly undermined by its own, inevitable tendencies toward escalation, which lead to new forms of social de-stabilisation on the societal level and to new forms of alienation on the part of subjects. I will return to this idea in the fourth section of this contribution, which advances the claim that, in the cultural self-perception of late modernity, a turning-point has been reached beyond which growth, acceleration and innovation no longer figure as motivating goals and inspiring promises, but instead as 'blind' forces and imperatives which need to be met in order to avoid chaos and disaster. Instead of moving forward, modern subjects feel they must run faster and faster just to stay on pace; they are not running towards a goal, but fleeing from an abyss. Fear, not promise, is the dominant dynamising force on the cultural plane.

On the basis of the ensuing analysis of patterns of de-synchronisation and alienation, I hope to gain a more clear-cut analytical grasp as well as a richer empirical foundation for my diagnosis of the current growth-dependent structural and cultural predicament.

In the fifth section, I will briefly sketch out the contours of a possible solution to the problem of incessant escalation caused by the mode of dynamic stabilisation by introducing the concept of resonance as a new yardstick for measuring the quality of life and of social arrangements. A short conclusion will then wrap up the argument by summarising the findings in four successive steps.

2. DYNAMIC STABILISATION: TOWARDS A NEW DEFINITION OF MODERNITY

As a first step in developing my argument, I wish to slightly modify the approach to modernity developed in the first three sections of this book, and at greater lengths in my book on social acceleration[2] by shifting the focus from acceleration to dynamic stabilisation. This approach holds that the central problem of modern, capitalist societies is no longer acceleration *per se*, but as the tendency toward escalation that accompanies dynamic stabilisation. This necessitates a re-definition of modernity at the 'macro-level' of social analysis and a redefinition of the contours of a 'good life' and the obstacles to it at the micro-level. I will begin with the former.

In the social sciences, the debate about the defining criteria of what constitutes modernity or what defines modern societies is as old as the disciplines themselves. A core problem of most definitions is their (intended or unintended) inherent normativity and ethnocentricity: regardless of whether one follows the suggestions of 'modernisation theories' in the vein of Parsons, or the more philosophical definitions of the 'project of modernity' provided by authors like Habermas or Taylor (often centred around conceptions of the Enlightenment), a normative and Eurocentric bias appears inevitable. Furthermore, most conceptions of modernity appear ill-equipped to grasp the vast differences between the social and cultural fabric of, say, eighteenth-century societies on the one hand and late modern culture on the other. Yet the conceptions of 'multiple' or 'entangled' modernities developed to resolve these problems are often highly successful in identifying the vast differences and diversities between conceptions of the 'modern' over time and space while simultaneously being incapable of defining any essence or commonality of 'the modern' underlying these differences. In countering this, I would like to suggest the following modest and simple definition: *a society is modern when it functions according to a mode of dynamic stabilisation, i.e., when it systematically requires growth, innovation and acceleration for its structural reproduction and to maintain its socio-economic and institutional status quo.*

At first glance, this definition appears to contain a contradiction: how can we talk of maintaining the status quo through innovation, acceleration, growth – that is, through change? What changes, and what stays the same? What is dynamic, and what is stable? I have already dealt with this problem at great length in my book on social acceleration. With structural reproduction and reification of the status quo I mean, firstly, the stabilisation of the basic institutional fabric of society, in particular the competitive market system, the political and legal framework, as well as educational and welfare institutions. Secondly, I refer to the basic structures of socio-economic stratification: the reproduction of class hierarchy and what Bourdieu termed 'class fractions'. Thirdly, and perhaps most importantly, the status quo is

---

2 H. Rosa, *Social Acceleration: A New Theory of Modernity*, New York 2013

defined by the operational logics of accumulation and distribution: the logic of capital accumulation and the very processes of growth, acceleration, activation and innovation themselves – for obviously some political, economic, educational etc. institutions change their shape, form or composition over time. What does not change, however, are the systemic compulsions to augmentation, increase and escalation. This answer, however, raises another serious question: is modern society, then, equivalent to capitalist society? Do I simply mean 'capitalism' when I refer to the basic structure of modern society?

Certainly, the systematic need *to grow, to accelerate* and to *increase the rates of innovation* in order to maintain the social structure and the socio-economic status quo can most easily be seen in capitalist economies. Absent constant increase and escalation, jobs are lost, companies close down, and tax revenues decline while welfare expenditures go up, states go bankrupt and the political system incurs de-legitimation. While this need for growth, increase and escalation results from several interrelated factors such as the logic of profit and competition, the competitive drive to increase productivity, the credit system itself, etc., it is nevertheless undeniable that no known form of capitalism could do without it. In the end, it may very well boil down to the simple formula of 'money–commodity–money' as the driving motor of economic escalation. Thus, the self-valorisation of capital, as Marx says, can still be interpreted as the real subject of change and as the dynamic motor of modern society. Interestingly, however, the logic of dynamic stabilisation also holds sway in other sectors of society. In the reproduction of science, for example, the logic of novelty, innovation, increase and escalation has completely replaced the older notion of knowledge as something with innate worth that must be preserved and handed down from one generation to the next. Knowledge – and in particular the most essential and most highly esteemed form of knowledge – is no longer something that has been revealed in an original act, or something that is rooted in the wisdom of the ancients and must be restored, but rather is dynamically recreated in a process of dynamic progression. No one would be rewarded institutional recognition or research grants without presenting his or her achievement as something that goes beyond what is already known. The exact same shift can be observed in the nature of law, as well: modern society does not seek to restore and preserve the 'eternal' or 'holy' law given to us by the Gods or by the ancients; it does not even seek to find and establish the best set of laws for mankind, as Plato sought to do. Instead, legislation is considered to be a perennial task; laws, as well as the legislating bodies that make them, are legitimated by the very idea of dynamic stabilisation – that is to say, by the idea that law is something that has to be improved and adjusted (and often: extended) incessantly. Similarly, our entire conception of art has likewise changed: modern society considers innovation and originality to lie at the very heart of artistic activity[3] – this stands in sharp contrast to forms of artistic aspiration known from other (pre- or non-modern) cultures, for whom artistic achievement was defined by ideals of mimesis or imitation. The same is true for political modernity: democracy operates by definition on a mode of dynamic stabilisation, i.e., a repetitive cycle of elections – in sharp contrast to all previously known forms of monarchical regimes, which aspired to preserve the existing political order. Moreover, political programmes and political competition invariably follow the logic of overbidding and outpacing competitors, the logic of promising increase and escalation:[4] this is just as valid for the logic of modern democracy and legislation ('law' as something that needs to be dynamically re-created on a permanent basis). It follows that parties, universities and artists alike cannot survive and reproduce their institutional structures without promising and achieving 'progress' in the form of innovation, increase and escalation, growth or acceleration. Collectively, then, they follow a logic of escalation. In all these cases, society no longer aims at the preservation of the given or the realisation of some 'static' goal, but at its constant transgression to such an extent that the arts, the sciences, the economy etc. could no longer exist without it. Moreover, and finally, the logic of increase and escalation is a defining cultural moment in individuals' pursuit of the good life and the best course of action: social actors inevitably strive for an increase in wealth, but also for an increase in the range of options and contacts. In a society whose central mode of allocation (not just for wealth and money, but also for positions and privileges, life chances, contacts and friends, status and recognition) is competition, this strategy eventually becomes a necessity for the individual reproduction of the status quo: for subjects, standing still (with respect to knowledge or relationships, money or health, tools or fashions, etc.) inevitably entails sliding backwards (or falling down) with respect to their position in the social order.

Now, of course, one could claim that this whole array of dynamic stabilisations is simply the consequence of the unleashed logic of capital(ist) reproduction. This is the Marxist or materialist interpretation of modernity and society. But one might just as well claim that the roots of this epochal shift in the logic of social stabilisation and reproduction are cultural; that it is triggered by a process of cultural re-interpretation closely linked to the ideas that emerged in the age of the Enlightenment. As we know from the long-standing debates between Hegelians and Marxists, Taylorists and

---

3   B. Groys, *On the New*, London 2014.
4   N. Luhmann, *Politische Theorie im Wohlfahrtsstaat*, Munich 2011.

Foucauldians, Habermasians and Adornites etc., it is currently impossible to decide who is right or wrong. I tend to side with Max Weber and simply observe that there seems to be an 'elective affinity' between these material and cultural developments. Thus, I am agnostic with respect to the question of whether or not dynamic stabilisation is caused by capitalism (and by capitalism alone). In any case, dynamic stabilisation is the current mode of stabilisation in all relevant spheres of contemporary social life, and will not be replaced absent a fundamental change in the economic fabric of modern society.

In sum, then, we can call this co-evolutionary shift towards dynamic stabilisation in the dominant spheres of society *modernity's logic of escalation*.

As I have argued in my book *Social Acceleration: A New Theory of Modernity*,[5] this results in an all-encompassing process of acceleration that transforms the material, the social and the mental worlds at ever-higher rates. However, one need not be particularly imaginative to recognise that this mode of dynamic stabilisation creates its own de-stabilising tendencies at ever-increasing rates. At least three resultant, fundamental problems appear to have become pathological in the twenty-first century:

1) First, it comes as a physical and experiential truism that escalation grows more and more difficult with every successive step: the faster, the more innovative and the more voluminous (or the more dynamic) we already are, the more energy, power and effort it takes to grow, accelerate and increase innovation rates: i.e., to dynamise even further. In the end, obviously, we will have to invest all our individual and collective (that is to say: all our mental and political) energies[6] to feed the engines of dynamisation – and even then, there will ultimately be a limit to how much dynamic is possible. As we will see shortly, these limits can perhaps be observed in the rising rates of psychological burnout. Furthermore, there is also a physical and material side to this process: obviously, dynamisation requires not just individual and social energy, but also oil, carbon and other natural resources, at ever-increasing rates. Thus, the more successful we are in terms of growth and acceleration, the deeper we get into the ecological crisis.

---

5   H. Rosa, *Social Acceleration: A New Theory of Modernity*, New York 2013.

6   This, in my understanding, is the central point made by Stephan Lessenich in his contributions to this volume: The activating state is defined by a welfare regime that musters all available political energies for the purpose of inspiring or forcing citizens to invest and feed their mental, emotional and bodily energies into the engines of growth, acceleration and innovation.

2) Even if and where late modern capitalist societies still manage to dynamise, i.e., to keep the engines of growth, acceleration, and innovation running, the requirements of reproduction and stabilisation become problematic. This means that we can observe new forms of dynamisation without stabilisation – for example, where jobless growth occurs and where gross domestic product increases, while poverty and scarcity persist or even intensify for significant segments of the population; or where dynamisation comes at the expense of political legitimation, undercutting social integration instead of securing it. Thus, while the first problem is the increasing difficulty in further dynamisation, the second problem is the lack of stability in the face of ongoing dynamisation – or: dynamisation at the expense of stability.

3) The third problem might appear to be more academic in nature, but in my view, understanding it is absolutely crucial. It consists of a deep cultural break in the self-perception of modern societies. When the mode of dynamic stabilisation and the logic of escalation became operative in the eighteenth century, the emphasis in cultural self-interpretation as well as in social experience was on the dynamic side of this: growth, acceleration and innovation, at least to some extent and for significant segments of the population, were inherently connected to the promise of *progress* and thus to the prospect and promise of a better life. They clearly carried some potential for (or at least the possibility of) liberation, for new spaces of self-determination, for the overcoming of scarcity, and so on. Quite obviously, the democratic aspiration to acquire the individual and collective resources and liberties needed to lead self-determined lives was dependent on the success of this threefold process of dynamisation. Furthermore, as the new mode replaced the older, static and estate-based social and cultural orders, growth, acceleration and innovation were perceived to be elements of change (and progress), they obviously *could not* be perceived as necessities to simply preserve the status quo.

All of this, however, has changed in the twenty-first century. The promise has been turned into a threat, or even a nightmare, at least in the so-called developed economies: if we do not grow, accelerate and innovate, things will become worse; we will encounter crisis and disaster. Thus, individuals and collectivities today are no longer moving towards some goal or promise or better horizon; instead, they are running away from the abyss coming up behind them. This reality is reflected in empirical data: for perhaps the first time in modern history, parents on a grand scale and in all of the Western countries no longer believe in a *better life for their children* – all they hope

for is that life will not be too much worse for them. Thus, growth, acceleration and innovation have lost their inherent cultural potential, appeal and
promise: of course (or at least: *we hope*), the economy will keep growing –
but no one (at least no one of a sane disposition; in other words, no one but
the economists) believes that this will put an end to poverty, scarcity or the
ever-intensifying struggle for economic survival. Of course, technological
inventions will give us faster tools and further increase the speeds of social
life – but no one believes that this will put an end to the scarcity of time.
Scientific innovations and political reforms will come about at a relentless
pace – but no one really believes that these will improve our lives. I will
return to this aspect in the fifth section of this contribution.

   In short, then, the prospect of progress has been replaced by the horizon
of crisis and catastrophe, and this catastrophe has two possible faces: one
scenario is that we could fail to dynamise, and hence to stabilise; thus, our
economies, welfare-states and democratic systems could break down, and
we would slide back into poverty, darkness and even warfare. The other consists of a scenario in which *we do* manage to keep up growth, acceleration
and innovation rates. This would lead to ecological disaster or, at the very
least, require transhumanistic beings who are capable of running faster and
faster each year just to keep up.

3. DE-SYNCHRONISATION: THE FOURFOLD CRISES OF LATE MODERN CAPITALIST SOCIETY

The problems I have dealt with in the preceding sections are obviously
vexing, inherent, long-term problems of dynamic stabilisation intrinsic to
this very mode of stabilisation. However, in the current, late-modern state
of dynamisation, they manifest themselves predominantly in the form of
insoluble symptoms of de-synchronisation, i.e., in the temporal realm.
Hence, I now want to move on to the claim that the four major crises of
contemporary society – the core crises of our late modern, global age – can
best be grasped from a temporal perspective, from which they are seen to
be crises of de-synchronisation, inherently caused by and connected to the
irresistible logic of social acceleration. The reason for this, in a nutshell, is
the fact that time is the one factor in (or dimension of) social life that cannot
be increased or extended – it can only be compressed.[7]

   Thus, while we can obviously increase the *number of goods* we produce
and consume (the average European or North American household today

---

   7   See David Harvey's concept of 'time-space compression', in D. Harvey, *The
Condition of Postmodernity*, Cambridge, MA 1990.

contains about 10,000 objects, as opposed to only a few hundred in 1900) as well as the *number of options* for action and the *number of contacts* almost indefinitely,[8] the time we can dedicate to all these goods, options and contacts remains virtually the same (namely 24 hours a day, 365 days a year). Therefore, modernity's logic of escalation necessarily results in an ever-greater scarcity of time: time can only be compressed, and this is what we are all trying to do in our lives.

Therefore, it is within the dimension *of time* that the limits of the modern mode of dynamic stabilisation become more noticeable and pressing. But in order to understand this properly, we need to first establish the claim that growth and acceleration can be seen as two sides of the same coin. Basically, my argument is this: acceleration can be defined as *quantitative growth* or *increase in quantity per unit of time*. This is exactly the definition I arrived at in my books on social acceleration.[9] Taking transportation as an example, acceleration figures as an increase of kilometres traversed per hour; with respect to communication, it might refer to the number of signs transmitted per microsecond; in production, acceleration refers to the material output per hour, day, month or year. Thus, the very phenomenon of increasing productivity is just as much a phenomenon of social acceleration – definable as increased output per unit of time. Moreover, the phenomena of accelerated *social change* can be likewise be interpreted as an instance of this form of acceleration: if people change jobs or spouses at higher rates, this will amount to an increase in the average number of jobs or spouses (or newspapers, or bank accounts, or cars, or telephone numbers) per lifetime. Should the temporal validity of legal orders or bureaucratic regulations be shortened, this can be read as a rise in institutional 'rates of decay'. Read the other way round: rising rates of innovation inevitably result in an acceleration of social change. Finally, the acceleration of the pace of life, I have argued, amounts to an increase in the number of episodes of experience or action per unit of time (be it a day, a month, a year or a life-time). Consequently, all forms of growth can be interpreted or experienced as forms of acceleration, and vice versa. Thus, when I describe modern society as dependent on growth,

---

8   Thus, American psychologist Kenneth Gergen in his book on the saturated self calculates that the average North American commuter (from, say Connecticut to New York) encounters more people on his way to and from work on an average day than the medieval village-dweller did in the whole of his life. Cf. K. Gergen,*The Saturated Self: Dilemmas of Identity in Contemporary Life*, New York 1991. Gergen includes in this calculation the people encountered in and through the radio, the newspaper, and social media.

9   Rosa, 2013, pp. 63–73; also H. Rosa, *Alienation and Acceleration: Towards a Critical Theory of Late-Modern Temporality* 2010, pp.13–26.

acceleration and innovation, this only serves to distinguish experientially, or phenomenologically, three aspects of the same underlying phenomenon, which perhaps is best grasped by the term 'dynamisation'.

The basic problem of endemic and escalating dynamisation is this: accelerated systems or actors systematically put pressure on the slower ones – risking de-synchronisation and friction at the points where they intersect. Whenever there is a temporal juncture or 'fit' between two systems, actors or processes, and one increases its velocity, the other one appears too slow, seeming a brake or hindrance, and synchronisation is impaired. On the one hand, this helps to explain the deepening of social stratification. In fact, those who are well-equipped with economic, social and cultural capital successfully use these items as resources in the game of acceleration: they enter the accumulative race for their children before they are even born, while those who lack such resources are 'left behind', resulting in a further widening of the social gap. But de-synchronisation also lies at the heart of the four major crises of late modern societies in the twenty-first century. If we loosely follow a 'systems-theoretical' approach,[10] we can envision the 'social system' as being located between the overarching ecological system(s) and the individuals' psychosomatic systems. The acceleration of society places stress and pressures of de-synchronisation on both these other systems. Furthermore, even within society, some processes or subsystems are more 'accelerable' than others: economic transactions, scientific progress and technological innovations can be accelerated relatively easily, while the processes of political democracy and cultural reproduction cannot – thus, democracy in particular (and perhaps education as well) is in increasing danger of being 'de-synchronised'. Finally, the problem of de-synchronisation reappears even within separate social subsystems. Thus, while the financial markets can be accelerated to almost the speed of light, altering how transactions are conducted and profits can be made, the 'real economy' of material production and consumption is much slower. Hence, potentially harmful de-synchronisation lurks even within the economic realm itself. Let us take a closer look at these processes.

i) Macro-Level: The Ecological Crisis

Surprising as it may sound, I claim that virtually all aspects of what we call 'the ecological crisis' can be re-interpreted as problems of de-synchronisation. Thus, on the one hand, it is not at all a problem that we cut down trees and catch fish – but it *is* a problem that we cut down the trees in the

---

10   I take this idea from Fritz Reheis' seminal book *Die Kreativität der Langsamkeit: Neuer Wohlstand durch Entschleunigung*, Darmstadt 1996.

rainforest and catch the fish in the oceans at rates too high to keep pace with their natural reproduction. Obviously, the discrepancy vastly increases when we look at the rate at which we deplete oil and carbon-based energy supplies and the time needed for nature to reproduce them. Similarly, most of what is considered to be a 'poisoning' of the environment is only a problem because we produce these substances and emissions at speeds that are higher than nature's capability to dispose of them. Finally, even the problem of 'global warming' can be read as a form of physical and material de-synchronisation: heating the atmosphere literally means making the molecules in these layers of air move faster; thus, the physical heat produced through technological acceleration on the ground leads to atmospheric acceleration in the skies. In other words, the process of material dynamisation, driven by the consumption of physical energy, leads to a 'de-synchronisation' in the earth's atmosphere that results in the earth's warming.

ii) Inter-Social De-synchronisation: The Crisis of Democracy

Alas, the speed of socio-economic life is not only too high for our natural environment, but it also creates problems for the slower spheres of society itself. As I have argued at length elsewhere,[11] the current weakness of western democracy – as can be seen in both its unattractiveness for non-western states in Africa and Asia as well as the decline in support and credibility it receives in its core countries[12] – basically arises from the fact that the democratic processes of political will-formation, decision-making and implementation are by their very nature time-consuming. In fact, the more pluralistic and post-conventionalist society gets – and the more complex its networks, chains of transaction and contexts of action and decision-making become – the *slower* democracy proceeds. Thus, while the speed of cultural and economic life and technological change increases, the pace of democracy slows down. Hence, we can observe a frightening level of de-synchronisation between politics and the social systems it tries to control or steer. Democracy no longer appears to be a pace-maker of social change; rather, it has shifted to a role of 'fire-extinguisher' and to a mode of 'muddling through': reacting to the pressures created elsewhere, rather than shaping our shared world. Nowhere could this be seen more clearly than in the recent financial crisis, when political decisions always came too late and too slow for the markets – and yet too fast for legislatures to even have a say. Parliaments, it seems, are reduced to ex-post facto yes-men or naysayers, leading to increasing frustration and alienation on the part of voters – who (at least

11   Rosa 2013, pp. 25–76.
12   cf. C. Crouch, *Post-Democracy*, Cambridge 2004.

in some cases) tend to elect xenophobic or populist parties in response, or to abstain from voting altogether. The de-synchronisation between politics and the economy, or its markets, thus results in a state of affairs where citizens have lost faith in political self-efficacy; for them, political institutions no longer respond to their needs and aspirations.

iii) Intra-Social De-synchronisation: The Financial Crisis

Yet, this is not all there is to de-synchronisation. In addition to acceleration producing problems between the natural and the socio-technical processes and between the different spheres of action, temporal pathologies can arise *within* single spheres of action as well. Even after two hundred years of technological acceleration, producing cars or houses is still a time-consuming process, as is, to some extent, the design and production of, for instance, clothes or computers. Furthermore, it is not only the production, but also the *consumption* of these commodities that is time-consuming. Compared to its price, it takes ages to really 'consume', i.e., *read*, a book, and the ratio for the other consumer goods mentioned is not much better. However, the need for growth and speed in global competitive markets is insatiable. Hence, it is little wonder that the financial economy discovered ways and means to dynamise the speed of the flow of capital and the creation of profits way beyond these material speed barriers. By buying and selling 'financial products', and thus by 'virtualising' production and consumption, transactions could be accelerated to an extent approaching the speed of light. In fact, in many ways the speed of financial transactions has become too high for human agents to understand or steer any more; they are left to computer algorithms that harvest surplus profits by exploiting fluctuations in the market within micro-seconds. Alas, this necessarily led to a serious de-synchronisation between the financial markets and the 'real' or material economy, to a point where the two had little connection with one another at all. In this way, 'the bubble' was a temporal bubble, too, and its bursting had dramatic consequences that are yet to be resolved. Re-synchronisation seems inevitable, even to economists, but it comes at a high price. The world-economy, it seems, is still seeking a temporal balance – not just between the financial industry on the one hand and the 'real industries' on the other, but also between markets and governments or politics. And it may very well be that such a re-synchronisation is only possible at the price of a significant slow-down of the (financial) economy.

iv) Micro-Level: The Global Burnout-Crisis

If the mode of dynamic stabilisation entails the incessant acceleration of material, social and cultural reproduction of society, then this cannot leave the structures of the individual psyche (and body) and the character of the human subject untouched. Thus, the question arises as to how much acceleration individuals can take before they 'break', so to speak. Here the evidence for pathological forms of de-synchronisation appears to be overwhelming as well. Thus, while drugs that slow people down ('downers' like heroin, alcohol) are on the decline, amphetamines and other drugs that promise 'synchronisation' (Ritalin, Taurin, Focus Factor, etc.) are on the rise. In fact, most forms of 'human enhancement' have to do with increasing the accelerability of human bodies and minds – from 'fixing' whose who are viewed as 'disabled' to transhumanist fantasies of reconciling the speed of technology with the speed of social actors.[13] Signs of growing pathological de-synchronisation, in the form of burnout and depression, are alarming. In fact, even the WHO now realises that – alongside other pathological stress-reactions like eating and sleeping disorders and chronic anxieties – depression and burnout are the fastest-growing health problem on a worldwide scale.[14] One of the most striking features of both burnout and depression is the resulting lack of dynamics: for those who fall into the trap of a burnout or depression, time stands still; the world and/or the self appear to be 'frozen', void of motion and significance.[15] This has led researchers like Alain Ehrenberg[16] to suppose that depression is a stress-induced reaction of a de-synchronised psyche to the speed requirements of modern life. The fact that magazines all over the world regularly double their sales by featuring stories about stress, burnout, depression and exhausted selves on their covers should serve as a warning signalling an impending state of de-synchronisation, even for those sceptical of the diagnostic practices of our medical services. I will come back to this in the next section.

---

13   cf. J. Savulescu, and N. Bostrom, (eds), *Human Enhancement* 2011.

14   Wittchen and Jacobi calculate that there are five to six million adult Germans (aged 18–65) and more than 20 million Europeans affected by depression every year. cf. F. Jacobi, J. Hoyer, H-U. Wittchen, 'Seelische Gesundheit in Ost und West: Analysen auf der Grundlage des Bundesgesundheitssurveys.' *Zeitschrift für Klinische Psychologie* 33:4, 2004, pp. 251–60.

15   cf. T. Bschor et al., 'Time experience and Time Judgement in Major Depression, Mania and Healthy Subjects', in *Acta Psychiatrica Scandinavia* 109, 2004, pp. 222–29.

16   A. Ehrenberg, *Das Unbehagen in der Gesellschaft*, Berlin: Suhrkamp, 2011. [Original French title: *La Société du Malaise*, Paris 2010.]

4. ALIENATION AND THE CRISIS OF LATE MODERN LIFE

As I sought to demonstrate in the preceding passage, modernity's compulsion toward escalation has grave consequences for people's lifestyles, life conduct and life experience.

I have attempted to point out that these consequences change progressively over the course of modernity, or rather, change according to modernity's degree of dynamisation. From the Enlightenment to the mid- or even late twentieth century, the hope for a self-determined life constituted the *fundamental promise* of modernity. As a normative and political project, modernity represents the opportunity to free oneself from the authoritarian conventions imposed by tradition on the one hand, and from scarcity and natural constraints on the other, in order to realise a self-determined way of life. In the same sense, neither God nor King should dictate to us how we live, nor should the constraints set by the natural world (we decide, independently of nature, whether a room is warm or cool, light or dark, when we eat strawberries or go skiing, and even whether we are a man or a woman).[17] Growth, acceleration, and the proliferation of options in life were historically motivated and legitimated by this objective. Related to this is the modern conception of *authenticity*, according to which we seek, and are indeed compelled, to utilise scopes and spaces of autonomy to be this or that and behave in this or that way in a manner that truly corresponds to our talents, capabilities and preferences, to our personalities and dreams. We wish to not be forced to bend or break under the weight of society's whims, but instead to be true to ourselves. In short: the drive to escalation incipiently served (at least in theory) to acquire and expand spaces of autonomy (and to protect these through the welfare state) in order to pursue one's own plans in life.

Today, by contrast, we can observe the complete surrender and even reversal of this relation: the individual life plan serves the purpose of keeping up in the game of escalation, of remaining or becoming competitive. Fantasies of, and energies invested in, shaping one's life are increasingly aimed, individually as well as collectively, at maintaining the capacity to increase and escalate and to use this in the process of competition. The fundamental promise of modernity is thus being betrayed. Individual and political spaces of autonomy are being drained by the compulsion to increase and escalate.

---

17   See H. Rosa, 'Historischer Fortschritt oder leere Progression? Das Fortschreiten der Moderne als kulturelles Versprechen und als struktureller Zwang', in U. Willems, D. Pollack, H. Basu, T. Gutmann, U. Spohn (eds), *Moderne und Religion, Kontroversen um Modernität und Säkularisierung*, Bielefeld 2013, pp. 117–42.

However, the conception of autonomy is not only a *victim* of the game of escalation; it is also among the culprits, as it is one of the motivating factors behind this game. The concept of autonomy is intrinsically linked, via its specific notion of freedom, to the idea that growth, movement, and especially an increasing availability of options and opportunities raises the overall quality of life. This is why the modern desire for autonomy urgently requires modification, or at least complementation, in the form of a re-discovery of the desire for resonance: if we accept that life is successful when it allows for experiences of resonance[18] (at work, within a political community, in a familial setting, in nature, art, etc.), then even if autonomy does not necessarily become irrelevant, the blind multiplication of life options does not imply a gain in quality of life *per se*. I will return to this argument shortly.

If growth, acceleration and the increase in innovations represent the structural dynamisation imperatives of modern society, they are also mediated culturally via the competitive distribution not only of goods and resources, but also of privileges and positions, of status and recognition, of friends and life partners, etc. The logic of competition leads to an endless dynamisation of all spheres of society organised along competitive lines. Individual subjects are expected to always perform a bit better and invest slightly more energy than their competitors – who are then of course obligated to follow suit.[19] This logic can be observed virtually everywhere: in educational practices in particular, but also in relation to one's own body. What is referred to as 'doping' in professional sports is mere 'human enhancement' in other areas. This competition-induced spiral of increase and escalation becomes interminable. If we do not overcome this dominant mode of dynamic stabilisation – by means of an economic, political and cultural revolution – it seems quite likely that in a few years time we will have begun 'upgrading' our children with biotechnological and information-technological forms of enhancement.

As I have already pointed out, the flipside of the game of escalation is its excessive demands on the mind and body, as can be witnessed in the increasing rates of pyschological burnout found in modern society. The logic of the

---

18 'Resonance' is a term I use to depict the opposite of alienation; cf. H. Rosa, *Weltbeziehungen im Zeitalter der Beschleunigung: Umrisse einer neuen Gesellschaft-skritik*, Berlin: Suhrkamp, 2012 (*Global Relationships in the Age of Acceleration – Outlines for a New Social Critique*).

19 This is the subjective correlate to what Stephan Lessenich describes as the welfare state's activation policy: the policies he identifies take effect in the subject mainly via the 'competification' of life, i.e., via the circumstance that subjects are permanently forced to improve, or at least not diminish, their resource input during competition.

hamster wheel has such a tight grip on people in 'late modernity' that not even physical impairments can stop them (be it the flu, a broken leg, or a prolapsed disc). We push ourselves further – we plan a Caesarian section for childbirth and a cremation for our funeral to ensure that they will be well-timed and fit neatly into a schedule – up until the point at which we experience the 'slow and desperate temporal standstill', falling into a depressive burnout. Burnout syndrome is neither the product of simply having a lot of work to do nor of the compulsion to run faster, but rather of the utter absence of any long-term goals on one's individual horizon. The fact that one 'must keep running faster just to keep up' is literally making people sick. To have to constantly grow, accelerate and innovate simply to be able to actually pause once in a while, just to avoid sliding into crisis, culminates in an existential impossibility. Thus far, we have managed to avoid developing a collective burnout by seeking comfort in the idea that *things are only this hectic for now,* but *they will get better soon.* At this point, however, we as a culture are realising that this is an illusion: *nothing is getting better.* From this perspective, burnout can be considered an extreme form of alienation: it is not the amount of work, but instead the *relations of work themselves* that have a tendency to result in stress and burnout illnesses. There is overwhelming evidence that burnout appears where 'nothing is given in return' at our places of work, when there are no longer any 'resonances'.[20] Burnout arises when successes are no longer acknowledged or celebrated, but instead viewed as mere 'intermediate steps in an endless sequence'; when one receives no recognition (also known as a 'crisis of gratification'[21]); when genuine personal relationships and interactions erode or are instrumentalised; when progress at work is no longer intrinsically motivated; when an authentic passion for work as a meaningful activity is lost. In short: *burnout is the result when the 'axes of resonance' at the workplace fall silent* (*Verstummen*) – or, as is sometimes the case, when these axes fall silent due to the loss of the workplace altogether. This falling silent of all axes of resonance represents the embodiment of a condition of alienation in which the world faces the subject in a rigid, harsh, cold and silent form – a world in which the latter perceives of him or herself as pale, dead, empty and mute.

Psychologists have observed that individuals suffering from depression and burnout are often characterised by two features: firstly, by the loss of intensive, meaningful, 'resonant' social relationships (which in many cases may have been sacrificed for the sake of one's career in the first place), and

---

20   M. Burisch, *Das Burnout-Syndrom: Theorie der inneren Erschöpfung* 2006. For more elaboration on this cf. also J. Bauer, *Arbeit: Warum unser Glück von ihr abhängt und wie sie uns krank macht,* Karl Blessing, 2013.

21   Cf. J. Siegrist, *Medizinische Soziologie* 2005, pp. 71–6.

secondly, by a growing cynicism towards themselves and the world: neither in art or in nature, nor at work or within the family do they experiences spaces of resonance – the world becomes strange, silent, cold and external to them.[22] This alienation from one's family and work, spaces and things, from one's own body and self, is a frequent and quite obvious consequence of escalation compulsions, precisely because resonant relationships require stability as well as adequate time to maintain them.[23]

Granted, not all subjects fall victim to burnout syndrome, even in late modernity. There are three (problematic) 'alternative' patterns of life conduct that can be identified: one entails the modern ideal of autonomy being substituted by a *'surfer' ideal*. The point here is no longer to find a 'safe harbour' or an island in the ocean of life at which to dock one's proverbial boat, but rather to stand on a proverbial surfboard while making the greatest effort possible to read and master the wind and waves, jumping from crest to crest and 'staying afloat'.[24] 'Surfers' are frequently considered to be the 'victors and winners' of the system. I, however, consider them to be *susceptible to burnout* in the near future because they are no longer connected to society, and unhappy because they are neither 'autonomous' in the old sense nor 'resonant' in the new.

Perhaps late modern subjects are really more akin to *pinball players* than to surfers: they keep the ball in the game as long as possible and hope to encounter advantageous contacts and opportunities while playing.[25] Whoever does not manage to 'stay afloat' runs the risk of being flung back and forth uncontrollably by the wind and waves; he or she then becomes a 'drifter' – incapable of controlling, planning or steering his or her destiny and life, but likewise unable to find or acquire new spaces of resonance.

Those who are neither able to become a surfer nor willing to be a drifter may attempt to gain stability, orientation and perspective through a kind of transcendental anchor, i.e., to adopt a more or less fundamentalist religious or political identity. ('Whatever the future may bring, Jehovah's Word is eternal' – or, if religion is not to one's liking, perhaps a people's liberation struggle instead). In my view, at least some of the appeal of terrorist groups

---

22   Cf. A. Ehrenberg, *The Weariness of the Self: Diagnosing the History of Depression in the Contemporary Age*, New Baskerville, McGill-Queen's University 2010; V. King and B. Gerisch (eds): *Zeitgewinn und Selbstverlust, Folgen und Grenzen der Beschleunigung*, Frankfurt a.M., New York 2009.

23   For more elaboration cf. Rosa, 2010, pp. 83–101.

24   Cf. the preface to K. Gergen, *The Saturated Self: Dilemmas Of Identity In Contemporary Life*, New York 2000.

25   cf. U. Schimank, 'Flipperspielen und Lebenskunst', in *Identität und Moderne*, H. Willems, A. Hahn (eds), Frankfurt aM., Suhrkamp, 1999, pp. 250–72.

lies in their capacity to articulate precisely such a 'counter-horizon' in oppo-sition to the capitalist logic of dynamisation and flexibilisation (this is true for both the NSU[26] as well as Al Qaeda and ISIS). The essential question, then, is whether other, positive life plans can be observed in late modern society, at least in an embryonic stage. In my view, they would have to aim towards establishing and protecting those spaces of resonance which do not conform to the logic of escalation, while at the same time exhibiting some resilience in the face of dynamisation imperatives. This is precisely the point at which many alternative communes, movements and oppositional projects fail. But if it is true – as is reported by all kinds of major media outlets these days – that even (and particularly!) highly qualified and talented employees are increasingly refusing to assume leadership positions in the economy, in politics, or in the academy out of fear of becoming trapped in the hamster wheel, then perhaps the cultural resources of resistance against the rule of the logic of escalation do exist after all.

5. CONTOURS OF A BETTER WORLD: THE CONCEPT OF RESONANCE

The argument developed in the preceding section seeks to establish the opposition between experiences and spaces of resonance and forms of alienation as central to a new definition of the quality of life, and hence to developing a new standard for measuring the quality of life. This stand-ard is intended to replace the (often unacknowledged) criterion of growth and increase as the guiding normative principle applied in the evaluation of social conditions. However, to come up with a clearly delineated, solid defi-nition of this central concept of 'resonance' turns out to be a tremendously difficult task. I cannot provide such a definition at this point in time, but I can at least identify some of its basic elements. This is what I want to turn to in this last section of my contribution.

Quite obviously, modern conceptions of well-being and standards of living (the 'good life') are drivers for growth. In economic and politi-cal terms, well-being is all too often measured by the relative size of gross domestic product alone. Prosperity is then assumed to rise in tandem with the latter: life gets better with rising economic output. But even beyond such narrow forms of economism, the good life, or the quality of life, in

---

26   NSU stands for *Nationalsozialistischer Untergrund* (National Socialist Underground), a neo-Nazi terrorist cell that committed at least nine execution-style murders of immigrants across Germany between 2000 and 2006, and is suspected of committing numerous bombings, including the 2004 nail bomb attack in a district of Cologne heavily populated by Turkish immigrants.

philosophical as well as in everyday narratives, is usually measured (explicitly and implicitly) by the quality and quantity of options and commodities at hand. This, I believe, stems from a conception of the good life that is based on the idea of autonomy. According to this conception, quality of life rises along with rising means and commodities at our disposal; in short, with our increased access to resources. The happy life, then, is one well-equipped with economic (wealth), cultural (education), social (relationships) and physical (health, attractiveness, fitness) resources. After all, these resources increase the range of our relationship to the world: We prefer the city to the countryside because it gives us more options, we prefer higher to lower education because it provides us with more opportunities, we prefer the smart phone to the mobile because it has more capabilities, we adore money because it increases our control and reach over segments of the world, etc. ad infinitum. Thus, increase and escalation, growth, acceleration and innovation appear to be attractive and desirable for modern subjects *per se*. Consequently, it comes as no surprise that individuals, when asked about life satisfaction, tend to answer that question in terms of the resources they have at their disposal: I am (not) well equipped with economic, cultural, social and resource-based capital, so yes, I am (not) happy.[27] Therefore, a post-growth society, i.e., one that operates according to a mode of stabilisation different from the current one, requires a re-definition of the quality of life as well. Making a post-growth society possible depends on the introduction of a standard of measure for the good life that is different from the one that measures it against the range of options (for consumption, recreation, etc.) available to individual subjects. The starting point for this is the simple intuition that the happiness of people can be read from their sharing of laughter, song and dance rather than from their ranges of available options. But of course, this is an old and in itself quite unsustainable idea. We require something more substantial to formulate a compelling argument. So, what alternatives are available to develop a conception of the quality of life that is not resource- or options-centred and thus not growth-related?

The answer I am trying to develop stands in line with a long tradition in social philosophy, particularly in critical theory and phenomenology, but also in other variants of social philosophy. The basic idea is that the quality of life ultimately depends on the quality of relationships between the self and the world. It depends on how the self and the world (as the totality of the subjective, the objective and the social worlds) are related, on how the self experiences and approaches the world. This does not imply a return to Cartesian dualism; rather, as can be learned from the phenomenological

---

27   Cf. B. Schwartz, *The Paradox of Choice: Why More Is Less*, New York 2003.

tradition from Merleau-Ponty to Charles Taylor, this line of thinking does not presuppose a self and a world which only *subsequently* enter into a relationship, but on the contrary, proceeds from the assumption that the relationship exists *prior* to both the world and the self.

Thus, the concept of resonance takes as its starting point the observation that there are different modes of self-world relations: The first mode of encounter between the self and (a particular sphere or segment of) the world can be characterised by *indifference*. In this mode, the self is disengaged from an indifferent world which it might seek to control (or to shape or to use) while it is subjected to its effects. The relationship between self and world here are either instrumental or causal in nature. Secondly, the subject might experience the world as *repulsive*. In this mode, a subject feels thrown into a remorseless, hostile, cold, inimical and merciless world full of obstacles and dangers. The mode of existence, then, is one of struggle and suffering. Thirdly, subject and world might fall into a mode of *resonance*. In this mode, the subject experiences the world (or a specific segment of it) as 'answering', responding to and supporting him or her. The connection here is of an intrinsic nature and meaning, it is not just causal and instrumental, but constitutive for who the subject is. In this mode, the subject is capable of 'appropriating' the world in a manner that transforms the self's essence through 'connection' (*Anverwandlung,* as opposed to the simple instrumental *Aneignung* [appropriation]). Thus, the mode of resonance can be defined as a mode in which the self is moved, touched, 'meant to be' or 'addressed', but also feels capable of reaching out and touching or moving the external world. Hence, resonance is a mode of liquefaction in the relationship between self and world.

While it is exasperatingly difficult to define these modes of self-world-relationships (*Weltbeziehungen*) in a philosophically precise way, they prove to be rather easy to specify phenomenologically. Everyday language as well as everyday experience tell us what it means to say that something 'resonates' with us. It means that we are moved or touched by a thing, a person, an action or a physical surrounding in a way that triggers an internal 'response' from us. Thus, resonance specifies a relationship of 'benevolent' mutual response between self and world. It requires a certain openness on the part of the subject, but also a 'responsive' environment. In modern society, there appear to be specific, often institutionalised contexts in which subjects seek and experience such moments of resonance. In particular, these can be found in the spheres of art, nature and religion. Thus, people seem to experience a 'responsive world' in the mountains, at the ocean when the waves crash against the shore, and sometimes in forests and deserts. Furthermore, they are regularly touched and moved (to tears) in concert halls and cinemas (or in museums and theatres). Finally, for believers, the religious service provides assurance of being seen, heard and answered by a superior power who listens to and cares for us. By contrast, we all are familiar with those other experiences in which the world turns cold and indifferent, in which 'nothing speaks to us'. The most clear-cut example of the mode of indifference is the state of burnout or depression, which I have discussed at length in the preceding section. Subjects regularly describe it in terms of emptiness, bleakness, coldness, numbness and void, which apply to the experience of the outer world as well as their own inner states. In my view, this mode of (distorted) self-world relationship is not categorically different from the second mode of *repulsion*, in which the world is experienced as hostile, dangerous and adverse. Sometimes bad weather is sufficient to give us this feeling of being thrown into a world that is an aggressive challenge to our very existence.

Now, obviously, everyone knows episodes of all three modes of self-world-relationship. They are relative to specific contexts of life and transitory in nature. However, the basic tenet of resonance theory is the idea that these modes can be generalised into modes of existence and thus be used to evaluate and criticise the quality of life and social conditions. This would mean that modes of life can be measured in terms of their 'resonability'.

If we accept that this constitutes a viable route of exploration, then the good life could be defined as a life that allows and provides not just for experiences of resonance, but also for reliable 'axes' of resonance. At this point, we have to introduce a crucial distinction: while experiences of resonance are always and necessarily temporary, transient and fleeting, they are regularly sought and made along more or less stable 'axes' of resonance. In modern societies, those axes are generally not found in the everyday life of politics and the economy, law or science, but in the more poetic and remote realms of *nature*, *art* and *religion*, which are conceptualised as 'pure' spheres of resonance, standing in marked contrast to a 'hostile' or at least indifferent world of social competition and instrumental interaction. However, it is important to realise that there is an inherently elusive element to all experiences of resonance: they cannot be controlled and intensified or even brought about at will – and most significantly, they cannot be accumulated. Thus, if you listen to your favourite song every day, or ten times in a row, you will not maximise your experience of resonance, but minimise it; the same is true if you visit your favourite summit in the mountains every day, or while you are in a bad mood. Consequently, social conditions deserve criticism when they close off the axes of resonance for subjects. Repression, for example, almost certainly leads to a mode of self-world relationship that is repulsive. The same holds true for exploitation and deprivation. However, the history of modern social philosophy, from Rousseau to Charles Taylor or Axel Honneth, impressively and almost uniformly demonstrates that the deepest fear of modernity is the experience of a world turned completely mute and silent: from Rousseau's and Marx's conception of *alienation* to Weber's notion of dis-*enchantment* and Lukács's idea of *reification*; from Adorno and Horkheimer's plea against *bourgeois coldness* and *instrumental reason*, to Camus' interpretation of the *absurdity* of existence; from Habermas's verdict of the *colonialisation of the lifeworld* by the *cold and mute imperatives of the system*, and finally to Honneth's struggle against misrecognition and Charles Taylor's qualified plea for 're-enchantment' – the spectre of a world which has lost its propensity to 'resonate' appears to be the central theme, albeit expressed in many variations.

On the other hand, modernity is just as much characterised by a major rise in the desire for resonance and the sensibility to experience it. Thus, the three core spheres of modern resonance – nature, art and religion – are genuinely romantic 'inventions', and so is the modern understanding of love (between lovers as well as between parents and children) as a matter of pure and mutual 'resonance'.

But this is exactly where a systematic critique of the contemporary conditions of resonance should depart from. (Late-)modern life is characterised by a sharp and marked contrast between non-resonant, competitive, instrumental spheres of public (economic, political, legal etc.) life on the one hand, and secluded 'oases' of resonance on the other hand. Modern subjects seek reassuring moments of resonance in the concert hall or the football stadium, in weekend getaways to the countryside or in Sunday services at church, while in their everyday work lives – and all too often in their actual family lives as well – they operate in the modes of indifference and repulsion. Modern work life in particular is non-resonant, and as compensation modern culture provides small niches of 'pure resonance'. However, a core problem of these conditions of resonance – or alienation – lies in the fact that those niches or oases are constructed in a way that denies experiences of self-efficacy: subjects want to be 'touched', moved or affected, for example, at the opera or in the cinema, but their own role in this sphere is almost entirely passive. They might be moved, but they do not experience their own capacity to reach out and move themselves in such contexts. This underscores a central requirement of the resonating mode: resonance is a two-way relationship between self and world, not a 'one-way affection'.

If we draw on the musical metaphor, it becomes clear that resonance is a phenomenon resulting from a particular relationship between (at least) two bodies. It is different from echo, for resonance is not a form of 'resounding', rather, it is a mode of *answering*: the two bodies sound in their own, distinct 'voices', they are not aligned or connected in a mechanical or linear fashion. Hence, resonance as a mode of relationship can fail in two forms on either side of the relationship: if the self is solidly closed and buffered, it will not be able to 'resonate' with anything. On the other hand, if the self is completely open and fragmented, it will be unable to answer or sound 'in its own voice'. And conversely, if the world (in the form of social and material conditions) is over-regulated, fixed and solid, it will not resonate, but if it is chaotic and completely unpredictable, it will be impossible to discern its voice. Hence, the quality of self-world-relationships depends on this 'two-way resonability'.

In this way, resonance can replace the notion of 'identity' as a standard of measure for the quality of life. The good life, then, is not one that requires subjects to have and to maintain a fixed and stable identity, and it does not require 'identification' between the individual and his or her community, but it requires responsive, vibrant relationships between (a changing) self and (a changing) world – in other words, it requires reliable 'axes of resonance'. This, in turn and finally, allows the re-introduction of a non-essentialist conception of alienation: alienation, in my view, denotes a mode of existence in which subjects experience an indifferent or repulsive world – it is defined by a decisive lack of resonance.

Thus, resonance theory aims at a new form of social critique that is a critique of the conditions of resonance. If we find this conception to be convincing, then alienating conditions represent the most serious obstacle to the realisation of a good life. Consequently, efforts to increase and sharpen individual and political sensibility for experiences and spaces of resonance alongside the identification of alienating institutional contexts would be of crucial importance to any attempt at establishing a post-growth society. The subjective drive for escalation and increase could vanish if, through establishing and securing spaces of resonance, subjects would feel capable of re-appropriating the (public and political) world. Hence, for the political and philosophical analysis and normative critique of social and political change, the focus could and should be shifted to the background conditions enabling resonance and preventing (structural) alienation. Such a shift of attention could in fact herald the beginning of a fundamental alteration to the cultural, but also the structural and institutional, fabric of modernity.

6. Conclusion

In this contribution, I have sought to substantiate four claims:

1) Modern societies can be defined by their mode of stabilisation, which is dynamic. This means they need to grow, to accelerate and to innovate just to stay in place, i.e., to reproduce the status quo in the current socio-economic structure. This holds true for modern societies in all parts of the world and, for Western countries, at any given point in time since the eighteenth century.

2) This mode of dynamic stabilisation, and the ensuing logic of escalation, generate their own instabilities: the longer the system persists, the more difficult it becomes to keep it going. This is most evident from a temporal perspective: since time cannot be extended, but only compressed, time-scarcity (which lies at the heart of social acceleration) moves to the centre of social attention. In fact, the essence of dynamic stabilisation can be re-interpreted in terms of social acceleration.

3) Social acceleration inevitably creates problems of social de-synchronisation, which grow increasingly acute as modernity ages. Thus, the four major crises of our current age can be adequately understood as crises of de-synchronisation. This reveals their inherent connection: ultimately, they are all pathologies of acceleration and dynamisation. This, in turn, suggests that those crises will not be solved unless modern societies adopt a different mode of stabilisation (which, incidentally, would make them truly 'postmodern'): they must adopt a mode which would allow for growth, acceleration and innovation where it is socially and culturally desirable for the attainment of a certain goal or end, but which would not require escalation for the sake of maintaining the status quo. A post-growth society, obviously, is one that is *capable* of growth, acceleration and innovation if it needed or wanted to *change* the socio-economic, cultural or ecological *status quo* (e.g., to overcome some form of scarcity or fight a disease), but which is not dependent on escalation for systemic reproduction, for *preserving the status quo as such*. To sketch out the as-yet-unknown cultural, political and economic contours of such a society – one that is liberal, democratic and pluralistic in its cultural fabric, but has moved beyond the social totalitarianism of escalation – is what our research in Jena is all about.

4) An alternative mode of stabilisation that is both modern in the sense of being democratic, pluralistic and liberal, but not dependent on growth and escalation for reproduction, would require a new cultural definition of the

good life, a new measurement of the quality of life. I have sought to introduce the idea of resonance as such a benchmark and to juxtapose it with two forms of alienation. Alienation and resonance, so the argument goes, describe different modes or relationships between self and world, and a shift of mode in this realm might be the first and decisive step in any attempt to stop the endless spirals of escalation and, in so doing, to realise a better world.

Structural Problems of Growth Capitalism

STEPHAN LESSENICH

> I could feel at the time
> There was no way of knowing
> – Bill Murray sings Roxy Music
> in *Lost in Translation*

1. CAPITALISM, CRISIS, ACTIVATION: WHAT HAS HAPPENED SO FAR?

Five years have passed since the publication of *Sociology, Capitalism, Critique*; five years in which global capitalism, in its seemingly uncontrollable dynamic, has utterly ignored the sociological critique emanating from the German university town of Jena. Of course, one could argue that five years is not a very long time: was it not just yesterday that the German government passed the 'Growth Acceleration Act' (*Wachstumsbeschleunigungsgesetz*) in order to counter the most dire effects of the 'most severe financial and economic crisis since the founding of the republic' (as stated by the law's preamble states) through fiscal-political intervention? It certainly feels that way. But then again: thanks to the Bologna Reform(s), which challenged universities and their clients to contribute to the success of the EU Development Strategy as agreed upon in Lisbon (the 'most competitive and dynamic knowledge-based economy in the world', etc.), five years is enough time to complete both a BA and an MA in sociology. What I am trying to say is that a lot can happen in five years. Studious pupils can – if things go well – be trained to become critical sociologists, and financial market-driven capitalism can – absent any unforeseen developments – take its socially devastating business model to a new historical level. So, has nothing changed since 2009? Well, not quite.

As the reader will recall, I countered, or rather *complemented*, the two perspectives on the logic of movement and imperatives of escalation found in capitalist modernity put forward by my Jena colleagues in

Sociology, Capitalism, Critique. I sought to expand Klaus Dörre's politico-economic interpretation, as well as the cultural-philosophical perspective of Hartmut Rosa, with a politico-sociological interpretation drawing upon the neo-Marxist theory of late capitalism, as developed in the late 1960s and early 1970s. At the heart of this approach lay, or rather *lies*,[1] the analytical assumption that the capitalist mode of socialisation is thoroughly and deeply political, or rather, *politicised*. This politicisation of the capitalist economy has two dimensions. On the one hand, the capitalist logic of capital accumulation and valorisation (which occurs on an ever-expanding scale) rests upon a multiplicity of preconditions concerning ownership rights, infrastructure, regulations and reproduction, which can only be reasonably and reliably established and guaranteed by an entity or authority that is detached from the immediate process of capital valorisation – that is, by the modern state and its means of coercion and administrative apparatuses. The state becomes particularly important in times of economic crises (i.e., the cyclical stagnation of capital accumulation or the cyclical slump in that accumulation, accompanied by the corresponding dynamics of capital destruction), when state intervention seeking to, at least temporarily, pacify the resulting needs for social security and to restore capital's conditions for profitability (basically, capital's 'business confidence' regarding the 'general political/economic climate')[2] becomes more or less indispensable. The capitalist economy is thus constitutively dependent on (re-)productive contributions from the political-administrative system for its continued functional capacity. The political-administrative system is, in its controlling capacity and ability to intervene, itself of course tied to those same economic valorisation processes; the bureaucratic institutional state places the utmost priority on, the promotion and stabilisation of these processes which the bureaucratic institutional state places the utmost priority on – not least because it the system is, at least in fiscal terms, dependent on thissaid capital accumulation in the first place.

The politicisation of the capitalist economy in 'advanced societies'[3], however, has another dimension beyond the bureaucratic: namely, the *democratic* dimension. The democratic constitution of politics in the

---

1 In the context of the Jena research group 'Post Growth Societies' (*Postwachstumsgesellschaften*), I have worked extensively on a systematic reconstruction and update of the theory of late capitalism. Together with Jens Borchert I am publishing the findings of this work in 2015 (*Claus Offe and the Critical Theory of the Capitalist State*, New York).

2 Cf. T. Skocpol, 'Political Response to Capitalist Crisis: Neo-Marxist Theories of the State and the New Deal', in: *Politics and Society*, 10: (2), 1980, p. 183.

3 A. Giddens, *The Class Structure of the Advanced Societies*, London 1973.

western-industrial model of society, which has typically been neglected or even disregarded in social analyses emerging from the Marxist tradition, deserves to be at the heart of any investigation into the theory of late capitalism. The actually existing social opportunities for participation and inclusion in decision-making within capitalist democracies may be rightfully criticised from a normative viewpoint as being merely formal, limited or distorted. Yet from a functional perspective, it is nevertheless beyond doubt that state intervention, structurally crucial for the expanded reproduction of the capitalist economy, is (and must be) implemented by political entities which are bound in their actions to the compliance of those subjected to their rule, and that they rely on the latter's acceptance of decisions founded on collective commitment and obligation.

To follow Weber (the theory of late capitalism can in this sense be understood as that of a Weberian neo-Marxism): it is people's faith in the legitimacy of the state upon which 'successful' state activity (each according to specific criteria, of course) is in turn based. Capitalist state activity is just as dependent on this democratic legitimation as an ideational resource as it is on the material resources which the 'public sector' siphons off from the surplus product that is created in every economic cycle. Essentially, the state is only capable of conducting what amounts to an intervention into capital's right of disposition due to its relative autonomy vis-à-vis the interests of capital, through which it obtains its legitimacy in the eyes of the 'will of the people'. The latter can, of course, begin to demand so much from the democratic state that state institutions run the risk of outrunning or overburdening the economy's performance as a whole (or, more precisely: over-stretching the willingness of capital's side to forego opportunities for profit realisation in the interests of relative social harmony).

According to the theory of late capitalism, then, the democratic-capitalist state's *accumulation* function is complemented by its *justificatory* function. The said state is thereby functionally tied to the structures and dynamics of both the capitalist economy as well as democratic civil society, leading to – a *double bind,* which simultaneously works as the constitutive source and the systematic boundary of political-administrative actors' scope of action. In its interventionism, the democratic-capitalist state always follows, albeit in historically varying mixtures and degrees of mediation, a capitalist, a democratic *and* a bureaucratic rationality – that is to say, an intrinsic political-institutional logic – *at the same time.*[4] In this sense, the state is continuously confronted with conflicting interests of different social actors: capitalist interests of profit realisation (and, if possible, maximisation) as

---

4   Cf, R.Alford, R. Friedland, *Powers of Theory: Capitalism, the State, and Democracy,* Cambridge 1985.

well as democratic interests of political participation, which it then needs to mediate while taking into account the interests of *both* sides, as well as its own *self*-interest in institutional stability (and, if possible, the expansion of the state's scope of action).

The aforementioned dimension – namely, the rationality of an intrinsic logic of the field of politics – helps to avoid notions of the institutional order of the state as being merely an 'arena' of social, or rather class conflict – as well as an oversimplified reading of state activity as a mere manifestation of the balance of social forces, or even as a 'hegemonic project' ensuring the materialisation of prevailing dominant interests. The theory of late capitalism draws our attention to the fact that the rational *intrinsic logic of the political* must be a central focus of analysis of contemporary capitalist society and its developmental dynamic. This intrinsic logic feeds off of and draws from various sources; it is thus fragmented, as well as limited (or rather, 'multiple').[5] In this regard, the theory makes it quite plain that the democratic-capitalist state's interventionism is a highly multi-functional arrangement, even a *structurally contradictory* undertaking, systematically (or perhaps unsystematically) pervaded by conflicting goals and unintended effects, fault lines and 'gaps of indeterminacy'[6] of all kinds.

Should If we adopt this perspective, then the late capitalist constellation is marked on the one hand by its fundamental, essentially ineluctable and *permanent crisis-proneness*: the democratic-capitalist social formation is caught in a permanent systemic balancing act between competing organisational principles and conflicting interests which are expressed in the constantly changing, yet nevertheless always acute problems of control and the ever-new justificatory requirements accompanying democratic-capitalist state activity. The structural crisis-proneness of both capitalist accumulation and democratic legitimation is reflected in crises of the 'second order' – in incessant, alternating 'crises of crisis management':[7] in the political space of contemporary society, 'after' the crisis is always 'before' the next crisis, and alleged 'solutions' inevitably become the catalysts of renewed crisis dynamics. The political-administrative institutional field is where economic crisis

---

5 The fact that this instance of intrinsic logic is not systematically included in his argument represents the main weakness of Wolfgang Streeck's otherwise quite illuminating crisis analysis, which he nominally bases on the theory of late capitalism (cf. Streeck, 2014, Lessenich, 2014).

6 G. Vobruba, *Die Gesellschaft der Leute: Kritik und Gestaltung der sozialen Verhältnisse*, Wiesbaden 2009.

7 C. Offe, 'Crises of Crisis Management: Elements of a Political Crisis Theory', *International Journal of Politics*, 6:3; Political Legitimacy in Advanced Capitalist Countries (Part 1), Fall 1976, pp. 29–67.

tendencies and social experience of crisis – or rather, the resulting capitalist requirements and democratic demands[8] directed towards 'the state' or
'politics' – intersect. It is here, at this point of convergence in a political-
administrative system (which is regularly called upon and turned to for
problem resolution even by those who criticise it for both its excesses as
well as its insufficiencies), and confronted with incessant requirements for
control and legitimation, that the contingent crises of the economic and the
social become *crises of the political*.

On the other hand, it is precisely this constitutive crisis-proneness of
democratic-capitalist state interventionism – its contradictions, functional
gaps and rationality boundaries of political-institutional activity – which
opens up spaces for the unplanned and incongruous, the unintended and
undesired; these in turn constitute evolutionary-historical gateways for the
unexpected. If state interventionism in democratic capitalism is an expression of a specific political 'project', then it is subject to all the problems and
uncertainties that accompany any such project – regardless of which social
field it takes place in (one could think of, for example. university research
projects in this context). These problems range from ever-scarcer resources
to target planning, and time schedules that inevitably require revision and
alterations, substantially complemented in the political sphere by the limits
of control over social processes, or rather the inescapable reality that every
state intervention relies on social implementation.[9] This reality confronts
any attempt at socio-political intervention and frequently (even usually)
prevents them from occurring. Thus, the perspective offered by the theory
of late capitalism on contemporary society – despite all of its seemingly
functionalist or intentionalist excesses and its focus on the intrinsic macro-
social logics of social subsystems ('state', 'capitalism', 'democracy') – does not
hinder or prevent us from taking a closer look at the intrinsic micro-social
logic of the addressees of democratic-capitalist state intervention, the obstinacy of the 'policy takers[10], or those 'emancipatorily opportune moments'[11]
that emerge in the interplay between society and state activity.

But let us return to my contribution to *Sociology, Capitalism, Critique*, or,

---

8   Cf. C. Offe, *Berufbildungsreform: Eine Fallstudie über Reformpolitik*,
Frankfurt a.m., Suhrkamp, 1975.

9   G. Lenhardt, C. Offe, 'Staatstheorie und Sozialpolitik: Politisch-soziologische
Erklärungsansätze für Funktionen und Innovationsprozesse der Sozialpolitik', in
C. Von Ferber and F-X. Kaufmann (eds), *Soziologie und Sozialpolitik, Kölner Zeitschrift
für Soziologie und Sozialpsychologie*, 19, Opladen 1977, pp. 98–127.

10   W. Streeck, K. Thelen, 'Introduction: Institutional Change in Advanced
Political Economies', in Wolfgang Streeck; Kathleen Thelen (eds), *Beyond Continuity.
Institutional Change in Advanced Political Economies*, Oxford 2005, pp. 1–39.

11   G. Vobruba, *Politik mit dem Wohlfahrtsstaat*, Frankfurt a.M., Suhrkamp, 1983.

more precisely: to its inner core of analysis of the present and its diagnosis of the times. In that text, I described 'activation', or rather the 'activating' transformation of the institutional order of the welfare state, as the dominant mode of socio-political crisis regulation in contemporary late capitalism. In this political-institutional context, 'activation' signifies a *double movement*. This pertains, on the one hand, to the phenomenon of mobilising labour power hitherto unvalorised by capital – housewives, immigrants, the elderly – into labour markets. In fact, this is a classical process of commodification of previously non- (or not yet) commodified forms of social labour power (which, in the words of Klaus Dörre, could be described as a tendency towards a '*Landnahme*', or conquest, of areas in society or social milieus that have thus far been exempted from capital valorisation through private or welfare-state based forms of socialisation). This is the *economic* dimension of a politics of 'activation': market imperatives are intensified and expanded, non market-conducive social conditions and lifestyles are de-legitimated and made insecure, while the social model of a 'society of precarious full-time employment'[12] is institutionally flanked and actively promoted. Beyond this economic dimension, however, 'activation' also possesses a *social* dimension, which, although mediated via the socio-political 'shifting of market boundaries',[13] hardly ever proves successful in an increasingly 'marketised' way of life: corresponding policies are framed by relevant political actors as acts of 'inclusion' of socially marginalised social groups into the structures of recognition and promises of prosperity offered by the system of the social division of labour. In a self-proclaimed market society, market citizenship becomes the decisive moment and motive of social participation. A type of 'activation' that opens up opportunities for (or rather, *obligates*) these citizens to enter the market functions as a sort of political contribution, not only for system integration (through realisation of capital's interest in valorisable labour power), but also for social integration (in the sense of a collective desire for a legitimate position within the structure of social labour).[14]

Utilising the theory of late capitalism, the political 'activation project' can be interpreted as a specific, contemporary variant of democratic-

---

12 K. Dörre, 'Auf dem Weg in die prekäre Vollerwerbsgesellschaft?', in *Arbeitsrecht im Betrieb*, 34:5, 2013, p. 275.

13 U. Brinkmann, 'Die Verschiebung von Marktgrenzen und die kalte Entmachtung der WissensarbeiterInnen', in Klaus Schönberger; Stefanie Springer (eds), *Subjektivierte Arbeit: Mensch, Organisation und Technik in einer entgrenzten Arbeitswelt*, Frankfurt, New York 2003, pp. 63–94.

14 Cf. R. Castel, *From Manual Workers to Wage Labourers: Transformation of the Social Question*, London 2002.

capitalist state intervention, as the latter serves both the accumulation and the legitimation function(s) of state politics, capitalist requirements as well as democratic demands – and claims to do so in equal measures. Moreover, 'activation' also corresponds to the categories of late capitalist political intervention in that it exhibits a strategic selectivity[15] of state institutions. After all, only those individuals, social categories and action motives which are required and desired by and acceptable to market society are – or rather, are supposed to be – mobilised: a political filtering structure which, in *Sociology, Capitalism, Critique*, I attempted to grasp with my description of the 'dialectic of mobility and control'. Finally, 'activation' also shifts the mode of political intervention as a whole. And this occurs, as it were, not only or at least not exclusively by adhering to the prototypical neo-liberal pattern of 'shedding of state responsibilities'[16] in the sense of the state's abandonment of any social or material responsibility for large parts of its population. Instead, the re-privatisation of previously public services points towards something more, namely to a 'neosocial' agenda – linked to the neo-liberal renunciation of intervention – of shifting even system-integrating and socially integrating functions from the public hand into the hands (as well as minds and hearts) of individual subjects.

This new mode of intervention, or rather mode adapted to the new historical era of flexible capitalism, of a 'subjectification' of the social[17] – the regulative and motivational utilisation of social individuals constructed as 'active citizens' for the production of collective goods, the preservation and maintenance of economic competitiveness, and labour on behalf of a 'common good' (*Gemeinwohl*) – does indeed suggest a limitation of the theory of late capitalism. For this theory assumed – during the late 1960s and early 1970s – that the 'self-adaptive instrumentarium' of system-stabilising state action had been 'categorically exhausted'[18] in the existing apparatus

---

15   Cf. C. Offe, *Strukturprobleme des kapitalistischen Staates. Aufsätze zur Politischen Soziologie*, Frankfurt a.M 1972; B. Jessop, 'The Strategic Selectivity of the State: Reflections on a Theme of Poulantzas', in *Journal of the Hellenic Diaspora*, 25:1–2, 1999, pp. 41–78.

16   C. Offe, 'Die Aufgabe von staatlichen Aufgaben. "Thatcherismus" und die populistische Kritik der Staatstätigkeit', in Dieter Grimm (ed.), *Staatsaufgaben*, Frankfurt a.M 1994, pp. 317–52.

17   S. Lessenich, 'Social Subjectivity. The new Governmentality of Society', *Eurozine*, 20 August 2003, http://www.eurozine.com/articles/2003-08-20-lessenich-en.html; S. Lessenich, *Die Neuerfindung des Sozialen. Der Sozialstaat im flexiblen Kapitalismus* (*Reinvention of the Social: The Welfare State in Flexible Capitalism*), Bielefeld 2008.

18   Cf. C. Offe 1972, p. 24. In West Germany, the Law to Promote Economic Stability and Growth of 1967, as well as the 20th constitutional amendment to the

of intervention; that the toolbox of economic and social policies relied upon until that point had nothing left to offer. 'Activation' policy, which set in during the late 1990s as a form of subjectification of system rationality and social rationality, renders such a claim rather dubious.

At the same time, an analysis based on the theory of late capitalism (that is, in the sense of an empirical research hypothesis) suggests that this concrete historical variant of (attempted) political mediation between requirements of accumulation and legitimation within democratic-capitalist societies is subject to the 'evolutionary pattern of the formation of systemic elements alien to the structure but functionally necessary for the maintenance of the system;[19] a mode of political intervention aiming at the stabilisation, or rather revitalisation, of the capitalist economy for reasons of functionality and/or legitimation, operates with regulatory instruments and discursive rationalisations which in turn may ultimately jeopardise the original objective. Current state 'activation' policies would thus also be exposed to the same rationality boundaries, systemic contradictions and social conflicts – that is to say, that structural logic of intrinsic crisis-proneness – that were already described decades ago by theoreticians of late capitalism as the 'signature' of the late capitalist age.

This assertion will be further elaborated and substantiated in the following, framed and influenced by changes that occurred during the 'long five years' that have passed since the publication of *Sociology-Capitalism-Critique*: changes of both a social-historical nature as well as my own personal conceptual development, influenced by the institutional structures in which I conduct my research.[20] In terms of more recent social history, we should first name that which could be called 'the return of the crisis': though already present in 2009, the crisis as such has continued in the form of the banking, financial, currency, economic and sovereign debt crisis (cf. the contribution by Klaus Dörre), which in turn has meant that crisis as such

---

Grundgesetz (Basic Law for the Federal Republic of Germany, Germany's equivalent to a constitution) of 1969 had, under the impression of the first major economic crisis of the post-war era, prepared the (constitutional) legal foundation for a 'global control' of economic transactions seeking the 'the prevention of any impediment to the overall economic balance'.

19   19 Cf. Ibid., p. 38.

20   Building upon our joint publication in 2009, all three authors of this volume established and co-chaired a research group ('*Landnahme*, Acceleration, Activation. Dynamic and (De-) Stabilisation of Modern Growth Societies') at the Institute of Sociology of the Friedrich Schiller University of Jena in 2011 with funding from the German Research Foundation (DFG), in the context of which the three eponymous concepts have been further elaborated.

– that is, as concrete historical occurrence – has returned to the general awareness and horizon of society's lived experience. Society has once again grown accustomed to the permanent democratic-capitalist crisis and its (no less permanent) management by the state. In a way, the last few years have confirmed one of the main hypotheses of the theory of late capitalism – namely, that the crisis dynamic of late capitalist societies moves from the economic to the political system, where it takes on the form of a crisis of control, and of political legitimation in particular.[21] Following 2007–2008 and the collapse of Lehman Brothers, it was not long before the financial market crisis magically became a financial crisis of the state.[22] Rating agencies and institutional investors – that is to say, 'the markets' – have exerted such massive pressure on state actors ever since that, in some places, the organisational capacity and even the state's very political sovereignty have been lost.

Simultaneously, a vague unease has befallen the populations of the democratic-capitalist societies; a feeling, as repeatedly mentioned by Hartmut Rosa (though still partially subconscious and certainly not yet sufficient for collective action) that something is wrong, that things are not going as they should, that 'something is rotten in the state of late capitalism'. As a consequence, public receptiveness to academic social critique and critical social sciences has grown. This increased receptiveness is not due to our own intervention in this respect (at least not to any significant extent), but is just as unlikely owed to the contingent effects of a spectacle-driven media economy alone. Over the past five years, the impression that things cannot continue the way they have been, that the 'something' wrong in society stems not just from the financial crisis and its consequences, but that in fact a great deal of things are wrong. That there are logical and historical causal links between the countless varieties and locations of society's 'multiple crises'[23] has established itself in academic as well as non-academic discourse. This impression is one of the main reasons for the revival of sociological debate about the future of capitalism.

The debate about the future of the capitalist mode of socialisation is concentrated, as if through the lens of a magnifying glass, in a question the theory of late capitalism would describe as one of *structural problems*

21   Cf. J. Habermas, 'What Does a Crisis Mean Today? Legitimation Problems in Late Capitalism', in *Social Research* 40:4, Winter 1973, pp. 643–67.

22   J. O'Connor, *The Fiscal Crisis of the State*, New York 1973.

23   Cf. P. Bader, F. Becker, A. Demirovic, J. Dück, 'Die multiple Krise – Krisendynamiken im neoliberalen Kapitalismus', in Alex Demirović et al., *VielfachKrise Im Finanzmarktdominierten Kapitalismus*, Hamburg 2011, pp. 10–28.

of the growth society. The focus on democratic capitalism as a historically specific, politically mediated growth regime presents us with new perspectives on 'activation's' mode of intervention, its structural preconditions and process dynamics, and on the embedding of late capitalist crisis management (and its own crises) into broader contexts – a task that has been systematically neglected in the relevant attempts at theorising the crisis thus far. On the one hand, growth-societal contextualisation aids in illustrating the economic rationality and historical *timing* of 'activation' policies even more precisely. Against this backdrop, 'activation' appears even more convincingly as a politics of the productive potential of late industrial society, through the implementation of which a new economic growth cycle is to be set in motion. Considering the ongoing slow growth of the 'advanced' and increasingly financialised capitalist economies, an abandonment of the socio-political logic of 'activation' hardly seems likely – far less likely, that is, than an on ongoing intensification and differentiation thereof.

On the other hand, to think in categories of the growth society necessitates an expansion of a late capitalist theoretical analysis in at least two respects. For the arrangement of growth society, which constitutes itself in the field of tension between state, capitalism and democracy as well as in its corresponding intrinsic logics, must be understood, in terms of its functional capacity and crisis-proneness, not least in relation to, in a stricter sense, its material concerns, i.e. its substance-related and biophysical preconditions – ranging from fossil fuels to land and water consumption to human resources (the latter of which are henceforth to be activated on an expanded scale).[24] Moreover, the specific forms of crisis management in the historical growth centres of the capitalist world economy can also only be comprehended in both their functional capacity as well as their crisis-proneness if we take into account their anchor in the structures and mechanisms of the global division of labour and economic redistribution: the fact that democratic-capitalist growth societies in twentieth-century Europe were able to be institutionalised, and are now searching for the new modes of political dynamisation, cannot be explained through recourse to these societies' peculiarities of state intervention alone, but must also take into account the specific form of its embedding into global networks of international relations and hierarchies of power.

Such extension, deepening and – yes – complication of a sociology of late capitalist growth society and its political 'activation' agenda cannot be elaborated in this brief addendum to my original analysis developed in *Sociology-Capitalism-Critique* – not even as an attempt at (adequately)

---

24   Cf. B. Mahnkopf, *"Peak Capitalism?" Wachstumsgrenzen als Grenzen des Kapitalismus'*, in *WSI-Mitteilungen*, 67:7, 2014, pp. 505–12.

problematising the subject at hand, let alone as a clarification of the theoretical-conceptual problems this entails. Therefore, in the following remarks, I will limit myself to two specific questions contained in this wider problematic. First, I will deal with a reformulation of the 'activation' hypothesis in the context of growth society's logic of escalation – and thus with a corresponding variation of the question, arising out of late capitalism theory, of how great a contribution democratic-capitalist state intervention makes to the stabilisation of modern societies as *growth societies*. Subsequently, I will explore the question of what one should, against this backdrop, include in the notion of socio-political intervention toward a *post-growth society* – and why potential steps in this direction are for the time being prevented or structurally impeded, not only by the structures and selectivities of the late capitalist state, but also through the entanglement – institutional, normative, as well in terms of the interests of competing social groups – of late modern 'active citizens' within growth society's relations of function and legitimation. The focus on the 'growth subject' (*Wachstumssubjekt*) in late capitalism, then, ultimately poses the question about the mode of critique, or rather the function of critical sociologists, within democratic-capitalist growth society itself.

2. GROWTH, STATE, SUBJECT: THE POLITICS OF THE 'POTENTIAL'

Modern, democratic-capitalist societies are growth societies. That this is the case is due to the intrinsic logic of its (capitalist, democratic and bureaucratic) subsystems, which relate to one another and historically converge in a specific, growth-based and growth-oriented social arrangement.

As *capitalist* societies, modern societies exhibit a built-in compulsion to material growth, the ineluctable structural dynamic of escalation of which lies at the heart of the Marxian analysis of the logic of capital. What Marx identified as both source and driving force of the relentless, and necessarily expansive, movement of capitalist economies is capital's compulsion toward ongoing accumulation and valorisation, i.e. the need to repeatedly re-create a surplus to then in turn be re-valorised, to a permanent 're-establishment of a rate of profit adequate for further accumulation'.[25] Klaus Dörre's concept of *Landnahme* proceeds from this dynamic of economic movement: those needs, spheres of life and social milieus that have either not yet been capitalised and commodified, or which have been intentionally exempted from assuming a commodity form, constitute the non-capitalist 'exterior', the

---

25   P. Mattick, *Economic Crisis and Crisis Theory*, New York 1981, p. 58.

colonisation of which – in a valorisation cycle of appropriation, exploitation and sale – ensures those impetuses for accumulation, the continued
sequence of which represents the lifeblood of all capitalist economies.

The continued and historically unprecedented prosperity of capitalist
societies depends on a constantly expanding and accelerating capital accumulation whose modus operandi (as micro-economically rational as it is
macro-economically *irrational*) is the competition between individual units
of capital. It is, however, tied to effective profit realisation in particular;
that is to say, to the possibility (which itself must be repeatedly re-created)
of re-investing the accumulated capital at a profit, thus ensuring that the
surplus value siphoned off in one cycle can actually materialise in the next.
Thus, capitalism's expansive dynamic contains not only a socio-spatial, but
also a spatio-temporal dimension: individual capital units competing with
one another are forced to grow 'to produce not for an *existing* but for an
expected market'.[26] The accumulation invariably represents a form of betting
on future developments, and in a capitalist economy the future must always
have more to offer than the present.[27]

This compulsion to expand inherent in capitalism is accompanied and
flanked by a specific action pattern of permanent social comparison, rooted
in the *democratic* constitution of modern societies. The social-scientific *locus
classicus* locating this second distinct source of social dynamics of escalation
are Alexis de Tocqueville's studies of the young US-American democracy.
According to Tocqueville, the tendency to formal as well as material equality, as realised in the democratic type of society, stands in a paradoxical
relationship to an insatiable social desire for social equality, despite the fact
that this abstract desire contradicts virtually all lived experience. He argues
that the greater the degree of equality achieved over the course of a given
society's development, the more citizens find persisting inequalities to be
appalling – and the stronger their desire for more equality and demand for
the elimination of every last bit of inequality becomes.[28]

What may rightfully be ascribed, on the one hand, to aristocratic reservations vis-à-vis an effective democratisation of social relations, also
depicts, on the other hand, the same social dimensions of growth society
that Hartmut Rosa refers to in his diagnoses of the times: the social dynamic
of escalation, inherent in the guiding notions of a fair and potentially equal

---

26   Ibid. p. 68; emphasis in the original.

27   H. Holst, 'Die Konjunktur der Flexibilität – Die Temporalstrukturen
des Gegenwartskapitalismus', in Klaus Dörre, Dieter Sauer, Volker Wittke (eds),
Arbeitssoziologie und Kapitalismustheorie, Frankfurt, New York 2012, pp. 140–57.

28   S. Van Dyke, S. Lessenich, 'Unsichere Zeiten: Die paradoxale "Wiederkehr"
der Unsicherheit', in *Mittelweg*, 36 17:5, 2008, pp. 13–45.

access of all social groups and individuals to the promises of prosperity and security granted by democratic capitalism. The desire of the worst-positioned to improve their access to these promises, however justified that desire may be, corresponds with the desire of the better-off to distinguish themselves and set themselves apart on the other end of the social redistributive structure. However, the realisation of said desire, achieved through utilisation of political power, in turn further heightens the desire of the under-privileged to equalise social conditions. This dynamic, in a complex interplay of correlating socio-structural objectives, constantly fuels the capitalist engine of material production of wealth. Fred Hirsch has condensed this complex relationship into a basic formula of social positional goods which become devalued through widespread ownership and usage: 'If everyone stands on tiptoe, no one sees better.'[29] Seen from this angle, it is essentially impossible to achieve a state of equilibrium in terms of a general satisfaction of needs within modern citizenship societies granting equal rights of social participation. The social-structural problem of mutually escalating consumption preferences and conflicts over social status would in fact be 'heightened rather than relieved by the dynamic process of growth'.[30]

Robert Castel has identified a similar social mechanism of escalation in contemporary advanced capitalist societies, in which the renaissance of the semantics of precarity represents the 'downside of a society based on security'.[31] At the same time, this is instrumental in identifying the *political* arrangement, which mediates between the dynamic of economic accumulation and social grievances: the Fordist 'growth state', which 'linked together private property and social property, economic development and the acquisition of social rights'.[32] The 'social state [was] established'[33] at the institutional centre of the growth society, and organised the intra-social redistribution of a share of the constantly generated economic surplus product via myriad socio-political programmes, particularly in the post-war boom decades – thereby developing into an essential functional and justificatory pillar of late industrial societies.

The historically unique increase in overall prosperity achieved in these

---

29   F. Hirsch, *Social Limits to Growth*, London 1977, p. 5.

30   Ibid., p. 6.

31   R. Castel, *Die Stärkung des Sozialen. Leben im neuen Wohlfahrtsstaat*, Hamburg 2005, p. 10. [Originally published in French: *L'Insécurité Sociale: Qu'est-ce qu'être Protégé?*, Paris 2003.]

32   Castel, *From Manual Workers to Wage Labourers*, p. 343.

33   Ibid., p. 344.

societies, together with its social 'elevator',[34] or rather 'escalator effects'[35] of expanded material participation for broad layers of the population, was only possible through the combination of constant economic growth, increased trade union power and an expanding welfare state. The institutional arrangement of the democratic-capitalist welfare state, and the constant expansion and intensification of its socio-political interventionist activities, cannot be properly understood if viewed merely as dependent variables of capitalist accumulation imperatives and requirements for democratic legitimacy to be registered, adapted, and channelled by a purely 'ancillary' state administration. Rather, the modern state should be analytically regarded as a third, independent source of the development and establishment of growth society's structural dynamic. Oriented towards servicing both capital's need for further valorisation as well as popular aspirations for political participation engendered by economic and social competition, capitalist-democratic state action is also determined by an intrinsic systemic logic, namely the *bureaucratic* rationality geared towards the preservation of the status quo and – where possible – the expansion of the state institutions' scope of intervention.[36] It is the modern growth society's embedding into and stabilisation by the welfare state's institutional structure that ensures its ability to function satisfactorily. The welfare state itself, however, is by no means simply compelled forward by the conditions of growth society. It is constitutively involved in the former's genesis and reproduction; the institutions of the state thus not only *serve* growth capitalism and growth democracy, but are also created *by* them at the same time.

It would be an error of logic, however, to equate these functional and normative interdependencies between growth economy, growth democracy and growth bureaucracy with a pre-established harmony located within modern growth society. The growth state's intrinsic logic of acting on behalf of both capitalist functionality and democratic 'responsiveness' does not add up over the long term: state welfare production is, firstly, expensive and, secondly, selective, a fact that eventually leads to crises of welfare-state intervention, which in turn give occasion to their institutional restructuring and re-orientation, most recently in the form of a policy of 'activation'.

As far as *economic costs* are concerned, the welfare state historically withdraws (at least initially, and certainly at first glance) certain social milieus and categories from economic valorisation: this includes exempting

---

34   Cf. U. Beck, 'Beyond Status and Class?', in: U. Beck and E. Beck-Gernsheim, (eds), *Individualization: Institutionalized Individualism and its Social and Political Consequences*, London 2001, Ch. 3, pp. 30–42.

35   Cf. Offe, 1975.

36   Cf. Ibid.

children from factory labour or relieving the elderly of the compulsion to work, as well as extensively subsidising the cost of health care and (if society is clever) protecting pensions and security in old age from the logic of the market. In this sense, the welfare state and growth society have always also been a growth *impediment* – an impediment only conceivable and feasible in the context of a growth economy in the first place. Today capitalism is confronted with the reality that economic growth rates in the late industrial societies have been declining for decades and are now approaching zero; lately, due to the crisis, they even run the risk of turning negative (and in some cases already have). In this low- to no-growth constellation, the welfare state's redistribution-based collective rationality no longer seems affordable, or, for that matter, desirable. This argument, legitimised with reference to the *social selectivity* of welfare-state benefit systems, is becoming increasingly widespread. The various social provisions of the welfare state are being problematised against the backdrop of low growth, precisely because of their de-commodifying character that allows for possibilities of life conduct outside of the immediate compulsions of the market – a sociopolitical programme that is increasingly seen as counter-productive not only in economic, but also in social terms. According to the new neo-liberal consensus, the market-restricting welfare state overburdens not just the material capacity of the capitalist economy, but also the democratic society's moral commitment to perform and succeed in this economy. This functional and normative challenge to the welfare state's previous strategy of intervention ultimately prepared the ground for a comprehensive re-programming of the welfare state – from a social policy of 'providing' to an activating politics of the 'potential'.

The beginnings of this politics date back much further than the outbreak of the financial crisis. It began with the discovery of female human capital, which, particularly in former West Germany, had lain idle in private households over a long period, relegated to caring for children, parents, and the breadwinner husband. For the last two decades, this human capital has been mobilised onto the labour market in a peculiar feminist-productivist double movement.[37] A similarly ambivalent liberal-progressive alliance is pursuing the political objective of the social integration – in plain language, this really means integration *into wage labour* – of immigrant communities. The realities of competition in the globalised knowledge society allegedly necessitate the training and education of all potentially suitable persons and their utilisation to the benefit of the national economy. Moreover, we

---

37   S. Lessenich, 'Ökonomismus zum Wohlfühlen: Gøsta Esping-Andersen und die neue Architektur des Sozialstaats', in *PROKLA. Zeitschrift für kritische Sozialwissenschaft*, 136, 2004, pp. 469–76.

now find an extensive scientific-political consensus that older people have numerous resources at their disposal which, taking into consideration the demographic shift and resulting labour supply problems found in an ageing society, should also be productively deployed.[38] In line with this socio-political philosophy, the same is true for the already overburdened young generation, who from an early age are expected to serve the reproduction of a historically evolved economic model, and are thus bombarded with public and private interventions aiming at the discovery and promotion of their productive potential.

The politics of activation commands both women and children, the elderly and the immigrants, to *make something of themselves* (or rather, to let something be made *of* them): namely, a productive, useful market subject. Surely, the politics of the potential knows how to differentiate; it knows how to separate the 'good' market subjects from the 'bad' ones. This is particularly obvious when observing the contrast between recruitment efforts directed at the labour power of international 'high potentials' and the proactive politics of deterrence, deportation and debasement that target seemingly less desirable immigrant and refugee populations (at least with respect to economic productivity). Similar dualisms structure other potential-mobilising activities of the activating welfare state: for those with few job skills, the regime of labour promotion acts mainly as a regime of entitlement reduction; the state provision of *Elterngeld*[39] aims at demographic growth (preferably of the educated milieus), public praise for voluntary charitable work in old age is complemented by public criticism of the high social costs incurred by pensioners, as well as the explosive costs of caring for the elderly and infirm.

Where productive potentials are suspected in the active society, the standard motto is: 'Go for it!' This is valid – quite literally – for health-related fitness, exercise and nutrition programmes (can we all not do a little bit more 'for ourselves'?) as well as – in a more figurative sense – for the 'trimming down' of companies, administrations and organisations (where there are basically *always* possibilities for potential increases in 'efficiency'). This same logic is applied to all of the potentially infinite situations in which people could surely make more of themselves: they could write more job applications, pursue higher qualifications and further job training, and participate in lifelong learning, thereby bringing their lives more into line with the requirements of work. If all this be considered 'natural' in growth society,

---

38   T. Denninger, S. Van Dyke, S.Lessenich, A. Richter, *Leben im Ruhestand. Zur Neuverhandlung des Alters in der Aktivgesellschaft*, Bielefeld 2014.

39   [Trans. Note] *Elterngeld* ('parent money') is a tax-financed payment, found in Germany and some other European states, for couples raising children; it is somewhat similar to Statutory Maternity Pay in the UK.

then it is not least because of the evident analogy to the social domination of the natural world: human potentials are like natural resources – under no circumstances can they be left buried beneath the earth, but must instead be extracted. Though this extraction can ('unfortunately') never be absolute, the active society seeks to get as close to this unattainable goal as possible.

In a growth capitalism in which expansion appears to be ending, the compulsory drive to seek out more and more sources of social potential becomes a threat to society itself. For wherever the political apparatus for discovering social potential is set into motion, the citizens addressed by it can expect a further commodification of their working conditions and economisation of their conditions of life. In the exploitation of natural resources, no expense or effort is spared to penetrate the deepest layers of the earth's crust and exhaust the planet's potentials to the greatest possible extent. The same is true in the exploitation of human potentials: ever new and more complex forms of socio-political intervention are developed in order to adequately valorise people's potentials, thus far either hidden or intentionally concealed from the great social alliance of productivity. 'Fracking' is thus, by this logic, also a social technology.

On the other hand, this objectively dangerous vision could not take hold subjectively if it did not also reflect some sort of positive goal or objective – or at least allow for the projection of such positive objectives onto it. There can be no doubt that this is effectively the case; it would be a sign of professional hubris to explain away the social acceptance of the activating state's strategy of potential utilisation largely with the latter's discursive refinement by means of the sociological justificatory formula of 'inclusion'. Granted, the general understanding of the term 'inclusion' has gradually morphed into a notion that equates the (selective) integration of people into the functional spaces and operational mechanisms of labour and consumption markets, via guarantees of social inclusion, social recognition, economic independence and political participation. Yet what ultimately allows a politics of the potential to succeed in the first place is the latter's structural proximity to the collective self-understanding and 'mental infrastructures'[40] of the growth society, its compatibility with material and ideational interests, and the habitual dispositions of subjects in this society.

It was Max Weber who a century ago spoke of capitalism as 'the most fateful force in our modern life'[41] and grasped it as a structure of subject formation: 'Thus the capitalism of today, which has come to dominate

---

40   H. Welzer, *Mental Infrastructures: How Growth Entered the World and Our Souls*, Berlin 2011.

41   M. Weber, *The Protestant Ethic and the Spirit of Capitalism*, 23rd print, London, New York 2001, p. xxxi.

economic life, educates and selects the economic subjects which it needs through a process of economic survival of the fittest'.[42] Both aphorisms must be understood as historical-sociological specification of the social – for our purposes, 'growth-social' – interplay between 'system' and 'action'. After all, capitalism is socially 'fateful' in the sense that it has the tendency to force its economic rationality onto all spheres of life: the imprint of its structure formations and self-descriptions effected by the economic order (i.e. emanating from the field of economic action itself) renders modern society a capitalist society – despite its complex differentiation into diverse functional domains and action fields (cf. Schimank 2014). Furthermore, the capitalist social order has a 'subject-forming' effect in the sense that social actors are forced to orientate their seemingly individual goals of action around the former's action prescriptions (which apply to all individuals equally) – that is, assuming they desire to either make profits as an entrepreneur or earn an income as a wage earner, and to do so not only sporadically but continually and over the long term.

The social actors of capitalist societies are – *nolens volens,* and all the more so the more subaltern their position in the social hierarchy may be – oriented towards the action logic imposed by the former's systemic compulsion for growth. It is not least the welfare state's conversion of economic growth into material prosperity (though still distributed unequally, it has nevertheless proliferated to a previously unprecedented extent) that binds the actors' interests to the growth system. Both individually and collectively, it creates a growth-oriented hierarchy of social preferences, and fixes the cultural normality of a permanent, endlessly repeated, constantly intensified increase in action options and life chances within the social subjects' repertoire of values. Democratic welfare capitalism thus historically forms that social type of the growth subject that growth capitalism requires – which is why growth, as Ulrich Beck lamented with regard to social phenomena of individualisation, may count as 'a historically contradictory *process of socialisation*'.[43] Beck depicts the tendency towards individualisation as such a process, since it leads to 'individualized lifestyles and life situations', though the 'standardized collective character of these individualized life situations is certainly difficult to comprehend'.[44] A structurally analogous point can also be made, then, with regard to a modernity of industrial society conceived as a systemic growth arrangement: it pursues the collective individualisation of growth subjects who cannot spontaneously become aware of the social contradictions – contradictions which threaten to turn on them, resembling

42   Ibid., p. 20.
43   Beck, 'Beyond Status and Class?', p. 31. Emphasis in original.
44   Ibid.

a kind of collective-individual self-impairment – inherent in their mode of existence. Or, to put it more precisely: growth subjects who (at least for the time being) are not aware of this contradictory constellation to the extent necessary to base collective action upon it.

3. SUBJECTIVITY, CRITIQUE, POST-GROWTH: DO WE HAVE A RIGHT TO BE LAZY?

If we understand late capitalist, late industrial societies as societies in which people's everyday action strategies and lifestyles are systematically geared towards systemic dynamics of escalation via an amalgamation of capitalist, democratic, and state-bureaucratic functional logics, in which notions of and interest in growth are socially institutionalised in multiple ways, then two points become clear: Firstly, transcending this social arrangement will not be an easy task; and secondly, an analysis committed to promoting such a transformation cannot focus exclusively on the analytical pole of the 'system', but must also take into account that of the 'lifeworld'.

My reference to the 'system in/on the subject' in my concluding contribution to *Sociology, Capitalism, Critique* already suggested this necessary doubling of a critical sociology's analytical focus. Hopefully, this reconstruction of the democratic welfare-state capitalism of the past decades as a multifactorially-driven growth capitalism helps to accentuate my point more clearly: namely, that the insinuation of a quasi-'external', compulsive and ultimately inescapable systemic logic (which has always been as sociologically inadequate as it has been politically unproductive) clearly does not do justice to the social process mechanisms of growth society's structural formation. The 'system' of growth society is not a mere 'opposite' or 'counterpart' (*Gegenüber*) of social subjects, not an 'Other' that remains external to them. Rather, the production and reproduction of a specific social type – namely the *growth subject* – represents a process institutionalised in the growth society itself. In this sense, the growth subject follows a systematic pattern. The reverse is also true: just as 'the devil is in the details', so the growth system is *in* the subject. Thus, anyone who seeks to break through this arrangement must start from the structures and mechanisms of growth society's constitution of the subject itself – and from people's very own ideas and interests as constructed by the institutions of growth society.

In other words: once the subjectification of the growth logic (i.e., its effective integration into the world of ideas and interests of late modern subjects) is identified as a fundamental element of the growth society's structural problems, the analytical approaches for dealing with this structural problem must in turn adequately address the subjectivity of the late modern 'growth human (being)'. However, one essential quality criterion of such an approach would be that it does not – as the neo-liberal discourse of the past decades did incessantly – construct human beings as being either self-responsible, obliged to perform, or as being implicated in and thus in a sense responsible for said growth logic – even if this is done in the interest of breaking with it. A perspective of social transformation worthy of the name cannot simply take up and reverse neo-liberal means for its own ends. It cannot seek to appeal to people – or rather, seek to lead them by use of more or less authoritative means – to behave in the sense of a 'better', non growth-oriented mode of socialisation in the future. What is needed is rather a break with that neo-liberal programme of directing subjects to self-governance, and in its place an entirely new approach in terms of social analysis and social policy: an exploration of actors' unfulfilled needs and their secret (or, as the case may be, not so secret) desires, their daily experience of deprivation and the resulting 'individual imaginary' – which may not actually be individual, but instead, once articulated, may prove to be a collective imaginary after all.[45]

The critical questions concerning the contemporary constellation of growth society[46] and its subject construction would thus have to read: 'What are the specific historical deprivations confronting people in growth society that directly or indirectly determine the collective-individual choice of material or immaterial compensation? What material and immaterial goods are people forced to forego or sacrifice in this game of capitalist growth, and how do they cope with that loss? And does the manner of dealing with this loss perhaps play a role in prolonging the very game responsible for it in the first place? What would people choose if they were in the position to imagine a different social lifeworld?' It is questions like these which point toward subjectively accessible conceptualisations of a 'different society' – and which may possibly even suggest a path to its realisation.

Thus, in light of the activation state's aforementioned politics of the potential that virtually all citizens of the advanced capitalist democracies are confronted with sooner or later, one might suspect (pending empirical verification, of course) that there could in fact be something like an unspoken hope not for 'more', but indeed for a little 'less': to not have to always 'go that extra mile', to not be constantly 'available', to be left in peace from time to time. From this perspective, an idea that may seem nonsensical or indeed

---

45   Cf. H. Wolf, 'Gesellschaftskritik und imaginäre Institution: Zur Aktualität von Cornelius Castoriadis (Social Critique and Imaginary Institution. On the Topicality of Cornelius Castoriadis)', in *PROKLA. Zeitschrift für kritische Sozialwissenschaft* 167, 2012, pp. 267–86.

46   I owe many thanks to Tine Haubner for this valuable insight.

quite ludicrous in the context of growth society begins to appear quite reasonable; that is, an idea that has been evoked sporadically throughout the history of capitalism, but whose time may finally have come as growth society carries its reproductive logic to absurdity. I am referring to the idea which Paul Lafargue provocatively termed the 'right to be lazy'.

Modern capitalist wage relations as a regime of forced labour, modern industrial capitalism as one gigantic workhouse: this is the image Lafargue depicted, quite accurately, of late nineteenth-century society.[47] Admittedly, he was first inspired to write a polemic against the regime of wage labour by his impression that the workers of his time had reconciled themselves to the industrial-capitalist workhouse. According to Lafargue, the proletariat had succumbed to the modern dogma of work; it had let itself be deceived by the love of work; and even more, it had appropriated the work cult to such an extent that it had in fact incorporated the 'right to work' into its agenda as a supposedly revolutionary principle since 1848.

Lafargue's criticism of the workers, or rather of the working class movement of his time, is without a doubt unfair and exaggerated: after all, workers' seemingly peculiar addiction to work makes perfect sense in the context of an industrial-capitalist transformation of the European societies and the economic constraints this engendered. The fact remains that behind the demand for a statutory right to an opportunity to work lay the very fundamental demand for a guaranteed existence extending beyond the working day of the average wage-labourer. In this sense, the 'mania for work' displayed individually as well as collectively by the workers of that era was neither surprising, reprehensible, or condemnable – but cheap talk seems to have come easily to Lafargue, as is commonly the case with theoreticians, intellectuals and philosophers throughout all epochs.

Nevertheless, Lafargue did touch upon an element of truth, both generally and specifically. In a general sense, there can be no doubting his correct observation that, over the course of the nineteenth century, a working class movement which had aimed at the abolition of the wage system gradually morphed into one that instead struggled for its general implementation.[48] There is no need to deny the objective systemic constraints and social complicity of actors (who were ultimately responsible for this historic strategic shift on the part of subaltern groups) while still pointing out this development's historical irony, as well as the twists and turns it took. Without conceding to what appears to be a certain spitefulness on Lafargue's part, we can still agree with his analysis that the labour movement's revolutionary

---

47   Cf. P. Lafargue, *The Right to Be Lazy: Essays by Paul Lafargue*, Edited by Bernard Marszalek, Oakland 2011.

48   Cf. A. Przeworski, *Capitalism and Social Democracy*, Cambridge 1985.

and liberatory impetus has, over capitalist time, been ground down and changed into a rights-based labour reformism that has nevertheless – who could deny it? – historically done a great deal of good for workers and their families.

Lafargue's argument also contains a valid point as concerns what could be called the productivity paradox of labour in capitalism: more precisely, that over the course of its history, never has an increase in labour productivity been matched by a corresponding reduction in working hours and overall expenditure of labour power – not even remotely. Rather, what we have seen and will certainly continue to see is the opposite: the more productive the social organisation of labour becomes, the stronger the social pressure to mobilise even more labour power becomes as well. What may seem perfectly natural in the context of capitalist valorisation rationality in fact becomes rather difficult to comprehend from a common sense perspective: why should people continue to perform ever more work if their labour output and productivity has been steadily increasing over time? It seems appropriate to play dumb with regard to this question, as Lafargue would have intended: 'work, in order that becoming poorer, you may have more reason to work and become miserable. Such is the inexorable law of capitalist production'.[49] This 'law', however, is a purely *economic* law, the *social* logic of which is rather difficult to decipher.

It seems fair to ask why this gigantic arrangement of labour mobilisation still manages to function today. At least two elements in Lafargue's treatise suggest an answer to this question. In his view, the labour movement (and why should it be treated any better than other, no less competent actors such as, say, academic science itself?) had allowed itself to become infected by 'that scientific society [...] which disseminated among the masses the nonsense of bourgeois economics and ethics'.[50] Yet Lafargue also addresses another, second essential mode of reproduction of the capitalist work-centred society (*Arbeitsgesellschaft*) beyond this ideological-political moment, namely the working people themselves. Whoever seeks the transformation of the regime of labour growth must address not only 'capital', but also (and perhaps primarily) 'labour' itself. He or she will, on the one hand, have to account for the historico-cultural entanglement of people in their work, the symbiosis in their everyday lives with their jobs, their workplaces, and their working conditions. On the other hand, he or she will have to acknowledge the quotidian suffering (sometimes lesser, sometimes greater) of working people under wage labour – the experiences of deprivation and disenfranchisement, stress and disregard related to both their specific work situations,

---

49   Lafargue, *The Right to Be Lazy*, pp. 31–2.
50   Ibid., p. 29.

as well as the social organisation of labour as a whole. One consequence of this paradoxical configuration – suffering caused by something one loves – are psychological disorders and illnesses.[51] Yet it is also the source of the development and articulation of normative expectations and demands directed toward and within one's work.[52]

It remains an open question – and one that will ultimately have to be demonstrated empirically – as to whether (and if so, how) a social dynamic of labour transformation, in the sense of a break with the potential-based growth logic of the society of full-time employment, may arise from this constellation. It is quite obvious, though, that there are institutional arrangements which are not only an expression of such a dynamic, but which are actually capable of advancing it: institutions that increase the chances for the question of people's unsatisfied needs and secret desires, and that of an individual and collective imagination of a 'different society' to make it onto the socio-political agenda.[53] What Lafargue called the 'right to be lazy' – the proposal of institutional measures to facilitate a liberation of work-centred society (*Arbeitsgesellschaft*) from the self-imposed constraints of wage labour, were really nothing more than a polemical and provocative metaphor for a massive reduction in working hours.

Lafargue, being the sceptical *étatist* that he was, specifically called for the forging of 'an iron law forbidding every one to work more than three hours a day'. Three hours of socially necessary labour, and the rest of the day is left 'to be lazy', for leisure time – or let us say: for *life*. Over the past decades, similar concepts have been formulated and reformulated. Authors such as André Gorz have gone even further than Lafargue, advocating a 'path to paradise' through a model of lifelong employment that would amount to a ten-hour workweek.[54] The British New Economics Foundation (NEF), whose motto is 'economics as if people and the planet mattered', is currently following Lafargue's brazen proposal in its '21 hours' campaign

---

51   Cf. C. Dejours, *Souffrance en France: La Banalisation de l'Injustice Sociale*, Paris: Editions du Seuil, 1998; S. Neckel, G. Wagner, 'Burnout. Soziales Leiden an Wachstum und Wettbewerb', in *WSI-Mitteilungen* 67:7, 2014, pp. 536–42.

52   Cf. F. Dubet, *Ungerechtigkeiten: Zum subjektiven Ungerechtigkeitsempfinden am Arbeitsplatz* (Injustice: Subjective Perceptions at the Workplace), Hamburg 2008. [Originally published in French as *Injustices. L'Expérience des Inégalités au Travail*, Paris, 2006]; S. Hürtgen, S. Voswinkel, *Nichtnormale Normalität? Anspruchslogiken aus der Arbeitnehmermitte*, Berlin 2014.

53   Cf. G. Vobruba, 'Soziologie und Kritik: Moderne Sozialwissenschaft und Kritik der Gesellschaft', in *Soziologie* 42:2, 2013, pp. 147–68.

54   Cf. A. Gorz, *Paths to Paradise: On the Liberation from Work*, London 1985.

– albeit without making direct reference to him.[55] Admittedly, this proposal would not directly lead the 'old earth, trembling with joy' – as Lafargue once believed – to 'feel a new universe leaping within her'.[56] But it would build upon, in the same way that Lafargue did, the everyday experience we are all familiar with – that labour only gains subjective as well as social value within the horizon of non-work, i.e. when workers also have the necessary free time to reflect on and truly appreciate their labour. 'Work will become a mere condiment to the pleasures of idleness … a passion useful to the social organism only when wisely regulated and limited to a maximum of three hours a day'.[57]

So, how then should we progress down the path toward the 'right to be lazy'? If people in work-centred growth society – seeing as they can neither live *with* growth nor *without* it – are entangled with it in a dilemmatic sense, then the same is ultimately true for intellectual and scientific reflection as well. In a way, the fact that sociology is itself part of the very object it observes contributes to sociology's appeal as a discipline. However, it also means that sociologists really have no epistemological object, but instead 'it has us'.[58] The sociology of the growth society is therefore also always a sociology *within* the growth society. Taking this into account, it seems perfectly reasonable (and long overdue) to subject sociology's role as an observer to closer scrutiny. The issue would then be to clarify what role sociology itself has in the preservation of the functional interrelations and legitimatory practices of the growth society. 'As long as this option is deemed to be without alternative under the given conditions, the system's preservation appears as a practical necessity'.[59] In the light of this insight, the self-description of an observant social science would have to include working toward the illumination of the current social formation's structural problems, the highlighting of self-imposed limitations of the possibilities for social development and the collective imagination of alternative modes of socialisation. Sociology has to leave the rest to others – and in the process 'theoretically internalise that people, within certain limits, ultimately do what they want'.[60] But then again, perhaps only theoretically.

---

55   Cf. http://www.neweconomics.org/publications/entry/21-hours, last accessed 7 November 2014.

56   Lafargue, *The Right to Be Lazy*, p. 58.

57   Ibid., pp. 34–5.

58   L. Eichler, 'Von der Kritik der Akkumulation zur Akkumulation der Kritik. Reichweite und Grenzen der drei Jenenser Modelle kapitalismuskritischer Soziologie', in Julia Gruhlich et al. (eds), *Soziologie im Dialog. Kritische Denkanstöße von Nachwuchswissenschaftler_innen*, Berlin 2012, p. 61.

59   Vobruba, *Politik mit dem Wohlfahrtsstaat*, p. 177.

60   Vobruba *Die Gesellschaft der Leute*, p. 70.

Index